Quick (and Healthy) Dinner Tricks

Get dinner on the table in 10 minutes: Microwave a frozen dinner like macaroni and cheese or three-bean chili. While it's cooking, sauté small or large amounts of mushrooms, chopped onions, peppers, diced lean ham, cooked or uncooked diced tomatoes (or all of them) and add to the top of the macaroni. For the frozen bean chili, add sautéed diced tomatoes, onions, corn, raw chopped scallions, cilantro, and slices of avocados.

Forget slicing meat: Grab some of the new meat assortments of ready-sliced and usually very lean fondue-cut, diced, or thin-sliced beef, pork, turkey, and chicken for easy vegetable and meat stir-fries with no meat slicing.

Avoid buying too much: Prewrapped packages often have more cut vegetables like broccoli, carrots, cauliflower, onions, and mushrooms than you need. Get them from the salad bar for precise amounts for stir-fries or vegetable dishes.

Create lean bacon bites with no mess: For lean, tasty, real, no-fuss bacon bits, breakfast bacon, and BLT sandwiches, purchase namebrand bacon already cooked, now available in large markets where the uncooked bacon is displayed. Scissor off all fat, microwave in 10 seconds, and voilà, no greasy pan, little fat, and lots of flavor (some brands are more fatty than others).

Have time for barbecue: Buy already cooked barbecued pork in tubs in your meat department. It's almost all lowfat (look on the label) and, depending upon the brand, fabulous. Don't want so much pork? Add it to canned baked beans.

Enhance canned stews: To canned stews, add fresh sautéed versions of what is already in the can such as onions, tomatoes, peas, and green beans.

Make canned chili zing: Sauté extra onions and tomatoes and add corn and a teaspoon of chili powder and cumin.

Refresh canned cream soups: For soups like cream of broccoli and celery, add 1 cup lightly steamed fresh broccoli florets or chopped celery and onions. For mushroom, add sautéed mushrooms and leeks.

Quick and Healthy Salad Tips

Improve packaged salads: For fresher flavor and less fat, purchase store-packaged, ready-made salads, such as cole slaw, and add double the amount of your own large-cut fresh cabbage, diced apples, and nuts. Storeboughts almost always contain too much fatty dressing. For potato or macaroni salad (or chicken, tuna, crab, or shrimp salad), add fresh diced celery, shredded carrots, chopped onions, and peppers to dilute the fat and add more crunch and fresh flavor (already cut up and in the amount you want from the salad bar, of course).

Rev up the flavor in lowfat or diet salad dressings: Add a tablespoon or two of your own fresh lemon juice, wine, or balsamic vinegar, a dash of fresh herbs and spices like basil, tarragon, or oregano, a little minced garlic, and, if a cheese dressing, a sprinkle of blue cheese or Parmesan (where you can control the amount of cheese).

Make a quick turkey, chicken, shrimp, or crab salad: Purchase deli-cooked chicken, turkey, tuna, and already steamed and chilled shrimp, crab, or lobster for quick, no-effort meat salad. Just add chopped onions, celery, lowfat mayo or sour cream, and whatever else you like.

Quick & Healthy Cooking For Dummies®

Cheat Sheet

Quick and Healthy Breakfasts

Make quick pancakes: Buy lowfat frozen ready-made or frozen easy-pour (in cartons) pancakes. Toast the ready-made or make the pourables. Add tons of fresh blueberries or raspberries to regular sugar-free syrup and drizzle the berry-filled syrup on the pancakes.

Add fiber, fiber, fiber: Look at bread labels. Bread with 3 grams of dietary fiber per slice (you need about 25 to 35 grams a day) is a nutritious buy. (Be sure it's per slice and not 3 grams for two slices.) Also look at cereal labels (Nutrition Facts panels) to find out which cereals have the highest fiber and the fewest calories. Try Spelt, an ancient grain breakfast flake, or all bran for taste and fiber. With whole-grain cereal or toast for breakfast, a sandwich for lunch, and any kind of rice or pasta for dinner, you already have had the USDA Food Pyramid guidelines of six or more servings of whole-grain, enriched or fortified, grains a day.

Choose fruit over juice: One quart of juice has 500 and sometimes more calories; two cups of juice has 250. For half the calories and twice or more the fiber, eat the whole orange.

Quick and Healthy Ethnic Flavors

Avoid trouble when flavoring tofu: Get fresh tofu and look for tofu flavor packets now available right near the tofu. Add the packets to sautéed onions, bok choy, snow peas or sugar snaps, peppers, and other veggies, plus strips of lean meat already cut in your meat department

Try great new vegetables: Visit several Asian markets, smell the wonderful authentic smells, and get their interesting vegetables such as types of foot-long beans, unusual greens, different types of broccoli-type vegetables, radishes, and especially edamame, which are fresh, bright green soybeans. (Lightly steamed, they taste like a cross between peas and lima beans, only sweeter.)

Add authentic Hispanic flavors: Hispanic markets are wonderful, offering beans, lots of canned items, and often freshly made tortillas. Their spices and herbs like saffron chicken blends are terrific and are easy ways to add authentic flavor to your Tex/Mex meal.

Create Mediterranean foods: Purchasing fresh-spiced pitas and flat breads in Mediterranean markets offers fabulous quick and easy breads in deliciously piquant flavors. While there, get some pickled lemons, olives, and authentic desserts such as baklava, usually in smaller pieces than in American markets (or cut in half), and always delicious.

For Dummies™: Bestselling Book Series for Beginners

Quick & Healthy Cooking

FOR

DUMMIES®

Quick & Healthy Cooking FOR DUMMIES®

by Lynn Fischer

Photography by Tim Turner

IDG BOOKS WORLDWIDE

IDG Books Worldwide, Inc.
An International Data Group Company

Foster City, CA ◆ Chicago, IL ◆ Indianapolis, IN ◆ New York, NY

Quick & Healthy Cooking For Dummies®

Published by
IDG Books Worldwide, Inc.
An International Data Group Company
919 E. Hillsdale Blvd.
Suite 400
Foster City, CA 94404
www.idgbooks.com (IDG Books Worldwide Web site)
www.dummies.com (Dummies Press Web site)

Library of Congress Catalog Card No.: 99-67265

ISBN: 0-7645-5214-7

Printed in the United States of America

10 9 8 7 6 5 4 3 2 1

1O/QT/QR/QQ/IN

Distributed in the United States by IDG Books Worldwide, Inc.

Distributed by CDG Books Canada Inc. for Canada; by Transworld Publishers Limited in the United Kingdom; by IDG Norge Books for Norway; by IDG Sweden Books for Sweden; by IDG Books Australia Publishing Corporation Pty. Ltd. for Australia and New Zealand; by TransQuest Publishers Pte Ltd. for Singapore, Malaysia, Thailand, Indonesia, and Hong Kong; by Gotop Information Inc. for Taiwan; by ICG Muse, Inc. for Japan; by Intersoft for South Africa; by Eyrolles for France; by International Thomson Publishing for Germany, Austria and Switzerland; by Distribuidora Cuspide for Argentina; by LR International for Brazil; by Galileo Libros for Chile; by Ediciones ZETA S.C.R. Ltda. for Peru; by WS Computer Publishing Corporation, Inc., for the Philippines; by Contemporanea de Ediciones for Venezuela; by Express Computer Distributors for the Caribbean and West Indies; by Micronesia Media Distributor, Inc. for Micronesia; by Chips Computadoras S.A. de C.V. for Mexico; by Editorial Norma de Panama S.A. for Panama; by American Bookshops for Finland.

For general information on IDG Books Worldwide's books in the U.S., please call our Consumer Customer Service department at 800-762-2974. For reseller information, including discounts and premium sales, please call our Reseller Customer Service department at 800-434-3422.

For information on where to purchase IDG Books Worldwide's books outside the U.S., please contact our International Sales department at 317-596-5530 or fax 317-572-4002.

For consumer information on foreign language translations, please contact our Customer Service department at 1-800-434-3422, fax 317-572-4002, or e-mail rights@idgbooks.com.

For information on licensing foreign or domestic rights, please phone +1-650-653-7098.

For sales inquiries and special prices for bulk quantities, please contact our Sales department at 800-762-2974 or write to the address above.

For information on using IDG Books Worldwide's books in the classroom or for ordering examination copies, please contact our Educational Sales department at 800-434-2086 or fax 317-572-4005.

For press review copies, author interviews, or other publicity information, please contact our Public Relations department at 650-653-7000 or fax 650-653-7500.

For authorization to photocopy items for corporate, personal, or educational use, please contact Copyright Clearance Center, 222 Rosewood Drive, Danvers, MA 01923, or fax 978-750-4470.

is a registered trademark under exclusive license to IDG Books Worldwide, Inc. from International Data Group, Inc.

About the Author

Lynn Fischer has written 23 healthy cookbooks since 1989, which includes thick recipe pamphlets, product line cookbooks, appliance and special foods cookbooks, the in-flight menus for the new and excitingly revised National Airlines, her online "cookbooks" for AOL with more than 500 original recipes, her "cookbooks" on her own Web site (Lynn Fischer.com), plus cookbooks for various regional cooking shows and other requests. Her nationally published healthy cookbooks number seven now, with most, like *Lowfat Cooking For Dummies,* becoming bestsellers. She writes healthy tips for *Modern Maturity* magazine and was the host of *The Low Cholesterol Gourmet* for The Discovery Channel with 200 shows, airing from 1991 to 1995, and Lynn Fischer's *Healthy Indulgences* on PBS from 1995 to 1998. She resides in Largo, Florida, but is thinking about moving to New York where a few hundred years ago she was Miss New York and a top model appearing on the cover of *Esquire, TV Guide, Women's World,* and others.

ABOUT IDG BOOKS WORLDWIDE

Welcome to the world of IDG Books Worldwide.

IDG Books Worldwide, Inc., is a subsidiary of International Data Group, the world's largest publisher of computer-related information and the leading global provider of information services on information technology. IDG was founded more than 30 years ago by Patrick J. McGovern and now employs more than 9,000 people worldwide. IDG publishes more than 290 computer publications in over 75 countries. More than 90 million people read one or more IDG publications each month.

Launched in 1990, IDG Books Worldwide is today the #1 publisher of best-selling computer books in the United States. We are proud to have received eight awards from the Computer Press Association in recognition of editorial excellence and three from Computer Currents' First Annual Readers' Choice Awards. Our best-selling *...For Dummies®* series has more than 50 million copies in print with translations in 31 languages. IDG Books Worldwide, through a joint venture with IDG's Hi-Tech Beijing, became the first U.S. publisher to publish a computer book in the People's Republic of China. In record time, IDG Books Worldwide has become the first choice for millions of readers around the world who want to learn how to better manage their businesses.

Our mission is simple: Every one of our books is designed to bring extra value and skill-building instructions to the reader. Our books are written by experts who understand and care about our readers. The knowledge base of our editorial staff comes from years of experience in publishing, education, and journalism — experience we use to produce books to carry us into the new millennium. In short, we care about books, so we attract the best people. We devote special attention to details such as audience, interior design, use of icons, and illustrations. And because we use an efficient process of authoring, editing, and desktop publishing our books electronically, we can spend more time ensuring superior content and less time on the technicalities of making books.

You can count on our commitment to deliver high-quality books at competitive prices on topics you want to read about. At IDG Books Worldwide, we continue in the IDG tradition of delivering quality for more than 30 years. You'll find no better book on a subject than one from IDG Books Worldwide.

John Kilcullen
John Kilcullen
Chairman and CEO
IDG Books Worldwide, Inc.

Steven Berkowitz
Steven Berkowitz
President and Publisher
IDG Books Worldwide, Inc.

Eighth Annual
Computer Press
Awards ≥1992

Ninth Annual
Computer Press
Awards ≥1993

Tenth Annual
Computer Press
Awards ≥1994

Eleventh Annual
Computer Press
Awards ≥1995

IDG is the world's leading IT media, research and exposition company. Founded in 1964, IDG had 1997 revenues of $2.05 billion and has more than 9,000 employees worldwide. IDG offers the widest range of media options that reach IT buyers in 75 countries representing 95% of worldwide IT spending. IDG's diverse product and services portfolio spans six key areas including print publishing, online publishing, expositions and conferences, market research, education and training, and global marketing services. More than 90 million people read one or more of IDG's 290 magazines and newspapers, including IDG's leading global brands — Computerworld, PC World, Network World, Macworld and the Channel World family of publications. IDG Books Worldwide is one of the fastest-growing computer book publishers in the world, with more than 700 titles in 36 languages. The "...For Dummies®" series alone has more than 50 million copies in print. IDG offers online users the largest network of technology-specific Web sites around the world through IDG.net (http://www.idg.net), which comprises more than 225 targeted Web sites in 55 countries worldwide. International Data Corporation (IDC) is the world's largest provider of information technology data, analysis and consulting, with research centers in over 41 countries and more than 400 research analysts worldwide. IDG World Expo is a leading producer of more than 168 globally branded conferences and expositions in 35 countries including E3 (Electronic Entertainment Expo), Macworld Expo, ComNet, Windows World Expo, ICE (Internet Commerce Expo), Agenda, DEMO, and Spotlight. IDG's training subsidiary, ExecuTrain, is the world's largest computer training company, with more than 230 locations worldwide and 785 training courses. IDG Marketing Services helps industry-leading IT companies build international brand recognition by developing global integrated marketing programs via IDG's print, online and exposition products worldwide. Further information about the company can be found at www.idg.com.   1/24/99

Dedication

To my daughter Lisa and son Cary, and especially to my grandson Wolf, who like all children will both influence and are the hope of our future. I, too, hope I have influenced theirs toward health. And to people who respect and take care of their bodies, the only thing, regardless of what we were born with, we really have total charge of.

And to those lucky people who will see three centuries.

Author's Acknowledgments

I would like to thank the people with whom I worked most closely on this terrific book — my personal recipe testers. One recipe tester is my long-time nutritional analyst for my last five cookbooks, Chris Loudon, who is a registered dietitian. Chris does it right, she does it fast, and she can be relied on to give appropriate, necessary, helpful suggestions, and most important, accurate information. Her nutrition and science knowledge is always needed in a book like this because Chris has to check every single one of my statements to be sure that they are accurate and essential so that you get the best possible and most updated information. Occasionally, we differed in opinion and mine prevailed, so if you disagree with something, blame me.

I also want to thank Polly Clingerman who has herself over 1 million books in print. I was enormously lucky to get her as a tester for the short time period she had in between writing cookbooks and selling them on television. Polly is a total professional, helpful, funny, and creative, and cooks deliciously and as fast as a bat out of heaven wearing a chef's hat. Polly is just a very special, giving, and nice person. The recipes are better because of her.

Others who helped are Debra Murray and June Hughes. Debra is a terrific food person who is a great cook in her own right and who tested several recipes giving a very different, creative, and youthful view. I appreciate her efforts greatly. June is a computer online acquaintance and member of my weekly lowfat recipe chats (Tuesday night 9 p.m. `Peachtree Lounge.aol.com`) who sent me dozens of recipes to look at. We tested several and used a couple of really good ones. Also a genuine appreciation of and special thanks for my friend and literary agent of ten years, Gail Ross. Now if I could just find a boyfriend or husband as nice as Gail.

I think I have published more healthy and lowfat cookbooks than anyone in the world, so I have worked closely with a great many editors. I sincerely say (you have no idea how sincerely) that I am especially fortunate to have had Kelly Ewing as mine. She is not only a new mother and busy gal, but a gentle task master, a terrific editor, always asking the right questions that I forgot to address, making insightful but helpful comments, and giving constructive criticism. She is very patient and just plain sweet. She made sure I did a better book than I would have on my own, that the recipe instructions are as clear as possible (she complimented me on those — thank you, Kelly), and that there were no loose ends. Writing a good cookbook is a synergistic relationship, not a one-man band. I really do love working with IDG.

Heather Prince, also at IDG, was particularly helpful regarding a task more difficult than changing husbands — my changing computer programs. Thank you, Heather. She was patient beyond words, telling me, "Don't worry, Lynn, everyone does that." Sure, Heather. She actually sent me a book on Word in pictures because I was still using DOS. She realized I learn visually better than audibly or reading endless directions. Nice people at IDG.

Holly McGuire is the IDG acquisitions editor who hired me a second time for a second Dummies book. My last IDG cookbook, the best-selling *Lowfat Cooking For Dummies,* was one of IDG's first cookbooks, one of the top four bestsellers of all Dummies books in 1998, and, having set the pace, it is one I now have to keep up with.

Others who helped are the fabulous artist Liz Kurtzman, also a brand new mother. Liz does the illustrations. Liz makes *Quick & Healthy Cooking For Dummies* look as fun, clear, and easy as it really is. I love her clear illustrations. I also thank the photographer Tim Turner, who is one of the best in the world. I mean that. I am very lucky. I also thank food stylist Lynn Gagné, prop stylist Renée L. Miller, assistant food stylist Cindy Melin, and assistants Rod La Fleur, Paul Pela, and Andreas Larsson. You can't do this without them. One picture of good food is always better than a thousand words, and they all made it happen.

After my three recipe testers tested every single recipe, IDG (smart people as they are) always gets its own tester, and I thank Laura Pensiero for making even more good suggestions.

Thank you, Lynn Fischer

Publisher's Acknowledgments

We're proud of this book; please register your comments through our IDG Books Worldwide Online Registration Form located at `http://my2cents.dummies.com`.

Some of the people who helped bring this book to market include the following:

Acquisitions, Editorial, and Media Development

Project Editor: Kelly Ewing

Acquisitions Editor: Holly McGuire

Illustrator: Elizabeth Kurtzman

General Reviewer: Laura Pensiero

Acquisitions Coordinator: Heather Prince

Editorial Director: Kristin A. Cocks

Editorial Coordinator: Michelle Hacker

Photography: Tim Turner

Production

Project Coordinator: Regina Snyder

Layout and Graphics: Jill Piscitelli, Janet Seib, Brian Torwelle, Maggie Ubertini, Dan Whetstine, Erin Zeltner

Proofreaders: Laura Albert, Corey Bowen, John Greenough, Arielle Carole Mennelle, Marianne Santy, Charles Spencer

Indexer: Sherry Massey

Special Help

Lynn Gagné, Food Stylist; Renée L. Miller, Prop Stylist; Cindy Melin, Assistant Food Stylist; and Rod La Fleur, Paul Pela, and Andreas Larsson, Assistants

General and Administrative

IDG Books Worldwide, Inc.: John Kilcullen, CEO; Steven Berkowitz, President and Publisher

IDG Books Technology Publishing Group: Richard Swadley, Senior Vice President and Publisher; Walter Bruce III, Vice President and Associate Publisher; Joseph Wikert, Associate Publisher; Mary Bednarek, Branded Product Development Director; Mary Corder, Editorial Director; Barry Pruett, Publishing Manager; Michelle Baxter, Publishing Manager

IDG Books Consumer Publishing Group: Roland Elgey, Senior Vice President and Publisher; Kathleen A. Welton, Vice President and Publisher; Kevin Thornton, Acquisitions Manager; Kristin A. Cocks, Editorial Director

IDG Books Internet Publishing Group: Brenda McLaughlin, Senior Vice President and Publisher; Diane Graves Steele, Vice President and Associate Publisher; Sofia Marchant, Online Marketing Manager

IDG Books Production for Dummies Press: Debbie Stailey, Associate Director of Production; Cindy L. Phipps, Manager of Project Coordination, Production Proofreading, and Indexing; Tony Augsburger, Manager of Prepress, Reprints, and Systems; Laura Carpenter, Production Control Manager; Shelley Lea, Supervisor of Graphics and Design; Debbie J. Gates, Production Systems Specialist; Robert Springer, Supervisor of Proofreading; Kathie Schutte, Production Supervisor

Dummies Packaging and Book Design: Patty Page, Manager, Promotions Marketing

◆

The publisher would like to give special thanks to Patrick J. McGovern, without whom this book would not have been possible.

◆

Recipes at a Glance

Dressings

Pasta

Pork

Poultry

Red Meat

Rice

Salads

Sandwiches

Sauces and Condiments

Seafood

Soups

Vegetables

Contents at a Glance

Cartoons at a Glance

By Rich Tennant

The 5th Wave — By Rich Tennant

"Do you want your salad shaken, throttled or just tossed?"

page 43

The 5th Wave — By Rich Tennant

"I'm not sure we're getting enough iron in our diet, so I'm stirring the soup with a crowbar."

page 217

The 5th Wave — By Rich Tennant

"It's a microwave slow cooker. It'll cook a stew all day in just 7 minutes."

page 319

The 5th Wave — By Rich Tennant

"I'm sure there are some canned staples in the food pantry. That's what it's there for. Just look next to the roller blades, below the bike helmets above the back packs but underneath the tennis balls."

page 7

Fax: 978-546 7747
E-mail: richtennant@the5thwave.com
World Wide Web: www.the5thwave.com

Table of Contents

Introduction

• •

This book contains all kinds of recipes: Italian foods, Asian foods, Mexican fare, Greek dishes, Arabic foods, French cuisine, vegan food (a form of vegetarianism), and food as American as apple pie and the Fourth of July.

I wrote this book because I hate paying high prices for food or going to a restaurant or friend's house and being served food that will make me ill, fat, give me indigestion, or if eaten often may contribute to heart and artery disease.

Because I like delicious, simple, straight-forward food and excellent sauces prepared in just a few steps, I have created some wonderful recipes based on that concept. This is an effortless food-making book. (Who has the time for anything else?)

About This Book

This book is a reference, a way to cook healthful foods quickly, and can be read starting at the middle or with the acknowledgements, as bedtime reading, or standing on your head trying to find a spatula that slipped under the table, your foot keeping your place on the open page. (I also suggest exercise along with good food to be really healthy.) You can go back to any part at any time, as I do continually because I forget half the stuff I said.

Keep in mind that the recipes are simple, and all are tested, some several times. Their greatest benefit is that you will soon get the hang of how to make your own dishes lowfat yet taste rich and thick even when you use skim milk . . . and how smaller meat portions can look and taste appetizing.

Cooking healthfully and quickly at the same time, plus making it taste good, can be tricky. Make sure that you read each recipe before trying it.

Conventions Used in This Book

There are some "givens" in this book — conventions I have used when writing the recipes that I want you to know about.

- Use lowfat or fatfree butter substitutes to lower cholesterol and calories.

- Change vegetables you like for those you don't. Be cautious not to use vegetables like watery zucchini in place of drier green beans, or the dish may end up as mush. And keep in mind that it takes carrots longer to cook than asparagus unless you shred or thinly slice the carrots.

- Meats, fish, and poultry can often be interchanged. Use the same sized pieces and same amount or weight. There is little change in the nutritional analyses except for saturated fat (with red meat usually having more than fish or turkey breast). Seafood cooks faster than meat and poultry, so slice accordingly.

- All red meats used here are lean, lowfat, and zero trimmed (meaning no edge fat).

- All poultry (except quail) is without skin; usually I use just the breast, with all additional fat removed.

- All bacon has the fat cut off before or after cooking.

- Prepared meats like sausage, bologna, chroizo, and other luncheon meats are used only in lowfat or lean varieties.

- All meats, poultry, and seafood are portioned at approximately 3½ to 4 ounces before cooking.

- No salt is listed in the ingredients, and it isn't in the nutritional analyses. I make the assumption that you know how much salt you want to use. I do suggest, however, where to add it in the recipes if you're using it. Most foods taste better with a little salt, and salt is no longer considered the bogeyman for most people that it once was.

- Pepper is listed only when necessary for the recipe, but you can add it in any recipe you choose.

- Butter, egg yolks, cream, whole milk, and high-fat cheeses are not used or are used sparingly. Milk is skim, and half-and-half is fatfree. Use reduced-fat or fatfree dairy for sour cream, cream cheese, ice cream, and frozen yogurt. Plus, use butterlike sprays (not the same as cooking spray).

- Few high-cholesterol egg yolks or high-cholesterol products are used. Instead, egg substitutes are nearly always used, with only an occasional yolk.

- Although many fresh herbs are listed, most are common, such as basil, rosemary, parsley, and tarragon, and can easily be purchased or grown at home. There's no fresh oregano here. It is the only herb I don't like fresh. It's listed only as dried, but use what you like.

- To keep the ingredient list uncluttered, water is not included in the ingredient list. If needed, the instructions give the amounts and where to add it.

✔ Cooking spray also isn't listed in the ingredients. I hope folks who want to cook lowfat will have it available. (Cooking spray comes in many types such as canola, olive oil, and butter flavored, although canola will do for almost everything.) The recipe instructions explain when to use it.

✔ Flour is all purpose unless otherwise noted.

✔ All onions are white or Spanish yellow unless otherwise noted.

✔ Minced or whole garlic can be fresh, bottled chopped, or bottled minced.

✔ Usually fresh vegetables are used, and frozen is always acceptable. You can use some canned foods, such as mushrooms, corn, tomatoes, and beans. Try not to use canned green beans, asparagus, or peas. The texture and taste is different, and that will impact the recipe.

✔ I take for granted that you have certain tools: Microwaves, stoves, oven broilers, skillets, saucepans, large pots and skillets or Dutch ovens, knives, aluminum foil, plastic wrap, forks, bowls, spoons, rubber spatulas, and whisks. I let you know when you need a food processor or hand chopper, blender, or grill.

✔ Nutritional analyses is given only for the first item of two or three choices. If the recipe says, "1 cup fatfree or lowfat sour cream," the analysis is for the first listed, fatfree sour cream, only.

What You're Not to Read

You don't have to read all this book or in any order. Read whatever you like — skip from Chapter 2 to Chapter 10 and then back to the Intro or go to the Glossary. You don't have to read sidebars; I just put them there because they might interest you.

Foolish Assumptions

My own foolish assumptions are that you can read. Therefore, you can cook. I assume that you want to eat good food without getting a master's degree in it. I also assume that you don't want to always eat out. (It's expensive and fattening, and what's in this stuff anyway?)

Instead, I assume that you want to eat glorious meals in the quiet of your own home, meals that take 2 minutes to fix and cost 50 cents each. Most are actually under 20 minutes, and most cost about $3.50 a serving, which isn't at all bad. All are, of course, glorious (they really are pretty good), and at the least are very good tasting and nutritiously sound. What more could you ask for?

I suspect that you have little time or patience and just want to get good and tasty food on the table — food that doesn't contain a case of fat, salt, or sugar. In fact, this book is so handy and contains so many tips and hints, if you follow just a bit of it, you will know what healthy is all about, what quick cooking is all about, and be able to write your own sequel to it and add scintillating information to any conversation about food.

In addition, you need this book if:

- ✔ You think healthy cooking must be done from scratch with alfalfa sprouts and cranberries.

- ✔ You think cooking healthy is expensive. (It's cheaper.)

- ✔ You think that cooking foods quickly and without fat means it won't taste good. (I use regular easily available food and know how to make lowfat delicious.)

- ✔ You think quick cooking means you are running around your kitchen like a crazy person. (You are actually more relaxed.)

- ✔ You want to prepare meals more efficiently. (Some recipes use partially prepared foods, precut meats, convenience foods, and mixes, all common items from local chain supermarkets. The book tells you how to find them, what's healthy, and how to use these shortcut foods in your daily cooking.)

- ✔ You think healthy cooking means saying goodbye to the golden arches and taco emporiums. (No! It tells you how to turn those favorite hamburgers, tacos, and pizzas into healthy, lowfat meals. And it tells you what to order and not order — so much for fast food snobbery.)

- ✔ You think healthy cooking is self-righteous and boring and that it is a sort of penance and isn't any fun. (No! No! No! It is both fun and clever.)

- ✔ You want quick and healthy cooking to be enjoyable and easy. It is full of light-hearted facts, illustrations, and comments about foods and the way we used to eat and the way we eat now.

How This Book Is Organized

Quick & Healthy Cooking For Dummies is a quick read for those who have an interest in both health and easy food prep. It follows standard cookbook formats with recipes on everything from hors d'ouevres to desserts and everything in between. The health part is proven, double-checked with doctors, registered dietitians, and health experts, but alternatives are given.

Part I: Cooking the Quick and Healthy Way

Part I tells you what healthy cooking means and what it doesn't mean. Deep-fat frying isn't healthy; a quick spritz of a cooking oil to the skillet is. It gives lots of tips and hints such as also spritzing the vegetables or adding a tablespoon of water. It is full of information about what the big markets now offer, which is plenty, and how to spot and take advantage of thousands of new products for fast prep. You find out how to read Nutrition Facts panels (labels), what to look for quickly, what you might want in your pantry to make healthy cooking easy, and even the types of pots and pans and knives for quick clean and breezy heating. I list handy appliances because certain ones can speed up any meal while others just sit in the cupboard like last year's juicer, which took an hour to clean. This is equipment that stands the test of time.

Part II: Quick & Healthy Recipes

Here are all the basics: hors d'oeuvres, salads, soups and sandwiches, lots of vegetables, a chapter on red meat, poultry, fish and shellfish, pasta, grains and rice chapters, and fabulous fruit and dessert recipes.

Part III: New Fast and Easy (And Healthy) Ideas

Wanting to add a few more recipes but in very different categories, I give you remakes of old favorites, one-skillet and one-pot meals, vegetarian and vegan recipes, bright breakfasts, and slow cooker recipes. I also tell you everything you want to know about spices, herbs, and spirits.

Part IV: The Part of Tens

In this part, I help you find the ten best health newsletters and the ten best health Web sites.

Icons Used in This Book

Throughout this book, I use icons to make the text more clear and easier to read and to highlight certain points.

This icon tells you of a special suggestion, like how to make something even quicker or easier, or another addition that might work in a certain recipe, or any other info I think you'd like to know.

Unlike a tip, a warning icon means I have added this in a particular place because I noticed something to look out for. Last night, there was a huge BOOM in my kitchen, alerting me that my eggplant blew up in my microwave (it really did) because I didn't pierce it. I now have this warning icon in my head when I see eggplants, but I have also placed them here and there in the book to alert you not only about the proclivity of eggplants, but why you might want to wash all produce carefully.

This icon gives you a hint on how to save even more time, which is hardly possible as all these recipes are so fast. However, when there are even more timesaving ways, they are beside this icon.

I use this icon to mark things you'll want to remember during your cooking adventures. It's in the book because I forget stuff and think you may also occasionally.

This little guy, which you find in the recipes list at the beginning of each chapter, marks vegetarian recipes.

Where to Go from Here

You can begin almost all *For Dummies* books anywhere — the middle, end or just one chapter — but what are you interested in? Want to first organize your kitchen and pantry? Chapter 2 can tell you that. A favorite is the spice and herb chapter (Chapter 11) because it is so complete, telling you exactly when and how to use them and test recipes with them. There are tips and hints about speeding up both your shopping and cooking in Chapter 2, or if it's the best health newsletters, medical sites, and cooking sites, Part IV tells you that. Or just read the jokes and look at the illustrations.

Part I
Cooking the Quick and Healthy Way

The 5th Wave   By Rich Tennant

"I'm sure there are some canned staples in the food pantry. That's what it's there for. Just look next to the roller blades, below the bike helmets above the back packs but underneath the tennis balls."

In this part . . .

This part tells you how to make nutritious meals quickly and easily. It explains the Food Pyramid and label reading. I also give you tips and hints on what equipment to buy, what is easiest to clean and cook in, and what gadgets speed up the whole process.

Chapter 1

Quick and Healthy Cooking: The Beginning

. . . .

In This Chapter

▶ Examining the Food Guide Pyramids

▶ Reading food labels

. . . .

*Y*ou want your meals quick. And you want them healthy. How do you do that? First, I tell you about the quick recipes I give you throughout the book. Second, I tell you about the different kinds of Food Guide Pyramids because there is more than one way to be healthy, and if you're very young or a senior, you may want something different, but still healthy. Knowing what the Food Guide Pyramids are and how to interpret them helps greatly in the healthy area. And quick and healthy is what this book is all about. You also find out about Nutrition Facts panels and package ingredient's lists (all easy to decipher when you understand them).

Recipes in a Flash

The recipes in this book are quick. Quick because I know how to make almost everything fast and easy. Fast to me means skipping unnecessary steps, using one pan instead of three, and sometimes combining fresh foods with other ready-made, frozen, or canned foods (canned foods are all long cooked) as a base to give flavor and save time, steps, and effort. It is the way I live, not scurrying or hurrying, but relaxed, enjoying preparing food, using every shortcut gadget (like garlic mincers, serrated knives, and slicers) to hasten or reduce food prep steps, all to make the recipe easier — or almost as important, the recipe's cleanup faster and simpler.

The recipes are healthy, but what about taste?

Taste is very important to me. I take special care in that. A discerning cookbook writer tests each recipe. If there was *any* question as to taste from my testers, I dumped the recipe.

I don't have the time or patience to spend an hour grinding up shrimp shells in a mortar and pestle and then adding cream, cream cheese, and butter, which I've done and can do — especially not when I can make a fabulous and far healthier chicken and vegetable stir-fry to get on the table for myself or my family or friends in 10 minutes!

Although the food preparations in this book are quick because the recipes are easy (but not rushed), they are also as healthy as current science recommends. And they're healthy because I have enormously reduced the fat (especially the saturated fat) and cholesterol, substituted skim, lowfat, or nondairy creamer for whole milk dairy and lean meats for fatty, and reduced some but not all meat protein, whole-fat cheese, egg yolks, salt, and sugar in all my recipes. The recipes fill most dietary needs for nutrition.

Healthy (for me) is straightforward. I try to be sure every statement I make has a scientific, well-proven underpinning. The recipes are also holistic and practical. You won't find fiddlehead ferns as a vegetable because, although delicious, they aren't available everywhere and are very expensive when you do find them. Most of what I say is backed by many years of experience (this is my seventh healthy cookbook). The recipes are tempered with good-tasting, lush, and simple foods that take both your lifestyle, your family needs, and your large local markets offerings into account — holistic because I integrate ease and health with really beautiful-looking and tasting food, plus, the recipes are all easily adaptable to your own favorite foods. Once you know how to make a fast and delicious chicken and pepper recipe, you can substitute lean pork and broccoli, adding some of your own secrets or favorites. I add quick-cooking tips throughout the whole book.

What You Need to Know about Healthy Eating

Healthy eating doesn't just happen. The following sections tell you how to pick and follow a Food Guide Pyramid and how to understand Nutrition Facts labels or ingredient's lists.

Pyramid basics

The Food Guide Pyramid basics aren't a fad like bellbottoms, which blast on the scene, soon go out of style, and return again 30 years later only to fade away again. The Food Guide Pyramid may be tweaked every few years, but it is a basic good health plan from opinions of the best scientists from around the world who have studied and researched diet for decades with thousands of people. They help you understand what works, who recommends it, and why. You don't want too much meat, eggs, and whole milk dairy to make up the bulk of your diet if you're over age four.

The Food Guide Pyramid is a research-based food guidance system developed by the USDA (United States Department of Agriculture), supported by the Department of Health and Human Services, and recommended by numerous health researchers. The Food Guide Pyramid (and my recipes and my own pyramid) focuses primarily on fats as they pertain to heart and artery disease, as well as good nutrition and a variety of different foods. The government researchers concluded Americans eat too much fat.

Because more than 50 percent of the American population carry too much weight and almost 20 percent are considered obese, a large number of people subsequently experience diet-related health problems. Unnecessary heart and artery disease, diabetes, osteoarthritis, and other diet-related diseases costs everyone about 10 percent of the one trillion dollars spent on medical care each year. And this doesn't count the excess costs in growing, producing, trucking, storing, or selling all this extra food for people who physically don't need it.

A diet appropriate in calories and low in saturated fats, total fats, and cholesterol can play a role in preventing, controlling, or reversing heart disease, and a diet low in total fat can both help one keep weight down and lose weight.

The following sections describe several Food Guide Pyramids and help you get on the right road to healthy eating.

How much fat is in my recipes?

My quick and healthy recipes, taken in total, have less fat than the government recommendation of 30 percent fat from calories. Most are less than 20 percent. I do this because it is the way I need to eat, because of heart studies, and because over half of Americans are too heavy.

Lower your protein intake

Every time I suggest limiting protein intake, especially animal protein like meat, cheese, milk, and so on, I get the answer, "I won't get enough protein." Yes, you will. Americans already eat double the protein recommended. With some of these newly popular high-protein diets, now many people are eating too much protein. Getting too much animal protein can cause the following problems:

✔ Additional and severe kidney or liver damage if you're even slightly debilitated before going on a high-protein diet

✔ Bone loss

✔ Heart and artery disease

✔ High cholesterol

To *lower* your protein intake, keep meat, fish, and poultry portions small or less than 3½ ounces per serving and eat these items only four or five times a week with vegetarian meals and beans for other meals. Lower your intake of cheese and eggs and other animal products, too. To maintain your animal protein, examine the Food Guide Pyramids. Lowering portion sizes of meat can be the biggest step.

USDA Food Guide Pyramid

The government suggests you eat a wide variety of foods, with plenty of grains, vegetables, and fruits to provide the needed fiber, minerals, and vitamins in a diet that is both low in fat and saturated fat and cholesterol. It isn't a rigid prescription, but a visual guide for healthy eating. This is the government's suggestion (see Figure 1-1).

✔ **Fats and sweets:** Eat sparingly.

✔ **Dairy, milk, yogurt, and cheese:** Eat 2 to 3 servings daily.

✔ **Fish, poultry, meat, nuts, eggs, and dry beans:** Eat 2 to 3 servings daily.

✔ **Vegetables:** Eat 3 to 5 servings daily.

✔ **Fruits:** Eat 2 to 4 servings daily.

✔ **Grains, breads, cereals, rice, and pasta:** Eat 6 to 11 servings daily.

USDA Children's Food Guide Pyramid

This pyramid (see Figure 1-2) is designed for children from ages two through six. Children need fewer calories and less food generally. However, I would give children over age four *only* skim milk, lean meats, and lowfat cheese. Why give them a taste for anything else, and studies show, especially for boys, that cholesterol plaque buildup begins in very early childhood.

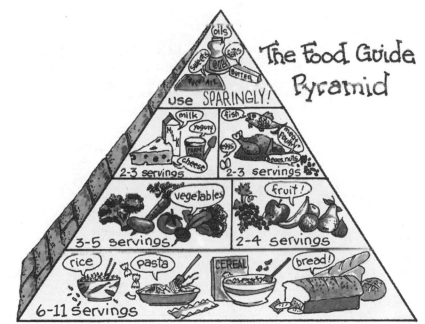

- ✔ **Fats and sweets:** Eat sparingly.

- ✔ **Dairy, milk, yogurt, and cheese:** Eat 2 cups milk or yogurt or 4 ounces cheese daily.

- ✔ **Fish, poultry, meat, nuts, eggs, and dried beans:** Eat two 2- to 3-ounce servings of cooked lean meat, poultry, or fish daily.

- ✔ **Vegetables:** Eat 3 servings daily.

- ✔ **Fruits:** Eat 2 servings daily.

- ✔ **Grains, breads, cereals, rice, and pasta:** Eat 6 servings daily.

Make the dairy servings skim milk, fatfree yogurt, and fatfree cheese. Increasing the vegetable servings to four is a good idea, but difficult. (Getting little kids used to eating vegetables early gives them easier dietary habits to continue throughout their lives, one of the best gifts parents can give a child.) Perhaps letting them pick the colorful ones they want that day, especially when they are tiny, would help finicky eaters eat vegetables. Although serving sizes might be small, they are introduced to many different tastes like asparagus and avocados, foods that are fun to eat.

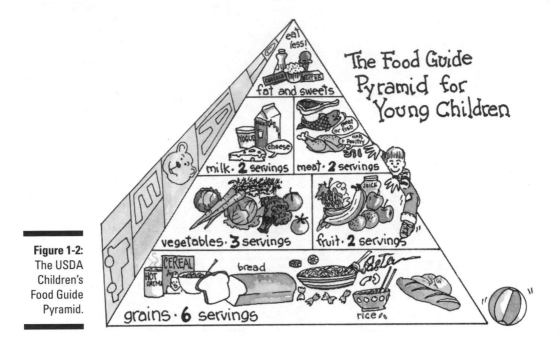

Figure 1-2:
The USDA
Children's
Food Guide
Pyramid.

Tufts University Human Nutrition Research, Center on aging Pyramid diet for people over 70

This is the Tufts University recommendation pyramid (see Figure 1-3), adapted to the needs of older people, which means less food and smaller servings. I personally would make it skim dairy and lean meats only. The addition of water or diluted tea is included.

✓ **Supplements:** Take calcium and supplements, such as vitamins D and B-12 daily.

✓ **Fats and sweets:** Eat small amounts daily.

✓ **Dairy:** Eat 3 servings daily.

✓ **Meat, poultry, fish, beans, eggs, and nuts:** Eat 2 or more servings daily.

✓ **Vegetables:** Eat 3 or more servings daily.

✓ **Fruits:** Eat 2 or more servings daily.

✓ **Grains:** Eat whole-grain enriched or fortified grain and eat 6 or more servings daily.

✓ **Water:** Drink eight or more glasses daily. (Older people tend to lose their sensation of thirst.)

Figure 1-3:
Tufts
University
Human
Nutrition
Research,
Center on
Aging
Pyramid diet
for people
over 70.

Center for Science in the Public Interest Healthy Eating Pyramid

After so much controversy over the first USDA Food Guide Pyramid and its subsequent revamping, the Center for Science in the Public Interest (CSPI), a nonprofit health-advocacy group based in Washington, D.C., came out with its own pyramid (see Figure 1-4). As I agree with it, I have included it. It is a four-sided pyramid with lots of detail, which makes everything very clear (see Figure 1-4). You can get a nice three-dimensional copy of this pyramid by writing to Pyramids CSPI, Suite 300, 1875 Connecticut Ave., N.W. Washington, D.C. 20009-5728. (A paper copy is $4; plastic $15.)

CSPI suggests making anytime foods the backbone of your diet, but the advantage of its food pyramid is that it has "sometime foods" and "seldom foods."

- **Dairy:** Eat 2 to 3 servings daily.
- **Fish, poultry, meat, nuts, and eggs:** Eat 0 to 2 servings daily.
- **Vegetables and beans:** Eat 4 to 6 servings daily.
- **Fruits:** Eat 2 to 4 servings daily.
- **Breads, cereals, rice, pasta, and baked goods:** Eat 6 to 11 servings daily.

Lynn's Food Guide Pyramid for Ages 40 to 70

Because I am asked so often, this pyramid (see figure) shows how I eat. It is more the CSPI pyramid, but slightly adapted for people from 40 to 70, the age group I am in. Staying fit is my most important work. Check with your doctor or registered dietitian before adopting any plan.

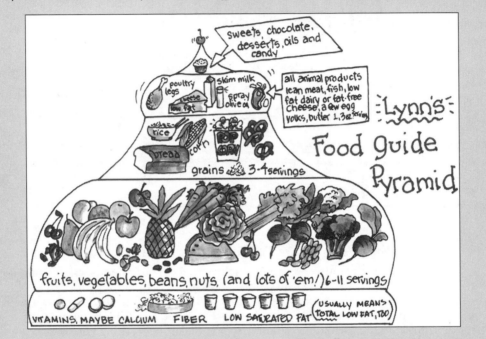

✔ **Multivitamin supplements and other tablets:** I take 1,200 mg daily calcium. I also take a multivitamin, extra vitamin E, and B12 or B complex, plus ginseng.

Regarding calcium, some new studies have come out questioning the use of calcium tablets at all. Keep your eyes open to more information on calcium pills to be sure that they are in your best interest. I am continuing personally but with a careful watch concerning new studies.

✔ **Fats such as butter, lard, almost all other animal fats (like the fat in gravy), and stick margarine:** I eat almost none except on rare occasions.

✔ **Fats such as tub margarine (the package will say without transfatty acids), butterlike sprays and cooking sprays, plus olive or other vegetable oils:** I use 1 to 2 tablespoon daily (of every fat combined).

✔ **Sugar:** Having a sweet tooth, I take care to eat about 2 tablespoons daily, which includes sodas, jams, honey, candy, chocolate milk, desserts, and so on, but doesn't include the sugar in orange juice, other fruit juice, or fruit. For lemonade, I combine Equal with very little sugar.

✔ **Dairy, cheese, fatfree half and half, and nondairy creamers:** I personally eat very little dairy. When I do, it's lowfat or a mixture of regular and lowfat such as adding more real blue cheese to lowfat blue cheese dressing. I limit it to about 100 mg cholesterol and 2 to 3 gm saturated fat in the cheese and dairy daily, perhaps getting more sat fat in other items.

- **Meat, fish, poultry, dried beans, and eggs:** I eat three to five servings a week of animal products. If eggs, I have only half a yolk or egg substitutes, or 100 mg cholesterol a day. Serving sizes are about 3½ to 4 ounces cooked ounces of lean fish, meat (including pork or beef), or skinless poultry.

- **Vegetables:** I eat 6 to 8 servings daily, usually in the form of one big salad, and mostly vegetarian meals at dinner.

- **Fruits:** I eat 1 to 2 servings daily, usually in the form of fresh OJ, maybe berries or bananas on my cereal, and perhaps a fruit tart (very little crust) for dessert.

- **Grains:** I eat 3 to 4 large servings a day made up of a high-fiber piece of toast or cereal at breakfast and perhaps a sandwich at lunch, or whole-grain crackers with an apple later.

- **Water:** At 5'2", I drink only 4 to 6 glasses water, diet caffeine free soda, juice, plain soda water, weak tea, or weak decaffeinated coffee daily.

- **Exercise:** I walk 10 to 20 minutes most days, make an effort to use stairs, park far away in mall lots, and religiously do weight and stationary exercise-equipment training with a professional trainer three times weekly. (Government guidelines are to walk 30 minutes daily.)

- **Sleep:** Getting at least 6 hours is my goal. Many days I get 7 hours, and I sleep easily, which I credit to my exercise regime.

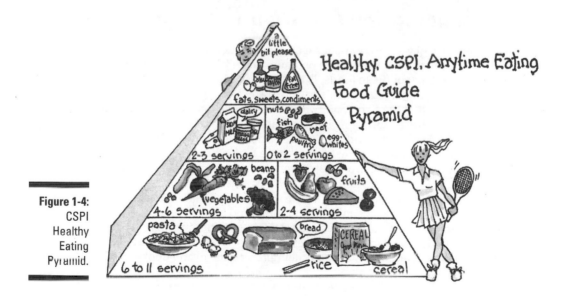

Figure 1-4:
CSPI
Healthy
Eating
Pyramid.

Reading ingredient's statements

Ingredient's statements are on every package, can, or frozen food, and they tell you what's actually included in the food you are eating. This is of passing interest to some people, especially when they notice a food marked apricot nectar and the first ingredient is water, the second corn syrup, and finally, the third ingredient is apricot puree concentrate. Ingredient's statements are of vital interest for those with certain fish or nut allergies, which can be fatal. They have to know that Worcestershire sauce contains fish (anchovies), or that some donuts may be made with peanut flour. Both these items can send them into anaphalatic shock and even death.

The ingredients on labels are listed as to amount by weight, the heaviest down to the lightest, so that you know relatively how much of one ingredient or another product it contains (although no exact amounts are given). As an example, a certain spice mixture may list salt first. You may decide to purchase another brand that lists the spice you want first and salt as the second ingredient. You may also notice very strange or chemical-sounding names, such as locust bean, which isn't a bug and is harmless, as are most of the chemicals. The amounts of the chemical, often added for shelf life or color, may be as small as one part per million and are usually harmless but must be listed.

Reading the Nutrition Facts panel

The grocery store food packages, cans, frozen goods and even meats offer great nutritional knowledge on almost every item — if you just turn it over. On the back of these foods, is the Nutrition Facts panel or label. Thanks to the Food and Drug Administration of the Department of Health and Human Services and the Food Safety and Inspection Service of the U.S. Department of Agriculture (and especially Dr. Michael Jacobson of Center for Science in the Public Interest and Dr. David Kessler, director of the Food and Drug Administration, who pushed for these labels), the food label offers more complete and more accurate nutrition information than ever before.

The label is in a distinctive, easy-to-read format that enables consumers to more quickly find the information they need to make good, healthful, and personal food choices. You need to read labels, including ingredients labels (correctly called *ingredient statements*), to find out whether the food is nutritionally sound, works with any allergies you have, and contains what you want.

Plus, labels include nutrient reference values, expressed as percent Daily Values, that help consumers see how a food fits into an overall daily diet. Uniform definitions are used for terms that describe a food's nutrient content. All this is to ensure that such terms mean the same for any product on which they appear.

So what's high and low in cholesterol, calories, fiber, sodium, and sat fat?

You may wonder what is considered high and what is considered low when it comes to measuring important nutritional values like cholesterol, saturated fat, calories, or sodium. Here are some tips.

- **Calories:** Calories are measured on packaging at 2,000 a day for purposes of figuring the percent of daily values. A small, slender woman who doesn't exercise and is about 5'0" tall might need only 1,200 calories a day. A large-boned, young, tall, and athletic man (not heavy) might need 2,800. Two thousand calories is a good average, so measure your intake against that, taking into account your age (over 60 would usually mean fewer calories), physical activity, build, and sex (women usually need fewer calories than men). If you are overweight, the most likely cause is that you are consuming too many daily calories.

- **Cholesterol:** A single serving of a food with 150 mg of cholesterol is high (one egg yolk contains between 215 to 275 mg, depending upon size). The body needs no dietary cholesterol, incidentally, because it makes enough naturally.

  Cholesterol intakes shouldn't exceed 300 mg a day, and some studies say it shouldn't exceed 200 mg. All meat, fish, poultry, and animal fat contain relatively the same amount of cholesterol, so having a chicken dinner instead of pork won't mean that you're eating less cholesterol. Only animal products contain cholesterol.

- **Saturated fat:** A food (such a slice of apple pie with ice cream or cheese) that contains 5 to 18 gm of saturated fat might be construed as being low. In fact, that single item would provide one-fourth to three-fourths the total Daily Value because 20 is the Daily Value for saturated fat for most.

- **Sodium:** A serving package with a big-appearing number of 150 mg of sodium shouldn't be mistaken for a high-sodium food. In actuality, that amount is small and represents less than 6 percent of the Daily Value for sodium, which is 2,400 mg.

- **Fiber:** A single food serving considered high in fiber would have 5 g (or more). Eating foods high in fiber can help you consume the daily recommendation of about 25 grams for 2,000 calories.

Information on the labels tells you the amount (per serving) of calories, total fat, saturated fat, cholesterol, dietary fiber, and other nutrients you may want to know.

The label can tell you that as there is also a declaration of total percentage of juice in juice drinks, which enables consumers to know exactly how much juice is in a product.

Serving sizes

Standardized and specific serving sizes make nutritional comparisons of similar products easier.

The serving size remains the basis for reporting each food's nutrient content. However, unlike in the past, when the serving size was up to the discretion of the food manufacturer, serving sizes now are more uniform, but may not reflect what people actually think is a serving. They also must be expressed in both common household terms and metric measures.

As a matter of interest, however, more than 133 serving sizes are recognized, and sometimes they differ only slightly. One package of six muffins might have smaller muffins than another package of six muffins; however, both would say, "6 servings." Make sure that you look at the label as the nutrient information will be for the serving size listed.

Here are some terms you might want to know:

- ✓ **Cholesterolfree:** Sometimes you see terms used on packages or cans of foods, and you aren't sure what they mean. For example, corn or olive oil will say cholesterolfree. But to say this term, the oil must meet certain government guidelines in regards to the saturated fat content, which both corn and olive oil contain. All vegetable oil is cholesterol-free. All animal oils or fats (butter, lard, bacon fat, cream, and so on) contain cholesterol. Although vegetable oils are cholesterolfree, they might not meet the saturated fat requirements. All vegetable oils contain some saturated fat, but if the number is too high, even though they contain no cholesterol, they cannot be labeled cholesterolfree.

- ✓ **Reduced in fat:** When a package proclaims, "Reduced in Fat" or "No Sugar or Fat Added," it isn't always clear to the consumer what that means. Does "Reduced in Fat" mean it is lowfat or healthy? No. Not necessarily. Usually, it isn't. "No Sugar Added" simply means the product, such as applesauce, has a trace amount of its own sugar and the manufacturer hasn't added any. As applesauce contains natural sugar, the manufacturer can't say, "Sugar Free." But it can say, "No Sugar Added."

- ✓ **Caloriefree:** Fewer than 5 calories per serving.

- ✓ **Sugarfree and fatfree:** Less than 0.5 g per serving. Synonyms for free include without, no, and zero.

- ✓ **Lowfat:** 3 g or less fat per serving and 15 percent or less of calories from saturated fat.

- **Low sodium:** 140 mg or less per serving.

- **Sodium free:** Less than 5 mg per serving.

- **Low cholesterol:** 20 mg or less of cholesterol and 2 g or less of saturated fat per serving.

- **Low calorie:** 40 calories or less per serving.

- **Lean:** Less than 10 g fat, less than 4.5 g saturated fat, and less than 95 mg cholesterol per serving and per 100 g. (Applies to the fat content of meat, poultry, seafood, and game meats.)

- **Extra lean:** Less than 5 g fat, less than 2 g saturated fat, and less than 95 mg cholesterol per serving and per 100 g serving. (Applies to the fat content of meat, poultry, seafood, and game meats.)

- **High:** Contains 20 percent or more of the daily value for a particular nutrient in a serving.

- **Good source:** One serving of a food contains 10 to 19 percent of the Daily Value for a particular nutrient in a serving.

- **Reduced in fat:** A nutritionally altered product contains at least 25 percent less of a nutrient or of calories than the regular, or reference, product. However, a reduced claim can't be made on a product if its reference food already meets the requirement for a low claim.

Calories and calories

How many calories does a bagel contain? Who knows? Because sizes can differ, calories can differ. Some bagels, for example, are 2½ ounces per serving; others may be 4, 5, or even 6 ounces each, more the size of a half loaf of bread. One bagel may contain 100 calories (without a spread); the other may contain closer to 500 calories (without a spread). Add a fatfree butter-like spray to the first, jelly and fatfree cream cheese, and you can have 160 calories. Add butter, gobs of cream cheese and jelly to the big bagel, and it can be between 700 and 1,200 calories for one bagel.

Chapter 2

Easy in the Kitchen, Easy Out of the Kitchen

. . . .

In This Chapter

▶ Kicking the fat out of your kitchen

▶ Getting "quick" in your kitchen and "healthy" in your shopping

▶ Filling your pantry and refrigerator

▶ Acquiring healthier and quicker cooking and prep methods   spoon it, trim it, skim it

. . . .

This chapter tells you what you need in your quick and healthy kitchen to make fast and healthful cooking a breeze. From fancy and simple appliances to speeding up the prep and cooking process to knowing what to look for on labels, stocking a healthy kitchen is easy.

I also cover food prep with a few quick and helpful tips and hints, such as how to partially cook a food in the microwave and finish it in the oven or on the stove top for the most taste and browning appeal.

Shopping Today — the Quick and Healthy Way

Today, my shopping lists, pantry, kitchen gadgets, and appliances look quite different than they did five years ago and very different from 25 years ago and *really* different from my grandmother's. As I've gained knowledge and experience in how to stock a kitchen primed for quick and healthy cooking, I've trimmed not only the excess fat in the food, but the fat in my kitchen — yet I'm still ready for occasional sumptuous (but healthy) dining.

Historical food gadgets

Horsehair and wooden sieve (1865), Raisin seeder (1895), pineapple eye snips (1901),   *— 300 Years of Kitchen Collectibles,* Linda Campbell Franklin

If you've ever seen the small and large kitchen gadgets your grandmothers or great-grandmothers used 100 years ago, you can see she, like you, wanted her food to be attractive and healthful.

They wanted information on what is healthy, what appliances or gadgets could make cooking quicker and easier, and recipes the family loved. We want that now. We also want food that is simple and fast and healthful. And we can have it.

Cupboards and refrigerators can be full of flavor with little fat. For food that tastes naturally wonderful, kick the fat out of your kitchen. You simply don't need it. It's expensive, takes up valuable space, and is hard to clean on every surface it touches — in your body as well as your cupboard.

The first step in buying more healthful food is to read the Nutrition Facts panel (see Chapter 1) because it's important.

For your good health, it is easy and important when shopping to compare fat grams on similar products. On seemingly identical foods such as pasta sauce, you can save 6 fat grams for the same ½ cup portion. Read the Nutrition Facts panel numbers on the black bordered label on most products before you make your selection. One may have calories at 100, another at 150 per serving.

Creating Lowfat and Fatfree Pantries

Knowing the right ingredients and having them at your fingertips can mean cooking quicker and more healthful almost effortless. I list the essentials you need for pantry, refrigerator, and freezer with tips for selecting and storing ingredients to help you get the most flavor for your money and the most ease and speed in food prep.

All the old pantry standbys that have served you well in the old way of cooking will continue to perform in your healthy, enlightened, and easy kitchen. Fresh fruits and vegetables will abound. Canned tomatoes and soups, condiments, flour, milk, eggs, cereal, and even granulated sugar are all found in quick and healthy kitchens.

In the pantry

TIP

I want to say something about storage: Storing foods neatly and separately is important.

If you can find foods easily, it will greatly speed up prep time. Looking for that box of popcorn for 20 minutes isn't fun and can spoil the party. Here's what I usually have in my 2-foot deep, 6-foot wide pantry. I store food in no other place except the refrigerator and spice cabinet.

The following basic pantry suggestions can help you keep a variety of healthy canned foods on hand in your pantry to use when fresh products aren't available or when it makes more sense to use fresh or frozen vegetables and a canned item as a side. When you can have a good canned applesauce available in 2 minutes at 100 calories instead of making apple fritters at 20 minutes and 400 calories, if you're like me, you'll go for the applesauce both for health and convenience. Remember, canned fruits and vegetables still contain lots of fiber (sometimes too much salt, however) and are quite nutritious.

- ✔ **Canned or bottled applesauce:** Use it as a side and to reduce the fat in baked goods. It works especially well in muffins, quick breads, and snack cakes. Serve it with many meats and vegetables. Cook lean pork right in it, adding a dash of fresh lemon juice, a little apple cider, and a sprinkle of cinnamon to spark up the flavor.

- ✔ **Canned or bottled fruit:** I keep many varieties for eating and adding to sauces and dishes. Mandarin oranges, plums, apricots, mangoes, clingstone peaches, Queen Anne cherries, tart cherries, cranberry sauce, and fruit mince pie mixes are my favorites. For those dieting or reducing sugar, use canned fruits packed in juice or light syrup.

- ✔ **Canned or bottled vegetables:** I keep a few cans such as corn, white and green asparagus, lima and butter beans, hominy, sauerkraut, lots of small cans of sliced or chopped mushrooms, beans of all kinds (about 20 varieties), three-bean salad, green chilies, ripe olives (both the black ripe, pale green ripe, and green varieties), and all kinds of tomato products, such as whole, wedges, diced, crushed, sauce, paste, puree, and Italian-style, which I use often in combination with fresh vegetables.

- ✔ **Pasta sauce:** Keep several jars of differently flavored lowfat brands handy (olive, mushroom, basil, garlic, and so on). Believe me, you can't tell the difference from most fresh sauces, and you definitely can't tell the difference between high-fat bottled or refrigerated sauces. I often add more onions, green peppers, fresh diced tomatoes, shrimp, or other foods to them.

✔ **Gravy:** I keep jars of fatfree beef and chicken gravy to extend my own homemade defatted meat drippings. Great for baked potatoes and dry chicken or turkey breast.

✔ **Canned soups and stews:** From vegetarian chili to pork-flavored baked beans (with 1 gram saturated fat), I have every soup possible, such as lowfat chicken broth, cream of celery and mushroom, tomato, chicken noodle, clam chowder, beef stew (lowfat), oyster stew (lowfat), and at least ten more for quick meals or as a base for my own additions. Having these canned foods handy means practically effortless soups, stews, gravies, sauces, casseroles, and grain dishes where you can add your own fresh vegetables (onions and fresh broccoli florets to cream of broccoli, as an example) to perk them up.

✔ **Canned meats and canned seafood:** Keep water-packed tuna, salmon, anchovies, sardines, and chicken for quick dishes, salads, and convenience.

✔ **Condiments:** Almost all piquant seasonings are fatfree and the life of the flavor party, whether just for me or a flock of folks. For speedy flavors, stock items such as salsas, dried chipotle peppers (to add to the salsa), bottled pepperoncini peppers (for your Greek salad), candied ginger (for fun and sprightly eating), liquid smoke (instead of bacon), green stuffed olives, Kalamata olives, lite soy sauce, oyster sauce, Worcestershire sauce, Bovril or other meat extract, Chinese hot oil, garlic chili paste or crushed garlic, capers, ketchup, and chili sauce, in addition to herbs, spices, pepper sauces, relishes, and French and Dijon mustard (and there are many more).

✔ **Cookies and candy:** I have lowfat varieties of cookies on hand, usually only one kind at a time (which keeps temptation down). It might be lowfat chocolate, minty, caramel, lemon, vanilla wafers, reduced-fat Oreos, reduced-fat Pecan Sandies, cinnamon and honey cookies, gingersnaps, or graham crackers.

For candy, again, I have just one kind on hand at a time. I keep marshmallows, jelly beans, Good and Plentys, and clear fruit hard candies, as well as Tootsie Rolls and sugarless candy for that sweet tooth when I don't want calories.

✔ **Coffee and tea:** I have both decaffeinated and regular hot and iced coffee, Postum (a World War II grain beverage), green tea, a few herb teas, and both decaffeinated and regular tea. Many teas come decaffeinated, including Earl Gray and Constant Comment. With coffee, you can mix decaffeinated with regular when you don't want a huge jolt. Postum is a fun winter drink and with the addition of a fatfree creamer, it's pretty good. My dad loves Ovaltine and skim milk.

Be wary of herb teas. Unless from a major name brand company, be cautious about their safety. For more on herbs, see *Herbal Remedies For Dummies* by Christopher Hobbs, L.Ac. (IDG Books Worldwide, Inc.).

- **Dried fruits:** Raisins, prunes, apricots, tart cherries, cranberries, blueberries, and dates all add sweetness and fiber (but no fat) for just eating or to put in baked goods, salads, and savory dishes alike.

- **Dry pasta:** Most dried pasta contains only 1 gram of fat per 2-ounce serving, and some contain more, such as egg noodles. But lower fat brands that contain 0.5 gram of fat per 2-ounce portion are also available and if dieting, a pasta with half the fat may be important. Get a brand you love — Italian-made pasta can be a little more chewy and flavorful. Stock a variety of shapes, including spaghetti, linguine, shells, tubes, and orzo. But put them all in bugproof containers. (I'll spare you my bug stories.)

- **Dry beans:** Keep lentils, barley, and several kinds of dried beans handy (in sealed containers). I cook them all from scratch, never soaking — however, that is bothersome to many as they blow up like balloons. I eat beans often and don't eat huge amounts at a time. I just put the beans on very low heat in the morning, flavor with plenty of garlic, onions, celery, and carrots, lots of water, cover, and go out all day — and when I get back, dinner is done. (Make sure that you test your "very low or lowest heat" to be sure it isn't too high [or too low] sometime when you can observe the all-day cooking.)

- **Evaporated skim milk:** Mimics the consistency of heavy cream in sauces, desserts, and soups, making for fast and easy preps. Mixing with fatfree liquid creamers helps with the flavor and thickish mouth feel.

- **Cocoa powder:** Here's deep chocolate flavor with all the cocoa butter removed. You can use cocoa powder in desserts, and you can enjoy chocolate and still eat fatfree treats. For hot cocoa, use skimmed milk, fatfree half-and-half, or nondairy fatfree creamers.

- **Garlic:** Whether cooked whole in a pot or pressure cooker for a stew or minced fresh for a salad, this powerful bulb, even when jarred, is essential for many dishes in the healthy kitchen. Store garlic in a cool, dry place but not in plastic and usually not in the refrigerator. Commercial garlic in a jar can stay on the shelf until opened (then refrigerate).

- **Jams, jellies, preserves, and reduced-fat peanut butter:** Just a spoonful of jelly can brighten toast and both sweet and savory dishes. And they're fatfree musts for topping English muffins, bagels, pancakes, and waffles. I defy you to tell the taste difference between reduced-fat peanut butter and regular. Why eat fat? Jams and preserves, unlike peanut butter, needs refrigeration after opening.

With peanut butter, use *only* reduced fat. It tastes the same and has 25 percent less fat — which in reality means 6 to 7 grams fat per tablespoon compared to 8 grams (every little bit helps). Check for the lowest reduced-fat peanut butter as they differ.

✔ **Juices:** Tomato juice, carrot juice, and vegetable juice cocktail are handy to have on hand for soup or stew bases or just for a nutritious snack. I also have peach nectar, apricot nectar, pear juice, papaya, mango mixes, and cranberry juice. Add a squirt of fresh lemon juice to the nectars. Avoid bottled lemon juice like the plague because it tastes awful compared to fresh juice and taints whatever it is added to.

✔ **Diet dressings:** Most aren't very good for dressing salads because they are a little gelatinous, but I keep a few anyway to cook turkey filets and make marinades. I do add other good things to them for salads like balsamic vinegar, a touch of olive oil, and fresh herbs and spices. (For some terrific salad dressing recipes, check out Chapter 4.) Refrigerate when opened.

✔ **Packaged foods:** Keep 10-minute brown rice, 5-minute wild rice, onion soup or dip mixes, ramen noodle mixes, pasta and rice mixes, and bean and rice mixes. Those with flavor packets are usually high in sodium and fat, so use only half the pack or, with macaroni and cheese, half the cheese (adding your own sautéed fresh foods like diced tomatoes and onions). Store them in bugproof containers if keeping them for longer than a week. Also have pie crust mixes (for speed, not fat reduction unless you use just the bottom crust), matzo meal, and crackers all stored in containers that won't allow bugs. (They love my cupboards, which is why I keep mentioning that.) I also have herbed breadcrumbs, oatmeal, and whole-grain cereals plus brown and white sugar and flour (forget the no-white-food nonsense; white sugar is 98 percent the same as brown, and an occasional white flour item, white rice, and white potatoes are just fine).

✔ **Nonstick cooking sprays:** Keep canola, vegetable, olive oil, and butter-flavored sprays if you want a variety. The flavored sprays really offer almost no difference in taste (I tested them all under different circumstances), except when sautéing very small amounts when you can really taste the difference. I keep them all on hand, which makes me feel better when I reduce the olive oil from 2 tablespoons to an olive oil spritz.

✔ **Oil:** Keep olive, canola, and maybe even walnut and grapeseed oils. The latter two need refrigeration upon opening. You can find a lovely salad with walnut oil in this book (see Chapter 4). Grapeseed oil makes wonderfully flavored meat dishes when you sauté lean meat with garlic or onions first.

✔ **Fatfree or lowfat sweetened condensed milk:** The fatfree version of this classic sweet milk is thick, which provides the rich consistency needed for some desserts (see Chapter 9) and perhaps a tablespoon or two in cocoa.

- **Syrups:** Corn syrup can be used in some desserts, but maple syrup, diet, and sugarfree syrups are my favorite. They're all fatfree. Lite syrups have half the calories, sugarfree even less. You can mix regular and lite for a fourth of the calories and more taste. I use them often heated with berries for drizzling on lowfat or fatfree ice cream desserts, grits, pancakes, waffles, French toast, lean pork, bacon, and turkey sausage.

- **Tapioca:** Two kinds, one is granulated for thickening pies, the other is various sizes of tapioca "pearls" for making puddings (fatfree or lowfat). For fruit pies, cook the granules for an hour and 15 minutes at 350°, or you'll still see white granules.

- **Instant flavorings:** Keep ham, chicken, fish and beef bouillon cubes, demi glacés, granules, flavor packets, and sprinkles (and there are other names), all handy for flavoring beans, soups, and stews. Yes, they're high in sodium, but the sodium is divided among several servings, and the added flavor is worth it. These can go bad within a few months, so don't purchase more than you need or refrigerate them after opening.

- **Vinegar:** Vinegar contains absolutely no fat and really brings out the flavor in foods. Try sweet-tart balsamic, cider, red wine, or white wine vinegars (see Chapter 4), plus malt (it's mild), rice wine (also mild), Spanish sherry, raspberry, tarragon, and several other flavored vinegars.

In the refrigerator

I don't always have time to plan meals, so I keep many items in my refrigerator. My refrigerator is full, and I have another junker refrigerator in the garage for pop, beer, and juice. Part of my bargain with myself is that I know some fresh produce will be wasted. For health and variety reasons, I always have a lot on hand, so I continually have a nice choice of the healthiest, freshest foods to choose from. You decide if you want to do that, too. A larger family would have less waste than I do (mine is about 10 percent, but I hate any waste). Plus, if I have 20 oranges and fresh broccoli, I'm more apt to make orange juice and cook broccoli often (sometimes together), so they won't go bad.

- **Citrus fruits:** I always have six to eight lemons, limes, and about twelve oranges, plus one half gallon or two of fresh-squeezed orange juice on hand. Store the fruit in a loosely closed plastic bag in the vegetable crisper for up to two weeks. Use the grated rind (scrub the lemon or orange well with soap and rinse before grating or juicing) and the juice to add zest to everything from appetizers to desserts.

- **Vegetables:** Keep as staples onions, garlic, potatoes, carrots (baby and long), celery, radishes, cabbage, maybe leeks and shallots, and parsley (along with fresh basil, which is in my garden, too) and often I keep fresh mushrooms, green beans, broccoli, artichokes, and asparagus, too.

- ✔ **Lettuce and greens:** Get the prewashed lettuce and greens in packages to save time in sorting and cutting. It's often bite-sized. Look for the latest date or the date furthest out. For example, May 12 will be fresher than May 10. Examine the package contents carefully for brown leaves. Wash again all packaged lettuce in a large bowl filled with cool water and two or three squirts of detergent swirled around. Rinse the lettuce well.

- ✔ **Condiments:** For perking up meals, certain dishes, stews, sauces, salads, or sandwiches, keep pickles (dill, sweet and butter), capers, horserad-ish, relish, roasted red peppers or pimentos (jarred), salsa, ketchup, Worcestershire sauce (which also comes in a low-sodium version. Regular Worcestershire contains less sodium than even lite or reduced sodium soy), Dijon mustard, fresh ginger, hoisin sauce, and hot-pepper sauce. These are kept, once opened, in the refrigerator, unopened in the pantry, so you may see some duplications in the book; however, these are what I currently have in my refrigerator door.

- ✔ **Eggs:** Egg whites are fatfree and cholesterolfree and indispensable for lightening and tenderizing cakes, souffles, and some cookies and for both stretching omelets and scrambled eggs made with egg substitutes. I use yolks *very* sparingly.

    Remember, you can make all your souffles with egg whites only. Just double the amount of egg. If your recipe calls for 4 eggs separated, sub-stitute 8 egg whites, and the souffle will be perfect.

- ✔ **Liquid creamers:** These fatfree nondairy creamers found in the dairy case mimic the consistency of heavy cream in soups and sauces. Choose plain (not flavored) for cooking. Land O Lakes even makes a fatfree half-and-half, which is great. Unlike cream, the liquid creamers will bake and boil without curdling.

- ✔ **Liquid egg substitute:** This convenient, pasteurized, good-tasting fatfree product, which is primarily made from egg whites (99 percent), is great for omelets, scrambled eggs, cookies, custards, quiches, frittatas, may-onnaise, Hollandaise, pancakes, waffles, French toast, and many more baked goods. You can substitute ¼ cup of egg substitute for each whole egg in a recipe.

- ✔ **Fatfree butter-flavored pump sprays (not cooking sprays):** These sprays make an excellent substitute for butter or margarine on breads, toast, bagels, English muffins, pasta, rice, popcorn (butter flavored), barley, mushrooms, or any steamed vegetables. If you haven't discovered them, you're in for a treat. I tell you when something is bad, and this is good and well worth the fat and calorie savings. Some of these fatfree sprays don't say fatfree on the front, but instead, on the label. New brands of soft tub margarines contain no hydrogenation and no trans fatty acids.

- ✔ **Mayonnaise:** When fatfree mayonnaise is well seasoned, you won't know it's not the real thing. Lowfat does taste better than fatfree, and it's so good you don't need to purchase the regular high-fat variety. Some Midwesterners will want the sweeter, lowfat Miracle Whip. Several brands make good lower fat sandwich spreads.

- **Milk and dairy:** Skim milk, skim milk, skim milk. Fatfree buttermilk is good for baking and sauces because it is thick anyway. Skim milk has suddenly become thicker and more palatable with no added calories, so if you haven't tried it lately, you're in for a surprise. Skim milks called "skim deluxe" and "Skim Plus" are creamier and have even more calcium than regular skim milk. Skim milk has slightly more calcium than the full fat variety (regular milk). Fatfree is also better than 1 percent. The additional fat in 1 percent is considerable. I mix skim with nondairy creamers for cereal, which does lessen the calcium, for consistency and to keep it fatfree.

- **Ready-made pudding and Kraft gelatin and Jello brand gelatin, lowfat and fatfree:** The pudding and gelatins are found both in the cold section and on the shelf near the cookies. They aren't as good as homemade, but fatfree chocolate or butterscotch pudding placed in your own dish, topped with fatfree topping and fresh sliced bananas, has only 170 calories. The same amount of pudding made with whole milk, whipped cream topping, and the half banana has more than double the calories at 273.

- **Parmesan cheese:** Fatfree is called a "topping." Look for fatfree brands that contain some real Parmesan or Romano cheese in the ingredient list. Frankly, it doesn't taste exactly like the real thing. So I buy both the fatfree and regular Parmesan and mix them equal amount of each and funnel them back into their shaker cans. Sometimes I get really good Parmesan, shred it, and mix with the fatfree, storing in airtight refrigerator containers. Even a little Parmesan has lots of flavor and goes a long way.

- **Polenta or grits (cooked from scratch or in a tube):** The tubed polenta is ready-to-serve polenta or grits is not only super-convenient but also fatfree. It comes in several flavors, including plain, mushroom, and sun-dried tomato. Instant polenta, which some think tastes better, takes only five minutes.

- **Meat, poultry, fish, and shellfish:** For red meat, always select *zero trim* and with no visible fat or marbling. Zero trim means no fat is on the edge. If you see some, have the meat cutter remove it. Best beef choices are select grade top round and sirloin, which have the least fat. Tenderloin is lean. Lean ham, pork, lamb, and Canadian bacon are also good choices.

  - **Fatfree or lowfat cold cuts, such as chicken breast, ham, bologna, or turkey breast:** These are convenient for sandwiches and salads. Add several slices fresh tomatoes, lots of lettuce, a good spread on a great bread with a good crust, and no one will ever miss the fat, which is mostly saturated anyway.

  - **Ground meat and ground poultry:** Check the labels carefully. Some ground turkey is high in fat because the skin and fat are included. With beef or pork, the fat content can be very high. If a ground product says 85 percent fatfree, it is a *very* high-fat product. Fifteen percent fat is an enormous amount, and it is nearly all saturated. Get a ground product that says "low fat," which has to meet government standards. Get meat that is 7 percent fat or less. Some chicken and turkey breast today is almost fatfree (and some is fatfree). If you can't find lowfat ground round, have the meat cutter remove all the fat from a top round and grind it.

- **Canadian bacon:** This is another handy staple for seasoning a variety of dishes, eating at breakfast, lunch, or dinner, adding to a sandwich, or flavoring soups and beans. One ounce of cured, smoked, and cooked pork tenderloin or ham contains only 2.4 grams of fat compared to 13.9 grams in regular bacon. It's always precooked, so it's ready when you are.

- **Boneless, skinless turkey breast:** Trimmed of all visible fat, this is as close to fatfree as poultry can be. (And some producers are marketing boneless, skinless chicken breasts with only 0.5 gram of fat in a 3-ounce cooked portion.) So read labels carefully to always choose the lowest fat cut possible and always trim off all visible fat. (For duck, remove the skin. Wild duck is always more fatfree than domestic.)

- **Fish and shellfish:** Most fish contains little saturated fat, and shellfish has almost no fat. The cholesterol content for all meats, fish, and poultry is about the same except for liver, other organ meats, shrimp, and squid. Dietary cholesterol isn't quite as important to reduce or even eliminate as is saturated fat. The fish with the least total fat is cod; the most is eel. The shellfish with the least fat and cholesterol is scallops.

✔ **Semifirm or hard cheeses:** Look for lowfat shredded Cheddar, mozzarella, and Swiss. A few years ago, fatfree cheese was a synonym for plastic or rubber, but now some major brands melt fairly well. I particularly like individually wrapped slices for melting and especially the tofu-based cheeses, which also melt well but are somewhat lacking in taste still. Check the fat content on tofu.

And remember, that unless you are on a severely fat-restricted diet, you can enjoy reduced-fat cheeses blended with fatfree cheeses. Each ounce of reduced fat cheese (such as Swiss or mozzarella) adds about 3.5 grams of fat to the total recipe. The shredded lowfat varieties are great for a variety of dishes and make for quick melting.

✔ **Soft cheeses:** Select lowfat or fatfree cottage cheese, reduced-fat cream cheese, or lowfat or fatfree ricotta or fresh mozzarella to add a creamy dairy flavor and consistency to a variety of dishes. In dips with cream cheese, many are already lowfat. For lowfat salmon cream cheese, I put in a bowl with the store salmon dip tub, add a few tablespoons of my own fresh smoked salmon, a few teaspoons lemon, a tablespoon chopped onion and a dash or two of hot sauce, and wow, is it good.

For cream cheese, I use one pack fatfree mixed with one pack regular. The end result is lower in fat and better tasting than the reduced-fat version, which is pretty high in fat and somehow doesn't have the same flavor as high fat.

- **Sour cream:** Choose lowfat or fatfree sour cream, which has the added bonus of not separating when heated, as full-fat sour cream does.

- **Tortillas:** Lowfat flour tortillas, which is naturally lower in fat than corn tortillas, keep well in the refrigerator for a week or more (and much longer in the freezer). Use for fajitas or tacos or serve with scrambled egg substitute or bean dishes.

- **Fatfree plain yogurt:** This is as good as high fat, whether flavored or unflavored, and essential for sauces and for making creamy, tangy yogurt dressings. Flavored and fruit fatfree yogurts are good with fresh fruit (add fresh lemon juice to the lemon) or eaten as snacks.

In the freezer

The freezer is a great place to keep many healthy foods that are quick and easy to prepare. Nuts (which spoil quickly after opening) don't even need defrosting.

- **Frozen bagels, whole-grain bread, and pita breads:** These are good to keep handy for sandwiches, toast, and recipes. Stock English muffins and crumpets, too.

- **Frozen pancakes and waffles:** Get the lowfat variety. Pop them in the toaster, add lots of berries, syrup or lite syrup, maybe fatfree or lowfat whipped topping, and more berries on top for delicious timesavers.

- **Frozen fatfree whipped topping:** Keeping them frozen is always great for impromptu desserts as they defrost very fast.

- **Frozen lowfat dinners:** I keep four or five, especially lowfat macaroni and cheese, which is very hard to make at home lowfat. Then I add fresh chopped tomatoes, onions, or other foods to these basically good if bland or incomplete meals — meals where someone else has done the long cooking, fat reduction, and flavoring.

- **Frozen phyllo dough:** These paper-thin sheets of fatfree pastry make wonderful pie crusts or appetizer wrappers for lowfat and fatfree fillings. Thaw according to package directions. Lightly coat each sheet of phyllo with nonstick spray so that the sheets will stay separate and crisp when cooked.

- **Frozen meat, poultry, and seafood:** It's convenient to have a small variety on hand in recipe-ready portions. I keep small chunks of already cut lean meat frozen in little plastic bags and all the little bags in a bigger zipper-style bag (easier to find), ready to pop into a stir-fry, soup, stew, and so on. If you crack them on the counter to separate, they need no defrosting.

✓ **Frozen vegetables and fruits:** These are good additions for sides or "greening up" long-cooking foods, rice, or pasta (which can get a little muddy or bland looking). Add fresh frozen broccoli spears, cut asparagus or green beans, peas, or limas right from the package during the last minute of cooking. Frozen fruits are great for cereals (cherries), pancakes (blueberries), dessert sauces (pureed raspberries or strawberries or added fresh cherries), quick pies (peaches and blueberries), and more interesting salads (frozen peas). Buying frozen pearl onions saves an hour of peeling the delicious little troublemakers.

Choosing Cooking Equipment

I want speed. I love most nonstick cookware, and I personally use the heavy kind such as Le Crueset nonstick. I like the heavy cookware because it holds the heat and doesn't burn as quickly at higher temperatures. (I'm a distracted and sloppy cook, which you know if you've seen my more than 300 half-hour television shows.) I get into less trouble with the heavier types. And because it's such a breeze to clean up, you may find yourself cooking much more often.

Lynn's favorite: Heavy cookware such as Le Crueset nonstick. It goes in the oven up to 450°.

Lynn's opinion: Stainless steel is terrific. It doesn't stick anymore, and I have some of that, too.

Least favorite: Pans that are too thin and warp.

Nonstick surfaces are tremendously improved from the original coatings that chipped and flaked soon after they were put into use. In general, the heavier the pan, the better the heat is kept. Steel doesn't conduct well, but many steel pans have an aluminum core base. Aluminum, cast iron, and stainless steel (with a bottom pad of aluminum or copper) are all good choices. Shop for the best pans you can afford. The best pans, by the way, aren't always the most expensive. (See Figure 2-1.)

I also have stainless steel and many, many glass covers. I also love pressure cookers (see Figure 2-2). T-Fal makes a terrific one called a Fusion Cooker. No little tiny pressure thingy top to lose with this one, and the cover works on more than the one size pan and they include both sizes. The rim is the same diameter on both the 4-quart and 6-quart sizes. The new pressure cookers of most brands have several, sometimes as many as five, really good safety valves. I also have an old aluminum 8-quart pressure cooker of my mother's, which I use for getting great flavor in less time.

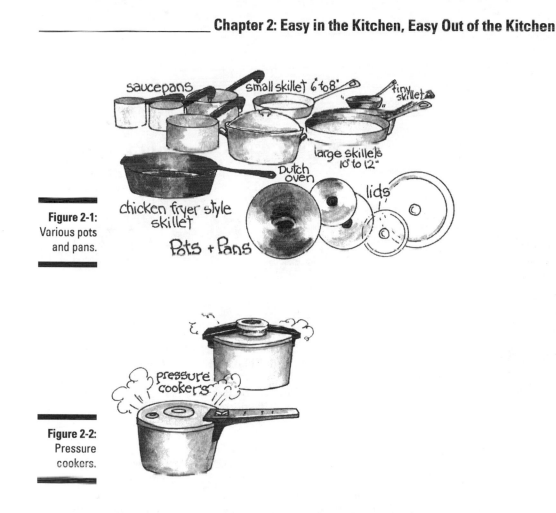

Figure 2-1:
Various pots
and pans.

Figure 2-2:
Pressure
cookers.

With just a spritz of nonstick spray in a nonstick or stainless steel pan, you can turn onions and other vegetables into flavor-gold as the base for great-tasting dishes. A spritz also browns turkey cutlets, chicken pieces, stewing beef, and fish fillets with little added fat. (The new stainless steel is easy to clean, by the way.)

Nonstick bakeware is nice to have but not essential. I use ovenproof glass, my grandmother's tin cake pans, nonstick cookie sheets, and many other kinds, whatever I have or someone has left (see Figure 2-3).

Scissors of all kinds are essential for cutting off bulky wrappers, rubber bands, and tie twists that won't untwist; cutting fat from chicken thigh and breast edges; cutting string; snipping herbs, such as parsley, rosemary, basil, thyme, and chives; cutting pizzas slices; cutting phyllo dough; and cutting pie crust designs.

Figure 2-3:
Nonstick
bakeware.

Bakeware

As far as knives (see Figure 2-4), here are my suggestions. High-carbon stainless-steel forged knives are durable, hold an edge, and won't rust as old-fashioned carbon-steel knives did. Good sizes include a 10-inch chef's knife, a 10-inch serrated knife, a 4-inch serrated knife, and eight or nine four 3-inch or 4-inch paring knives. An electric knife sharpener is also a good investment.

I prefer dishwasher-safe knives with molded polyurethane handles, placed carefully on the top shelf of the dishwasher away from the drying coils.

You may prefer to handwash and dry your knives to protect them from unwanted bumps that may dull the blades but if they won't go in the dishwasher, to heck with them.

Glass or plastic defatting pitchers (see Figure 2-5) are a must for removing fat from stocks, soups, and meat drippings. Large glass ones handle more liquid and remain transparent unlike some of the plastic cups, which can turn cloudy and crack with heavy use.

For more information on cookware, see *Cooking For Dummies* by Bryan Miller and Marie Rama (IDG Books Worldwide, Inc.).

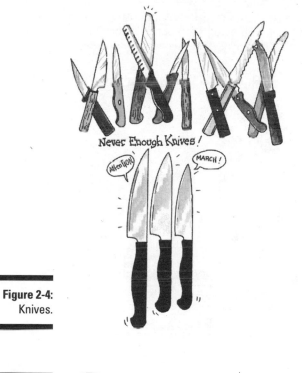

Figure 2-4:
Knives.

Figure 2-5:
A defatting
pitcher.

Getting Rid of the Fat

Trim it, skin it, and skim it. That's all you need to know to rid excess fat from your food before and after cooking. Plus, cleanup is quicker and easier without the fat. Getting rid of excess fat always means healthier cooking. That's where you can take extra time.

Before cooking, trim all visible skin and fat from seafood, poultry, and meat (see Figure 2-6). Don't trust your supermarket meat cutter with this important job. Your motivation to do a thorough job is the desire for improved health. Still buy lower fat cuts and products, however (see Figure 2-7).

Figure 2-6: Trim all visible fat from your meat.

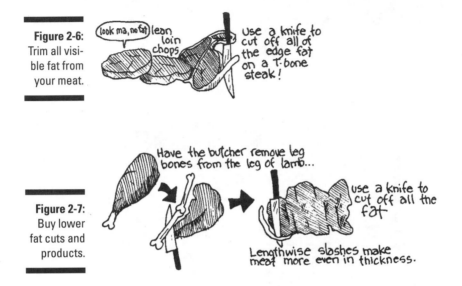

Figure 2-7: Buy lower fat cuts and products.

After cooking stocks, soups, stews, chili, a roast with pan drippings, or any other dish that contains melted fat, defat completely with a defatting cup before serving. Melted fat is clear and rises to the top of the pot, where it's easy to capture and discard.

You can spoon fat off by hand, but it takes time and isn't efficient. If you chill it in the refrigerator for even a few minutes, the fat rises to the top and can be easily removed; longer or frozen, it can be lifted off. Let time do the work for you. This method works especially well for stews and other dishes with lots of chunky ingredients. Even refrigerating the finished dish for several hours or overnight, until the fat hardens on the top, makes it easy to pick off and discard.

For lowfat and fatfree soups and gravies, use a large defatting pitcher. Pour the liquid into the pitcher, which has a spout that starts at the bottom. Wait a few seconds until the fat rises to the top. Slowly pour out the stock (which comes from the bottom of the pitcher), stopping just before the fat reaches the base of the spout. I usually do two passes with the defatting pitcher to get rid of every drop of fat.

Mastering Quick and Healthy Cooking Techniques

You might be surprised to find out that you already know a lot about quick and healthy cooking techniques and tools. You use them in your kitchen every day. You love rubber spatulas. You've found they make it easy to get batters and sticky liquids completely out of their bowls or cans. Your counters are probably already easy to clean, you may have a countertop grill (see Figure 2-8), you have a microwave, a whisk, even a blender, and an assortment of choppers, some electric. Toasters are automatic. However, here are some techniques and appliances you might want to consider. The techniques reduce the fat, and the appliances and tools speed up the process.

Figure 2-8:
Countertop
grill.

countertop electric grillers

✔ **Sautéing:** One method of quick cooking or sautéing is to dry-fry. This sears foods to seal in the moisture and make a slight crust without a lot of excess fat. Lightly coat the food, not the skillet. You sear these already lowfat foods, such as turkey cutlets or fish fillets with nonstick spray, in a hot skillet. Then you heat it at a lower temperature, uncovered, to completely cook the meat through, making sure it doesn't burn.

✔ **Grilling and broiling:** These direct-heat methods cook some vegetables and small cuts of meat, poultry, and seafood quickly, letting the fat and juices drain off for better health.

Brush the grill or broiler pan with a few drops of oil or lightly coat the food with nonstick spray before cooking. To add flavor to lowfat cuts, marinate or coat the food with defatted stock, barbecue sauce, marinades of lime juice, herbs or spices, and garlic, whatever you would like.

To grill small pieces of seafood or vegetables, place them on a special cooking rack, perforated with small holes, that sits right on top the grill rack. Or create your own perforated surface by punching holes in a double thickness of heavy-duty foil. Or do as the Chinese taught us — place the pieces of fish or tomato slices on lettuce leaves (high enough off the flames, burners, or coals so that they don't burn).

✔ **Roasting:** This method of oven-cooking food in a covered or uncovered pan is ideal for poultry, meat, and seafood. Enhance flavor before roasting with dry seasoning rubs or marinades. You can do it before leaving for work. Rub on the spice or place the meat with a marinade in a sealable plastic bag. Let time be your ally with flavored meat or vegetables ready to cook when you return home.

✔ **Braising:** Braising cooks foods in a small amount of liquid in a tightly covered pan or casserole on the stove top or in the oven. Seafood, poultry, and meat can be browned before braising using the dry-frying technique. This boosts the flavor of the finished dish. The liquid is often reduced after cooking as the base for an accompanying sauce.

✔ **Poaching:** This method cooks seafood, poultry, and vegetables submerged in simmering seasoned water, juice, wine, or other liquids. Always poach at a gentle simmer, never a boil. This is a no-fat cooking method that infuses flavor and moisture into food.

✔ **Microwaving:** A microwave is especially useful for moist-heat recipes such as braises, soups, and stews. Make sure that you have plenty of oven bags available for quickly cooking vegetables like green beans, asparagus, corn (microwave it unhusked to be twisted off after cooking), small pieces of meat, and so on.

✔ **Steaming:** A fast way of cooking seafood, poultry, or vegetables on a rack set over boiling liquid in a tightly covered pan can be accomplished using a variety of equipment (see Figure 2-9).

- Collapsible metal steamer with legs
- A heat proof plate or small metal baking rack set on a clean, empty tuna can
- A 2-inch thick bed of shredded carrots, cabbage, onions, or other vegetables (to serve as part of the dish)
- A pressure cooker
- A small electric rice steamer
- A small electric vegetable steamer
- An electric steam convection oven

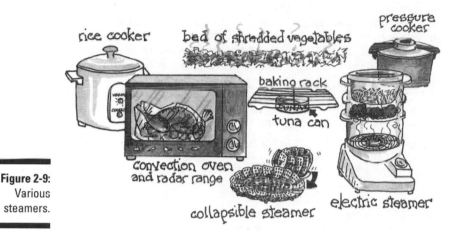

Figure 2-9:
Various
steamers.

The collapsible metal steamer unit must sit comfortably inside the pan with some room to spare around the sides so the steam rises both under and around the food. Fill the pot with about 1-inch of water. Place the steamer rack in the pan and put the food to be steamed on the rack. Cover and bring the water to a boil. Reduce the heat slightly and cook until the vegetable "greens up" or for the amount of time specified in the recipe.

Many foods can also be steamed on a grill or in the oven tightly wrapped in foil packets or in an oven bag, with some seasoned liquid and chopped vegetables added for flavor.

✔ **Stewing:** Stewing is a method of cooking several foods in a seasoned liquid, such as stock or wine. The liquid base, often thickened, is served as part of the dish.

✔ **Stir-frying:** Cutting seafood, poultry, meat, and vegetables into small pieces is the secret to successful stir-frying with just a coating of non-stick spray in a very hot skillet or wok. For best results, always stir-fry in small batches. If the pan is too crowded, the ingredients will steam instead of browning — which isn't bad either.

✔ **Pressure cooking:** Artichokes take 12 minutes whereas steaming takes 40, chicken 15, potatoes 6, beets 4, dried beans 20 minutes, green beans 3 minutes — and that's almost too long for some people.

Measuring Up

Sometimes you need to know measurements — especially when you're baking or making a dish where the ingredients and spices are tricky. Having measurements around is handy.

Fanny Farmer, who began the standardized measurement style of cooking in 1896, did a great service to everyone who has ever cooked. Imagine trying to decipher early instructions from various city and country cooks who called for "butter the size of an egg" or "one penny's worth of raisins" or told you to "cook until done." Today, an apple pie can almost be foolproof if you follow directions.

However, Fanny could make cooking intimidating. Measuring became a chore, something to fear. "Did I tap the side of the cup to get the flour down? Was it a level measurement?" was many a lament. You do need fairly good measurements for most recipes, always in baking and especially when you want to either reduce or increase a recipe, or you're not sure how much a pinch, dash, or dollop is.

You will know as much as you need to now because few measures call for a "peck" of something anymore. Although creative cooking is great fun and sometimes necessary when you have pasta but not the rice that was called for, it doesn't work with every recipe, especially baking, which is more a chemical process.

- A *pinch* is $\frac{1}{16}$ of a teaspoon - more if you like it.
- A *dash* is between $\frac{1}{8}$ and $\frac{1}{16}$ of a teaspoon - more if you like it.
- A *dollop* is 1 to 2 tablespoons, depending on whether you're adding it to a single serving or a very large tureen (when it could be nearly 1 cup).
- A *sprinkle* is 1 teaspoon to 2 tablespoons, depending on whether you're adding it to a single serving or a large tureen (when it could be $\frac{1}{4}$ cup if sprinkled over a very wide surface).
- A *handful* is about $\frac{1}{4}$ cup.
- Three teaspoons are in a tablespoon.
- Four tablespoons are in $\frac{1}{4}$ cup.
- Five and one-third tablespoons are in $\frac{1}{3}$ cup.
- Eight tablespoons are in $\frac{1}{2}$ cup.
- Twelve tablespoons are in $\frac{3}{4}$ cup.
- Sixteen tablespoons are in 1 cup.
- Two cups are in a pint.
- Four cups are in a quart.
- Four quarts are in a gallon.

Part II
Quick and Healthy Recipes

The 5th Wave   By Rich Tennant

"Do you want your salad shaken, throttled or just tossed?"

In this part . . .

This is the meat of the book. I cover sauces, spices, appetizers, grains, vegetables, pasta, soups, salads, sandwiches, and desserts, of course, and give you lots of quick-cooking tips as well as healthy recipes.

Chapter 3

Easy Hors d'Oeuvres, Appetizers, Dips, and Snacks

Appetizers are fun. The Spanish sometimes use appetizers (called *tapas*) for the whole meal. In this chapter, I tell you about delicious food that is often overlooked — dips, spreads, and even guacamole. I also share with you many tips on how to make those convenient store-bought dips taste better, go further, and become lower in fat, a real boon to making hors d'oeuvres easily and quickly. Because everyone loves appetizers, I make them each stars in their own right.

Having Fun with Appetizers

Appetizers, hors d'oeuvres, and dips and are just plain fun to eat. They quench that ravenous hunger at about dinnertime perfectly. At functions, dips and easy finger foods help make conversations with strangers and friends alike simple, instead of having to sit captive and fuss with knives and forks, chained to the partner you are next to. With cocktail parties, one can just walk, talk, and pop in a tasty bite-sized morsel.

Recently, wise people hadn't thought of fatty dips and party foods as being very rewarding healthwise. You eat them out of hunger and because there is nothing else, but you aren't happy. You know the chicken livers wrapped in almost uncooked bacon isn't in your best interest. But the healthy, lowfat good-tasting party foods in this chapter are the most fun of all.

Even 100 years ago, a hostess prepared special foods for guests

To pickle peaches, take 1 pound peaches, ½ pound sugar, 1 pint vinegar plus mace, cloves, cinnamon and boil the ingredients every day for six days and pour over the peaches.

— Mrs. F.D.G., 1879, _Housekeeping in Old Virginia_

Party foods are different than dinner foods, so do a little planning for big do's and have a few canned or frozen foods available for impromptus. Be sure if it's evening to light the candles or remove them as they cast a nice glow on food and add a sparkle to the evening. Be aware of the safety rules.

✔ **For the safety of those who are allergic, identify fish or shellfish dishes with a topping of shrimp, clam, crayfish, or lobster claw or a small sign in a holder.** The garnish or sign warns those guests with allergies about the food's contents; this isn't just a courtesy because fish allergies are serious.

✔ **For consideration of your guests who have problems with spicy foods, identify dishes that are peppery-hot by garnishing with a small, whole red pepper or adding a small sign.**

✔ **Serve only the freshest of greens, radishes, cucumbers, carrots, and other vegetables.** When you see one limp or brown thing, the imagination goes wild, so remove even that one.

✔ **To make them more attractive, lightly oil black and green olives to avoid them looking dry after about 10 minutes.** Don't spray them with cooking spray because the spray gets bubbly or beady-looking on the olives.

✔ **Use store-bought dips whenever you want, but "doctor them up" with attractive garnishes or thin them with lowfat or fatfree sour cream, yogurt, or mayonnaise.** You can also add chopped onions or green peppers or dilute the higher fat dips with lowfat sour cream or mayonnaise. Look on the ingredients list to see what is already in the dip and add more of that, such as more chopped fresh onions to an onion dip.

✔ **Place small dishes of nuts and dried fruit on tables.** Good mixtures include raisins and almonds, peanuts and dried blueberries, cashews and dried cranberries, dried cherries and filberts, and different kinds of nuts like pistachios.

If you're interested in throwing a party and want to make sure that you do everything right, check out _Cocktail Parties For Dummies_ by Jaymz Bee (IDG Books Worldwide, Inc.).

Jazzing Up Supermarket Dips

If you want to make a great dip, but don't have the time to make one from scratch, try buying a fatfree, lowfat, or regular supermarket dip and improving on it. Following are some dip improvements I've done often. Here's how you can either thin the fat, freshen the taste, or both.

- **Bean dip:** Look for the lowest fat or fatfree variety. They taste better than those made with lard (pig fat). Expand the taste by mixing in a smaller amount of mashed canned beans, finely chopped onions, and a dash of hot sauce. Garnish with items such as a few cilantro leaves, a dollop of lowfat sour cream, chopped black olives, and lime wedges around the edge.

- **Blue cheese dip:** Look for the lowest fat or fatfree variety, thin with fatfree or lowfat sour cream, and add crumbled fresh blue cheese of a better type. (Usually, the blue cheese in store bought dips is bought in bulk and may not be the finest but instead the type that best stores on the shelf.) This way, a little flavor of the best goes a long way.

- **Cheese dip:** Add more lowfat cheese dips such as Old El Paso Cheese and Salsa dip (it's very lowfat) to thin. Garnish with a puddle in the center of hot sauce or salsa, tortilla chips (the end stuck into the dip will get soft if it sits a while so do that at the last minute), chopped cilantro, or black olives around the edge.

- **Crab, salmon, or clam dip:** Add additional fresh-cooked crab, salmon, or clams, a teaspoon or so of lemon juice, and finely chopped chives or onions.

- **Curry dip:** Add chopped hot (spicy) mango chutney, ground ginger, diced cooked chicken or turkey pieces (skinless), and more of whatever the base ingredient is (read the label).

- **Dill dip:** Add chopped fresh dill and fatfree or lowfat sour cream or chopped green and red peppers and onions.

- **Hummus dip:** Add more well-mashed garbanzo beans, fresh lemon juice or just wedges of lemon, minced garlic, chopped onions, and a thin but noticeable swirl of fresh olive oil on top.

- **Tabbouleh:** Add fresh chopped parsley, onions, and more lemon juice.

- **Vegetable cream cheese dip:** Add chopped celery, onion, peppers, and carrots and thin with additional fatfree or reduced-fat cream cheese.

- **Vegetable sour cream dip:** Add more vegetables, such as chopped celery, onions, chives, and peppers, and thin if needed with fatfree or lowfat sour cream or yogurt.

Garnishing your dip

Your dip's garnishes can be simple. Try a few shakes of paprika, a single cooked chilled crayfish, mussel, or shrimp, a sprig of parsley, rosemary, tarragon, or other herb. A flower can connote a sweeter dip.

Trying Your Hand at Appetizers

I chose these recipes because people already love them. But better yet, I made them faster and easier — and definitely lower in fat!

Keep in mind that all dips taste better when allowed to chill for a few hours. The time allows for the melding or blending of flavors, which improves most dips, and chilling provides a longer time the dip can sit out without spoiling.

Deviled Ham

Guests love these bite-sized savory appetizers. Serve on small, thin cracked wheat crackers or thin round crackers. Usually, I buy those convenient little cans of deviled ham and serve them as a ham paté or ham spread, but the canned version is exceptionally fatty. This is so easy, especially if you have a little push chopper. If making large amounts, use a processor.

Preparation time: *10 minutes*

Yield: *2¼ cups*

¾ pound cubed lean ham	*2 small dill or sweet pickles, finely diced*
1 small onion, cubed	*½ teaspoon prepared mustard*
1 stalk celery, finely diced	*2 tablespoons lowfat mayonnaise*

1 Place the ham and onion on a cutting board and chop with a hand chopper or push chopper until the ham and onion is finely minced. Transfer to a medium bowl.

2 Add the celery, pickles, mustard, and mayonnaise and mix until well blended. Add more mustard or mayonnaise, according to preference.

Nutrition at a glance (per serving): *Calories 59.9 g; Protein 7.5 g; Carbohydrates 2.3 g; Dietary fiber 0.3 g; Total fat 2.1 g; Saturated fat .6 g; Cholesterol 17.7 mg; Sodium 625.3 mg.*

Lynn's tip: *To get a little fancy, top with a tiny sprig of parsley, a few sprinkles of chopped scallion, or a tiny slice of pimento. You can also make small tea sandwiches, each 2 inches round or square (crusts removed), with a little lowfat mayo on each piece of bread, and add a ¼-inch slice of chilled cucumber, plus arugula or watercress leaves instead of lettuce, and a sprinkling of salt and especially lots of pepper.*

Clam or Crab Dip

I put these two recipes together because the ingredients work perfectly with either clams or crab with only minor differences, which I note. Because they have several names, remember that spring onions are also called scallions or green onions. Both are great to spread on toast or crunchy bread or to use as a dip with celery or other dipping vegetables. You can sprinkle chopped walnuts, pecans, chopped parsley, or hot sauce (if you like it really spicy) on the dip.

Preparation time: *10 minutes*

Yield: *1½ cups*

8 ounces neufchatel or lowfat cream cheese, room temperature

¼ cup fatfree or lowfat sour cream

1 clove garlic, minced

2 7-ounce cans minced clams or baby clams, drained, juice reserved for the clams (or for crab, 12 ounces fresh picked crab meat)

1 tablespoon fresh lemon juice

2 teaspoons Worcestershire sauce

1 teaspoon dried oregano

¼ cup chopped parsley

2 spring onions, finely chopped

Several dashes hot sauce

2 tablespoons capers, drained (for crab dip only)

½ teaspoon celery seed (for crab dip only)

In a medium bowl, beat the softened cream cheese, sour cream, garlic, drained clams or crab, lemon juice, Worcestershire sauce, oregano, parsley, spring onions, hot sauce, and any salt and white pepper you want. (For the crab dip, also add the capers and celery seed.) If you need to thin the clam dip, use a few drops of clam juice (for the crab, use a few drops of skim milk).

Nutrition at a glance (per serving): *Calories 62.0 g; Protein 4.4 g; Carbohydrates 3.1 g; Dietary fiber 0.0 g; Total fat 3.1 g; Saturated fat 2.1 g; Cholesterol 15.1 mg; Sodium 126.6 mg.*

Tofu Egg Salad Dip

This great snack and dip came from one of my testers, Chris Loudon, who is also a registered dietitian and who always gives me terrific recipes from her own collection. Serve this with crackers or pita bread or even make it as a sandwich on bread with lettuce. Chris likes the taste better with the lowfat mayonnaise rather than the fatfree.

Preparation time: *15 minutes (plus chilling time)*

Yield: *1¾ cups*

1 package 12.3-ounces extra firm lite silken tofu, drained

2 tablespoons fatfree or lowfat mayonnaise

½ cup finely shredded carrot

½ cup finely chopped celery

¼ cup finely chopped green onions

1 teaspoon dried basil

½ teaspoon dried oregano

½ teaspoon dried tarragon or thyme

1 teaspoon turmeric

1 In a medium bowl, place the tofu and mash well with a fork.

2 Add the mayonnaise, carrot, celery, onions, basil, oregano, thyme, and turmeric and mix well. Chill before serving.

Nutrition at a glance (per serving): *Calories 25.5 g; Protein 2.7 g; Carbohydrates 2.5 g; Dietary fiber 0.5 g; Total fat 0.5 g; Saturated fat 0.0 g; Cholesterol 0 mg; Sodium 62.8 mg.*

Lynn's tip: *Add other interesting ingredients, such as slivered sundried tomatoes, sprinkle on capers, and surround with olives for an interesting and tasty party appetizer.*

Orange Granola

Orange juice and fresh ginger give this granola a spirited flavor of freshness without being overly sweet. For the fruit, use a mixture you especially like, such as raisins, dates, figs, tart cherries, cranberries, apricots, and prunes. Both old-fashioned rolled oats and the quick-cooking oats work fine. This granola is good for a quick breakfast, too — grab a handful along with a glass of fresh juice.

Preparation time: *45 minutes*

Yield: *4 cups*

1 tablespoon margarine, butter, or canola oil

¼ cup slivered almonds, chopped walnuts, or pecans

1½ cups finely chopped mixed dried fruit

¼ cup fresh orange juice

1 teaspoon grated fresh ginger

½ cup maple syrup, divided

2½ cups rolled oats

1 Preheat oven to 375°. Place the margarine and nuts in a large flat ovenproof dish or pan and place the dish in the oven during the preheating stage so that the margarine melts. After 5 minutes, remove the dish, swish the margarine and nuts around, and continue heating. Leave the pan in the oven for 10 minutes, or until you smell the aroma of the nuts.

2 Meanwhile, in a medium microwaveable bowl, combine the fruit, orange juice, ginger, and ¼ cup maple syrup. Microwave on high for 1½ to 2 minutes, or until hot.

3 Remove the baking pan from the oven, place the oats in the pan, and stir to combine. Drizzle with the remaining ¼ cup maple syrup; toss lightly to coat. Spread the oats and nuts mixture in an even layer and bake for 15 minutes, stirring once midway through baking.

4 Pour the fruit mixture over the oats and stir well to mix. Spread in an even layer and bake for 10 to 15 minutes, stirring every 5 minutes, or until the mixture is crisp and golden. Cool and store in an airtight container in a cool spot.

Nutrition at a glance (per serving): *Calories 126.7 g; Protein 2.8 g; Carbohydrates 24.2 g; Dietary fiber 2.5 g; Total fat 2.7 g; Saturated fat 0.4 g; Cholesterol 0 mg; Sodium 12.3 mg.*

Lynn's tip: *If granola becomes soggy in humid weather, you can re-crisp it by spreading it on a baking sheet and baking at 200° for 10 minutes. Turn off the oven and leave the granola in the oven for 1 hour. You can also use this as a muesli and mix it in yogurt or serve with skim milk and sugar.*

Snack Mix

Of course, you can eat this snack mix anytime, and guests and kids alike love it. You can find the salad dressing mix in many shake-style dressings. I use buttermilk-style mix. You can find the spicy Asian-dried peas in any Asian store. Or use miniature spicy Asian-style cracker slivers, found in any large market.

Preparation time: *10 minutes*

Yield: *12 cups*

(continued)

3 cups popped popcorn (light, low salt, lowfat variety)

2 cups lowfat goldfish

2 cups Cheerios

2 cups short thin pretzel sticks

1 cup spicy Asian dried peas or Asian-style cracker slivers

1 cup salted pecan halves, walnut halves, cashews, or macadamia nuts

1 1.1-ounce package Ranch salad dressing mix, or mixture of ½ teaspoon salt, ½ teaspoon sugar, ¼ teaspoon garlic salt, and ¼ teaspoon onion salt

1 Preheat oven to 350°.

2 In a very large bowl, add all ingredients and toss lightly. Spray lightly with canola oil or butter-flavored cooking spray and toss again.

3 Transfer to a large ungreased cookie sheet (or 2) that has a raised rim. Lightly spray again and bake for 5 minutes.

Nutrition at a glance (per serving): *Calories 107.2; Protein 2.3 g; Carbohydrates 13.9 g; Dietary fiber 1.3 g; Total fat 5.0 g; Saturated fat 0.8 g; Cholesterol 0 mg; Sodium 311.8 mg.*

Lynn's tip: *You can exchange any of the preceding foods for items you like better, including rice or wheat Chex, oyster crackers, other nuts or no nuts, raisins or dried cranberries, and lowfat broken Triscuits or other cracker pieces. Asian markets have the most interesting little spicy crackers.*

Yogurt Dill and Cucumber Dip

This is a great dip for a larger gathering. It takes only minutes to make, but needs to be refrigerated overnight. Although you can use either mayo or sour cream, my testers liked the mayo a bit better.

Preparation time: *15 minutes (plus chill overnight)*

Yield: *4 cups or about 12 to 14 servings*

1 large peeled cucumber

¼ cup vinegar

½ teaspoon salt

8 ounces reduced-fat cream cheese, room temperature

1½ cups plain fatfree or lowfat yogurt

1 cup fatfree or lowfat mayonnaise (or sour cream)

½ teaspoon minced garlic

1 teaspoon onion powder

1 teaspoon lemon juice

3 tablespoons chopped fresh dill

Pinch sugar

1 Finely dice the cucumbers. Add the vinegar and salt to the cucumbers and refrigerate overnight.

2 The next day, drain the liquid and press the cucumbers in a sieve. Discard the liquid.

3 In a medium bowl, add the cream cheese, yogurt, mayonnaise, garlic, onion powder, lemon juice, dill, and sugar, mix well with a whisk, and fold in the cucumbers.

Nutrition at a glance (per serving): Calories 28.6 g; Protein 1.4 g; Carbohydrates 2.7 g; Dietary fiber 0.1 g; Total fat 1.1 g; Saturated fat 0.8 g; Cholesterol 3.5 mg; Sodium 112.9 mg.

Lynn's tip: Garnishing large dip bowls can be fun. Try placing ripe olives around the dip edge, green olives in between or after every third olive, small sprigs of parsley or cherry tomato halves on top, a spiraled spread out cucumber to decorate the center, carrot sticks and celery stuck in all around the sides, or any number of interesting "dippers."

Bean Dip

Bean dips are always terrific at parties. Folks now know how healthy beans are, and because these are also tasty, they disappear fast. These are high protein, Tex/Mex in flavor, and delicious for a casual gathering. Serve with corn chips, pita bread, crackers, or as a sandwich filling. Celery, jicama (a crunchy root vegetable), or carrot sticks can be used to dip, too. As the dip is somewhat pale, add other garnishes such as sliced jalapeno peppers or the more mild light green bottled pepperoncinis peppers, both available in any large market.

Preparation/Cooking time: 25 minutes

Yield: 3½ cups

2 teaspoons ground cumin

1½ cups finely diced onion, divided

1 garlic clove, minced

2 16-ounce cans fatfree refried beans

1 4-ounce can chopped mild or hot green chilies, drained

¼ cup fatfree or lowfat yogurt

Paprika or cayenne

¼ cup diced tomatoes (for garnish)

¼ cup chopped scallions, green part (for garnish)

¼ cup chopped red or green peppers (for garnish)

1 Lightly spray a large skillet. Add the cumin and heat for 1 minute, stirring steadily, on medium heat. Raise the heat to medium-high. Add 1 cup onions and the garlic and cook and stir for 4 or 5 minutes, until the onions are cooked.

(continued)

2 Add the beans one-fourth at a time, mixing them well with the onions. Lower the heat and continue to cook for 2 to 3 minutes, stirring frequently, or until well heated.

3 In a large bowl, add the cooked beans and onion mixture, the remaining ½ cup chopped raw onion, chilies, yogurt, any salt and pepper you wish, and paprika or cayenne and mix well. Chill.

4 Serve in a bowl on a garnished tray with whatever "dippers" you have selected. Garnish with diced green or red peppers, diced tomatoes, chopped scallions, or several squirts hot sauce. For those who like spicy food, finely dice some jalapenos on the top. Sprinkle on additional paprika or cayenne and tuck in a sprig of cilantro.

Nutrition at a glance (per serving): Calories 85.2 g; Protein 5.1 g; Carbohydrates 16.0 g; Dietary fiber 3.7 g; Total fat 0.4 g; Saturated fat 0.1 g; Cholesterol 0.1 mg; Sodium 81.3 mg.

Lynn's tip: Sometimes I make this recipe and add an equal amount of the canned bean dip, which often has more fat. The dip has a better taste with the combination of canned bean dip and their commercial spicing plus my homemade freshness. This way, I get twice the amount with half the work and an improved taste, depending upon the brand.

Spinach Horseradish Dip

This is a refreshing dip, one everyone will want to dip into. Spinach just looks good. Use lowfat corn tortillas, potato chips, and vegetables like celery, jicama, or carrot sticks. Or fill hollowed cherry tomatoes. If using as a dip, dice some tomatoes or red peppers and sprinkle on top.

Preparation time: 25 minutes

Yield: 2 cups

1 8-ounce box frozen chopped spinach, defrosted and drained

1½ cups fatfree mayonnaise or sour cream

1 small chopped shallot, leek, or onion

1 clove garlic, minced

1 teaspoon lemon juice

¼ teaspoon white pepper

Several shakes hot sauce

2 teaspoons bottled horseradish

1 With paper towels, squeeze the water out of the spinach until dry. Transfer to a large bowl.

2 To a medium bowl, add the mayonnaise, shallot, garlic, lemon juice, white pepper, hot sauce, and horseradish and mix well. Add any salt you wish.

Nutrition at a glance (per serving): *Calories 35.9 g; Protein 1.5 g; Carbohydrates 6.1 g; Dietary fiber 0.6 g; Total fat 0.6 g; Saturated fat 0.0 g; Cholesterol 1.2 mg; Sodium 96.5 mg.*

Lynn's tip: *To drain defrosted chopped spinach, wrap the spinach in 2 or more layers of paper towels and squeeze. Repeat if needed.*

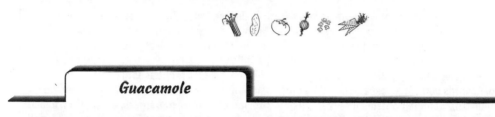

Guacamole

Guacamole in one form or another has been around for 2,000 years. Only the addition of lemon juice (which came from China) a few hundred years ago is new to the basic recipe. This is the best guacamole and is simple, without the unneeded American additives of sour cream, black olives, salsa, mayonnaise or garlic (which you can always add if they are your faves). If you aren't an onion lover, lower the amount.

Preparation time: *10 minutes*

Yield: *1¼ cups*

2 ripe medium to large Hass avocados	*½ cup finely chopped onion*
2 tablespoons fresh lime or lemon juice	*Hot sauce*

1 Cut the avocados in half around the pit and twist. Pull out the pit carefully with a knife tip. With the avocado in your palm and using a sharp knife, carefully score the flesh with crosswise cuts (but not through the shell) and spoon out all the flesh.

2 In a medium flattish dish, add the avocado and mash to desired consistency. Add the juice, onion, and hot sauce, plus any salt you wish.

Nutrition at a glance (per serving): *Calories 58.9 g; Protein 1.1 g; Carbohydrates 4.0 g; Dietary fiber 3.2 g; Total fat 5.0 g; Saturated fat 1.0 g; Cholesterol 0 mg; Sodium 0.3 mg.*

Lynn's tip: *Good additions to guacamole include a few tablespoons chopped cilantro, parsley, diced tomatoes or salsa, and a smaller amount of finely chopped jalapeno for spice lovers, or even a smattering of coarsely chopped black olives to garnish the top.*

Should I eat guacamole on a healthy lowfat menu plan?

Yes, you can eat guacamole even if you're watching your weight. Just don't eat two large servings a day! I have interesting foods such as guacamole in all my healthy cookbooks simply to encourage you health watchers to widen the variety of foods you eat — especially if they are fun foods. Guacamole contains little saturated fat, which is the artery-damaging fat. Its fat is primarily monounsaturated. The total fat amount is between 8 and 17 percent if it is the small pebbly black Hass avocado, about half of that if it is the big shiny light green Fuerte avocado. And yes, the fat in an avocado is high compared to lettuce, a radish or a carrot. But it is low compared to the usual serving of Southern fried chicken, ribs, or a cheeseburger. More important, the avocado, unlike chicken, turkey, ribs, fish, lamb, cheese, or burgers, contains no cholesterol. Plus, the avocado contains fiber. Meat has none. And it tastes so good. So enjoy an avocado, guacamole, or a few slices now and then. I do at least once a week.

Chapter 4

Speedy Salads and Salad Dressings

In This Chapter

▶ Choosing salad greens

▶ Enhancing salads with additions

▶ Making superb salad recipes

▶ Preparing great-tasting healthy dressings

This chapter contains all my favorite salads — many of which I've relied on for decades, updated now to incorporate new methods and ingredients. None of them are oddities, like the time I was served a Caesar with strawberries. And there aren't ingredients you can't find in any major chain. Several may be enticingly different, and I include Asian, Thai, and Tex/Mex tastes.

In addition, my good-tasting dressings are amazing. That they are both lowfat and delicious isn't an oxymoron. A fatfree Caesar is my signature salad dressing, so good it has been borrowed by many a friend/chef for their cookbooks, so I've put it in my own book. You can always add a dash of good olive oil as I occasionally do, but the original version is fatfree.

You find full meal or entree salads (where you won't be hungry in an hour) and small side salads. These aren't your ordinary salads and salad dressings.

Just so you can try something new if you've a mind to, I include descriptions of all the different kinds of greens. Plus, I recommend why you should take advantage of all those prepackaged salad fixings sprouting in your markets' cold bins. Gadgets and appliances for the ideal salad kitchen are also included.

Why Eat Salads?

Salads of vegetable and fruit are bundles of color, variety, texture, fiber, minerals, vitamins, and carbohydrates that are loaded with good stuff. You will taste just how delicious good nutrition can be.

Salads, at least the fruit and vegetables part, make up the whole second layer of the USDA Food Guide Pyramid (see Chapter 1). Salads are the most refreshing reason to really enjoy healthy eating. Salads are natural fat fighters. Rather than calorie-rich, nutrition-poor candies, cakes, or cheese doodles, let the hundreds of salad varieties fill your stomach. You'll eat fewer calories and get more nutrition.

Composed primarily of fresh vegetables and fruits, salads can easily help you fulfill the USDA Food Guide Pyramid recommendations of three to five servings of vegetables and two to four servings of fruit a day.

Salads are easy to make because almost anything can go on them. Salads are generally an *assembly*. You just assemble a lot of delicious fresh ingredients, make it look reasonably pretty, pour on a tasty dressing, and dig in. They take little time and use nutritious food with a modicum of effort.

Add a small amount of protein-rich canned or cooked beans, lean poultry, lowfat or fatfree cheese, or seafood to a simple vegetable or fruit salad, and it turns into a feast that is low in fat and high in nutrition and protein.

2,000 years of salads

A little salad-history points out that salads have been relished for a long time because scientists have proven today what our ancestors instinctively realized 2,000 years ago.

. . . Some drops of olive oil he next instills; Then vinegar with caution scarcely less And gathering to a ball the medley mess, Last, with two fingers frugally applied, Sweeps the small remnant from the mortar's side And thus complete in figure and in kind, Obtains at length the Salad he designed.

Virgil, from Romans 70-19 B.C. (*Food for Thought,* Joan and John Digby)

Tossing the Green

The usual way you serve a salad is tossed. The Caesar, garden, mixed greens, mesclun, potato salad, pasta salad, carrot, and raisin salad are all mix-it-all-together-in-a-bowl salads for a reason. They're easy, quick, and a great way to include the last of the carrots or a handful of leftover sliced asparagus.

A tossed salad (see Figure 4-1) can also include something special on top, like a small delectable mound of diced lean, skinless chicken, turkey, or duck breast, hunks of fresh chilled cooked salmon, a lobster claw, pieces of fresh crab, or a few huge shrimp. Tossed into the salad, a small shrimp can get lost. Sitting on top, it's a treat.

Figure 4-1:
A tossed
salad.

Salads can be formal like the Nicoise (see Figure 4-2) or informal like the Caesar. Greens or lettuces are also formal or casual. Bibb or Boston lettuce is formal; the sturdier romaine isn't. French Mache is formal probably because it is expensive, originally from France, and delicate in texture; while iceberg is hardy, common, plentiful, and usually inexpensive.

Figure 4-2:
A Nicoise
salad.

Nicoise Salad

Washing, peeling, and seeding

Tomatoes need to be washed like every other vegetable, but they don't need to be peeled or seeded. Long carrots need peeling, baby carrots don't. Cucumbers don't need seeding, but they do need peeling if they are waxed.

The only technique you really need to know when making a salad is to carefully cut or pick off all the bad spots. Nothing is more unappetizing than lettuce with brown edges or tomatoes with dark spots. The rest, whatever you do, is fine. When thinking of the ingredients, just be a little wary of mixing some sweet fresh fruits with savory salads. Dried you can mix. If you aren't sure whether one ingredient goes with another, place them on the side of the plate instead of mixing them in.

You don't need to know anything special to make a salad. Chop or tear the lettuce. (They used to say chopping rather than tearing turns the leaf edges brown, but you're eating the salad within hours so chop away.) You can leave some water on it (especially if the dressing is very vinegary or lemony) or spin it or pat dry so that the dressing clings better. You can slice carrots in the round, in short sticks, cubes, diagonally, or shred them (not my favorite way except in carrot and raisin salad) — it doesn't matter.

Choosing Your Ingredients

When it comes to salad greens, the darker the green the more beta-carotene. The more beta-carotene, the more vitamin A. Eat all kinds of salad greens because they are all healthful. If you prefer pale iceberg, white asparagus, or light romaine leaves, try a darker green vegetable occasionally. The darker green leaves are more vitamin and mineral rich.

Some greens are available only at fancy food markets, but many, like baby spinach and mesclun, are now available in every large market. Especially, take advantage of all the different prepackaged greens. Just examine the quality and date carefully. Table 4-1 and Figure 4-3 lists some salad greens.

Figure 4-3:
A variety
of salad
greens.

So easy to eat. salads with so many kinds of greens
and lettuce! Lettuce is filled with calcium, iron,
Vitamins A+C.(The darker the green, the more nutrients!
Not all lettuce is considered a green!

Table 4-1	Types of Usual Salad Greens
Salad Green	**Description**
Arugula	Dark green, slightly peppery, smallish 4-inch long leaves. A striking taste, but not bitter and oh so good. I make a whole salad of them when I can find them
Baby spinach	Smaller leaves, about 3 inches, flat, and more tender than regular. Much like the very special French mache and available everywhere. A big plus is that they are prewashed.
Belgian endive	Cylinder-looking with pointed ends with a white base and pale green tips. The leaves, which look like a cone cut in half lengthwise, have a bitterness I don't particularly like.
Beet greens	Dark green and flavorful, these are terrific if you can find them still on the beets, fresh-looking, and not wilted. They are something like a softer, more rubbery romaine in texture, but thicker and with mucho vitamins and minerals. (They steam nicely whereas romaine doesn't.) Serve tossed with chilled cooked beet chunks and other salad ingredients and any good vinaigrette.

(continued)

Table 4-1 *(continued)*

Salad Green	Description
Chicory	A curly, slightly prickly, dark green head with a white heart, which has a bitter tang that can occasionally be a welcome change from some of the more bland lettuces. Use a strong dressing.
Bibb or Boston lettuce	These are two different kinds of lettuce, but most markets mix them up anyway. Also called butter lettuce or butterhead and sometimes limestone lettuce. An elegant bright green, fluffy soft-headed lettuce with a sweet mild taste. You don't get much per head as, unlike iceberg, it grows more loosely. Tastes best with a delicately flavored dressing.
Cabbage, red and green	Always nice additions to salads for crunch. The red is especially pretty, but cut it into bite-sized pieces because it is too hard to break with a fork. Perfect for slaws where it is shredded anyway.
Escarole	Curly leaves of all colors, sometimes red curly ends, green curly ends, and mixtures of red and green in the same leaf. A sweet pretty lettuce with more texture and crispness than bibb or mache. Good in any salad, alone or mixed with other greens.
Iceberg lettuce	Grandma's old standby. A hard, tightly packed head of light green leaves. Look for the darkest green heads for the most vitamins and minerals. Perfect for sandwiches and especially salads like the Cobb salad, where the lettuce needs some structure to be finely chopped. Can be served in wedges, too. Light leaves don't contain as much nutritional value as do darker leaves.
Mache	Also known as lamb's lettuce, a dark green, tender French lettuce that melts in your mouth. Very expensive and worth it. You usually add it to other greens for interest and to save money. It is about the same size as baby spinach and arugula, both of which are tougher.
Mesclun mixture	Fancy stuff here. Usually an expensive mixture of six or seven different greens, such as the tender French mache, a little red radicchio for color, some baby spinach and arugula, and a couple of light colored lettuces for contrast. Handy when it's already mixed and considered quite elegant if you can stand the price.

Salad Green	Description
Parsley	Add small amounts of either the darker green Italian flat leaf or green curly leafed parsley to any salad or chopped to any dressing. Too much parsley, and its distinctive flavor takes over.
Prepackaged greens	These are fabulous boons for busy people. Most are ready for the table. (I rewash anyway.) Often they come in resealable bags, which is an advantage right there. Look at the dates (usually in the upper right-hand corner or ask the green grocer) and pick the one furthest out. Look to see whether they are prewashed and especially inspect it carefully to see whether there are any brown edges. I select the one closer to the bottom as they have been kept colder than those on top. Look also for the addition of sulfites, which they are often dunked in to keep them fresh longer. It doesn't bother most people, but you may want to select another brand if you are sensitive to this chemical. These packages of spinach, romaine, iceberg, and mesclun are so easy to work with.
Radicchio	Red and bitter. Fun to add in small amounts (and in small pieces) to add color to a salad. Too much, and it's left on the plate.
Romaine lettuce	Dark green, crunchy long leaves shaped like hounds ears. Tough and crisp, but easily bitable. No other lettuce stands up to a really good Caesar dressing full of garlic and anchovies (not that wimpy bottled creamed stuff — use iceberg for that).
Spinach	Dark, dark, dark curly or flat rugged leaves that can be eaten with many kinds of dressings, such as in a spinach salad. (Greatly reduce the bacon grease for better health, please, as it is almost all saturated fat.) Very good with lowfat ranch dressings. Spinach is often extremely dirty and terribly difficult to clean. Getting a jarring, sandy crunch with every bite and wasting your good dressing is no fun. Get it prewashed and perhaps prepackaged, ready for eating instead. Letting them do the washing makes time and effort sense.
Watercress	A peppery flavored bright green, tiny flat leaf on a stem, it is my personal favorite along with romaine and arugula. Nice in any fruit or vegetable salad. (I eat it alone with avocado chunks, yellow cherry tomatoes, and a good Italian dressing.) Use it also to garnish any fruit, fish, or vegetable salad, meat, soups, or cooked vegetables.

Why sulfites

Sulfites are a chemical used to preserve lettuce (and other produce), however, some people may be allergic to it. A package ingredients will say whether the produce has been dipped in sulfites.

You can find other greens like dandelion greens, nasturtium leaves, fiddleheads, and sorrel, but they are either too mysterious for me or a weed I am used to destroying. Fiddleheads are another story. I do love the sweet and tender fiddleheads, which are more a hunk of curvy hard fern than a lettuce green. Unfortunately, they are found only in very upscale markets once a year.

Some folks like a lot of fresh herbs, such as dill, mint, rosemary, tarragon, oregano, and sweet basil, in salads. I like some but in limited quantities, more as part of the dressing (unless it is a mozzarella, tomato, and basil salad). For more on herbs and spices, see Chapter 11.

Adding Onions and Garlic

You can find many different kinds of onions and garlic, and all can be eaten raw (or cooked). From purple garlic to red onions, they add a piquancy to salads whether fruit or vegetable. Onions, however, can taste terrible. Tell the green grocer. They were of poor quality, and your taste buds were right. Table 4-2 lists the different types of onions and garlic.

Table 4-2	Onion and Garlic Varieties
Type	*Description*
Sweet Spanish onions	Usually very big, yellow, and mild; good for those that don't like a strong onion flavor.
White onions	Medium-sized and strong. Usually better for cooking than for salads.
Pearl	Tiny, white and purple, sweetish, and musty flavored. Can be used raw in a pinch.

Type	Description
Vidalia and Maui	Two different sweet onions, which both come large and small, although large is the usual variety. The baby Vidalias look like huge scallions with a big 2 to 3-inch bulb. More of these onions can be used without upsetting the stomach. Since the Vidalia, Georgia onion became so popular, many onions are now called Vidalia, but aren't grown there. Buy from a reputable dealer if you want real Vidalias.
Chives	Little green 10-inch sprigs that can nicely flavor dressings when snipped. They can also be used as an attractive garnish laid across a salad.
Scallions	Larger, green 14-inch members of the onion family. Better raw in salads than cooked in dishes where they lose their flavor.
Leeks	If you haven't discovered this fat, oversized scallion-looking onion sliced thin and raw in any dressing or salad, you are in for a treat. It will soon become a favorite.
Shallots	A mild, small, sweet onion with a little bite in white, yellow, or purple. Dresses up any salad when thinly sliced or chopped.
Wild spring garden onions	These are the kind that sprout in your lawn each year. Whew, they are really hot, but a treat. Wash them well in case they were sprayed, walked on, or worse.
Garlic	All sizes, all colors from purple to yellow to white, tiny to elephant (less flavor there). Whether roasted and pureed, minced, chopped finely, or lightly sautéed and thin sliced, any type of garlic adds to any salad (except a few maybe).

I implore you to wash *all* produce (eaten raw especially) with detergent. Fill a large bowl with water, add a squirt of detergent, swish around *all* produce you will be eating raw (whether lettuce, celery, cherry tomatoes, carrots, peaches, raspberries — every single one). Rinse them well and drain. If you are going to eat the skins of potatoes, wash and scrub them, too. Wash delicate raspberries, mushrooms, mache lettuce, and a few other very tender items just before eating. Wash your oranges and lemons, too, especially if you zest. All produce can be washed and stored in plastic bags or the fruit bin.

My Favorite Salad Additions

Healthiest salad additions include any vegetable or fruit, but here are the most common and the ones I use. Healthiest means items lower in saturated fat and higher in vitamins, minerals, and perhaps fiber.

Fuerte avocados, large, shiny green, which often come from Florida, contain only 4 grams of fat per serving or ⅙ of an avocado, which isn't that much. Haas, the smaller, almost black pebbly-skinned avocado, has 8 grams. Both have vitamins and minerals, plus their fat is nearly all monounsaturated fat, the same fat that predominates in olive oil and canola oil.

Also keep the following in mind:

- ✔ **Serving sizes matter.** A small amount of meat — 1 ounce of diced lean ham — is fine. Four or 5 ounces in a salad wouldn't be, especially if you are eating another meat any other time of the day. A small amount of cheese, 1 ounce, would be okay, but 3 or 4 ounces, which is nearly 1 cup of cheese, has way too much saturated fat and calories.

- ✔ **All cuts and types of meat, poultry, and fish contain almost identical amounts of cholesterol, with shellfish having a little more.** The differences lie in the saturated fat content. Most red meat, such as beef, lamb, and pork, and some poultry contains lots. Roasted skinless chicken or turkey breast are the exception, and a serving contains less than 1 gram. The meat with the least saturated fat is dense pork cuts such as lean ham and Canadian bacon. Shellfish and most other swimmers contain less saturated fat than most red meat.

I would use these every day, including avocado, if I had them handy.

artichokes	asparagus slices	avocados (1 to 2 ounces — higher in fat, but not saturated fat)
baby corn	bamboo sprouts	beans; fresh green, string, wax, pole, fava, foot long, sprouts
beets	canned beans; kidney, garbanzo, navy, red, any kind	capers
carrots, baby carrots; not shreds but hard slices orchunks (hard for teethand jaw health)	cherry or grape tomatoes; red yellow	chicken, (1 to 2 ounces, lean or skinless breast)
chow chows	cod (1 to 2 ounces)	cooked potatoes

corn	crab (1 to 2 ounces)	dried fruits like raisins, cranberries
fatfree cheese (2 ounces)	fruit like grapes, dried fruits, fresh apples	garlic
hard-cooked egg whites	high-fat cheese (½ to 1 ounce)	lean skinless chicken (1 to 2 ounces)
lean ham or Canadian bacon (1 to 2 ounces)	lobster (1 to 2 ounces)	lowfat cheese (1 to 2 ounces)
mushrooms	nuts (1 ounce)	okra
olives, (4 or 5 green or ripe)	onions, scallions, leeks, chives, shallots, any onions	peas
peppers; red, green, yellow, purple, orange, hot, mild	pickles	pimentos
radishes, hot small ones, big white ones, in large slices or halves	relishes	roasted red peppers
salmon (1 ounce)	sardines (1 to 2 ounces)	scallops (1 to 2 ounces)
shrimp (1 to 2 ounces)	smoked or canned fish packed in water (2 to 3 ounces)	snow peas
sundried tomatoes packed in water, smaller amount packed in oil	turkey (1 to 2-ounces, lean, skinless breast)	water chestnuts
winter or yellow squash	zucchini	any diet or lowfat dressing

And here are some more commonly used salad additions that are okay (okay here means having the items occasionally, about once a week depending on the rest of the diet).

bacon (1 slice crumbled)	chicken, lean, skinless breast (2 to 3 ounces)	crab (2 to 3 ounces)
croutons (¼ cup)	diced lean ham (3 ounces)	lobster (2 to 3 ounces)
lowfat cheese (2 to 3 ounces)	nuts (1 to 2 ounces)	regular cheese (1 to 2 ounces)

(continued)

salad dressing of
regular Italian,
2 T. thousand island,
blue cheese, ranch,
creamy Italian,
French, 1 T. Caesar

shrimp (3 to 4 ounces)

turkey, lean, skinless
breast (2 to 3 ounces)

Lastly, here are the least healthy salad additions (this means items that are
very high in fat, especially when eaten in larger amounts):

chicken with skin and
fat (2 or more ounces)

cheese (2 or more
ounces)

duck with skin and fat
(2 or more ounces)

hard-cooked egg
yolks, 2 or 3
especially if eating
any meat, chicken,
poultry, fish or other
high cholesterol
items that day)

large amount bacon
(2 or more slices
crumbled)

lowfat cheese (4 or
more ounces)

luncheon meats like
bologna, salami

medium amount
lowfat cheese (2 or
more ounces)

medium amount regular
cheese (1 or more
ounces)

nuts (2 or more
ounces)

shredded cheese
(handful or 2 or
more ounces)

steak (2 or more
ounces)

turkey with skin and
fat (2 or more ounces)

Beware of Salad Dressings

Salads can indeed be lowfat wonders, but salad dressing is the serpent lurk-
ing in this Garden of Eden. Just 1 tablespoon of vegetable oil — less than
many people unthinkingly pour on a salad — and you have added 13.5 grams
of fat. You can see that by liberally pouring on the oil-based dressing, you can
quickly send the fat content of a salad into the double digits.

If you still think you must have oil, mist it lightly on your salad from a plastic
spray bottle or a salad sprayer. Choose an oil that offers plenty of flavor, such
as extra-virgin olive oil or a dark Asian sesame oil (instead of the
Mediterranean variety, which doesn't have as much flavor). You can use nut
oils, but they are fragile and need refrigeration after opening.

I often dress my own salads with only herbed vinegar, especially when I am in
a weight-reduction mode. I suspect that most people don't care for salads
quite that sharp. You can thin it with fatfree chicken stock. Vinegar or citrus

juices should heighten natural flavors without overpowering them. Unlike most other vinegars, both balsamic and malt vinegar have a natural sweetness that makes them mellow enough to drizzle alone on a salad, without any oil. Brands of balsamic vary widely.

Fortunately, great-tasting lowfat salad dressings are a cinch to make when you know how and are far less expensive. My Creamy Italian Dressing, Thai Peanut Dressing, the Caesar, and several others will attest to that.

Salad dressings highest in fat are Thousand Island, blue cheese, ranch, creamy Italian, regular Italian, sour cream, mayonnaise, French, cream cheese, Cheddar cheese, or a dressing that is mainly fat (bacon fat) or oil (even olive oil). A Caesar dressing is fine if it's tossed onto the greens, and the excess dressing drained.

Table 4-3 lists the different types of salad dressing and their calories and fat for 2 tablespoons.

Table 4-3 Calories and Fat for 2 Tablespoons of Various Dressings		
Type	*Calories*	*Fat*
Regular Italian	137	14.2
Thousand Island	117	11.2
Blue Cheese	154	16.0
Ranch	109	11.3
Creamy Italian	143	15.5
French	134	12.8
Caesar	107	10.5

Dressing up store-bought dressings

Forget the old high-fat store-bought salad dressings just as they come from the bottle or packet. Expand on them. Give them your personal touch and make them healthy, too.

As an example, to make a quick blue cheese vinaigrette, to bottled Italian dressing, add ½ cup vinegar (balsamic if you choose), 2 tablespoons each water and olive oil, and 2 ounces blue cheese or Roquefort. Pour over tomatoes or bibb lettuce.

For a quick creamy Italian dressing, mix together ½ cup lowfat Italian bottled dressing with 1 cup lowfat mayonnaise.

If you want to reduce calories and keep taste in salad dressing, make your own or use store-bought dressing as a base (see the sidebar and recipes later in this chapter).

Here are some tips for making your own dressings:

✔ When making your own favorite dressing, reverse the oil to vinegar ratio from the usual ⅔ oil and ⅓ vinegar to ¼ oil for every cup of vinegar. You may have to adjust the acidity with water or fatfree chicken stock or slightly more oil, but it won't be as fatty as before — and remember, fat adds more calories than any other food because fat has double the calories as protein and carbohydrates.

✔ Use any oil you want — walnut, olive, canola, corn, or safflower. I personally don't care for many flavored oils such as garlic oil because they get rancid too quickly. There are some exceptions. Several companies have put out some gorgeous looking oils in long slim bottles filled with red chili peppers and thyme sprigs, and those I use up quickly.

The oil with the lowest saturated fat is canola and then safflower. Those with double the saturated fats are olive, corn, and walnut. Both olive oil and canola are high in monounsaturated fats.

Table 4-4 tells you how different types of vinegar differ in flavor and intensity.

Table 4-4	Different Types and Flavors of Vinegar
Type	*Flavor*
Distilled white vinegar	Clear and strong. Made from grains such as corn and rye. Can be diluted with water, tomato, or fruit juice. A tart vinegar, good for gift bottles with herbs.
Rice vinegar	Clear and mild. Ideal for those who like a less pungent vinegar flavor.
Cider vinegar	Amber colored, strong, and clean tasting. Made from apples and has the rich smell of apples.
Wine vinegar	Varies in consistency, taste, and color and can range from very strong for some of the reds to more mild. Some wine vinegars are excellent, but others are too strong for salads. Wine vinegars can be made from red and white wine such a Burgundy and Chablis, as well as from sherry and champagne.
Spanish sherry vinegar	Excellent, depending on the quality of the sherry. A little sweet with a pleasant pungent aroma.

Type	Flavor
Malt vinegar	Made from barley, it is actually mild but with a more thick aromatic smell and taste. Excellent with fish, cooked spinach and other greens, and cooked or French fried potatoes.
Balsamic vinegar	Varies greatly in quality. Dark, aromatic, sweet, and mellow. One of the vinegars popular as far back as the 1200s. Aged for years in wooden casks, which gives it its unusual flavor. Different brands range greatly in taste and flavor, and pure balsamic is too costly for most.
Flavored or herbed vinegars	Made by soaking or making extrusions of herbs, fruits, and spices right in the vinegar. Excellent as flavorings for soups and stews and often don't require oil on a salad.

Instead of the awful tasting diet salad dressings, add your own additions to liven and freshen store-bought dressings. Try these additions in small amounts of the dressing to first be sure that you like the taste.

- **Caesar:** To a bottle of fatfree Caesar salad dressing, add a minced clove or two of fresh garlic, a dash of Worcestershire, a tablespoon or two of fresh lemon juice, a squirt of anchovy paste (whisk in), and a teaspoon of grated or slivered Parmesan cheese. Top with freshly ground black pepper.

- **Italian:** To a bottle of diet or lowfat Italian dressing, add a minced clove or two of fresh garlic, ¼ to ½ cup wine, cider, balsamic, or a mixture of vinegars, a tablespoon or two of olive oil, and even a pinch of sugar if you like sweet dressing. Shake in a dash or two of dried oregano and a teaspoon of dried or chopped fresh basil. You can also add a pinch of tarragon and other spices and herbs.

- **Creamy Italian:** To a bottle of diet or lowfat creamy Italian dressing, add a minced clove or two of fresh garlic, 1 to 2 tablespoons wine, cider, balsamic, or a mixture of vinegars, ¼ cup fatfree or lowfat sour cream, (whisk in), ½ teaspoon dry mustard, ¼ cup fatfree nondairy creamer, ¼ teaspoon dried oregano, ½ teaspoon dried or fresh basil, and a tablespoon or two of chopped parsley.

- **Vinaigrette:** To a bottle of diet or lowfat vinaigrette, add a minced clove or two of fresh garlic, 2 or 3 tablespoons wine, cider, balsamic or a mixture of vinegars, 3 tablespoons fresh lemon juice, ½ teaspoon dry mustard, ¼ teaspoon dried oregano, ½ teaspoon dried or 1 teaspoon fresh basil, and a tablespoon or two of chopped parsley.

- **Blue cheese:** To a bottle of diet or fatfree blue cheese dip or dressing, add to a blender ¼ cup lowfat sour cream, 2 tablespoons wine or cider vinegar, ¼ cup fatfree cottage cheese, and a tablespoon or two of skim milk or buttermilk to thin. Blend in a blender until velvety smooth, about 4 minutes. Stir in 3 to 4 tablespoons fresh crumbled blue cheese.

- **Buttermilk:** To a bottle of diet or lowfat mayonnaise dressing or other creamy dressing, add 1 cup lowfat buttermilk, 1 tablespoon grated or slivered Parmesan, ¼ teaspoon each garlic powder, onion powder, ground pepper, and 1 tablespoon each fresh chopped chives and parsley.

- **Horseradish:** To a bottle of diet or lowfat mayonnaise dressing or other creamy dressing including buttermilk, add ¼ cup lowfat or fatfree sour cream and stir in 2 to 4 tablespoons prepared horseradish.

- **Thousand Island:** To a bottle of diet Thousand Island to freshen it or full-fat Thousand Island to dilute it more, add 2 or 3 chopped egg whites (discard the yolks), 3 or 4 chopped green olives, a tablespoon or two each of chopped parsley, sweet relish, chili sauce, lowfat or fatfree mayonnaise, and skim milk to thin, if needed.

- **To all bottled dressings:** Freshen the diet dressing or dilute the full-fat or regular dressing with any kind or mixture of vinegar, lemon juice, orange juice, grapefruit juice, fatfree chicken stock, olive or canola oil, lowfat or fatfree sour cream, buttermilk, skim milk, plenty of finely chopped or minced garlic, onions, shallots or leeks, raspberries, chutney, pureed fruits like mangoes, Dijon mustard, and herbs and spices like dried oregano or fresh or dried tarragon, mint, dill, chives, sage, thyme, or basil.

Vinegar alternatives

For those who don't like or can't tolerate vinegar, try thinned lemon or lime juice, tomato juice, and herbed fatfree chicken stock. They're all excellent on salads.

Lemon juice is the basis for many popular salad dressings, such as the Caesar salad, and predominates in many fruit salad dressings, such as lemon and honey.

The Asian influence has helped those who don't like vinegar with their slivered fresh ginger or ground ginger added to soy sauce and lemon juice with a pinch of sugar, which makes an especially good dressing.

Making Your Own Salads and Dressings

 I happen to like a tart salad and the recipes are geared to that, but you may not. If you desire a gentler-tasting salad, substitute half the vinegar for half water or fatfree canned chicken broth. The chicken broth dressing keeps only for four days refrigerated. You can also use the more gentle rice wine vinegar.

Crunchy Salad

When you feel like crunching away on great vegetables (much like you feel when you tackle the crudités at a cocktail party), then this is the perfect salad. No mushy foods here. Instead, you have a terrific salad. You can choose from the 2 dressings recipes that follow — one is more like the familiar cocktail party dip, and the other is a vinaigrette.

Preparation time: *15 minutes*

Yield: *4 servings*

Leaf lettuce to line plates

4 Roma tomatoes, sliced

3 large carrots or 18 baby carrots, cut into ½-inch slices

12 radishes cut in quarters

2 4 inch pickling cucumbers (don't peel if not waxed), cut in half lengthwise and then sliced in ¼-inch slices

3 stalks celery, cut into slices

2 scallions, cut into slices

4 teaspoons drained capers

1 Arrange the lettuce on the 4 plates. Place the tomatoes on the lettuce.

2 Arrange the vegetables mound-style — the carrots (divided for 1 serving) in 1 area, cucumbers in another, radishes in another, and celery in another.

3 Sprinkle on the scallions and capers and salt and pepper and pour on the dressing.

Nutrition at a glance (per serving): *Calories 52.59; Protein 1.93 g; Carbohydrates 11.78 g; Dietary fiber 3.73 g; Total fat 0.53 g; Saturated fat 0.08 g; Cholesterol 0 mg; Sodium 141.19 mg.*

Creamy Dressing for Crunchy Salad

Try this dressing on the Crunchy Salad.

Preparation time: 5 minutes

Yield: 1 cup

1 cup fatfree or lowfat sour cream or plain yogurt

2 tablespoons skim milk (to thin)

2 tablespoons chopped scallion

¼ cup chopped parsley

2 cloves garlic, minced

2 tablespoons fresh chopped dill

In a small bowl, mix all ingredients.

Nutrition at a glance (per serving): Calories 19.34; Protein 1.13 g; Carbohydrates 3.34 g; Dietary fiber 0.06 g; Total fat 0.01 g; Saturated fat 0.00 g; Cholesterol 1.28 mg; Sodium 14.24 mg.

Crunchy Salad Vinaigrette Dressing

This dressing is easy and has a healthy feel with the crunchy tastes.

Preparation time: 5 minutes

Yield: ¾ cup

2 tablespoons parsley

2 cloves garlic, minced

1½ teaspoons sugar

⅔ cup red wine vinegar

½ teaspoon chopped dried or fresh tarragon

¼ cup olive oil

In a small bowl, mix the ingredients together well.

Nutrition at a glance (per serving): Calories 43.36; Protein 0.08 g; Carbohydrates 0.83 g; Dietary fiber 0.04 g; Total fat 4.51 g; Saturated fat 0.61 g; Cholesterol 0 mg; Sodium 1.80 mg.

Lynn's tip: If you want a thicker dressing, mix the parsley, garlic, sugar, vinegar, and tarragon in a blender. Drizzle the olive oil slowly into the running blender.

Peas and Celery Salad

A strikingly pretty salad with a creamy style dressing, this is a favorite of one of my testers. She tweaked this until it was just right.

Preparation time: *10 minutes*

Yield: *2 servings*

¼ cup fatfree or lowfat mayonnaise	¼ cup chopped onion
1 teaspoon fresh lemon juice	2 tablespoons chopped pimento or red pepper
Pinch dry mustard	
½ teaspoon sugar	2 ounces ¼-inch diced or crumbled feta cheese
1 cup frozen peas, separated	2 tablespoons parsley
1 cup chopped celery	

1 In a small bowl, add the mayonnaise, lemon juice, mustard, and sugar and whisk to blend. Add any salt or pepper you wish.

2 Add the peas, celery, onions, and pimento and mix gently to coat.

3 Using a rubber spatula, fold in the cheese and parsley.

Nutrition at a glance (per serving): *Calories 184.24; Protein 9.14 g; Carbohydrates 22.66 g; Dietary fiber 6.15 g; Total fat 6.50 g; Saturated fat 4.30 g; Cholesterol 25.23 mg; Sodium 652.61 mg.*

Lynn's tip: *Try this with fresh English peas and carrot slices, too.*

Cabbage and Kidney Bean Cole Slaw

You will be surprised at how nice kidney beans go with this slaw. Let it sit a few hours for best flavor, although I can never wait that long. I always wish I had because the leftovers are even better. Beans, with all their protein, fiber, and very little fat, are always a good salad addition. Rinsing them can mean almost no tummy upset.

Preparation time: *15 minutes*

Yield: *4 to 6 servings*

(continued)

1 tablespoon white wine vinegar or cider vinegar

¾ teaspoon sugar

⅓ cup fatfree or lowfat sour cream

¼ cup fatfree or lowfat mayonnaise

2 cups shredded cabbage

1 small onion, shredded or finely chopped

1 cup shredded carrots

¼ teaspoon crushed red-pepper flakes (optional)

1 16-ounce can dark kidney beans, drained

1 In a large bowl, add the vinegar, sugar, sour cream, and mayonnaise and whisk to combine.

2 Add the cabbage, onions, carrots, and pepper flakes and toss to coat well.

3 Add the kidney beans, gently tossing to coat. Cover and let sit refrigerated for a couple of hours.

Nutrition at a glance (per serving): Calories 162.11; Protein 9.01 g; Carbohydrates 30.93 g; Dietary fiber 6.89 g; Total fat 0.55 g; Saturated fat 0.08 g; Cholesterol 1.65 mg; Sodium 322.06 mg.

Lynn's tip: A tablespoon of fresh poppy or caraway seeds and a handful of raisins or dried cranberries always makes a nice addition to coleslaw.

Bean Salad

Unlike most salads, this attractive dish of beans, fennel, and scallions can be marinated overnight in the refrigerator for use the next day, but it isn't necessary. The fennel or celery and the scallions give it a nice crunch, and the red pepper flakes have just the right bite if you like spicy salads.

Preparation time: 15 minutes

Yield: 4 to 6 servings

½ cup cider vinegar

¼ cup sugar

1 cup canned dark red kidney beans, rinsed and drained

1 cup canned white kidney beans, rinsed and drained

1 cup canned garbanzo beans, rinsed and drained

½ cup chopped scallions

½ cup chopped or diced red bell pepper or pimento

¼ cup drained and chopped pepperoncini peppers

½ cup chopped fennel or celery

½ teaspoon chopped hot pepper flakes

1 In a large bowl, add the vinegar and sugar and mix for a minute to help begin to melt the sugar.

2 Add the beans, scallions, peppers, fennel, hot pepper flakes, and any salt and pepper you wish.

3 Just before serving, season liberally with black pepper.

Nutrition at a glance (per serving): Calories 233.06; Protein 9.44 g; Carbohydrates 46.55 g; Dietary fiber 9.95 g; Total fat 1.85 g; Saturated fat 0.05 g; Cholesterol 0 mg; Sodium 573.42 mg.

Lynn's food fact: Fennel is a vegetable that looks something like a big bulb version of celery but with fuzzy fanned out green fronds instead of celery's straight tall stalks with its pale green leaves. Fennel is delightful with a mild licorice taste. It can be used raw or cooked. It is especially good in winter dishes baked in combination with potatoes and cheese.

Fresh Tomatoes, Basil, and Buffalo Mozzarella

If you use the best home-grown summer tomatoes, garden basil, and fresh buffalo mozzarella, I guarantee you will swoon with ecstasy over this dish (and won't notice that I use less cheese). Serve it on a platter decorated with sprigs of basil or on individual plates with 2 slices of mozzarella cheese per serving, which is plenty.

Preparation time: 10 minutes

Yield: 4 servings

2 to 3 large very ripe home-grown tomatoes, thickly sliced

¼ cup shredded or chiffonaded fresh basil leaves, plus 4 sprigs basil (at top of plant), divided

4 ounces fresh buffalo mozzarella, very thinly sliced

½ to 1 teaspoon dried oregano

¼ cup red-wine or cider vinegar

2 tablespoons olive oil

4 sundried tomatoes in olive oil, drained, patted dry, and thinly sliced

(continued)

1 On each plate, place a slice of tomato, a little shredded basil (use half here), another slice of tomato, and a slice of mozzarella on the plate, overlapping in design. There should be 2 tomato slices for every mozzarella slice.

2 Mix the remaining shredded basil and oregano with the vinegar and oil and drizzle over the salads. Sprinkle generously with black pepper and a little salt and garnish with the sundried tomato slices and a basil leaf cluster.

Nutrition at a glance (per serving): Calories 185.70; Protein 6.98 g; Carbohydrates 7.95 g; Dietary fiber 1.87 g; Total fat 14.90 g; Saturated fat 4.93 g; Cholesterol 22.23 mg; Sodium 147.49 mg.

Lynn's tip: You can buy fresh buffalo mozzarella in Italian groceries or specialty or fancy food markets. It's worth the effort. It is kept in water, so just ask for a ball and they will weigh and wrap it. Slice it as needed. It doesn't keep long — just a few days. Use the rest in a good lasagna or other pasta dish.

Greek Bean Salad

Although Americans use only 1 version of a Greek salad, trust me, the Greeks really know how to make many delicious salads. Here is a bean salad, just as pungent and flavorful. You can make this salad the night before or refrigerate it for a couple of hours for more flavor. Garlic lovers can add a minced clove or 2.

Preparation time: 10 to 15 minutes

Yield: 4 servings

2 16-ounce cans fava beans, drained, or 3 pounds fresh beans in their pods, shelled and steamed (in hot, salted water for 1 to 2 minutes, until their skins start to peel off, and then drain)

12 Amfissa, Kalamata, or ripe black olives, pitted and cut in half

1 medium red onion, slivered or thinly sliced and cut in half

½ cup chopped or finely sliced fennel bulb

¼ cup chopped flat-leafed parsley

2 tablespoons olive oil

½ cup fresh lemon juice

Lettuce to line plates

2 ounces feta cheese, crumbled (optional)

1 *If marinating in the refrigerator:* In a large bowl, add all the ingredients except the lettuce and cheese, add salt and pepper, mix to blend, cover, and refrigerate from 1 hour to overnight. When serving, place on the lettuce and add the crumbled cheese.

2 *If eating immediately:* In a large bowl, add all the ingredients except lettuce and cheese and mix to blend.

3 Line 4 plates with lettuce, add the bean mixture, and sprinkle on salt and pepper and cheese.

Nutrition at a glance (per serving): Calories 195.07; Protein 8.32 g; Carbohydrates 22.79 g; Dietary fiber 7.24 g; Total fat 9.06 g; Saturated fat 1.33 g; Cholesterol 0 mg; Sodium 552.09 mg.

Lynn's tips: If steaming the fava beans, you don't need to remove the skins (although the Greeks prefer to do so because of the pretty green color of the bean). You can pit olives easily with a small $10 cherry pitter available in kitchen-supply stores.

Nicoise Salad

This country simple salad done as only the French can has many versions, but the ideal is cold boiled red potatoes, green beans, tuna, and olives. This recipe has a little more lettuce, but is very similar.

Preparation time: 20 minutes

Yield: 4 servings

1 head Boston or bibb lettuce

½ to ¾ pound small red or white potatoes, unpeeled and cooked, or 1 16-ounce can, drained

½ pound haricots verts (tiny string beans) or regular string beans, lightly steamed

4 small hard-cooked eggs, halved, yolks discarded

1 6.5-ounce can water-packed tuna, well drained

4 tablespoons capers, drained

2 ripe tomatoes, cut into wedges

4 anchovies, patted dry

12 black olives

½ cup wine vinegar

2 tablespoons olive oil

½ teaspoon sugar

¼ teaspoon prepared Dijon mustard

1 tablespoon chopped herb mixture (such as fresh thyme leaves, basil, and tarragon)

(continued)

1 Line 4 large dinner plates with a layer of lettuce.

2 Cut the potatoes into bite-sized pieces. Arrange the food in separate areas on each plate. Place the potatoes on 1 side, next to the potatoes going around the edge of the plate, and place the beans in a neat bunch. Then place 2 egg halves each filled with ½ tablespoon capers. Place the tuna next to the eggs.

3 Put the tomato wedges in the center, top with an anchovy, and place 3 black olives together on the largest empty spot on each plate.

4 In a small bowl, add the vinegar, olive oil, sugar, and mustard and whisk. Drizzle as much dressing as you wish over the salads and sprinkle on the herbs and any salt and pepper you wish.

Nutrition at a glance (per serving): Calories 235.75; Protein 17.51 g; Carbohydrates 22.10 g; Dietary fiber 4.64 g; Total fat 9.49 g; Saturated fat 1.38 g; Cholesterol 14.32 mg; Sodium 777.67 mg.

Lynn's fun food fact: Haricots verts are tiny slender (and usually more expensive) French-style green beans with a slightly sweeter taste.

Making croutons

Using 4 pieces of toast to make 2 cups croutons, spray both sides of the toast with nonstick olive oil spray. Sprinkle with garlic salt and rub in finely chopped parsley. Cut into cubes. You can also add a dash of red pepper flakes and bake for 10 minutes in a 350° degree oven to "set" the flavors.

Orange Lentil and Wild Rice Salad

This is the best lentil and bean salad (see photo in color section). You can substitute barley or canned rinsed white beans. This is quick because these new brands of fast-cooking wild rice and lentils are excellent. Incidently, see my tip at the end of the recipe on cooking lentils, which takes 30 minutes. You can cook the 2 in the same pot at the same time by taking notice of cooking times for each, adding one after the other.

Preparation/Cooking time: *15 minutes*

Yield: *4 servings*

1 packet 5-minute wild rice (makes 1 cup)

1 clove garlic

¼ cup orange juice

1 teaspoon Dijon mustard

2 tablespoons olive oil

½ cup nonfat plain yogurt

1 teaspoon Worcestershire sauce

¼ teaspoon cumin

½ teaspoon ginger

1 16 to 18-ounce can lentils, drained, or ¾ cup dry (1½ cups)

1 large orange, peeled, seeded, and cut into bite-sized pieces

½ cup chopped carrots, walnuts, or pecans

3 scallions, some green, sliced diagonally (about ½ cup)

Lettuce to line plates

½ cup crumbled feta cheese (optional)

1 In a large saucepan of boiling water, cook the wild rice. Drain and place the cooked rice packet in the freezer to chill for 5 minutes while you prepare the rest of the salad.

2 In a blender or food processor, puree the dressing ingredients of garlic, orange juice, mustard, olive oil, yogurt, Worcestershire sauce, cumin, and ginger.

3 In a large bowl, add the lentils, wild rice, orange segments, carrots or nuts, and scallions. Add the dressing and coat to cover.

4 Serve on lettuce-lined plates and sprinkle on the feta cheese, if using.

Nutrition at a glance (per serving): *Calories 434.88; Protein 18.76 g; Carbohydrates 64.99 g; Dietary fiber 10.37 g; Total fat 12.26 g; Saturated fat 4.21 g; Cholesterol 17.24 mg; Sodium 867.23 mg.*

Lynn's tip: *Making lentils from scratch is easy. The red ones take only 10 minutes, and they disintegrate, which is fine for soup but not salads, so check while cooking. Small brown and green versions take about 20 minutes.*

Spinach Salad

This is that crunchy tangy salad you used to love but without all the bacon grease. I do use real bacon, just very little bacon fat. You can also add 1 8-ounce can drained mandarin oranges, ½ cup crumbled feta cheese, a handful of sunflower seeds, or slivered hard-cooked egg whites and croutons.

Preparation/Cooking time: 20 minutes

Yield: 4 entrée servings or 8 side salads

12 slices bacon

½ cup cider vinegar

3 tablespoons canola oil

1 teaspoon sugar

¼ teaspoon dry mustard

1 pound spinach, cut or torn into bite-sized pieces

½ cup red onion, thinly sliced, slices cut in half

12 ripe, very small pitted olives

1 If the bacon isn't cooked already, in a large skillet, fry the bacon over medium-high heat until crispy, pouring off the fat often and reserving 2 teaspoons of the fat.

2 Pat the cooked bacon dry with paper towels and remove all the fat by hand. Break or chop the remaining lean bacon meat, all visible fat removed, into 1-inch long pieces (if the bacon is already cooked, scissor off all the visible fat).

3 In a small bowl, add the vinegar, oil, sugar, mustard, and reserved 2 teaspoons bacon grease and mix well.

4 Place the spinach in a salad bowl, add the bacon and onion slices, pour on the dressing, and toss. Add salt and pepper to taste. Garnish with olives.

Nutrition at a glance (per serving): Calories 102.95; Protein 4.80 g; Carbohydrates 3.96 g; Dietary fiber 1.33 g; Total fat 8.06 g; Saturated fat 1.27 g; Cholesterol 9.24 mg; Sodium 345.46 mg.

Lynn's tip: If you want to use olive oil and want a bacon flavor, marinate the cooked bacon in the olive oil for several hours before removing the fat from the bacon. By carefully removing all the fat from the bacon, you're saving about 10 grams of saturated fat — as much sat fat as some people should consume in a whole day.

Pasta and Tomato Salad

This easy Midwestern-style salad suggested by Darlene Diederich can be dressed up and served on lettuce or plain on a bare plate. It is her adult daughter's favorite, and my testers liked it, too. My hint? If you're from the Midwest like I am, you'll want to use light Miracle Whip instead of mayonnaise.

Preparation/Cooking time: *25 minutes*

Yield: *4 servings*

½ pound uncooked pasta	*⅓ cup chopped celery*
½ cup fatfree or lowfat mayonnaise	*½ cup chopped parsley*
½ teaspoon celery salt	*2 summer ripe medium tomatoes, cubed*

1 In a large pot of boiling water, cook the pasta according to package instructions, drain, and set aside.

2 In a large bowl, add the mayonnaise, celery salt, celery, and parsley and mix to blend.

3 Add the tomatoes and pasta, any salt and pepper you wish, and mix gently to coat.

Nutrition at a glance (per serving): *Calories 162.01; Protein 5.20 g; Carbohydrates 32.66 g; Dietary fiber 2.04 g; Total fat 0.85 g; Saturated fat 0.12 g; Cholesterol 0 mg; Sodium 279.79 mg.*

Lynn's tip: *For a full meal or entree salad, add ¼ cup each diced lean ham or Canadian bacon and barely steamed and chilled peas or green beans. Garnish with a few sprigs watercress or parsley.*

Egg Salad with Dill

My very persnickety testers loved this really terrific egg salad. Plus, it is healthy, uses real eggs, and is a great sandwich filling. You can serve it on lettuce, in a ripe tomato, or on fanned avocado slices (looking like more than it is). If you aren't a dill lover, substitute chopped parsley.

Preparation/Cooking time: *15 minutes*

Yield: *6 servings*

(continued)

1 cup substitute egg

8 hard-cooked eggs

½ finely chopped medium red onion

½ cup finely chopped celery

½ cup chopped fresh dill or parsley

½ cup fatfree or lowfat mayonnaise

½ cup fatfree or lowfat sour cream

2 tablespoons prepared Dijon mustard

1 Lightly spray a large nonstick skillet with a lid. Add the substitute eggs and a little salt and pepper and cook over low heat, covered, until firm, about 10 to 12 minutes. Don't stir while cooking. With a rubber spatula, continually lift and check the bottom to be sure the egg "pancake" doesn't burn.

2 When the substitute eggs are cooked but still in the pan (and if you have a skillet finish that doesn't mar easily), take a knife and make slices ½-inches apart across the whole pan in 1 direction. Then do the same the other way or crossways across the first slices making ½-inch cubes of cooked yellow eggs. If unsure of your finish, slide the pancake off on a cutting board and slice, dicing the pancake into ½-inch cubes. Transfer to a large bowl.

3 Peel the hard-cooked eggs, cut in half, and discard six of the yolks. Quarter the other 2 yolks and set aside.

4 Cut the hard-cooked egg white halves in fourths and add them, along with the 2 hard-cooked yolks, to the bowl with the egg substitutes. Add onions, celery, dill, lots of pepper, and some salt if needed and toss gently.

5 In a medium bowl, whisk together the mayonnaise, sour cream, and Dijon mustard. Add the mayonnaise mixture to the egg and vegetable mixture, stirring gently to blend.

Nutrition at a glance (per serving): Calories 112.39; Protein 11.53 g; Carbohydrates 9.99 g; Dietary fiber 0.49 g; Total fat 2.26 g; Saturated fat 0.57 g; Cholesterol 72.33 mg; Sodium 485.95 mg.

Lynn's tip: To save time, you can buy hard-cooked eggs in the deli department of large markets. If you precook your own hard-cooked eggs like I do and have them on hand for weeks (and then can't tell the difference between the cooked and uncooked), either mark them after cooking with a felt tip X or spin them on the counter. Hard-cooked eggs will spin fast and even. Uncooked eggs wobble.

Seafood Salad

You can make this special seafood salad with shrimp, lobster, crab, scallops, surimi (real fish made to look like shrimp and crab), or a combination of seafood. It makes a wonderful appetizer or sandwich filling with a dash of red pepper flakes and lettuce. Serve with chilled fresh melon slices and grapes for a refreshing summer luncheon salad.

Preparation time: 15 minutes

Yield: 4 servings

¼ cup fatfree or lowfat mayonnaise

¼ cup fatfree or lowfat sour cream

2 tablespoons freshly squeezed lemon juice

2 tablespoons water

¼ teaspoon hot pepper sauce

1 tablespoon chili sauce or ketchup

½ cup diced cucumbers

2 large stalks celery, diced

1 medium onion, diced

2 tablespoons diced dill pickles

1 tablespoon capers, rinsed and drained

1 tablespoon chopped fresh dill

8 ounces cooked and chilled shrimp cut into bite-size pieces

Paprika

1 In a small bowl, add the mayonnaise, sour cream, lemon juice, water, hot pepper sauce, and chili sauce. Whisk until smooth.

2 In a medium bowl, add the cucumbers, celery, onions, pickles, capers, and dill. Toss lightly to mix. Add the shrimp and toss again.

3 Add the dressing and the shrimp or whatever seafood you are using and toss gently to mix. Season to taste with salt and pepper and paprika.

Nutrition at a glance (per serving): Calories 107.88; Protein 13.68 g; Carbohydrates 10.73 g; Dietary fiber 1.25 g; Total fat 0.76 g; Saturated fat 0.20 g; Cholesterol 111.82 mg; Sodium 452.51 mg.

Lynn's tip: To make dilled green peppers or baby corn, use the liquid left over from a jar of store-bought dill pickles. (Make sure that the first or second ingredient on the label is vinegar.) Add large slices of fresh green peppers or whole baby corn to the jar and submerge them in the liquid. Put the lid on and refrigerate for at least a month. The peppers and baby corn will stay green and crisp, but will have a mild pickled taste. Serve them as a condiment or slice for sandwiches. Incidently, you can use the juice from any pickle to "pickle" your own pickles if the first ingredient is vinegar.

Chicken Salad with Orange Dressing

I have served this chicken salad at showers, weddings, and birthday celebrations, and it always gets raves (so I know no one misses the usual fatty dressings in chicken salad). Use it as a cool main-dish summer salad served with a rainbow of fresh fruit: grapes, strawberries, cantaloupe, honeydew, watermelon, or fresh pineapple.

Preparation/Cooking time: *20 minutes*

Yield: *6 servings*

½ cup orange juice

½ cup fatfree plain yogurt

2 cloves garlic, minced

2 teaspoons fresh lime juice

2 teaspoons low-sodium soy sauce

1 teaspoon Dijon mustard

1 teaspoon dried tarragon

8 ounces cooked and boned skinless chicken breast, trimmed of all visible fat and cut into ½ to 1-inch cubes

1 teaspoon lemon pepper seasoning

1 cup coarsely chopped celery

1 cup seedless red or green grapes, halved

1 cup coarsely chopped fresh pineapple

¾ cup canned sliced water chestnuts, cut into matchsticks

⅔ cup thinly sliced scallions

6 hard-cooked egg whites, sliced into wedges

1 head bibb lettuce

¼ cup chopped pimentos

1 ½ cups garlic sourdough croutons (optional)

1 In a small bowl, combine the orange juice, yogurt, garlic, lime juice, soy sauce, mustard, and tarragon. Cover and refrigerate.

2 Season the chicken with the lemon pepper seasoning. Place in an ovenproof plastic cooking bag. Microwave on high power for 4 minutes, or until pieces are no longer pink in the center when tested with the point of a sharp knife (or you can poach the chicken breast in broth or water for 15 to 20 minutes). If you have time, refrigerate for 30 minutes, or until chilled.

3 Add the celery, grapes, pineapple, water chestnuts, scallions, and cooked egg whites to the bowl.

4 Remove 6 lettuce leaves and place on a platter. Chop the remaining lettuce and add to the chicken mixture.

5 Pour the dressing over the salad. Toss gently to coat. Spoon over the lettuce. Sprinkle with the pimentos and croutons (if using).

Nutrition at a glance (per serving): *Calories 164.13; Protein 18.17 g; Carbohydrates 19.34 g; Dietary fiber 2.21 g; Total fat 1.97 g; Saturated fat 0.51 g; Cholesterol 32.50 mg; Sodium 320.17 mg.*

Lynn's tip: Take advantage of deli-cooked or packaged cooked chicken in chicken salad recipes. Chicken pieces are easy to microwave in just a few minutes, but the deli variety is easier. Be sure to always skin the chicken and then wipe, cut, peel, and pull off all the fat with knives, scissors, and paper towels.

Potato Salad

This scrumptious old-fashioned potato salad will be asked for again and again. Chock full of potatoes and crunch, you can use sweet pickles instead of dill pickles if you prefer a sweeter salad.

Preparation/Cooking time: 15 minutes

Yield: 4 large servings

8 tiny red potatoes

½ cup chopped kosher dill pickles, plus 1 tablespoon liquid

½ cup finely chopped scallions

¾ cup diced celery

⅔ cup corn kernels, frozen and thawed

⅓ cup fatfree or lowfat mayonnaise

½ cup fatfree or lowfat sour cream

2 teaspoons Dijon-style mustard

½ teaspoon cumin

Lettuce to line plates

1 cup cherry tomatoes, halved

1 Cut the potatoes in half or bite-sized chunks. In a medium pot of gently boiling water, add the potatoes and cook for 20 minutes or until soft when pierced with a knife. Check for doneness after they have boiled 15 minutes.

2 Drain and set aside. Place in a medium bowl the pickles, scallions, celery, corn, mayonnaise, sour cream, mustard, and cumin and mix well.

3 Add the potatoes, gently stirring to coat, cover, and refrigerate for 10 minutes to 2 hours to chill. Line serving plates with the lettuce leaves. Just before serving, garnish with cherry tomatoes.

Nutrition at a glance (per serving): Calories 161.85; Protein 5.32 g; Carbohydrates 34.18 g; Dietary fiber 3.57 g; Total fat 0.70 g; Saturated fat 0.09 g; Cholesterol 2.50 mg; Sodium 578.73 mg.

Broccoli Salad

If you love a broccoli, green beans, or asparagus salad, this is the right dressing.

Preparation/Cooking time: *15 minutes*

Yield: *6 servings*

1½ cups egg substitute

3 10-ounce packages frozen chopped broccoli

6 tablespoons fatfree or lowfat mayonnaise

¼ teaspoon Dijon mustard

1 cup chopped celery

1 small chopped onion

1 Lightly spray a large skillet and place over low heat. Add the egg substitute, cover, and cook over low heat until set, about 10 minutes. Do not stir, but check the bottom frequently to be sure that it doesn't burn.

2 When the eggs are cooked through and while they are still in the pan, cut them crosswise with a sharp knife to make ½-inch squares. Transfer to a medium bowl.

3 Meanwhile, in a saucepan with ½-inch water, cook the broccoli, covered, until separated and hot, about 2 minutes. Drain well.

4 In a medium mixing bowl, add the broccoli, mayonnaise, mustard, celery, and onion to the bowl with the eggs. Mix gently. Thoroughly chill.

Nutrition at a glance (per serving): *Calories 99.34; Protein 10.21 g; Carbohydrates 15.67 g; Dietary fiber 4.34 g; Total fat 0.22 g; Saturated fat 0.03 g; Cholesterol 0 mg; Sodium 258.33 mg.*

Lynn's tip: *You can exchange 1½ cups of diced tofu for the substitute eggs.*

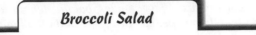

Endive, Romaine, Orange, and Artichoke Salad

This is for endive lovers (which, I admit, I am not, but in this salad I like it). It's the only good endive recipe I've ever had. Don't use olive oil in place of the canola — it detracts from the flavors. When I make it, I sometimes add diced avocados and switch the oranges to grapefruit segments cut into bite-sized pieces, adding a teaspoon of sugar and a pinch of salt to the dressing. I even tried tangerines. Yum.

Preparation time: *20 minutes*

Yield: *6 servings*

2 heads Belgian endive

1 head romaine lettuce, broken or cut into bite-sized pieces

½ large red onion, cut in rings

1 jar (6 ounces) marinated artichoke hearts, drained and halved

2 oranges, in segments or slices, cut into bite-sized pieces

¼ cup fresh orange juice

2 tablespoons lime juice

1 teaspoon grated orange zest

¼ teaspoon garlic salt

⅛ teaspoon dry mustard

1 tablespoon canola oil

1 With a small, sharp knife, cut off the bitter white end of each endive head and separate the leaves.

2 In a salad bowl, place the endive, romaine, onions, artichokes, and oranges.

3 In a small bowl, whisk together the dressing ingredients of orange juice, lime juice, zest, garlic salt, and dry mustard. Drizzle in the canola oil, whisking very fast to emulsify. Drizzle as much dressing as you wish over the salad and toss to combine.

Nutrition at a glance (per serving): Calories 84.37; Protein 2.56 g; Carbohydrates 11.98 g; Dietary fiber 4.00 g; Total fat 3.93 g; Saturated fat 0.40 g; Cholesterol 0 mg; Sodium 176.59 mg.

Lynn's tip: To easily zest an orange (lime or lemon) without much clean up, wash the orange and rinse, place a thin sheet of plastic wrap over the grate tightly, and zest away. Then, just lift off the plastic wrap. The little cutters make enough holes in the plastic to make the zester work just fine. The plastic doesn't get into the food, and wrapping keeps the grater clean, needing just a rinse instead of the usual heavy scrubbing.

Waldorf Turkey Salad

Crisp and cold, a fruit and poultry salad doesn't get any better than this. You can use skinned turkey, chicken, duck, or any other poultry — all visible fat removed, of course. You can leave the raisins or green grapes out and serve a small bunch of 1 or the other on the side.

Preparation time: 12 minutes

Yield: 4 servings

(continued)

2 Granny Smith apples

2 red apples (not Red Delicious unless you love them)

¼ cup lemon juice or sherry vinegar

¼ cup fatfree or lowfat mayonnaise

¼ cup fatfree or lowfat sour cream

1 teaspoon sugar

1 cup chopped celery

2 scallions cut into ½-inch pieces

¼ cup raisins or green grapes cut in half

6 ounces cooked skinless turkey breast, diced

½ cup lightly chopped walnuts plus 4 walnut halves

4 large romaine or bibb lettuce leaves

dash nutmeg

1 Wash the apples and rinse well. Don't peel but do halve them and then core. Chop or dice the apples and toss with the lemon juice or vinegar.

2 In a large bowl, add the mayonnaise, sour cream, and sugar and mix well. Add the celery, scallions, raisins or grapes, turkey, chopped walnuts (only), and apples. Using a rubber spatula, carefully stir to coat.

3 Serve on lettuce and top with a half walnut and a sprinkle of nutmeg.

Nutrition at a glance (per serving): Calories 317.75; Protein 17.32 g; Carbohydrates 40.10 g; Dietary fiber 5.77 g; Total fat 11.51 g; Saturated fat 1.17 g; Cholesterol 36.55 mg; Sodium 173.27 mg.

Beans and Salsa Salad

Colorful and easy, this is one of my testers favorite salads, and it became mine, too. Use any 2 kinds of beans you like, but make them different. Black beans will color the other beans black, so you may want to use them alone.

Preparation time: 5 minutes

Yield: 4 to 6 servings

2 cups salsa

1 cup wine or cider vinegar

1 16-ounce can navy or garbanzo beans, drained

1 16-ounce can dark red kidney beans, drained

1 green pepper, cored and chopped

1 red pepper, cored and chopped

4 scallions (including green), chopped

2 medium tomatoes, chopped

1 In a large bowl, add the salsa and wine vinegar and stir to mix.

2 Add the beans, peppers, scallions, and tomatoes and mix gently but well.

Nutrition at a glance (per serving): *Calories 253.60; Protein 15.26 g; Carbohydrates 48.36 g; Dietary fiber 12.70 g; Total fat 1.28 g; Saturated fat 0.23 g; Cholesterol 0 mg; Sodium 587.25 mg.*

Lynn's tip: *You can add a teaspoon of chili powder and a dash of lemon juice and hot sauce for more intense flavor. Chili powder can be mild, medium mild, or very hot, slightly sweet, acrid and smoky, or pungent with a depth of flavor. Find a brand you like because it can make or break a dish.*

Gelatin Fruit Salad

A great way to get kids to eat fruit, this fabulous fruit salad is easy because the gelatin is premade (and not by you). Although you can find flavored gelatin cups on the shelf and not in the refrigerated cases, I usually refrigerate them because they hold up better, especially when sliced. You can fancy this up by serving it on lettuce.

Preparation time: *5 minutes*

Yield: *4 servings*

4 individual premade 4-ounce refrigerated red gelatin cups (found in all large markets)

2 tablespoons lemon juice

2 bananas, sliced

1 cup fresh hulled strawberries

½ cup blueberries

½ cup raspberries

4 mint sprigs for garnish

1 Run a thin sharp knife around the edge of the plastic cups with the gelatin and remove and place into individual dishes or bowls.

2 With the same knife, cut the gelatin into squares, which fall apart nicely as you cut.

(continued)

3 Sprinkle the lemon juice on the cut bananas and add to the top of the gelatin. Add the blueberries, strawberries, and raspberries. Top with a sprig of mint.

Nutrition at a glance (per serving): Calories 162.14; Protein 2.18 g; Carbohydrates 40.23 g; Dietary fiber 4.35 g; Total fat 0.52 g; Saturated fat 0.12 g; Cholesterol 0 mg; Sodium 46.39 mg.

Lynn's tip: If you like another flavor, buy the orange gelatin and add canned, drained mandarin oranges; for yellow gelatin, add green and red seedless grapes.

Seafood Dressing

This dressing is excellent on any seafood mixture such as shrimp, crab, lobster, and cold chilled fish such as cod or any white fish.

Preparation time: 5 minutes

Yield: 1½ cups

½ cup fatfree or lowfat mayonnaise

½ cup fatfree or lowfat sour cream

2 tablespoons skim milk

3 tablespoons lemon juice

½ teaspoon hot sauce

¼ teaspoon dry mustard

½ teaspoon dried dill, or 1 teaspoon fresh chopped

¼ cup finely chopped celery

2 tablespoons finely chopped onions

1 tablespoon chopped dill pickles

3 teaspoons chopped chives or parsley

1 In a small bowl, add the mayonnaise, sour cream, milk, lemon juice, hot sauce, and mustard and whisk thoroughly.

2 Stir in the dried dill, celery, onions, dill pickles, and chives. Add any salt and pepper you want.

Nutrition at a glance (per serving): Calories 8.21; Protein 0.32 g; Carbohydrates 1.54 g; Dietary fiber 0.04 g; Total fat 0.02 g; Saturated fat 0.00 g; Cholesterol 0.33 mg; Sodium 35.10 mg.

Lynn's tip: Although both are always offered, lowfat rather than fatfree versions of both mayonnaise and sour cream usually taste better or have more of a taste that you are used to. But if you're dieting or just watching your health, with this particular dressing the other flavors add greatly to the fatfree version, and it is excellent fatfree.

Creamy Italian Dressing

This creamy and flavorful Italian dressing is also lowfat and is quite something. If you don't have fresh basil for this dressing, you can substitute 1¼ teaspoons dried.

Preparation time: *5 minutes*

Yield: *About 1 cup*

½ cup fatfree or lowfat sour cream

¼ cup fatfree buttermilk

1 tablespoon olive oil

2 tablespoons red wine vinegar

2 tablespoons thinly sliced fresh basil

2 cloves garlic, minced

1 tablespoon garlic salt

¾ teaspoon dried oregano

¼ cup chopped or diced pimentos or tomatoes

1 In a small bowl, combine the sour cream, buttermilk, olive oil, vinegar, basil, garlic, garlic salt, and oregano. Whisk to combine. Season to taste with pepper if you wish.

2 Stir in the diced pimentos or tomatoes.

Nutrition at a glance (per serving): *Calories 19.88; Protein 0.73 g; Carbohydrates 2.14 g; Dietary fiber 0.11 g; Total fat 0.90 g; Saturated fat 0.14 g; Cholesterol 0.76 mg; Sodium 350.74 mg.*

Lynn's tip: *Commercial herb vinegars are expensive and may not be a good investment, although they make a great gift because they are so pretty. To make your own herbed vinegars, use a neutral white cider or red or white wine vinegar. Then customize the flavoring for each as your taste buds dictate by adding chopped fresh or dried herbs, spices, lemon juice, small whole garlic cloves, chopped leeks, tiny red peppers, raspberries, and perhaps a pinch of dry mustard and sugar. Add a few long sprigs of the main herb just for looks.*

Thai Peanut Dressing

A gently spiced Thai peanut dressing is wonderful over greens, sprouts, snow peas, carrots, sugar snap peas, and many other vegetables (see photo in color section). It's also great spooned over fish or poultry grilled with a brushing of soy sauce. Make sure that you get the Oriental type sesame oil because my testers said the Middle Eastern brands don't have the flavor appropriate for salads.

(continued)

Preparation time: 10 minutes

Yield: ¾ cup

2 tablespoons reduced-fat chunky peanut butter

6 tablespoons fresh-squeezed lime or lemon juice

2 tablespoons low-sodium soy sauce

2 tablespoons Oriental sesame or olive oil

1 teaspoon sugar

¼ teaspoon red pepper flakes or hot pepper

sauce

3 tablespoons chopped fresh cilantro

2 tablespoons thinly sliced fresh basil

2 teaspoons chopped fresh mint

3 cloves garlic, minced

3 tablespoons chopped chives or scallions

1 In a medium bowl, add the peanut butter and gradually add the lime or lemon juice, whisking constantly until smooth.

2 Add the soy sauce, oil, sugar, and red pepper flakes or hot pepper sauce. Whisk to blend.

3 Add the cilantro, basil, mint, garlic, and chives. Stir to combine.

Nutrition at a glance (per serving): Calories 40.90; Protein 1.01 g; Carbohydrates 2.48 g; Dietary fiber 0.28 g; Total fat 3.24 g; Saturated fat 0.52 g; Cholesterol 0 mg; Sodium 104.46 mg.

Lynn's tip: Add cubes of diced firm tofu to the dressing to add more soy, but don't whisk in unless you want a creamy dressing.

Thousand Island Dressing

An old-time favorite, almost a salad in itself it is so nutritious, this is the dressing that men especially adore and also the dressing that usually adds all the calories to salads. But not this version.

Preparation time: 20 to 25 minutes

Yield: 2¼ cups

1 cup fatfree or lowfat mayonnaise

¼ cup skim milk

⅓ cup chunky or regular chili sauce

3 hard-cooked eggs, 2 yolks discarded, remaining yolk and whites chopped

2 tablespoons finely chopped green peppers

3 tablespoons finely chopped parsley

3 tablespoons sweet pickle relish, drained

2 tablespoons finely chopped green olives

¼ cup finely chopped onion

1 In a small bowl, mix with a whisk the mayonnaise, milk, and chili sauce.

2 Add the eggs, peppers, parsley, relish, green olives, and onion and gently mix. If too thick, add more skim milk; if too thin, add more mayonnaise.

Nutrition at a glance (per serving): Calories 13.62; Protein 0.53 g; Carbohydrates 2.25 g; Dietary fiber 0.10 g; Total fat 0.22 g; Saturated fat 0.06 g; Cholesterol 5.92 mg; Sodium 109.59 mg.

Lynn's tip: Named after the Thousand Islands in the St. Lawrence River, this dressing is even healthier cholesterol-wise by dropping out 2 of the yolks. You lose over 400 mg of cholesterol but very little of the flavor.

Italian Dressing

This is my personal signature dressing when I only want the simplest and most flavorful vinegar-based dressing. It is so good on any salad of lettuce or greens mixture with tomatoes, carrots, onions, and maybe a ¼ cup drained, rinsed beans.

Preparation time: 5 minutes

Yield: 1¾ cups

1 cup cider vinegar or mixture of vinegars such as cider, balsamic, wine, and so on

2 tablespoons water (optional)

2 tablespoons fresh lemon juice

¼ teaspoon dry mustard

2 cloves garlic, minced

1½ teaspoons fresh chopped basil, or 1 teaspoon dried

½ teaspoon dried oregano

Pinch dried tarragon

½ cup olive oil

(continued)

1 In a blender or small processor (or bowl if you don't want it emulsified or thickened), add the vinegar, water, lemon juice, mustard, garlic, basil, oregano, tarragon, and any salt and pepper you want.

2 Turn on the motor and slowly drizzle in the oil.

Nutrition at a glance (per serving): Calories 63.70; Protein 0.06 g; Carbohydrates 1.38 g; Dietary fiber 0.05 g; Total fat 6.77 g; Saturated fat 0.91 g; Cholesterol 0 mg; Sodium 0.32 mg.

Lynn's tip: You can use more or less suggested oil, and you can add a pinch of sugar. Personally, I don't emulsify, and I keep it in a bottle on the counter. The oil can become rancid, so use it up within a few days or refrigerate. (After refrigeration it takes a few minutes for the olive oil to become clear.) For a cheese flavor, add ½ cup crumbled blue cheese or feta cheese.

Ranch Dressing

Most people love ranch dressings, and this mixture, so fast and easy, is far less expensive and much better-tasting than bottled versions. If you don't have dried celery flakes (which are great for soups and stews), use chopped celery leaves or finely chopped celery.

Preparation time: 5 minutes

Yield: 2 cups

1 cup fatfree or lowfat sour cream	*1 tablespoon finely chopped fresh parsley*
½ cup fatfree buttermilk	*1 large clove garlic, minced*
2 tablespoons canola oil	*½ teaspoon celery seeds*
2 teaspoons cider vinegar	*½ teaspoon dried celery flakes*
¼ teaspoon sugar	*½ teaspoon garlic salt*
½ cup shredded carrots	*½ teaspoon onion salt*

1 In a medium bowl, add the sour cream, buttermilk, oil, vinegar, and sugar and mix to blend.

2 Add the carrots, parsley, garlic, celery seeds, celery flakes, garlic salt, and onion salt. Stir to combine.

Nutrition at a glance (per serving): *Calories 19.14; Protein 0.66 g; Carbohydrates 1.98 g; Dietary fiber 0.06 g; Total fat 0.90 g; Saturated fat 0.08 g; Cholesterol 0.76 mg; Sodium 67.64 mg.*

Lynn's tip: *When feeding many people, add this ranch dressing recipe to expand bottled fatfree or regular ranch dressings to extend them and give them some punch without all those drutted calories. Use some ranch dressing as a zippy sandwich spread instead of high-fat butter.*

Poppyseed Dressing

This tangy dressing is great for cole slaw. Toasting the poppyseeds in a small skillet for a few minutes over medium heat brings out their flavor.

Preparation time: *5 minutes*

Yield: *¾ cup*

½ cup cider vinegar

2 tablespoons honey

2 tablespoons canola oil

1 tablespoon freshly squeezed lemon juice

1 teaspoon poppyseeds

In a small bowl, add the vinegar, honey, canola oil, lemon juice, and poppyseeds. Mix well with a whisk.

Nutrition at a glance (per serving): *Calories 25.37; Protein 0.04 g; Carbohydrates 2.75 g; Dietary fiber 0.03 g; Total fat 1.79 g; Saturated fat 0.13 g; Cholesterol 0 mg; Sodium 0.23 mg.*

Lynn's tip: *You don't want olive oil in this dressing because it can overpower the honey flavor. The color and flavor of honey are affected by the flower the bee visits. Dark buckwheat honey is intensely flavored. Thyme flowers make a clear and golden honey. Sage is a lightly pungent taste. Wildflower honey is "vigorous." Orange blossom is light and delicate. If you are highly allergic (and because you don't know what the bee has been on), substitute corn syrup.*

Chunky Tomato Dressing

This is a great dressing (see photo in color section). Tomatoey rich, and full of chunks and flavor, this dressing will become a favorite over greens. It is also good over cold pasta and other vegetables like celery and onions, which go well with tomatoes.

Preparation time: *5 minutes*

Yield: *3 cups*

4 medium tomatoes, 2 chopped and 2 quartered

½ cup vinegar

2 tablespoons lemon juice

2 tablespoons olive oil

1 large clove garlic, minced

½ teaspoon sugar

1 small onion, shallot, or 2-inch leeks, chopped

2 tablespoons chopped fresh basil leaves or ½ tablespoon dried

1 tablespoon dried oregano

Red pepper flakes (optional)

1 In the processor bowl, add the 2 chopped tomatoes, vinegar, lemon juice, olive oil, garlic, sugar, and any salt you wish (¼ teaspoon will do). Puree the ingredients.

2 In the same processor bowl, add the 2 quartered tomatoes and onion and process to a large chunk.

3 Stir in the basil, oregano, and red pepper flakes, if using. Add any salt and pepper you wish.

Nutrition at a glance (per serving): *Calories 8.72; Protein 0.12 g; Carbohydrates 0.91 g; Dietary fiber 0.19 g; Total fat 0.61 g; Saturated fat 0.08 g; Cholesterol 0 mg; Sodium 1.03 mg.*

Lynn's tip: *I also like this dressing on cottage cheese and cucumbers, and over diced tofu on greens, all with lots of black pepper.*

Chapter 5

Swift and Savory Soups, Snacks, and Sandwiches

Soups and sandwiches go together nicely. This chapter shows you how to make both soups and sandwiches healthier. Simple basic steps show you how to make meat-based soups and sandwiches lower in fat without losing flavor. Plus, you find several tips to speed up the soup process and easy-to-read substitutions and suggestions on how to change a high-fat sandwich or soup into a lowfat version. Easy suggestions and great recipes round out the chapter.

Transforming the New and Retro Sandwich into an All-American Healthy Meal

A soup and sandwich is a favorite casual meal for lunch or dinner, but both have continually changed as America has become more affluent. The changes may look on the surface to be good, but they aren't.

Sandwiches

Sandwiches, as some history buffs tell us, began when John Montagu, the fourth Earl of Sandwich in the 1700s, found that he didn't want to leave the gaming tables or get his fingers soiled while eating. So he placed the meat part of a haunch between two slices of bread. Pretty convenient.

From a thin peanut butter and jelly on one or two slim slices of 5-inch by 4-inch bread, society has "advanced" to larger and thicker bread and sandwiches that are stacked 4 to 6 inches high. These meat, tuna, bacon, and cheese towers have unfortunately also gotten everyone used to eating some extremely large, very high-fat meals. Some cheese and meat subs are so big that they contain a thousand calories, several hundred milligrams of cholesterol, and 50 to 60 grams of fat. Add to that a cream soup, and you have 2,000 calories in one lunch.

Yet eating half a sandwich and half the soup occurs to only a few. In speaking to a diet specialist, she said the No. 1 reason people eat too much when dining out even when it's soup and sandwich is "I paid for it, I should eat it." The second reason for overeating is that the meal isn't planned. One solution is to make soups and sandwiches at home — the way you want and the way that tastes best to you.

Sandwiches can be a perfect food

You can make delicious and familiar sandwiches quickly and healthfully. With just a little planning about the selection and amount of the meat (or whether to use meat at all), the kind of dairy products, and the kind and amount of sandwich spread, sandwiches really are the perfect food. Table 5-1 shows you a few improvements you can make.

Ways to lower fat in sandwiches

Eliminate butter and high-fat spreads by instead substituting fatfree and lowfat spreads, lessening the meat slices, and using a lower fat meat like lean ham or roast beef instead of salami. Remove the edge fat, add more tomatoes, onions, and lettuce, and get a good, whole-grain or high-fiber bread.

Table 5-1	Making Sandwiches Healthier
Improve This Sandwich:	*By Doing This:*
Peanut butter sandwich	Use reduced-fat peanut butter
Bacon, lettuce, and tomato	Cut the fat off the bacon; use lowfat mayo
Club sandwich	Omit full-fat cheese, mayo, and bacon; use turkey or lean ham and lowfat cheese
Turkey club sandwich	Omit the turkey skin; omit bacon or cut the fat off the bacon and use lowfat mayo
Ham sandwich	Remove all visible fat; use fewer ham slices and lowfat mayo
Deviled ham sandwich	Use lowfat mayo and lots of lettuce; make your own deviled ham
Chicken salad sandwich	Use more lettuce, more celery, and onions; use less chicken or turkey; use skinless white meat; use lowfat mayo
Tuna salad or tuna melt sandwich	Use lowfat cheese and water-packed tuna for both; use more lettuce, celery, and onions; use lowfat mayo
Bagel with cream cheese	Use less cream cheese and make it reduced fat or fatfree cream cheese
Stuffed pita sandwich	Omit cheese or fatty meats; stuff with hummus, olives, and alfalfa sprouts
Submarines	Omit the fatty salami; use lean ham, add lots of lettuce and tomato and a squirt of vinegar; use lowfat mayo

Why are sandwiches the perfect food if made right? You get grains and fiber in the bread, vegetables with vitamins, minerals, and fiber in the lettuce, tomato, celery, onion, pickles, and any other vegetables, and protein and minerals in lean meat, with calcium in any added lowfat cheese. And you exercise your jaws with the concentrated and intense chewing. Perfect.

You can make sandwiches healthier by making modest reductions in fat, selecting high-fiber bread, using lower fat mayo (or less mayo) or substituting mustard or olive oil for mayo, and using both lean and less meat and lowfat cheese. With just minor shifts, sandwiches can be immensely healthy. If you are dieting, make a huge sandwich (see Figure 5-1) using oversized bread and cut it in half, making two servings. A half sandwich made of small bread slices looks too skimpy to halve, but if you have one brimming with lettuce, onions, grilled vegetable slices, pickles, and tomatoes piling out, you won't miss not eating the whole thing.

Figure 5-1:
Make a huge sandwich so that you can share half with someone.

Mastering Soups

Soup is an easy way to enjoy several good foods at once. Cooking foods together develops and changes their flavors. Soup is easy (usually taking just one pot), and while it is cooking, the aroma gives a home that rich, traditional feel that you are doing something really worthwhile.

Even on the most extreme lowfat eating plan, you can make soups with fatty meat such as salt pork, marrow bones, fat-filled knuckles, and smoked ham bones. You throw everything in the pot — the bones (if chicken), skin, fat, back, neck, bones, wings, even butter, and lots of water. You just need to defat the stock or broth (see next section). That way, you keep the flavor and lose the fat. With so many interesting ingredients, soup never suffers from the lack of fat — in fact, the lack of it enhances soup because you get a more pure vegetable flavor that's not marred by grease, fats, or oils.

Soups

Soups, called "soupe" in Europe, became immensely popular in the Middle Ages in France. In Italy and the British Isles, the contents of what was left in the cooking pot were commonly poured over a 6-inch block of coarse bread (or trencher), and the one who ate the sop bread was a trencher man. French onion soup with cheese-topped toast is a loose version today.

Too much salt?

Bouillon cubes, dry soup mixes, and prepared foods all contain sodium — and sometimes quite a bit. It is one of the reasons I have you dilute these foods with fresh vegetables, perhaps pasta and rice, and additional liquids. If you want to reduce your sodium, which affects fewer people than originally thought, you will want to look at the nutritional analyses at the end of each recipe carefully and either add many more vegetables and liquids or, like people with allergies, not eat what isn't in your best interest.

Defatting meat soups

To defat soups (see Figure 5-2) made with animal products, make them in two stages. In a large pot with a lid, simmer between 30 minutes and an hour a couple of quarts of water and whatever meat, bacon, fatback, skin, and bones of meat and poultry, along with herbs, spices, and vegetables such as onions, carrots, celery, and any other vegetables you want. Discard the vegetables and defat the stock by chilling and picking off the fat (it rises and congeals), which takes a few hours to chill. For more immediate results, spoon it off or use a large, glass defatting pitcher (available in most kitchen stores, or by calling 1-800-8-FLAVOR for a free catalog).

Wash the soup pot, add the defatted, flavored broth you just made and then whatever new vegetables, beans, herbs and spices, and any other ingredients you want. You now have a fatfree soup in any flavor you want.

Figure 5-2: Defat your soup.

Thin can be made thick and rich without fat

You can easily thicken thin soups without adding many calories. Use a few tablespoons flour (whisk into a cool liquid and stir into the hot soup cooking for 3 to 4 minutes) or cornstarch (whisk into a cool liquid and stir in cooking soup thickening it immediately). You can also use breadcrumbs, cooked rice, potato, rice or tapioca flour (available in specialty stores), and even raw finely shredded potatoes. Red/orange (Persian) lentils also help thicken thin soups, making them appear richer than a thin gruel (which is like a very watery oatmeal).

Soup flavoring and speed-up tips

You can easily use ready-made, frozen mixes to quick-start soups. Because they are often long-cooked, they do have flavor, but most lose that freshness good food has because of the canning, freezing, and drying process. With clever additions of herbs, spices, and fresh ingredients, you can add flavor back, thin the fat, dilute the sodium, reduce the calories, and make it taste great.

With many, you won't need extra sodium because they already may be high in salt, but adding chopped fresh parsley or other herbs can also spice up the look and flavor of the soup.

- ✔ Take advantage of canned soups by using them as a base, adding your own fresh vegetables (long cooking gives foods extra flavor).

- ✔ Use packaged frozen vegetables or dinner mixes (mixed foods, not compartmentalized TV dinners) and mix into canned soups or vegetable juices for extra flavor and easy-to-use ingredients.

- ✔ Use packaged soup mixes and mix not only with water, but with fresh sautéed vegetables and meat for extra flavor and fiber.

- ✔ Use powdered or granulated packet soup mixes with beans, canned soups, and fresh vegetables for extra flavor and more fiber.

- ✔ Put chicken or beef, bones and meat on a tray and bake for an hour or two in a 275° oven. Refrigerate in foil or use immediately as a soup base, along with all the other ingredients, such as fresh vegetables or more lean meat. Long-cooked bones make for a better soup flavor.

- ✔ Use a pressure or fusion cooker (same thing) to speed up the time.

- ✔ Use a rice maker, adding not only rice but small amounts of meat and fresh vegetables, plus extra liquid, making a rice-based soup rich in flavor and fiber (rice has almost none) instead of plain steamed rice.

✔ With canned beef soup, add beef granules or a bouillon cube for a flavor zip, along with plenty of quick white, brown, or wild rice, perhaps pasta or fresh cooked diced potatoes, and lots of fresh red, yellow, and green vegetables.

✔ With canned beans, rinse, use a ham bouillon cube and a teaspoon of liquid smoke plus diced lean ham and plenty of savory vegetables like peppers.

✔ For other quick flavors from long-cooked foods, use *demi glacés* (a reduced thick sauce usually made from beef or chicken, sometimes vegetables), bouillon cubes or flavor granules of ham, beef, lamb, chicken or vegetables, reduced meat and chicken powders, and other types of flavor packets.

Trying Your Hand at Soup Recipes

A great thick soup is scrumptious comfort food that's usually a winter dish. You can make it without almost any fat, so you just get the good flavor. Soups are my specialty, and I think the soups in this chapter are extra good. They are so basic that you can add extra onions or garlic or remove them completely, making these soups any way you like with the ingredients you want.

Corn Chowder

This hearty soup uses corn chowder as a base. You get a creamy taste with no fat. You can increase the ingredients to make more of this easy and colorful soup.

Preparation/Cooking time: *12 minutes*

Yield: *2 to 3 servings*

1 medium onion or leek, or 2 shallots, chopped

1 cup thinly sliced carrots

¼ cup chopped parsley

1 ear fresh-scraped corn kernels, or ½ cup frozen corn, defrosted

2 tablespoons diced green or red pepper or baby peas

1 16 to 18.5-ounce can corn chowder

1 cup fatfree half-and-half, fatfree nondairy liquid creamer, skim milk, or water

1 Lightly spray a large 4-inch high-sided skillet with cooking spray. Add the onions and carrots and sauté, stirring, over medium heat for 5 minutes.

2 Add the parsley, corn, peppers, chowder, and liquid and stir well. Heat just until the soup is very hot but be careful not to boil or burn the soup. Add any salt and pepper you wish.

(continued)

Nutrition at a glance (per serving): Calories 408.6 g; Protein 12.3 g; Carbohydrates 51.3 g; Dietary fiber 7.4 g; Total fat 14.5 g; Saturated fat 6.6 g; Cholesterol 23.1 mg; Sodium 983.9 mg.

Lynn's tip: You can make this very pretty with a few dashes of paprika and a sprinkling of chopped chives.

Chicken or Turkey Noodle Soup

This soup is simple and tasty, and you can add instant or leftover noodles, too. If you like rice better, switch to that.

Preparation/Cooking time: 15 minutes

Yield: 4 servings

1 medium onion, shallot, or leek, chopped

1 cup chopped celery

1 clove minced garlic

½ cup thin-sliced or shredded carrots

¼ cup chopped parsley

2 tablespoons sherry, or ½ teaspoon sherry extract (optional)

1 cup diced cooked skinless chicken or turkey, all visible fat removed, or one 6-ounce can chicken or turkey

1 10.5-ounce can fatfree chicken broth

1 16 to 18.5-ounce can chicken noodle soup

1 Lightly spray a large 4-inch high-sided skillet or wide pot. Add the onions, celery, garlic, and carrots, mist the vegetables with the spray, and sauté over medium heat for 5 minutes, stirring.

2 Add the parsley, sherry, chicken, chicken broth, and soup, stir well, and heat until the soup is very hot.

Nutrition at a glance (per serving): Calories 173.3 g; Protein 14.2 g; Carbohydrates 14.9 g; Dietary fiber 2.2 g; Total fat 5.6 g; Saturated fat 1.5 g; Cholesterol 32.0 mg; Sodium 1,309.6 mg.

Lynn's tip: Fresh noodles and tiny dried pastas like stars or orzo all cook in 5 or 6 minutes, so add a cup of them if you want more noodles.

How to avoid burning minced garlic

If you have experienced burned minced garlic in the past, which ruins a recipe, add the garlic at the end of the vegetable sautéing, cooking the garlic for just a minute or two, whereas the other vegetables cook for 4 or 5 minutes.

I add the garlic at the beginning of cooking, as it says in these recipes, cooking it with the onions or other foods. But if the pan appears a little dry, I often spritz only the minced garlic, which I dump in the center, with vegetable cooking oil spray, and then I stir the now coated spritzed garlic into the rest of the vegetables, cooking as usual. The spritz of oil slightly delays the cooking.

Onion Soup

You can add a tablespoon or two of sweet sherry or vermouth to this really fabulous soup.

Preparation/Cooking time: *10 minutes*

Yield: *4 servings*

1 large onion, thinly sliced	1 16-ounce can fatfree or lowfat beef or chicken broth
½ cup wafer-thin sliced carrots	1 16 to 18.5-ounce can onion or French onion soup
2 tablespoons parsley	

1 Lightly spray a large 4-inch high sided skillet or wide pot with nonstick vegetable oil spray. Add the onions and carrots, mist them with the spray, and sauté over medium heat, stirring, for 10 minutes or until transparent.

2 Add the parsley, broth, and soup, stir well, and heat until the soup is very hot.

Nutrition at a glance (per serving): *Calories 8.8 g; Protein 6.0 g; Carbohydrates 14.1 g; Dietary fiber 2.1 g; Total fat 1.7 g; Saturated fat 0.3 g; Cholesterol 0 mg; Sodium 1,517.0 mg.*

Lynn's tip: *Cut the crust off bread and cut into a round shape and toast. Add a rounded slice of lowfat Swiss cheese to the bread, place on a tray, and melt the cheese under the broiler for about 2 minutes. Add the cheese bread to the top of the soup.*

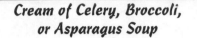

Cream of Celery, Broccoli, or Asparagus Soup

These are all separate soups and are very, very good. Adding fresh vegetables makes canned creamed soups quite delicious. Decide the soup you want and add more of same.

Preparation/Cooking time: *10 minutes*

Yield: *4 servings*

1 medium onion, shallot, or leek, finely chopped

1 cup finely sliced celery, 1-inch pieces of asparagus, or finely chopped broccoli florets

1 tablespoon flour

1 cup fat free or lowfat nondairy liquid creamer, skim milk, or evaporated skim milk

¼ cup chopped parsley

1 10¾-ounce can fatfree chicken broth

1 16 to 18.5-ounce can cream of celery, asparagus, or broccoli soup

2 tablespoons Parmesan shreds (to melt)

1 Lightly spray a large high-sided skillet or wide pot with nonstick vegetable oil. Add the onions and sauté over medium heat for 2 minutes, stirring.

2 Add the vegetable you have selected, lightly spray vegetables, and sauté with the onions over medium-high heat, stirring constantly, for 3 minutes.

3 Whisk the flour into the liquid creamer and add to the skillet, stirring over low heat for 2 minutes.

4 Add the parsley, broth, and soup. Stir well and heat until the soup is very hot. Stir in the cheese and serve.

Nutrition at a glance (per serving): Calories 175.2 g; Protein 3.8 g; Carbohydrates 16.0 g; Dietary fiber 1.6 g; Total fat 6.1 g; Saturated fat 1.9 g; Cholesterol 14.9 mg; Sodium 1,166.3 mg.

Lynn's tip: Stir in another tablespoon of flour or cornstarch and use as a sauce poured over a mound of cooked celery, steamed cauliflower, corn, rice, noodles, or hot polenta. You can top with hot diced cooked lean skinless chicken, turkey, or lean ham.

Creating Simple Sandwiches

Sandwiches are so simple, and I give you a few extra tasty ones. What you can discover in these recipes is how to make all your sandwiches lower in fat. (Also refer to Table 5-1.)

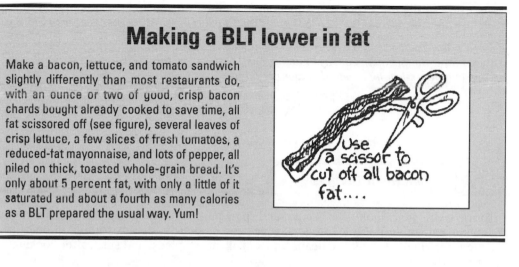

Making a BLT lower in fat

Make a bacon, lettuce, and tomato sandwich slightly differently than most restaurants do, with an ounce or two of good, crisp bacon chards bought already cooked to save time, all fat scissored off (see figure), several leaves of crisp lettuce, a few slices of fresh tomatoes, a reduced-fat mayonnaise, and lots of pepper, all piled on thick, toasted whole-grain bread. It's only about 5 percent fat, with only a little of it saturated and about a fourth as many calories as a BLT prepared the usual way. Yum!

Use a scissor to cut off all bacon fat....

East Indian Luncheon Sandwich

If you don't have pita bread, use any bread. Bean sandwiches are delicious, and if you like East Indian fare, you'll love this crisp, clean, crunchy, and flavorful sandwich (see photo in color section). Part hummus, part vegetables, it is an ideal way to get a tasty lunch that is also incredibly nutritious.

Preparation time: *10 minutes*

Yield: *4 servings*

1 cup fatfree or lowfat plain yogurt

1 tablespoon fresh lemon juice

2 tablespoons olive oil

½ teaspoon hot pepper sauce

¼ cup garbanzo beans

2 tablespoons chopped hot mango, peach chutney, or thinly sliced candied ginger,

½ large cucumber diced

1 narrow 6-inch carrot, thinly sliced or shredded

1 small-diced green bell pepper

⅓ cup chopped mint, dill, or parsley

4 pita bread pockets, sliced in half and opened

1 In a medium bowl, add the yogurt, lemon juice, olive oil, hot sauce, and garbanzo beans and mash until well mixed. If the mixture is too thick, you can make them less chunky by using a hand blender or food processor.

2 Add the chutney, cucumber, carrots, bell pepper, and mint and mix well.

3 Add the filling to the pita pockets and serve.

(continued)

Nutrition at a glance (per serving): Calories 307.4 g; Protein 10.7 g; Carbohydrates 48.6 g; Dietary fiber 3.6 g; Total fat 8.0 g; Saturated fat 1.1 g; Cholesterol 1.1 mg; Sodium 419.5 mg.

Lynn's tip: You can buy hummus already made in your deli department to speed this up even more. But because I always have canned garbanzos, this is also easy. If you don't have chutney, slice the candied ginger very thin.

Mexicali Burgers

Topped with guacamole, this is a fun and spicy burger. Serve with lowfat tortilla chips. If you make it with vegetarian burgers, which can be bought already formed or unformed in any large market, omit the beans and add cilantro, spices, and salsa after cooking. Serve with guacamole.

Preparation/Cooking time: *10 minutes*

Yield: *4 servings*

8 ounces top round, all visible fat removed, ground, or 4 vegetarian burgers

1 large onion, finely chopped, divided

½ cup canned pinto beans, drained

3 tablespoons chopped cilantro

2 tablespoons chili powder

1 teaspoon ground cumin

¼ cup salsa

4 hamburger buns

8 lettuce leaves

1 tomato thinly sliced

4 lowfat slices mozzarella cheese

1 In a large bowl, add the ground round, onions, beans, cilantro, chili powder, cumin, salsa, and salt and pepper, mashing the beans well and mixing thoroughly with the other ingredients.

2 Make into 4 hamburgers.

3 Grill, broil, or fry the burgers in a large skillet lightly sprayed with cooking spray over medium-high heat, making sure that they are well done and nicely browned. During the last minute of cooking, add a slice of cheese and grill, broil, or fry, covered, until the cheese is browned or nearly melted.

4 Toast the buns and add the lettuce and a tomato slice to the buns.

5 Add the burgers to the buns, add a dollop of guacamole, and sprinkle on extra onions.

Nutrition at a glance (per serving): Calories 361.0 g; Protein 27.1 g; Carbohydrates 36.6 g; Dietary fiber 6.2 g; Total fat 12.8 g; Saturated fat 5.4 g; Cholesterol 47.9 mg; Sodium 618.4 mg.

Lynn's tip: Not all chili powder is the same. Chili powder is different mixtures of chilies. Try more than one brand to see what you like the best. Some brands really are awful, and some are terrific. You may need a little more or less chili powder, depending on the density or taste. In a stew or chili, I may use ¼ cup when the recipe calls for 1 tablespoon, if it isn't too hot (spicy).

Walnut Chicken Salad Sandwich

Chicken salad sandwiches are terrific, and my testers said this was the best ever and hard to tell that it was reasonably low in fat. Serve chilled with fruit and cookies for dessert. If you don't have deli or home-cooked chicken, use canned.

Preparation time: 10 minutes

Yield: 4 servings

¼ cup fresh orange juice

1 cup fatfree, lowfat, or light mayonnaise

1 tablespoon chopped fresh tarragon or parsley, (½ teaspoon dried), or 1 teaspoon finely chopped thyme or ½ teaspoon finely chopped rosemary

2 cooked skinless chicken breasts, diced (about 8 ounces)

1 cup finely chopped celery

½ cup finely chopped scallions or mild onion

1 cup halved seedless green or red grapes

½ cup chopped walnuts

4 lettuce leaves

8 slices soft bread (can be crusty)

_1_ In a medium bowl, add the orange juice, mayonnaise, and herbs and mix well.

_2_ Add the diced chicken, celery, scallions, grapes, and nuts to the dressing and toss lightly.

_3_ Place a lettuce leaf on 4 bread slices, add the chicken salad, and top with the other piece of bread.

Nutrition at a glance (per serving): Calories 401.7 g; Protein 20.8 g; Carbohydrates 50.6 g; Dietary fiber 3.4 g; Total fat 13.5 g; Saturated fat 2.1 g; Cholesterol 35.3 mg; Sodium 765.4 mg.

Lynn's tip: You can stuff chicken salad into pita pockets, hard-cooked egg white halves, and in thin wheat tortilla wraps that you skewer to hold shut.

Vegetarian Summer Sandwich

Although this sandwich contains no meat, it is so lush and colorful. Bursting with delicious vegetables and a tangy dressing and topped with sprouts and onions, you don't miss the meat. I use a serrated knife or small hand slicer for the tomatoes and peppers. Wrapped, this sandwich can be chilled and served several hours later.

Preparation time: *10 minutes*

Yield: *4 servings*

1 cup fatfree or lowfat Cheddar, feta, or ricotta cheese, crumbled

¼ cup lowfat or fatfree plain yogurt

¼ cup diet or lowfat Italian salad dressing

3 to 4 drops hot sauce

1 small onion, finely sliced

½ cup small-diced green bell pepper

½ cup chopped lettuce or parsley

1 cup salsa

4 8-inch soft wheat tortillas

1 large tomato, thinly sliced

½ cup shredded Cheddar cheese

4 small handfuls alfalfa sprouts

1 In a medium bowl, add the cheese, yogurt, Italian dressing, and hot sauce and blend.

2 Add the onion, bell pepper, and lettuce or parsley and mix well.

3 Spread the salsa over the center of the tortillas, line with tomato slices, and evenly disperse the cheese mixture, Cheddar cheese, and alfalfa sprouts and roll tightly. Wrap and refrigerate or slice into 2-inch lengths.

Nutrition at a glance (per serving): *Calories 308.8 g; Protein 18.8 g; Carbohydrates 39.7 g; Dietary fiber 4.1 g; Total fat 8.6 g; Saturated fat 3.9 g; Cholesterol 19.8 mg; Sodium 954.1 mg.*

Lynn's tip: *For more heat, sprinkle on red pepper flakes or chopped jalapeño peppers.*

Cheddar or Blue Cheeseburgers

This tasty sandwich is lowfat and delicious. Grab the pickles, onions, lettuce, and ketchup and enjoy. If you opt for vegetarian burgers, fry with the steak sauce, onions, and mushrooms and then top with the steak sauce, onions, and mushrooms instead of mixing them in and omit the bread crumbs.

Preparation/Cooking time: *15 minutes*

Yield: *4 servings*

12 ounces top round, all visible fat removed, ground, or 4 vegetarian burgers

3 tablespoons steak sauce

1 medium onion, finely chopped

½ cup canned mushrooms, drained and coarsely chopped

2 tablespoons to ¼ cup herbed breadcrumbs

4 hamburger buns

2 tablespoons fatfree or lowfat mayonnaise

4 lowfat slices Cheddar cheese (about 2 ounces), or 2 ounces crumbled blue cheese

1 Preheat broiler. In a large bowl, add the meat, steak sauce, onions, mushrooms, and breadcrumbs and make into 4 hamburgers. Add any salt and pepper you wish.

2 Grill or broil (or fry) the burgers until medium-well done, about 3 to 4 minutes per side, depending on the thickness and distance from broiler. If frying, lightly spray a heavy skillet with nonstick vegetable oil. Make sure that the burgers are flattened. Brown well.

3 Toast the buns. When toasted, spread on mayonnaise.

4 Top each burger in the skillet with a slice of cheese or crumbled cheese. Place under the grill or broiler or continue frying and cover until the cheese melts, 1 to 2 minutes.

5 With a spatula, carefully place the burgers and melted cheese on the bottom bun and serve on a plate with any garnish such as lettuce, pickles, relish, tomatoes, ketchup, mustard, and onions you choose. Add the top bun to the side.

Nutrition at a glance (per serving): Calories 335.6 g; Protein 26.0 g; Carbohydrates 33.8 g; Dietary fiber 2.7 g; Total fat 10.4 g; Saturated fat 4.0 g; Cholesterol 54.0 mg; Sodium 760.6 mg.

Lynn's tip: You can find many brands of vegetable and lowfat burgers. Try Boca Burgers, Harvest Burgers, and Morningstar Farms Grillers.

Old-Fashioned Egg Salad Sandwich

This egg salad is easy to make and has very little cholesterol (which is found in the yolks) because you use primarily egg whites and a few substitute eggs for color. You get all the taste with this sandwich. Hard-cooking eggs takes about 20 minutes.

Preparation/Cooking time: 15 minutes

Yield: 4 servings

(continued)

7 medium hard-cooked eggs

½ cup substitute eggs

½ cup chopped celery

½ cup chopped onion

¼ cup chopped red bell pepper

1 cup fatfree or lowfat mayonnaise

8 lettuce slices

8 slices soft bread (can be crusty)

1 Cut the eggs in half, remove the yolks, and discard all but 2 yolks. Coarsely chop the egg whites and 2 yolks. Transfer to a large bowl and set aside.

2 Lightly spray a large skillet. Add the substitute eggs, don't stir, cover, and cook over low heat, checking the bottom often to be sure that they don't burn.

3 Add the celery, onion, bell pepper, and mayonnaise to the bowl with the eggs and gently stir to combine.

4 When the substitute eggs are cooked (about 4 minutes), while still in the pan, score with a sharp knife about ¼ to ½-inch apart, dicing them. Add the diced eggs to the egg white and vegetable mixture and toss again to coat. Season with salt and pepper.

5 Place the lettuce on the bread, add the filling and cover with the second piece of bread, slice diagonally, skewer with fringy toothpicks, and serve.

Nutrition at a glance (per serving): *Calories 278.7 g; Protein 15.3 g; Carbohydrates 41.4 g; Dietary fiber 2.4 g; Total fat 5.2 g; Saturated fat 1.6 g; Cholesterol 108.0 mg; Sodium 870.1 mg.*

Tuna Melt

Tuna melt fans have finally found a lower-fat, better-tasting version in this recipe.

Preparation/Cooking time: *10 minutes*

Yield: *4 servings*

2 6-ounce cans water-packed tuna, drained

¼ cup sweet relish, drained

2 tablespoons fresh lemon juice

2 tablespoons chopped scallions

½ cup fatfree or lowfat mayonnaise

4 Kaiser rolls

4 slices fatfree or lowfat cheese

1 Preheat broiler. In a medium bowl, add the tuna, relish, lemon juice, scallions, and mayonnaise and mix well but don't mash.

2 Place the rolls on a cookie sheet, add the filling on the rolls, add 1 slice cheese, and place under a broiler until the cheese melts, about 2 minutes, watching carefully to be sure it doesn't burn.

Nutrition at a glance (per serving): Calories 335.5 g; Protein 30.8 g; Carbohydrates 43.3 g; Dietary fiber 1.6 g; Total fat 3.2 g; Saturated fat 0.5 g; Cholesterol 27.3 mg; Sodium 1,213.7 mg.

Lynn's tip: Some lowfat cheeses melt better than others, but they often have no taste. Use a wafer-thin slice of a full-fat cheese along with a major brand slice of a lowfat variety. The major brand cheeses often melt better.

Chapter 6

Vegetable Pleasures for Any Occasion

In This Chapter

▶ Enjoying a variety of vegetables

▶ Discovering the right way to store vegetables

▶ Creating vegetable dishes the healthy way

*Y*ou may have noticed that there are more recipes in this chapter (and the salad chapter) than any other! In fact, this is not only chock-a-block full of great vegetable recipes (a few with optional meat), all thoroughly tested, of course, but it explains why vegetables, perhaps more than any other food group, are essential for good health.

This chapter offers several ways to get vegetables into your life, even if you don't especially love them. It shows how vegetables add excitement to cooking and eating. If their vivid colors, textures, and flavors still don't convince you that putting vegetables in your menu plan is a great idea, you'll change your mind when you discover that vegetables are naturally great timesavers and have the lowest calories of any food group.

Cultivating the Vegetable Habit

Some people loved vegetables from the first pea selected with tiny baby fingers eagerly aimed toward their mouths. But what if you or someone in your family doesn't like them? You know you should eat them because vegetables are important foods. You probably know that the Food Guide Pyramid (see Chapter 1) tells you to eat four or five servings of vegetables daily. Again, what if you don't like them?

No problem! Just try these suggestions, and you and your loved ones will soon have more vegetables in your diets.

- ✔ **Be brave.** Try a taste of something you previously didn't like. Most restaurant chefs know how to cook vegetables very well. Instead of ordering the suspicious dish (which is expensive), take a forkful from a willing friend's plate. And if you really hate vegetables, make sure that you're really hungry when you try something new!

- ✔ **Spend a little time in the vegetable or produce department.** If you see something new and different, buy it. Twenty-five cents to $1.50 is a small price to pay for a new delicious discovery and perhaps better health. Green grocers can give you suggestions or free recipes on preparing them. I discovered fiddlehead fern that way.

- ✔ **Ask a friend how they fix celeriac or whether they think you might like it.** Then no matter what they say, try it anyway.

- ✔ **If you like a particular vegetable, try another variety or vegetable with a similar taste or texture.** For example, if you like big red tomatoes, try yellow tomatoes or fried green tomatoes, Roma, pear, baby yellow, cherry, or little grape tomatoes. They all taste slightly different. (See Table 6-1 and Figure 6-1 for more ideas.)

Peas a little healthier today

Pease Pudding hot, Pease Pudding cold, Pease Pudding in the pot, nine days old.

— 11th-Century Rhyme

This 900-year-old poem underlines that vegetables such as good old peas have been a staple for a very long time. Can you imagine these peas (pease) cooking away endlessly, then going cold, then when wood is lit again, reheated, with some having been in the pot for nine days?

These cooking habits apparently lined many an early "doctor's" pockets because with so many sick patients, writings from the period indicate that in wealthy homes he always kissed the errant cook first. Nowadays, thank goodness, you know not to keep adding food to a perpetual cooking (and probably rotten) pot of peas. Yet for all their history, peas are one of America's (and England's) most popular green vegetable.

Figure 6-1:
If you like a particular vegetable, try other varieties of it.

Table 6-1	The Great Vegetable Exchange
If You Like . . .	*Try . . .*
Asparagus	White asparagus, purple asparagus, a salad with asparagus, asparagus soup
Artichokes	Okra, asparagus
Broccoli	White cauliflower, green cauliflower, broccoli rabe, brocaflower (or broccoflower)
Button mushrooms	Portabello, shitake, lobster, enoki, chantrelles in an omelet, morels in a stew, matsutakes, boletes, oyster mushrooms, mushroom soup or gravy
Cabbage	Red cabbage, Chinese cabbage, savoy cabbage, curly cabbage, bok choy
Carrots	Baby carrots, parsnips, sweet potatoes, yams
Celery	Bok choy, fennel, celeriac
Garlic	Roasted garlic, purple garlic, elephant garlic, shallots
Green beans	Haricot verte, wax beans, Chinese long beans, French cut beans, Italian flat beans, pole beans, string beans
Kidney beans	Black beans, black-eyed peas, can nelini (white kidney beans), fava beans, pinto beans

(continued)

Table 6-1 *(continued)*

If You Like . . .	Try . . .
Lentils	Barley, split peas, sweet beans like French flagolets, white beans
Lima beans	Kidney beans, butter beans, Christmas beans, cannelini (white kidney beans), fava beans, navy beans, pinto beans, white beans, pea beans, field peas, stubin yellow eyes (mild and sweet), French flagolets)
Okra	Artichokes
Onions	Shallots, scallions, spring onions, leeks, chives, cibolas (Mexican onions), elephant garlic (milder than regular garlic), wild onions (stronger than chives), Spanish onions, boiling onions, pearl onions (see Figure 6-2)
Potatoes	Sweet potatoes, pureed parsnips, pureed fennel, yuca or yucca root, jicama (eaten raw)
Rutabagas	Turnips, parsnips, kohlrabi, carrots
Spinach greens	Chard, collards, beet greens, turnip greens, kale, dandelion greens, bok choy
Zucchini	Yellow summer squash, fennel

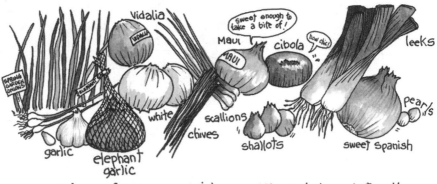

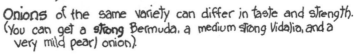

Figure 6-2:
Try different types of onions.

TIP

Get into the habit of trying at least one new vegetable a week (see Figure 6-3 for some ideas). I purchase almost every new item I see at some time or another and try it. By year's end, you'll have 52 stalwart friends who will support your good health efforts.

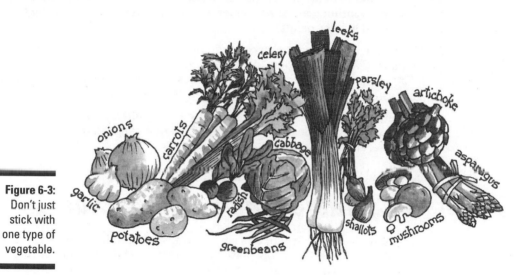

Figure 6-3:
Don't just stick with one type of vegetable.

Why Are Veggies So Healthy?

Healthwise, vegetables are practically perfect for humans. If you compare the human body's physiology with its closest mammal relatives (the chimpanzee, gorilla, and ape), you find that these creatures also have long intestines and flat back teeth — both better suited for eating plants than meat. So it isn't surprising that these animals are by nature primarily plant eaters or herbivores.

Eating vegetables has more than one health benefit. For more on how diet can affect your health, see *Healing Foods For Dummies* by Molly Siple, IDG Books Worldwide, Inc.

TIP

✔ **Vegetables contain less fat and cholesterol than meat.** All meat contains fat and cholesterol. Excess meat contributes to elevated blood cholesterol and weight problems. Vegetables do not contain cholesterol.

You don't need to give up meat, but you probably do need to eat less of it and more vegetables (plus grains and fruit).

✔ **With only a few exceptions, most vegetables are close to fatfree in their innate state.** It's when you gunk them up with high-fat sauces or butter that you run into trouble. (See Chapter 11 for some great lowfat sauces.)

✔ **Vegetables provide fiber.** Fiber is needed to help food go quickly through your long intestines. Fiber also gives you a nice full feeling that staves off hunger pangs.

✔ **Vegetables are a great source of vitamins.** Those vegetables highest in vitamin C are bell peppers, dark lettuce, sweet potatoes, and tomatoes. The vitamin A winners are sweet potatoes, pumpkin, spinach, plus beets, squash and carrots, romaine, and mixed vegetables.

✔ **Vegetables also contain powerful substances called antioxidants.** Antioxidants may destroy the free radicals that can lead to cancer, heart disease, and premature aging.

Storing Vegetables the Modern Way

If your family lived on a farm or in a small town, your grandmother might have had a root cellar. This was a cool, dark, unfinished room directly under the house, usually with a dirt floor. Root cellars were damp and cool in spring and summer, dry in fall and winter, and often full of bushels of different produce — potatoes, onions, beets, cabbages, and apples.

Electric refrigerators are far more handy for storing vegetables than the old root cellar. Unfortunately, refrigerator bins are small and drying. If they aren't too small in your house, perhaps you aren't purchasing enough vegetables.

Be particularly careful about washing all fresh produce with a few squirts of detergent in a large dishpan, adding the vegetables and swishing them around, and then rinsing them well with water (see Figure 6-4). Many people have handled your food, and many chemicals may have been sprayed on them while growing, storing, and shipping — before they get to your table. You can store vegetables and wash them just before preparing if you want.

Figure 6-4:
Wash your veggies well!

Here are several ways that you can store your vegetables.

- **On your counter:** You can store some vegetables outside the refrigerator. Potatoes, tomatoes, squash, onions, and garlic can all be stored in aerated bins or baskets. You can also refrigerate them.

- **In the refrigerator:** All leafy vegetables need refrigeration, as do avocados as soon as they reach ripeness if not eaten immediately.

  - **With wet paper towels:** Wrap very wet paper towels around washed and rinsed vegetables such as lettuce, watercress, and other leafy greens. You can do the same with carrots, rutabagas, and celery. Then place them, with the wet paper towels on them, in plastic bags, squeeze out the air (oxygen is the spoiling enemy), and refrigerate.

  - **In a glass of water:** Fill a glass or bowl with water and place the ends of celery, asparagus, watercress, and parsley (vegetables with distinct stems) in the water, making sure that the leaves are not in the water. Many restaurants use this method, although it may not be practical for your home.

  - **In green-colored chemically treated bags:** Use the new chemically treated green plastic bags, which apparently keep washed and patted-dry vegetables fresher for weeks, not just days.

  - **In shrink-wrap:** Oxygen is the enemy and with air squeezed out, spoilage will occur more slowly.

Freezing vegetables

Most vegetables can be frozen. Frozen vegetables are often processed very close to the fields where they are grown and can have more nutrients than even fresh vegetables. Some fresh vegetables are dunked in light chemical baths, trucked to a delivery or packaging point, sit on shelves sometimes in heat, are sprayed or radiated, waxed, and may not be as healthy or fresh as frozen. Frozen vegetables are more limp when defrosted and may have slightly less taste, and most need to be cooked. But freezing, if done correctly whether commercially or in your home, if the vegetables are used within a few weeks, doesn't appreciably affect their vitamin content.

Be aware that frozen vegetables are never static. They can get freezer burn or water crystals, dry out, shrivel, or get that awful refrigerator/freezer smell and taste. Even in store-bought packages, covered glass jars, or plastic and foil-covered vegetables you have frozen yourself, frozen vegetables change continually in their frozen state, so don't keep them for too long. Toss if you've had them many months or if you notice a strange color, white "burn" spots, unusual shriveling, or odor.

Freeze-drying is done commercially and is a controlled version of freezer burn where moisture is not lost by evaporation but natural moisture is forced out and the foods, such as soup mixes, retain much of the flavor. They are dry and sold in packets and not frozen.

Freeze drying vegetables, if kept covered or bottled, keeps vegetables longer, almost indefinitely. Although they still have fiber, they have lost many of their vitamins and some nutrients. Some dried or freeze-dried vegetables like onions can be very flavorful.

Table 6-2 tells you the best way to store each type of vegetable for maximum longevity.

Table 6-2	Storing Vegetables to Keep Them Fresh Long
Vegetable	*How to Store It*
Artichokes	Refrigerated in plastic bags or, if stems are long, stems in a glass of water
Asparagus	Refrigerated in plastic bags or stems in glass of water
Avocados	On the countertop until ripe or refrigerated to delay ripening or after cutting
Beets	Refrigerated in plastic bags
Broccoli	Refrigerated in plastic bags
Cabbage	Refrigerated in tightly wrapped plastic wrap
Carrots	Refrigerated in plastic bags

Vegetable	How to Store It
Cauliflower	Refrigerated in plastic bags
Celery	Refrigerated in plastic bags
Chard	Refrigerated in plastic bags
Cilantro	Refrigerated in plastic bags or stems in glass of water
Corn	Refrigerated in plastic bags
Cucumber	Refrigerated in plastic bags
Eggplant	Refrigerated in plastic bags
English peas in pods	Refrigerated in plastic bags
Fennel	Refrigerated in plastic bags
Garlic	On the countertop or refrigerated in plastic bags (they dry or sprout more quickly unrefrigerated)
Herbs	Refrigerated in individually sealed plastic bags or stems in glass of water
Kale	Refrigerated in plastic bags
Leeks	Refrigerated in plastic bags
Lima beans	Refrigerated in plastic bags
Mushrooms	Refrigerated in plastic bags
Okra	Refrigerated in plastic bags
Onions	On the countertop or refrigerated in plastic bags (they sprout more quickly unrefrigerated)
Parsley	Refrigerated in plastic bags or stems in glass of water
Parsnips	Refrigerated in plastic bags
Peppers	Refrigerated in plastic bags
Potatoes	Refrigerated or on the countertop (eyes grow faster unrefrigerated)
Pumpkin	Refrigerated or unrefrigerated for shorter time period
Rutabagas	On the countertop or refrigerated in plastic bags
Scallions	Refrigerated in plastic bags
Shallots	Refrigerated in plastic bags

(continued)

Table 6-2 *(continued)*

Vegetable	*How to Store It*
Squash	Refrigerated in plastic bags or unrefrigerated for shorter time period
Sweet potatoes	Refrigerated or on the countertop (eyes grow faster unrefrigerated)
Tomatoes	On the countertop; if cut, refrigerated in plastic bags
Turnips	On the countertop or refrigerated; if cut, refrigerated in plastic bags
Watercress	Refrigerated in plastic bags or glass of water
Wax or yellow green beans	Refrigerated in plastic bags
Yams	Refrigerated or on the countertop (eyes grow faster unrefrigerated)
Zucchini	Refrigerated in plastic bags

If celery, radishes, parsnips, parsley, and carrots get limp, rehydrate them by sprinkling a little water into their plastic bag. Reseal and refrigerate for several hours. Pour out any excess water within 12 hours and then use the vegetables as soon as possible.

Mechanically shrink-wrapping vegetables

You can mechanically shrink-wrap vegetables if you have the proper vacuum equipment.

To mock shrink-wrap (this comes from author and superb cook Polly Clingerman), almost close the plastic bag over the washed and rinsed vegetables. Insert a drinking straw into the tiny opening that remains and suck out the air. Pinch the bag just below the straw to keep the air from returning and quickly close off the straw opening.

You can also flop the vegetables to the very bottom of the bag and fold and squeeze the plastic until you've removed all the air you can. When freezing, shrink-wrapping causes less freezer burn.

Cooking with Flavor, Not Fat

Most vegetables are naturally low in fat, so you don't want to undo all of nature's good work by pouring on the fat during cooking or the butter, sauce, or cheese after cooking. Marinating is one good option.

Simply marinate vegetables separately from meat products because vegetables may not grill long enough to kill the bacteria that can be present in raw meat. Marinate vegetables such as onions, peppers, and others for two hours and then grill on an outside or indoor grill. If grilling corn, you can keep it more moist by soaking in the husk for several hours in a large tub of water and then grilling over the coals in the husk but near the edge of the grill.

In addition to marinating, many cultures have great secrets that you can adopt and adapt. Here are a few general tips.

✔ Before adding vegetables to other dishes, my French grandmother would sauté leeks, onions, shallots, mushrooms, peppers, zucchini, crookneck squash, potatoes, carrots, or celery (first spritz them with cooking spray). The water-filled vegetables "sweat" their sweet juices, which caramelize on the bottom of the pan, and the oil and juices create that wonderful flavor we associated with French cooking.

✔ A great cook from Rome told me that I should add a pinch of sugar or a small amount of shredded or thinly sliced carrots to dishes, especially ones that contained tomatoes. Even if the dish already contains minced garlic, chopped onions, celery, and sweet basil, sugar can bring out or add to the flavor in bitter or second crop tomatoes or other vegetables.

✔ I grew up with Asians in my household, and the parents of my Japanese friends, instead of using the higher saturated fat peanut oil needed for cooking at a higher temperatures, would cut the vegetables into very small pieces to get the quick-cooking properties. Today, lightly spritz the pan and the vegetables with cooking spray instead of greasing the skillet or wok. This way, they cook quickly without sticking, no matter what type or amount of oil you use.

✔ Europeans developed superb long-cooking recipes for vegetables (and meat). Carrots, cabbages, potatoes, squash, beets, celery, parsnips, leeks, and onions (root vegetables especially) can all benefit from long cooking as well as short cooking.

✔ Americans and Mediterranean love quick-steamed or microwaved vegetables such as artichokes (try pressure cooking these for speed), asparagus, broccoli, broccoli rabe, and cauliflower.

Flavor secrets

Small amounts of citrus juice (such as orange or lemon), combined with triple the amount of water, vegetable broth, or defatted chicken stock, can enhance many vegetables. If you like, add herbs, spices, ginger, onions, or garlic.

For carrots, parsnips, turnips, rutabagas, sweet potatoes, yams, or all the winter squash like acorn, banana, and others: Steam or microwave in small amounts of apricot juice or orange juice and water. Add a pinch of cinnamon, nutmeg,

Cajun spice blend, curry powder, or Chinese five-spice powder.

For spinach, beet greens, collard greens, kale, mustard greens, Swiss chard, or other greens: Steam or microwave in small amounts of cider vinegar, rice wine vinegar, or lemon juice combined with triple the amount of water, vegetable stock, or defatted chicken stock. Season with splashes of vinegar.

Making Superb Vegetable Pleasures

These recipes cover many popular vegetables, giving you ways to make your favorites less boring. I also give you suggestions to encourage you to try new ones.

Sugar Snap Peas with Mint

These peas in the pods have a delicate fresh glaze, making it an easy and simple embellishment for crispy steamed sugar snaps. These peas, according to my testers, are easy and absolutely wonderful (see photo in color section).

Preparation/Cooking time: 10 minutes

Yield: 4 servings

1 pound sugar snap peas	1 tablespoon honey
1 tablespoon freshly squeezed lemon juice	1 tablespoon finely chopped fresh mint

1 In a large saucepan, add 2 cups water and bring to a boil over high heat. Add any salt you wish.

2 Add the peas, cover, and cook 2 to 3 minutes, or until the peas are bright green and crisp-tender.

3 Drain and return to the saucepan. Add the lemon juice, honey, and mint. Stir to coat the peas. No additional cooking is needed.

Nutrition at a glance (per serving): Calories 67.58; Protein 2.96 g; Carbohydrates 14.07 g; Dietary fiber 3.12 g; Total fat 0.28 g; Saturated fat 0.06 g; Cholesterol 0 mg; Sodium 11.76 mg.

Lynn's fun food fact: Sugar snaps are a cross between the English pea and the snow pea. These sweet, completely edible peas in the pods are now widely available in supermarkets fresh and frozen. When I first grew them in 1970, my Labrador and I would sit between the tall vines and eat them raw off the vine. Sugar snaps need very little or no cooking. Like corn, they are usually best enjoyed within a few hours of picking. They are full of fiber and vitamin C.

Tomatoes with Herbed Crumbs

Some cooks stew tomatoes for hours over very low heat until they are mush, but these fresh varieties are too good to cook that long. My version is quicker and retains the fresh appeal of vine-ripened tomatoes. Serve over mashed potatoes or rice.

Preparation/Cooking time: 25 minutes

Yield: 4 servings

4 medium tomatoes, quartered	*2 tablespoons herbed breadcrumbs*
1 cup tomato juice	*¼ cup chopped parsley*
2 teaspoons sugar	*1 clove garlic, minced*
¼ cup fresh basil, or 1 tablespoon dried	*¼ cup shredded lowfat or regular Parmesan cheese*
½ teaspoon dried oregano	

1 In a large saucepan, combine the tomatoes, tomato juice, sugar, basil, and oregano. Bring to a boil over medium-high heat.

2 Reduce the heat to medium and simmer, uncovered, for 15 to 18 minutes, or until the tomatoes are very soft and the juices are slightly thickened. Stir occasionally. Season to taste with salt and pepper.

3 In a small bowl, combine the breadcrumbs, parsley, garlic, and Parmesan cheese. Sprinkle over tomatoes.

Nutrition at a glance (per serving): Calories 88.89; Protein 4.78 g; Carbohydrates 13.72 g; Dietary fiber 1.95 g; Total fat 2.45 g; Saturated fat 1.29 g; Cholesterol 4.96 mg; Sodium 446.35 mg.

Lynn's tip: Italian or flat-leaf parsley is darker green and more intensely flavored than the common curly-leaf variety, but the two types are interchangeable in cooking.

Beets with Greens and Oranges

Oranges bring out the natural sweetness of fresh beets. Make this dish when you feel like both greens and beets (see photo in color section). I have made this with beet greens, too. Just lightly steam the beet greens, chop, and continue.

Preparation/Cooking time: *15 minutes*

Yield: *4 servings*

10-ounce package frozen chopped spinach

1 cup fresh orange juice

1 tablespoon cornstarch

1 tablespoon dry orange peel or zest

2 15-ounce cans sliced beets, drained

1 11-ounce can mandarin oranges, drained

1 Place the frozen spinach package on a plate and cook on high in the microwave for 3 to 4 minutes, or until defrosted. Meanwhile, to a large cool saucepan, add the orange juice, cornstarch, and zest and whisk together. Cook over medium-high heat, whisking continually until the mixture clears and thickens, 3 or 4 minutes.

2 Open the spinach package and drain the excess water by placing in a micro sieve (fine mesh) and pressing out the water or by wrapping in paper towels and squeezing the water out with your hands.

3 Add the spinach to the orange juice mixture, whisking or stirring to break it up. Add the beets and cook over medium-high heat until the beets are hot, about 3 minutes.

4 Carefully add the mandarin oranges and cook for another 1 to 2 minutes, or until the oranges are heated.

Nutrition at a glance (per serving): *Calories 129.21; Protein 3.54 g; Carbohydrates 30.69 g; Dietary fiber 4.51 g; Total fat 0.53 g; Saturated fat 0.07 g; Cholesterol 0 mg; Sodium 316.88 mg.*

Lynn's tip: *Beets grow in colors of magenta, yellow, orange, pale pink, and white. The stunning Chioggia beet has concentric rings of red and white.*

How to pickle purple eggs

For red pickled eggs, add a dozen or more, peeled hard-cooked eggs to a large jar and fill with the red juice you cooked beets in plus 2 cups cider vinegar and 1 cup water. Add 2 tablespoons pickling spices and 2 tablespoons sugar. Leave on the counter covered for a month before eating. No need for refrigeration. The vinegar pickles them just fine. I personally omit the yolks in my diet. They will last for several months.

Steamed Okra with Lemon Butter

Are you an okra lover like me? This is easy and yummy. Make sure that the pods aren't stiff or hard but small and close to bite-sized. Trim only the stem tops. The ends don't need it. I use this same recipe for chard, every kind of spinach, broccoli, and collards. Sometimes I substitute vinegar for the lemon juice.

Preparation/Cooking time: *10 minutes*

Yield: *4 servings*

1 pound whole baby okra pods

1 tablespoon fatfree butterlike spray

2 teaspoons fresh lemon juice

1 Steam the okra for about 3 minutes, covered, in ½-inch water. Don't overcook.

2 In a small skillet, add the fatfree spray and lemon juice and heat until just hot, stirring to mix.

3 Add the salt and pepper, pour the topping over the okra, and serve.

Nutrition at a glance (per serving): *Calories 46.52; Protein 1.96 g; Carbohydrates 7.74 g; Dietary fiber 2.62 g; Total fat 1.68 g; Saturated fat 1.05 g; Cholesterol 5.00 mg; Sodium 22.74 mg.*

Lynn's tip: *Okra cooks quickly and turns brown just as fast, so be ready with your topping and your fork.*

Sweet and Sharp Spaghetti Squash

Here's a simple, savory way to prepare spaghetti squash. This can be a main dish. If you want meat, add diced lean cooked beef, lamb, ham, or skinless chicken or turkey. If you like a slightly less tangy mustard flavor, use the Dijonnaise, a combination of fatfree mayonnaise and Dijon mustard.

Preparation/Cooking time: *25 minutes*

Yield: *6 servings*

(continued)

1 spaghetti squash (about 2 pounds)

½ cup diced plum tomatoes

¼ cup currants or raisins

2 teaspoons Dijon mustard

2 teaspoons dry sherry, or ½ teaspoon sherry extract

1 tablespoon water

2 teaspoons white wine vinegar

1 teaspoon dried thyme. or 2 teaspoons chopped fresh

½ teaspoon sugar

1 Pierce the squash in several places so that it doesn't explode in the microwave. Microwave the squash on high power for 15 minutes, or until tender when pierced with a fork. Turn it over once or twice while cooking.

2 Let stand for 3 minutes. Cut the squash in half lengthwise. Scoop out the seeds and attached stringy membranes and discard.

3 Lightly spray a large skillet with cooking oil spray. Add the tomatoes, currants or raisins, mustard, sherry, water, vinegar, thyme, and sugar. Toss to combine.

4 With a fork, pull out the strands of squash and place in the skillet and mix with the other ingredients. Cook over medium heat, tossing frequently, for 3 or 4 minutes, or until hot.

Nutrition at a glance (per serving): *Calories 61.71; Protein 1.40 g; Carbohydrates 14.54 g; Dietary fiber 2.57 g; Total fat 0.58 g; Saturated fat 0.11 g; Cholesterol 0 mg; Sodium 68.64 mg.*

Lynn's food facts: *The pulp of the mild spaghetti squash resembles spaghetti, for which it's named. Pasta sauces can easily overpower its slightly sweet flavor. Spaghetti squash is also delicious simply spritzed with butter-flavored spray and a sprinkling of salt and freshly ground black pepper.*

Creamed Spinach

Creamed spinach has been almost everyone's favorite for decades. Serve it as a side dish, a stuffing for baked potatoes or tomatoes, or as a bed for poached fish. You can even chill and puree it for a dip.

Preparation/Cooking time: *10 minutes*

Yield: *4 servings*

1 1-pound package frozen chopped spinach

1 teaspoon minced garlic

1 cup fatfree half-and-half or skim milk

2 tablespoons flour

½ cup fatfree or lowfat sour cream

½ cup grated fatfree Parmesan cheese topping

3 tablespoons grated Parmesan cheese

⅛ teaspoon ground nutmeg

1 Place the spinach in a microwaveable dish. Cover and microwave on high for 4 minutes. Drain in a colander and squeeze out as much water as possible (an easy way to remove the excess liquid is to lay a piece of plastic wrap over the spinach and press — the spinach sticks to paper towels).

2 Lightly spray a large skillet. Add the garlic and sauté over medium-high heat for about 2 minutes, stirring, making sure that the garlic doesn't burn.

3 Measure the half-and-half or skim milk in a 2-cup glass measuring cup. Whisk in the flour, mixing thoroughly. Add the mixture to the cooking garlic, very slowly, whisking in the pan, heating, until the mixture is smooth and thick, 4 to 5 minutes.

4 Stir in the sour cream, both Parmesan cheeses, and nutmeg. Add any salt and pepper you wish. Add the spinach and cook for 1 to 2 minutes to reheat.

Nutrition at a glance (per serving): *Calories 194.07; Protein 9.82 g; Carbohydrates 28.68 g; Dietary fiber 2.37 g; Total fat 1.61 g; Saturated fat 0.94 g; Cholesterol 6.19 mg; Sodium 461.87 mg.*

Lynn's nutrition note: *Spinach is filled with vitamin A. In addition, it contains calcium. If you want, substitute kale instead of spinach because the calcium in kale is more readily absorbed by the body than that contained in spinach. Kale also contains substances called indoles that might help prevent cancer.*

Cauliflower Puree with Garlic

This recipe is perfect for impressing or to encourage family members that vegetables can be delicious, my testers raved over this recipe. Roasted garlic gives this earthy cauliflower dish a slightly different and wonderful flavor. I often just use store bought jar garlic. If all you have is fresh garlic, add 2 unpeeled cloves to the cooking cauliflower, peel, and puree as directed.

Preparation/Cooking time: *10 minutes*

Yield: *4 servings*

(continued)

1½ cups fatfree chicken or vegetable stock

1 medium head cauliflower, broken into florets

½ cup chopped onions

2 tablespoons chopped bottled garlic or

roasted garlic

1 tablespoon thinly sliced fresh basil

1 In a large saucepan, add the stock and bring a boil. Add the cauliflower and onions. Reduce the heat to medium, cover, and simmer for 5 minutes, or until the vegetables are very tender. Drain in a colander but reserve ½ cup stock.

2 Place the cauliflower, onions, and garlic in a food processor or blender and process until smooth. With a blender, add the cauliflower, onions, and garlic, plus the reserved stock, 2 tablespoons at a time until it reaches the desired thinness. (A blender needs more liquid to puree properly but it doesn't affect the taste either way.)

3 Season with the salt and pepper. Stir in the basil. If desired, return to the saucepan to reheat gently for 2 to 3 minutes (or puree with a wand or hand blender right in the saucepan).

Nutrition at a glance (per serving): *Calories 60.01; Protein 4.20 g; Carbohydrates 12.06 g; Dietary fiber 3.22 g; Total fat 0.03 g; Saturated fat 0.00 g; Cholesterol 0 mg; Sodium 285.60 mg.*

Lynn's tip: *For a variation, pour the puree into a casserole dish, dust with fatfree Parmesan cheese topping, and broil until the topping is golden.*

Roasting garlic

Make baked or roasted garlic by placing a plump garlic bulb on a 1-foot square of foil. Spritz it lavishly with a fine grade of good olive oil and lightly salt with plain or garlic salt and a teaspoon or so of dried parsley. Wrap the foil around it, loosely twisting at the top, and bake for 1 hour in a 300° oven. Do several bulbs at once if you choose. Then just squeeze the soft garlic. Use instead of butter on bread or add to dips and sauces.

Using purees

Purees have many applications in the quick and healthy kitchen. You can puree almost any vegetable or fruit. Blenders, hand blenders, and food processors make quick work of pureeing, but alternate methods include pushing foods through a sieve, grinding them in a hand-cranked food mill, or pressing them through a ricer. Purees can be hot or cold, cooked or raw. Use them as sauces, soup thickeners, entrees, or side dishes.

Mediterranean Vegetables

This lemony Mediterranean mixture is particularly good with grilled fish. My testers said you have the best of all worlds here, especially with taste. It is easy to make, has a really great flavor, has high-fiber beans, and the tomatoes and spinach are all filled with nutrients. Plus, garlic adds a touch of pizzazz, and lemon juice gives it that yum. Serve it topped with plain fatfree yogurt.

Preparation/Cooking time: 15 minutes

Yield: 4 servings

1 large onion, chopped

1 teaspoon minced bottled or fresh garlic

1 teaspoon ground cumin

1 teaspoon dried oregano

1 small plum tomato, diced

½ cup cooked chickpeas (garbanzos)

1 10-ounce package frozen cut leaf spinach

¼ cup diced jarred roasted red peppers or pimentos

2 tablespoons fresh lemon juice

Red pepper flakes (optional)

1 In a large saucepan, add the onions, garlic, cumin, and oregano. Cover and cook over medium-low heat, stirring occasionally for 5 minutes, or until the spinach is cooked and the onions are soft. If necessary, add 1 or 2 teaspoons water to prevent sticking.

2 Stir in the tomatoes and chickpeas. Cook for 1 or 2 minutes, or until the tomatoes soften.

3 Add the spinach, peppers or pimentos, and lemon juice. Cook over medium-high heat, stirring constantly, for 2 to 3 minutes, or until the spinach wilts and excess moisture evaporates. Add any salt and pepper you wish and any red pepper flakes (if using).

(continued)

Nutrition at a glance (per serving): *Calories 74.20; Protein 4.27 g; Carbohydrates 14.36 g; Dietary fiber 4.07 g; Total fat 0.93 g; Saturated fat 0.11 g; Cholesterol 0 mg; Sodium 95.28mg.*

Lynn's tip: *Few foods bring out the natural flavors of vegetables as well as a small amount of salt, fresh lemon juice, and grated lemon rind.*

Summer Succotash

Fresh happy flavors shine through in this traditional American dish. You can also add diced summer squash (yellow squash) or zucchini and diced lean ham. Sometimes you can find a frozen mixture of corn and limas so use that. I'm using garlic from jars to save time, but you can always use fresh.

Preparation/Cooking time: *20 minutes*

Yield: *4 servings*

¾ cup defatted chicken broth	*1 10-ounce package frozen baby lima beans, thawed*
1 large onion, chopped	*½ cup frozen whole kernel corn, thawed*
1 green pepper, chopped	*1 small tomato, diced*
1 medium potato, diced	*2 tablespoons chopped fresh dill*
¾ teaspoon minced garlic, or 1 large clove garlic, minced	*2 tablespoons chopped fresh parsley*

1 Coat a large saucepan with cooking spray. Add the broth, onions, peppers, potatoes, and garlic. Cook over medium-high heat, stirring occasionally, for 8 minutes.

2 Reduce the heat to medium. Add the lima beans and corn. Cover and cook for 5 minutes. Add the tomatoes; cook, stirring, for 5 minutes. Stir in the dill and parsley. Add any salt and pepper you wish.

Nutrition at a glance (per serving): *Calories 150.29; Protein 7.32 g; Carbohydrates 31.08 g; Dietary fiber 6.80 g; Total fat 0.55 g; Saturated fat 0.10 g; Cholesterol 0 mg; Sodium 149.43 mg.*

Lynn's tip: *Corn, potatoes, and onions all contain natural starches that thicken with cooking, making a tasty natural sauce. Cook for at least 15 minutes to release the starches. You can add several tablespoons of liquid, such as defatted chicken stock, vegetable stock, or water, to increase the saucing property of these vegetables. Or do as I do. Make a mixture of cornstarch and thicken it in 2 minutes.*

Orange Asparagus

Refreshing and pretty, this recipe works as a side or entree. You can add a tablespoon or 2 of small-diced pimentos or red pepper for extra color.

Preparation/Cooking time: *12 minutes*

Yield: *4 servings*

1 teaspoon margarine or butter	*2 tablespoons orange zest (about 2 oranges)*
1 pound fresh asparagus, tough stem part removed	*1 tablespoon cornstarch*
1 cup fresh-squeezed orange juice, divided	*1 11-ounce can mandarin oranges*

1 Add the butter to a large skillet and roll the asparagus around to coat, heating on high for 1 to 2 minutes.

2 Add ½ cup orange juice and zest, cover, and steam over medium heat for 3 to 4 minutes.

3 Whisk the cornstarch into the remaining ½ cup orange juice and oranges, add it to the skillet, and heat until thick. Add any salt and pepper you wish and stir in.

Nutrition at a glance (per serving): *Calories 107.34; Protein 2.36 g; Carbohydrates 23.87 g; Dietary fiber 1.90 g; Total fat 1.37 g; Saturated fat 0.25 g; Cholesterol 0 mg; Sodium 22.80 mg.*

Lynn's tip: *To make this recipe an entree, add 1 cup diced lean ham and a pinch of ginger. Serve it with rice or pasta. You can substitute broccoli for the asparagus as broccoli and oranges are also terrific.*

Spiced Carrots

These carrots have a shiny sauce that is very tasty. You can add broccoli florets, too. If someone doesn't like carrots, this recipe will change his mind.

Preparation/Cooking time: *20 minutes*

Yield: *4 servings*

(continued)

2½ cups or 1 pound baby carrots, diagonally sliced ½-inch

1 cinnamon stick, or ¼ teaspoon cinnamon

½ teaspoon ground ginger

2 teaspoons honey

½ teaspoon cumin

2 teaspoons fresh lemon juice

¼ teaspoon ground coriander (optional)

¼ cup orange juice

1 tablespoon cornstarch

1 Lightly spray a large saucepan with butter-flavored cooking spray. Add the carrots and spray them. Cook over medium-high heat for 2 or 3 minutes.

2 Add 1 cup water, the cinnamon, ginger, honey, cumin, lemon juice, and coriander (if using). Stir to mix.

3 Bring to a boil, lower to a simmer, cover, and steam for 5 to 7 minutes, or until the carrots are barely cooked.

4 For the sauce, measure the orange juice in a 1-cup glass measuring cup and whisk in the cornstarch. Remove the carrots with a slotted spoon and set aside.

5 Add the orange juice and cornstarch to the liquid in the pan and whisk to combine. Cook over high heat for 1 or 2 minutes, whisking constantly, until the sauce thickens. Add the carrots and cook for 1 or 2 minutes. Remove the cinnamon stick.

Nutrition at a glance (per serving): *Calories 63.07; Protein 1.16 g; Carbohydrates 14.23 g; Dietary fiber 2.15 g; Total fat 0.71 g; Saturated fat 0.12 g; Cholesterol 0 mg; Sodium 40.53 mg.*

Lynn's tip: *For extra pizzazz, you can add a teaspoon of dried or fresh chopped parsley, orange zest, chives, or caraway seeds just before serving.*

Zucchini and Onions

This recipe is light, fresh, and just a little different for zucchini lovers. You can use your processor for chopping both the onions and watercress (or parsley).

Preparation/Cooking time: *30 minutes*

Yield: *4 servings*

4 medium zucchini, sliced

1 cup chopped onion

1 cup fatfree chicken broth or water

1 cup chopped watercress or parsley

1 teaspoon lemon juice (optional)

1 Spray a large saucepan with butter-flavored or plain cooking spray. Over medium-high heat, swirl the vegetables around or stir with a spoon, cooking them for about 2 minutes.

2 Add the chicken broth. Cover, bring to a boil, reduce the heat to medium low, and simmer for 15 minutes.

3 Add the watercress or parsley and lemon juice and steam for an additional 5 minutes. Drain all excess liquid.

Nutrition at a glance (per serving): Calories 41.63; Protein 3.05 g; Carbohydrates 8.54 g; Dietary fiber 2.82 g; Total fat 0.33 g; Saturated fat 0.07 g; Cholesterol 0 mg; Sodium 170.10 mg.

Italian Green Beans with Tomatoes

Bright green, full of flavor, and looking like great fun, Italian-style green beans with tomatoes are lusty and colorful. If you can find them, use pole beans because they have so much more flavor.

Preparation/Cooking time: 15 minutes

Yield: 4 servings

1 tablespoon olive oil

3 cloves garlic, minced or very thinly sliced

1 medium onion, sliced

1 pound green beans, trimmed and cut into 1-inch pieces

2 medium ripe Roma tomatoes, diced or thin sliced

Pinch sugar

2 tablespoons chopped basil

2 teaspoons dried oregano

2 tablespoons capers

1 To a large skillet with a lid, add the olive oil. Over medium heat, add the garlic and onions. Swirl the vegetables around, coating them, for about 2 minutes.

2 Add the green beans and sauté over medium heat for about 3 minutes. Add ⅓ cup water, cover, and steam for about 5 minutes.

3 Add the tomatoes, sugar, basil, oregano, and any salt and pepper you wish and stir gently to mix, heating covered, for 3 to 4 minutes, adding additional water if necessary. Add the capers and stir gently.

(continued)

Nutrition at a glance (per serving): *Calories 88.20; Protein 2.79 g; Carbohydrates 13.12 g; Dietary fiber 4.36 g; Total fat 3.93 g; Saturated fat 0.57 g; Cholesterol 0 mg; Sodium 134.43 mg.*

Lynn's tip: *As a variation, instead of the basil and oregano, use crumbled or shredded fresh sage leaves or ¼ teaspoon dried sage. If using sage, add ¼ cup shredded Parmesan cheese to the top of the beans just before serving.*

Eggplant, Asparagus, and Tomatoes

This recipe is similar to but fresher than a ratatouille, and you can substitute or add other vegetables you like such as green beans, sliced green peppers, onions, zucchini, yellow squash, or parsley. Add cubes of lean ham or skinless turkey or chicken for an entree.

Preparation/Cooking time: *15 minutes*

Yield: *6 servings as a main dish, 8 servings as a side*

1 large eggplant, about 2 pounds	*½ teaspoon flaked red pepper*
1 tablespoon olive oil	*1 tomato, diced*
4 cloves garlic, minced	*¼ cup chopped basil*
1 pound asparagus or green beans, trimmed	*½ teaspoon dried oregano*

1 Cut the eggplant into sticks, ½-inch thick by 2 ½-inches long.

2 In a very large skillet or Dutch oven, add the olive oil. Over medium heat, add the garlic and cook for 1 minute, stirring, making sure that it doesn't burn.

3 Add the asparagus or green beans and coat. Add the eggplant and ¼ cup water, any salt and pepper you wish, and red pepper flakes. Cover and cook for 8 minutes, stirring occasionally.

4 Add the tomatoes, basil, and oregano, toss lightly, and heat for 2 minutes or until hot.

Nutrition at a glance (per serving): *Calories 60.55; Protein 1.86 g; Carbohydrates 10.50 g; Dietary fiber 3.86 g; Total fat 2.08 g; Saturated fat 0.31 g; Cholesterol 0 mg; Sodium 5.59 mg.*

Lynn's Tip: *Because this is an Italian dish, use the large fat purple eggplants, not the slim Asian (more lavender with pale light strias around the stem) variety. You can also use tiny sliced white eggplants, the original eggplant, named because they look like eggs.*

Cantonese Vegetable Stir-Fry

The word Cantonese is a tip-off that means gently flavored. (You do have an option of red pepper flakes, however.) Foods from that region of China aren't spicy but sooo good. The secret to good stir-fries is to cut all your vegetables before you begin cooking; to keep them small; and to not cook them for too long so that they get mushy. Substitute any vegetables but keep them colorful like green asparagus and thin-sliced orange yams or green beans and yellow pepper pieces. Garnish with chopped scallions or sprouts.

Preparation/Cooking time: *15 minutes*

Yield: *4 servings*

1 tablespoon cornstarch

½ cup fatfree chicken or vegetable broth, divided

2 large carrots, cut into thin diagonal slices

1 teaspoon minced garlic (1 large clove fresh)

2 teaspoons grated fresh ginger

2 teaspoons lite soy sauce, divided

5 scallions, cut into 1-inch diagonal slices

1 6-ounce can sliced water chestnuts or bamboo shoots, drained

2 teaspoons dry sherry, or ½ teaspoon sherry extract

8 ounces frozen snow peas

½ teaspoon sugar

½ teaspoon dark sesame oil

½ teaspoon sesame seeds or crushed red pepper flakes (optional)

1 Place the cornstarch in a glass measuring cup. Add ¼ cup broth, stir to dissolve the cornstarch, and set aside.

2 Coat a large skillet or wok with cooking spray. Add the carrots, garlic, ginger, 1 teaspoon soy sauce, and 2 tablespoons stock. Cook over medium-high heat, stirring, for 2 minutes.

3 Add the scallions, water chestnuts, sherry, and the remaining 2 tablespoons stock. Cook, stirring and tossing, for 2 minutes.

4 Add the snow peas, sugar, the remaining 1 teaspoon soy sauce, dark sesame oil, and the cornstarch mixture. Cook, tossing, for 1 minute, or until thickened. Sprinkle with the sesame seeds or red pepper flakes (if using).

Nutrition at a glance (per serving): *Calories 81.66; Protein 3.00 g; Carbohydrates 15.81 g; Dietary fiber 4.36 g; Total fat 0.97 g; Saturated fat 0.14 g; Cholesterol 0 mg; Sodium 189.87 mg.*

(continued)

Lynn's tip: Dark sesame oil (sold in Asian markets) imparts more depth of flavor than the light or Mediterranean Middle Eastern sesame oil. Store sesame oil in a plastic spray bottle in the refrigerator so that you can spray it in minimal amounts. You have to run it under hot water first.

Baked Potato Topping

So simple and good on a baked potato, this topping is also great on nachos and burritos.

Preparation/Cooking time: 5 minutes

Yield: 2 cups or 6 to 8 servings

2 cups fatfree or lowfat sour cream

3 scallions, chopped, including green

Dash garlic salt

2 tablespoons chopped parsley

1 In a small bowl, add all the ingredients except the parsley and mix.

2 If you're using on potatoes, slit each hot baked potato lengthwise. Push the ends to open and add the topping. Sprinkle on parsley.

Nutrition at a glance (per serving): Calories 95.31; Protein 5.46 g; Carbohydrates 16.43 g; Dietary fiber 0.16 g; Total fat 0.02 g; Saturated fat 0.00 g; Cholesterol 6.67 mg; Sodium 86.99 mg.

Lynn's tip: To encourage adding more vegetables to your menu plan, go for potatoes in a big way. You can add vegetables to your potato toppings easily.

Making potato wedges by hand

You can easily make thin potato wedges or slices by hand. Cut the potato in half lengthwise. Cut the halves in fourths. Lay each fourth on the cutting board, your palm pressed hard on the potato, thumb and hand perpendicular to your body. With the potato secured by your hand and sideways to your body, with a 6-inch knife, lean over so that you can see the exposed potato skin and slice it lengthwise as many times as you want. Or use a hand-held Feemster slicer or the slicer on your processor.

Western Oven Fries

Getting Western fries ready for the table in under an hour is a trick, and I've solved it. Use the best chili powder for these potatoes, because the seasoning is important. I often add wedges of scrubbed yuca, or yucca (from the cassava plant), a mild and delicious root vegetable available wherever there is a Hispanic market. Either spelling is correctly pronounced "youca."

Preparation/Cooking time: *25 minutes*

Yield: *4 servings*

3 large baking potatoes (8 ounces each), scrubbed

½ teaspoon dried oregano

¾ teaspoon chili powder

1 Preheat oven to 400°. Cut the potatoes into ¼-inch sticks (or wedges if you choose), making sure that no part is thicker than ¼ inch.

2 In a flat-bottomed dish, add the chili powder, salt, and oregano. Mix and add the potatoes, coating each well.

3 Cover a large baking sheet with foil and spray the foil with cooking spray. Place the potato wedges on the foil in a single layer.

4 Bake for 20 to 25 minutes, or until the potatoes are crisp on the outside and tender on the inside when pierced with a sharp knife.

Nutrition at a glance (per serving): *Calories 152.36; Protein 3.25 g; Carbohydrates 35.13 g; Dietary fiber 3.55 g; Total fat 0.24 g; Saturated fat 0.05 g; Cholesterol 0 mg; Sodium 15.79 mg.*

Lynn's tip: *You can make a type of homemade potato chip by thinly slicing potatoes, laying on the sprayed cookie sheet, spraying the potatoes, and baking for 10 to 15 minutes.*

Stuffed Sweet Potatoes

These sweet potatoes are rich and filling. Garnish with a dusting of nutmeg or a teaspoon of chopped parsley. This is a favorite at Thanksgiving or on chilly winter days or nights.

Preparation/Cooking time: *20 minutes*

Yield: *4 servings*

3 medium sweet potatoes

¼ cup drained canned apricots or peach or pear slices

½ teaspoon grated orange rind

⅛ teaspoon ground cinnamon

2 tablespoons brown sugar, divided

12 miniature marshmallows (optional)

1 Preheat oven to 400°. Pierce the sweet potatoes several times with a fork. Microwave on high, rotating twice for 8 to 10 minutes or until tender. Cut completely in half lengthwise and allow to cool for several minutes.

2 Using a thin teaspoon, carefully scoop out most of the potato pulp from 4 of the halves, leaving a ¼-inch shell.

3 Place the shells on the baking sheet and set in the oven for 10 minutes only. Meanwhile, scoop the flesh completely from the remaining 2 halves; discard the skins.

4 Place the flesh from all the potatoes in a medium bowl and mash. Add the apricots and mash again to mix. Add the orange rind, cinnamon, and 1 tablespoon brown sugar. Season to taste with salt and white pepper. Stir or mash to mix well again.

5 Remove the hot firm shells from the oven. Spoon the filling into the shells, mounding it above the top of the shells. Sprinkle with the remaining 1 tablespoon brown sugar. Dot each with 4 marshmallows (if using). Bake for 2 or 3 minutes, or until the marshmallows are melting and browned.

Nutrition at a glance (per serving): *Calories 124.13 ; Protein 1.56 g; Carbohydrates 30.15 g; Dietary fiber 2.88 g; Total fat 0.10 g; Saturated fat 0.02 g; Cholesterol 0 mg; Sodium 11.87 mg.*

Lynn's fun food fact: *Sweet potatoes are not the same as yams, although the terms are often used interchangeably and they look and taste similarly. Sweet potatoes are from a large edible root of the morning glory family. The two most commonly marketed in America are a pale yellow variety and a dark variety with moist orange flesh that's often referred to as a yam. True yams are sweeter and more moist and come from Africa and South America where they can vary in size from half a pound to 120 pounds. In those countries, they are cut up into large chunks and sold by weight.*

Ten easy baked potato toppings

You never have to settle for a baked potato with butter (which is full of saturated fat and cholesterol) and full-fat sour cream. You can find many lowfat baked potato toppings:

- **Chili:** Pour on a heated can of lowfat chili. To freshen the canned chili, first sauté onions, peppers, and a tablespoon of chili powder. When soft, mix in the canned chili, mixing well and heating them both.

- **Gravy:** Purchase bottled fatfree chicken gravy. First sauté plenty of fresh or canned drained sliced mushrooms and perhaps diced onions and celery. Then add the gravy, mix well, and heat.

- **Cheese and vegetables:** Melt Old El Paso lowfat Cheese 'n' Salsa or reduced-fat Velveeta cheese. Stuff the baked potato with lightly steamed florets of broccoli or cauliflower, shredded cooked cabbage, onions, or small-sliced green beans or asparagus. Pour the melted cheese over the vegetables in the potato.

- **Cheese:** Melt equal parts fatfree or lowfat shredded cheese with regular cheese. Mix with small amounts diced cooked skinless turkey breast, Canadian bacon, or lean ham.

- **Vegetables:** Steam frozen mixed vegetables. Make a cooked cream sauce with 2 cups fatfree half-and-half, skim milk, or fatfree nondairy liquid creamer and 2 tablespoons flour. Whisk together and heat for 4 minutes, stirring, over medium heat. Add the vegetables and mix well, heating until hot.

- **Giblets and gravy:** Finely dice partially frozen gizzards (only the gizzard part of giblets is available in most markets), toss in flour to coat, and sauté along with a few tablespoons each finely chopped onions, celery, and carrots for 10 minutes, spritzing

it all lightly with cooking spray. Add a bottle or two of fatfree chicken gravy and ½ teaspoon crumbled sage, mix well, and heat until hot.

- **Beef:** Finely dice lean, cooked, or raw beef. Toss the beef in flour to coat. Sauté the beef along with finely chopped onions, celery, firm tomatoes like Roma, and carrots for 10 minutes, spritzing lightly in cooking spray. Add a bottle or two of fatfree beef gravy, mix well and cook until hot.

- **Creamed chipped beef with peas:** Finely shred a 4-ounce bottle of chipped beef and make a cream sauce with 2 cups fatfree half-and-half, skim milk, or fatfree nondairy liquid creamer and 2 tablespoons flour. Whisk together for 4 minutes over medium heat. Add the chipped beef and ½ cup frozen peas and stir in, heating until hot.

- **Cream of mushroom soup:** Heat a lowfat can of cream of mushroom soup, skim milk, or fatfree nondairy liquid creamer instead of the water called for, plus 1 tablespoon flour whisked in. Heat for 3 minutes, stirring. Add 1 small can drained mushrooms and ½ cup any vegetable, such as peas, mixed vegetables, asparagus pieces. Stir until hot.

- **Creamed eggs:** Heat 1½ cups fatfree half-and-half, skim milk, or fatfree nondairy liquid creamer with 2 tablespoons flour whisked in. Heat for 4 minutes, stirring. Add ½ cup substitute eggs to a bowl. Pour half the hot mixture into the eggs, whisking well. Over low heat, add the mixture in the bowl slowly back into the heating roux and whisk for about 2 minutes, until thickened further. You can also add diced hard cooked eggs to this. Top with parsley or watercress sprigs.

Baking potatoes

Follow these tips for great baked potatoes. If you have

✔ **1 hour:** If you are oven-baking potatoes and want a crispy skin, first scrub with soap and water and rinse well, keeping them very wet. Put them in a preheated hot 400° oven. Turn the oven down immediately to 350° and bake for 1 hour.

✔ **25 minutes:** For speedier baked potatoes, after washing, place in a microwave for 3 to 4 minutes, turning often. Rinse again the now hot potato with cold water and put them in the 400° oven, turning it down to 350° immediately, for 20 minutes.

✔ **10 minutes:** You can always microwave washed, rinsed, and dried potatoes for 5 to 7 minutes, depending on the size and number of potatoes. Turn often. To crisp up the skin, rinse and place in a 400° oven for 5 minutes.

✔ **6 minutes:** This tip is from my editor Kelly Ewing, and I thought it was a great one. Place the washed potato in a vented microwavable container with a vented lid so that the potatoes steam. Cook on high for 5 to 7 minutes, depending on the size and number of potatoes.

Chapter 7

Meat, Poultry, Fish, and Shellfish

. . . .

In This Chapter

▶ Jazzing up prepared meat meals

▶ Getting to the heart of beef, lamb, and pork

▶ Preparing seafood safely

. . . .

1 n large grocery chains all over the country, markets are going to great effort to make your meat meals quicker and easier. And they're paying attention to health and what you want. In this chapter, I tell you about the meals you'll find already prepared and show you how to use them. A simple safety table shows you what temperature your meat thermometer should be for which cuts. I also tell you what meat, fish, and poultry are naturally lower in fat and which are higher and why cutting off all the fat is not just for the reduction of calories, total fat, or even saturated fat, but for a more important reason, which you see. And this is just some of the info you discover in this fact-filled, recipe-packed chapter!

Preparing Easy Meals with the Help of Your Local Grocery

If you're short on time, don't worry. You can literally find hundreds of varieties of fully cooked commercial meat dishes in your meat department. With meat department products from turkey jerky (snacks) to mint shrimp (entrees), your major chain meat departments have finely figured out what you want — quick, healthy, and easy to fix meats.

Spices are born

In ... 1570, "When spices (for meats) for the first time in a thousand years became expensive in Italy . . . it's cooks adapted with admirable promptitude (to) ... "nuova cucina," remarkable for it's lightly spiced simplicity . . . (kicked off with an) ... extravagant ... banquet given by Pope Pius V."

— *History in Food,* Rhey Tannahill

You can have some of these precooked meals on the table in about 10 to 20 minutes. You only need to heat them, and a microwave will work just fine. While these meals are heating, you can make a salad, steam a vegetable or two, set the table, and call the family to sit down.

Every grocery market is different, so you'll want to check out what your store offers. Some ready-made meals you'll probably find include pot roast, barbe-cued pork, chicken teriyaki, lemon garlic chicken, bacon, and snow crab legs, to name just a few.

You can also find cooked cold meats ready to serve or reheat. Examples include chicken, turkey, ham, steamed shrimp, and crab, to name just a few. You can even find cooked whole turkey breast.

If you're feeling ambitious and have the time, you can easily find uncooked pre-cutmeats at your grocery. Whole uncooked chickens and turkeys (and their separated parts), fish, and shellfish are available, as well as whole beef and pork ribs, chops, and roasts. But even though the meats are uncooked, you can still save time by using presliced uncooked meat strips. For example, you can find precut stew meat and precut strips of various meat, including beef, poultry, seafood, and pork. You can even find marinated meats, fish, shellfish, and poultry.

Are Alaskan king crabs too salty?

If you have had Alaskan king crabs that are too salty, don't give up — at least not if you are cook-ing them at home. Here's a tip. Nearly all frozen or unfrozen Alaskan king crabs need to be boiled in large pots of unsalted water for 2 to 3 minutes. Alaskan king crabs are caught, cooked, and salt-brine frozen, making boiling in clear water necessary to remove much of the salt. Otherwise, they aren't palatable. Some cooks use two large pots of boiling water, moving the crabs from one pot after 1 minute, adding them to another boiling pot, along with a teaspoon of sugar for another minute. They are already cooked, but they need desalting. Many profes-sional chefs (I've sadly discovered after ordering king crab in restaurants) don't know this.

Use store-ground (not commercially ground) turkey

I usually purchase store-ground turkey instead of commercial (asking my store to grind a breast without skin while I shop). Why? Store-ground turkey can be 99 percent fat free. On the other hand, regular commercial ground turkey can have 7 percent or more fat because it can contain everything, including skin and fat.

Here are two tips:

- You can transform market-cooked (deli) or packaged grilled chicken and turkey strips into a fast chicken salad with chopped onions, celery, and mayo. Or you can serve them cold, layered in strips over a lettuce salad or heated for a fast stir-fry, diced for a pebbly sauce, or warm to top rice or pasta.

- A sprinkle or toss of the new and tasty little morsels of ¼-inch small-diced store-cut lean ham (in vacuum pacs) can perk up everything from scrambled eggs, pancakes, quick soups like canned pea or bean, lettuce salads, potato salads, baked scalloped potatoes, and steamed broccoli or Brussels sprouts, cauliflower, or green beans. You can even use them to garnish mashed or baked potatoes

Cooking Meat, Fish, Shellfish, and Poultry

You can cook meat, fish, shellfish, and poultry in many ways, from the little-used poaching or braising method (cooking covered in liquid, or in an inch of liquid) to grilling on counter or stovetop grills in 5 minutes. Depending on the method you use, you'll want to keep certain guidelines in mind.

But no matter which method you use, keep in mind that countertop thawing is not good. Experts recommend not thawing frozen meat on the counter unless you pay very close attention to the time. Meat can sit already thawed at room temperature for several hours. Thaw in the refrigerator or microwave using the defrosting mode or cut partially frozen meat (when it's easier to cut anyway) and cook it then. Heating meat still partially frozen is fine as long as it is thoroughly cooked.

Healthy tips for quick cooking

Not all the things you need to know about cooking meat have as serious consequences as eating undercooked meat. However, the end result of your cooking will be so much better if you follow these tips as well.

✔ **Be sure to remove all fat on meat, poultry, and fish.** Also cook meat until it's well done (to kill any salmonella, listeria, or *E. coli*) and heat all shellfish and chicken until completely cooked. Removing the fat on meat not only means fewer saturated fats, but fewer chemicals such as PCBs and other contaminants, which are mostly contained in fat. A great many species of commercial

fish sold in America still contain contaminants, so remove the fish fat where it lodges in tuna and salmon or where you see it and cook all fish until opaque and it breaks apart easily with a fork (called flaky).

✔ **Don't overmarinate your meat.** According to some grilling experts, marinating most muscle meats for longer than an hour using a meat tenderizer causes mealiness or an unappetizing grainy surface when cooked. You're better off using seasoned rubs and a little oil. For more on marinating, *see Grilling For Dummies* by Marie Rama and John Mariani (IDG Books Worldwide, Inc.).

Make sure that you follow these guidelines when you're grilling, and you won't go wrong:

✔ **Place the food (if thicker than 1 inch) about 4 inches from the heat.** (If you're using a countertop grill, then just lay it on). Some grills have the heat closer, while some countertop grills have heat in the lid, too. With very thin slices and an open grill, you may want to have your meat just 1 inch from the heat.

✔ **Don't crowd the grill or broiler pan — you can't turn the food without messing it.** In addition, when the food is pushed together, it doesn't cook evenly, and it can steam instead of grill.

✔ **Put quicker cooking or smaller pieces of food closer to the outside of the grill grate or broiler pan where it isn't as hot.** Place thicker meat and poultry, which need a longer cooking time, in the center.

✔ **Cook wild game far more well done than domestic meats.** It may contain parasites, trichinosis, or salmonella.

✔ **No matter what method of meat cooking you opt for, make sure that you use a meat thermometer (see Figure 7-1).** The Center for Science in the Public Interest recommends the guidelines listed in Table 7-1.

Eating undercooked or raw meat, game, poultry, fish, or shellfish can be dangerous. Meats, especially hamburger and pork, should *always* be cooked well done. Meat can and does contain roundworms, listeria, and *E. coli* (*escherichia coli,* a bacteria). Undercooked, the latter can cause serious illness, including death. Undercooked pork or wild game can contain trichinosis, which can also cause death. Undercooked or cross-contaminating knives or basting sauce when cooking poultry or meat can contain salmonella, which causes illness yearly to hundreds of thousands with a recent study reporting several million each year.

Figure 7-1:
An instant-read thermometer.

Table 7-1	Safe Meat Temperatures
Type of Meat	**Temperature When Cooked**
Beef	160°
Fish	Until opaque and flaky, meaning you can easily separate it with a fork, cooking about 10 minutes per inch, flat fish just a minute or two, both sides or one side, not turning the fish.
Lamb	170°
Pork	165° to 170° (the lower temperature means less dry meat)
Poultry	180° to 185°
Stuffing	165°

Make sure that you follow these guidelines when you're pan-frying, and you won't go wrong:

✔ **Lightly spray nonstick, stainless steel, cast iron, enamel, aluminum, or other types of frying pans with cooking spray.** Or better yet, also spray the meat, poultry, or fish itself with cooking spray before adding it to the skillet pan (or spray the meat during cooking if it appears dry).

✔ **If you want your skinless chicken breast and legs to look, taste, and have a delicious crust just like chicken with skin, when you pan-fry it, first dust the skinless chicken with flour, spray with cooking oil spray, and add salt and pepper.** Turn often to brown every side. Add more spray to the chicken if necessary. Watch to be sure that the chicken doesn't burn, turn down the heat to low, cover briefly (10 minutes) to heat the chicken through (the last part ensures tender chicken inside the crusty coating), and then "crust it up" again by briefly cooking both sides uncovered on medium heat, turning often.

✔ **Watch all frying foods carefully.** Thin pans get to high temperatures very quickly. Thick or heavy pans hold the heat longer; even when you turn off the heat, the thick pan may still cause the food to burn or dry out unless it's removed from the heat fairly quickly.

Make sure that you follow these guidelines when you're pressure cooking:

✔ **You can use a pressure cooker for meat loaf, beef or lamb stew, pot roasts, pork roasts, and many chicken dishes.** It tenderizes tough cuts and quickly cooks all meat. There is almost no other way to get the long-cooking flavors or tenderizing from some meat except with long cooking, and pressure cookers do that well, shortening the time considerably. (For more on pressure cookers and slow cooking, see Chapter 15.)

✔ **When timing your food in pressure cookers, realize that it takes time to build up the pressure.** It usually takes about 5 minutes for smaller amounts of food and liquid to heat up and 10 or more minutes for larger amounts of food and liquid. Take that into account because the times given in most pressure cooker cookbooks (especially those that come with the cooker) don't always include that.

Make sure that you follow these guidelines when you're baking:

✔ **Use a meat thermometer to check temperature (refer to Table 7-1).** Except for Thanksgiving and when you're cooking large roasts, chicken, or geese, meats aren't baked as much as they used to be, and lean meats dry out when baked uncovered.

✔ **Bake most whole turkeys and whole chickens covered, whether in foil or large oven roasters with lids.** Crisp or brown poultry skin by uncovering it during the last 15 or so minutes of baking. Some (but not enough) whole chickens, Cornish game hens, and turkeys are leaner now and need to be baked covered tightly so that they almost steam.

✔ **Consider double-covering your pork and beef by wrapping them in foil first and then placing in a covered roasting pan.** Pork and beef are far leaner and need to be baked covered or in liquid to avoid ending up too dry.

✔ **Bake fish wrapped in foil (with vegetables and rubs if you choose).** Because most have been frozen, they, too, become dry when baked uncovered.

Make sure that you follow these guidelines when you're microwaving:

✔ **If you don't have a turntable in your microwave (which you can buy separately), move meats around several times while cooking.** Microwaves tend to cook the small or flatter areas of large pieces of meat more quickly, and they cook the edges of meat very fast.

Anyone for sushi?

Most home cooks, unless they are specialists in that area, should not prepare or serve raw oysters and clams, meat, fish, or shellfish. Leave the *sushi* (Japanese-style rice cakes usually topped with raw fish), *sashimi* (Japanese raw fish), *ceviche* (Latin American-style raw fish, usually marinated in lime), and *beef tartar* (thin slices, ground, or shreds of raw beef) to expert chefs and restaurants that specialize in those foods. Even then I'd use caution if you're unfamiliar with the restaurant or chef.

- ✓ **Lightly cover foods, especially fish.** Fish is easily cooked in a microwave and is more tender if cooked covered. (Microwaved fish tastes better when rubbed with spices or lemon juice. A friend cooks her fish in oven bags with sauces such as lowfat tartar sauce, Asian or Mexican sauces, Italian salad dressing, or bottled lemon or orange flavored sauce.)

- ✓ **Move hotdogs around often to avoid splitting.** Most hotdogs cook in 2 minutes. Wrapping in paper towels helps avoid splitting and also drains away some fat. The lowfat hotdogs are great cooked this way (or grilled).

- ✓ **Season a whole skinned chicken inside and out.** Stuff it with sprigs of rosemary and thyme and place it inside an oven bag. You'll end up with a tender, tasty, and beautiful chicken that cooks perfectly in just 15 minutes.

- ✓ **Cook chicken parts, flavored with spices or rubs, in oven bags.** They cook in 2 to 3 minutes, depending upon how much and how thick.

 And when you're *stewing* (which means cooking it in large amounts of water or other liquid), make sure that you remove all fat from the stewing meat. Or, before serving, chill it to remove the fat that has risen to the top.

Making Meat Look Like More than It Is

This is a secret section. Cooks know presentation is especially important. Eating healthy doesn't just mean lean, it also means eating less. Portion sizes should be no more than the suggested 4-ounces uncooked, about 3 to 3 ½ ounces cooked. But not everyone is happy about this. So smart family cooks often resort to subterfuge. (I did these things for two years before confessing, but meanwhile I brought my husband's cholesterol down 100 points. He felt like he was eating like he always did, and he had no idea why it came down so dramatically.)

Yeah, baby, cholesterol

All beef, pork, poultry, and fish have about equal amounts of cholesterol. It's the very low saturated fat content in some meats like turkey breast and most fish (but very little beef) that you look for in healthy food. Choose lean top round, pork cuts such as Canadian bacon, lean ham, and lean tenderloin to make them more acceptable healthwise.

Here are the secrets to cutting portion sizes without a lot of hollering:

✔ Slice the meat or poultry really thin and fan it out, making a big area.

✔ Purchase thin and flat but large-looking filets of turkey breast, fish, and beef. (Some 3 to 4 ounces of uncooked filets are 7 inches long and 4 inches wide — but only about ¼-inch thick.)

✔ Fill the plate to overflowing. Serve with lots of other foods such as three or four vegetables, a big heaping of potatoes (make one of the vegetables or potato varieties a favorite of the one you are cooking for), plenty of sliced tomatoes, and a sprig of something more exotic like rosemary, or a slice of candied ginger or plain twisted orange slice. No one will complain when you go to so much trouble and they end up feeling full anyway.

✔ Secretly use slightly smaller plates. The same pattern on both your big and slightly smaller plates (instead of having entirely different smaller plates) hides the size change so that it isn't noticeable. Conversely, when you have a child that says you give him too much food, use really large plates in the same pattern, putting just a little on each plate.

✔ Remove and hide the skin from cooked turkey and chicken. Hide the whole wing, too, before it gets to the table. Before cooking, remove every bit of edge fat from beef, pork, and lamb, even if it tears up the meat.

✔ Pour on lots of thick, really scrumptious mushroom, onion, or other vegetable-studded sauce or gravy. When the sauce tastes so fabulous and they have so much, no one notices the abysmally small portions of wafer-thin meat, fish, or poultry slices.

✔ Occasionally, serve large portions of almost zero fat protein foods like turkey breast, scallops, or cod to keep 'em guessing.

✔ Serve fruit on the plate with every meat meal. It takes up space, fills the stomach, contains fiber, and is relatively low in calories.

✔ In chili con carne, instead of hamburger or ground turkey, use lean, small-dice beef cubes. Also, use dark red kidney beans, which are firmer and more chewy than the lighter pinkish kidney beans. Or cook your own beans with salt, which toughens them. Getting a chunk of diced beef feels more meaty in the mouth than a paltry amount of ground meat.

✔ In meat loaf or burgers, instead of using all beef or pork hamburger meat, mix half or three-fourths with TVP (textured vegetable protein available in all large markets, a soy mixture). It tastes, looks, and feels just like meat. Sometimes I crumble up Boca Burgers (a vegetarian hamburger available in all large markets). For the meat part, use part ground turkey breast or lean pork (meat you have selected yourself to be sure it is lean), keeping the taste just a little different each time you lower the fat and meat amount.

✔ Instead of using regular sausage, get the lite or reduced-fat sausage. I saw some precooked lowfat sausage with 3 grams of saturated fat for 2 links, very reasonable compared to the 11 grams of sat fat in the sausage in the next package (brands were the same). Of course, vegetable sausage has no cholesterol, but most contain fat (and have a very different texture and taste).

Creating Easy, Healthy Meat Dishes

These recipes are the simplest, easiest, best-tasting, and healthiest. They are the result of taste comparisons and easy to find ingredients. My taste-testing experts loved this section.

Shrimp with White Wine Sauce

Drizzle this creamy wine sauce over grilled, broiled, poached, baked, or pan-fried shrimp. This dish (see photo in color section) immediately takes on a totally different flavor when you make it with grilled chicken or sautéed turkey cutlets. If you would rather not use wine, just add ¼ cup more broth.

Preparation/Cooking time: *15 minutes*

Yield: *4 servings*

1 tablespoon margarine or butter

2 tablespoons flour

¼ cup parsley

½ cup chicken broth

¼ cup white wine

1 cup fatfree, light, or lowfat sour cream

1 tablespoon finely chopped garlic, or 2 cloves, minced

12 large peeled shrimp

(continued)

1 To make the sauce, melt the margarine in a medium saucepan. Mix in the flour and cook for 1 minute. Add the parsley, broth, and wine, whisking out any lumps, and cook for 4 minutes on medium heat, or until thick. Stir in the sour cream and set aside.

2 Heavily spray a large skillet with butter-flavored or olive oil-flavored cooking spray. Add the garlic and toss for 1 or 2 minutes over medium heat, making sure not to burn it. Add the shrimp and sauté about 2 minutes, not quite cooking the shrimp through.

3 Add the sauce to the skillet and continue cooking for 1 or 2 minutes, or until the sauce is hot (don't let it boil) and the shrimp are pink.

> **Nutrition at a glance (per serving):** *Calories 146.99 g; Protein 8.80 g; Carbohydrates 17.02 g; Dietary fiber 0.27 g; Total fat 3.10 g; Saturated fat 0.62 g; Cholesterol 40.10 mg; Sodium 207.03 mg.*

> **Lynn's tip:** *Sometimes your meat market's peeled frozen shrimp is cheaper than their fresh shrimp (much of which has been prefrozen and thawed anyway).*

Grilled Turkey with Sweet and Sour Sauce

Sweet and sour sauce is used for cooking many Chinese dishes. Always a mixture of cider or rice vinegar and sugar with a cornstarch thickener, it can go orange, lemon, pineapple, ginger or Chinese Hot Oil spicy. For the latter, I add several drops Chinese hot oil or other type of hot sauce. Grill, broil, or pan-fry the chicken.

Preparation/Cooking time: *30 minutes*

Yield: *6 servings*

6 4-ounce skinless, boneless turkey breasts

½ cup cider vinegar

¼ cup white or brown sugar

½ cup thawed, frozen pineapple, lemon, or orange juice concentrate

½ tablespoon finely chopped ginger (optional)

½ cup finely chopped onions

½ clove minced garlic

½ cup finely chopped green pepper, plus the seeds

2 tablespoons cornstarch

2 tablespoons lite soy sauce

2 tablespoons finely chopped scallions

1 Cook the turkey by first adding salt and pepper if you want and either pan-fry, grill, or broil it, each of which takes about 12 minutes.

2 In a saucepan, add the vinegar, sugar, juice concentrate, ginger if using, onions, garlic, green pepper, and pepper seeds and heat over medium heat, until the onions, pepper, and garlic are cooked, about 5 minutes.

3 In a small bowl, add the cornstarch and soy sauce, whisk, and add to the mixture, stirring until it is thick, about 30 seconds.

4 Remove from heat and stir in the raw scallions. Serve under or over the chicken.

Nutrition at a glance (per serving): *Calories 229.75 g; Protein 29.21g; Carbohydrates 24.66 g; Dietary fiber 0.51 g; Total fat 0.57 g; Saturated fat 0.01 g; Cholesterol 70.88 mg; Sodium 257.68 mg.*

Lynn's tip: *To fancy it up, use a garnish of a few small chunks of fresh pineapple (if you used pineapple) or orange wedge (if you used orange).*

Turkey Chili Tacos

The nice crunch of a crisp taco shell filled to overflowing with tasty lowfat turkey or bean chili, chopped lettuce, and onions takes the place beautifully of any high-fat version (see photo in color section). It is so easy and stuffed so full no one notices that there isn't any unnecessary high-fat shredded cheese or sour cream. Serve with forks.

Preparation/Cooking time: *20 minutes*

Yield: *6 servings, 2 filled tacos each*

1 16- to 18-ounce can lowfat turkey or bean chili

1 package of 12 ready-made, lowest fat, taco-formed crisp taco shells

6 cups chopped lettuce

1 cup chopped tomatoes

1 cup chopped onions

1 avocado, diced, or 6-ounce tub commercial guacamole

Lemon wedges

Taco sauce, hot sauce, or salsa

(continued)

1 In a saucepan, add the turkey or bean chili and heat over medium heat, stirring occasionally, uncovered if there's a lot of liquid, for 10 minutes.

2 Meanwhile, set out the taco shells, 3 to a plate. On a large platter place a large mound of chopped lettuce, next to it the chopped tomatoes, next to that the chopped onions, next to that the diced avocado or guacamole, spread out, sprinkling the avocados with lemon. Have the hot sauce in a bottle or salsa in a pourable pitcher.

3 When the chili is cooked, place a large spoonful into each taco and let each person individually stuff his own with lettuce, tomatoes, onions, and avocado and sprinkle on his own amount of hot sauce or salsa.

Nutrition at a glance (per serving): Calories 377; Protein 8.32 g; Carbohydrates 27.28 g; Dietary fiber 6.12 g; Total fat 19.4 g; Saturated fat 2.16 g; Cholesterol 13.77 mg; Sodium 465.75 mg.

Lynn's tip: To either stretch and perk up canned turkey chili or chili without meat: In a large skillet, place 1 chopped onion, green pepper, 1 cup frozen or canned corn, and 1 teaspoon each minced garlic and chili powder. Spritz the vegetables with cooking spray and sauté, stirring, over medium heat for 5 minutes. Add the canned chili to the skillet, mix well, and heat for 5 more minutes. Other additions for tacos can include chopped jalapeño, cilantro, chopped ripe olives, and lowfat sour cream.

Pork and Apples

Pork cooked with apples is my favorite, and I update this recipe for every cookbook. A winter dish, it can be cooked in a pressure or fusion cooker, on the stovetop in a covered skillet, or baked in a covered casserole. Serve with green vegetables and mounds of bright yellow corn.

Preparation/Cooking time: 20 minutes

Yield: 4 servings

2 large onions, sliced

4 lean 4-ounce pork chops, all visible fat removed

2 large sweet potatoes, cut into 1-inch slices

3 tart apples, cored and cut into 1-inch slices

1 to 2 tablespoons brown sugar

½ teaspoon allspice

Several shakes cinnamon

½ cup apple cider, apple juice, or white grape juice

2 tablespoons cornstarch

2 cups seedless red grapes

1 Lightly spritz a pressure cooker with cooking spray (or for stovetop simmering, a large high-sided skillet with a cover; for baking, a large ovenproof casserole with a cover).

2 Add the onions, pork chops, sweet potatoes, any salt and pepper you wish, and apples.

3 In a small bowl, add the cider and cornstarch and whisk to mix. Add the brown sugar, allspice, and cinnamon, blend to mix, and add to the fusion or pressure cooker.

4 Cover and pressure cook for 10 minutes (or cook on the stovetop in a covered skillet 40 minutes on low, or bake covered in a 350° oven for 1 hour). At the end of cooking, add the grapes and stir in.

Nutrition at a glance (per serving): Calories 342.71 g; Protein 16.85 g; Carbohydrates 61.10 g; Dietary fiber 6.30 g; Total fat 4.88 g; Saturated fat 1.65 g; Cholesterol 38.66 mg; Sodium 40.27 mg.

Ham with Creamed Broccoli and Hard-Cooked Eggs

A little fancy looking but simple to do, this presentation can double as a one-dish family casserole or buffet party food. Ham and broccoli go together well in this easy casserole. The eggs halves are placed on the top across the center lengthwise, cream sauce over the eggs. Hard-cooking eggs take 20 minutes.

Preparation/Cooking time: 35 minutes

Yield: 6 servings

Eggs

6 hard-cooked eggs

1 cup substitute eggs

1 teaspoon finely chopped or minced onion

1 teaspoon Worcestershire sauce

½ teaspoon dry mustard

2 tablespoons lowfat mayonnaise

3 tablespoons grated Parmesan cheese

Casserole

4 slices cooked ham, 2 to 8 ounces each

1 pound long broccoli, stems left on, cut into spears

1 small onion, chopped

(continued)

Sauce

1 tablespoon finely chopped onion

2 cups skim milk

2 tablespoons flour

¼ cup Cheddar cheese

¼ cup lowfat Cheddar cheese

½ teaspoon dry mustard

¼ cup herbed breadcrumbs

Paprika for garnish

1 Preheat oven to 400°.

2 **Eggs:** If the eggs are hard-cooked already, place in a casserole dish to heat as the oven warms or in hot water in a saucepan. (If not hard-cooked, place them in a saucepan and cover with water. Simmer for 10 minutes after they begin to boil.) When hot, cut eggs in half lengthwise. Remove 4 yolks and discard, reserving 2.

3 Lightly spray a small skillet with cooking oil spray. Add the substitute eggs, break up the 2 reserved hard-cooked yolks, mashing and whisking them into the substitute eggs. Add the minced onion, Worcestershire, mustard, mayonnaise, and Parmesan cheese. Turn the heat on to medium high, scramble with a fork, and when firm, set aside.

4 **Casserole:** In a microwavable 8 x 12-inch casserole dish, add the ham and slice crosswise to make 6 servings. Place the ham in the bottom of the casserole. Then place the broccoli and onion side by side to cover the top of the ham. Add 2 tablespoons water.

5 Cover with plastic wrap and make several slits in it. Microwave on high for 3 minutes, turning the dish once or twice. Meanwhile, stuff the hard-cooked whites with the scrambled egg mixture.

6 Remove the ham and broccoli from the microwave. Place the stuffed eggs across the top of the broccoli.

7 **Sauce:** Make the cheese sauce by first adding the onions to a nonstick saucepan. Turn on the heat, spritz the onions with cooking oil spray, and heat for 1 minute, stirring. Meanwhile, in a small bowl, add the milk, whisk the flour into the milk, add the cheese, any salt and pepper you wish, and the mustard, pour over the onions and heat, stirring until thick, about 4 minutes.

8 Pour the sauce over the eggs, shake on paprika and breadcrumbs, place in the oven uncovered, to bake for 10 minutes.

Nutrition at a glance (per serving): Calories 237.0 g; Protein 25.5 g; Carbohydrates 17.4g; Dietary fiber 2.7 g; Total fat 7.3 g; Saturated fat 3.0 g; Cholesterol 96.2 mg; Sodium 917.7 mg.

Lynn's tip: If you don't wish to use a microwave and don't mind more thoroughly cooked broccoli and 20 minutes more baking preparation and cooking time, you can bake the whole dish, skipping the microwave step, add the eggs and sauce to the raw broccoli, and bake in a 350° oven (instead of 400°) for 20 minutes until brown and bubbling.

Whole Canadian Bacon with Marmalade

This is an easy way to serve a healthy but tasty meat because Canadian bacon is naturally low in fat. If your family doesn't cotton to marmalade (orange preserves), use apricot preserves. Make sure that you try it with the honey mustard sauce in the next recipe. The microwave preheats it slightly, and the oven slightly drys and infuses the flavor. If you have more time, bake with the sauce for 35 minutes.

Preparation/Cooking time: *25 minutes*

Yield: *8 servings*

1 2-pound Canadian bacon

½ 7.5-ounce jar marmalade

2 tablespoons Worcestershire sauce

1 Preheat oven to 400°.

2 Place the bacon in the bag. Reach in and cover the bacon with marmalade and sprinkle on the Worcestershire sauce.

3 Place the bag and meat in an oven-safe dish and microwave on high, turning at least twice, for 10 minutes to heat but not really cook.

4 Place the bag on foil in a baking pan, cut the bag open uncovering the meat, and place in the oven, baking for 10 to 15 minutes. Make several thin 1/4-inch slices and serve 1 slice per person. If serving 2 or 3 slices, fan them out when serving.

Nutrition at a glance (per serving): *Calories 213.58 g; Protein 23.40 g; Carbohydrates 11.43 g; Dietary fiber 0.03 g; Total fat 7.90 g; Saturated fat 2.52 g; Cholesterol 56.70 mg; Sodium 1,646.90 mg.*

Lynn's tip: *If making this dish for a party or buffet, add fresh mint sprigs for garnish and serve on a large platter along with plenty of corn, sweet potatoes, and green beans as side dishes.*

Handy foods to have around

Instead of always planning meals, keep lots of different kinds of healthy foods available so that you can spontaneously make foods like turkey tacos. A package of formed and cooked taco shells, hot sauce, canned taco sauce or salsa, frozen guacamole (which isn't that good on its own), and an assortment of the usual fresh vegetables like lettuce, onions and tomatoes will do it on a moment's notice.

Honey Mustard Sauce for Canadian Bacon

Great with Canadian bacon and especially fish, this sauce is easy to make. You can use a hot, Chinese-style mustard for a more spicy version. Heating it thins it, but it is just as good.

Preparation time: *5 minutes*

Yield: *About ½ cup*

6 tablespoons lemon juice or good dry white wine

2 tablespoons honey

2 tablespoons coarse-grain mustard

In a small bowl, add the lemon juice, mustard, and honey, mix well, and re-adjust taste to your liking.

Nutrition at a glance (per serving): *Calories 25.57 g; Protein 0.30 g; Carbohydrates 6.21 g; Dietary fiber 0.52 g; Total fat 0.04 g; Saturated fat 0 g; Cholesterol 0 mg; Sodium 59.91 mg.*

Lynn's tip: *Mustard is a true American spice, and although we can't grow black pepper, mustard flourishes. You can find hundreds of versions of prepared mustard, which means mustard with liquid such as water, honey, vinegar, eggs, wine, or other. Sometimes the seeds aren't all ground, which is called coarse-grained or bumpy mustard. Sometimes mustard is smooth. Dijon mustard, originally from Dijon, France, has a sharper taste and darker color than American. Mustard comes prepared (mixed) or dry powdered.*

Catfish with Mustard and Dill Rub

Use any great-looking fish in the market, such as snapper, striped bass, catfish, halibut, or flounder. Garnish with lemon wedges and dill sprigs. You can broil, microwave, grill, or pan-fry or skillet-cook with liquid (braise or poach) this fish. I include directions for all methods.

Preparation/Cooking time: *15 minutes*

Yield: *4 servings*

2 tablespoons fatfree or lowfat mayonnaise

2 tablespoons fresh chopped dill

2 tablespoons grated Parmesan cheese

2 teaspoons fresh lemon juice

1½ teaspoons Dijon mustard

1 pound red snapper or catfish fillets, cut into 4 pieces

1 In a small bowl, add the mayonnaise, dill, Parmesan cheese, lemon juice, and mustard and mix well.

2 Lightly spray a large skillet (or grill, broiler, flat oven, or microwavable dish) and turn the heat to medium-high.

3 Spread the mayonnaise mixture on both sides of the fish.

4 Place the fish in the skillet and cook until the fish is firm and opaque and has a slight crust, 4 to 5 minutes per side.

Nutrition at a glance (per serving): Calories 175.45 g; Protein 19.13 g; Carbohydrates 1.57 g; Dietary fiber 0.04 g; Total fat 9.72 g; Saturated fat 2.61 g; Cholesterol 55.76 mg; Sodium 218.30 mg.

Lynn's tip: If microwaving fish, microwave for 4 minutes total, not turning. If grilling or broiling, cook for 6 to 8 minutes 4 to 5 inches from the broiler, or until well browned, not turning. If baking, bake for 12 minutes in a preheated 350° oven, foil lightly resting on top.

Fish facts

For fish, cook for 10 minutes for each 1 inch of thickness — a slightly shorter time if thinner than an inch, slightly longer if thicker. (The Canadian Department of Fisheries developed this general timetable.) Overcooked fish is as good as disposal food — not for safety reasons but because it tastes terrible and is rubbery.

Pan-Fried Barbecued Chicken

This is so easy and good, and you don't have to fire up the barbecue grill (see photo in color section). I make it whenever I want quick-cooking, nicely flavored chicken. Use a sauce that is extra spicy or strongly flavored because it dissipates quickly with this form of cooking. Chicken drumsticks vary greatly, so pick the size right for your family.

Preparation/Cooking time: *20 minutes*

Yield: *4 servings*

8 small to medium chicken drumsticks, skin removed (large legs require slightly longer cooking)

2 cups bottled barbecue sauce, divided

1 tablespoon cornstarch

1 10-ounce can chicken broth

1 Lightly spray a 12-inch skillet with cooking oil spray. Add the skinned legs, spray the legs, season with salt and pepper, and over medium heat, brown all sides turning almost continually, about 6 to 8 minutes, making sure that they don't burn.

2 When the chicken is well browned, add 1 cup barbecue sauce and make sure that all the chicken is well covered. Turn down the heat, cover, and cook for 10 minutes. The chicken edges will be slightly crispy.

3 Meanwhile, in a medium bowl, add the cornstarch, chicken broth, and reserved cup of barbecue sauce and whisk together.

4 With a sharp knife, check to see if the chicken is pink near the bone. If there is pink, it's done. Remove to a plate and cover lightly with foil.

5 Turn up the heat, add the cornstarch, barbecue sauce, and broth mixture and stir, heating until hot and thick, about 3 minutes. Pour over the legs.

Nutrition at a glance (per serving): *Calories 255.68 g; Protein 27.45 g; Carbohydrates 18.12 g; Dietary fiber 1.52 g; Total fat 7.23 g; Saturated fat 1.64 g; Cholesterol 81.84 mg; Sodium 1,291.53 mg.*

Lynn's tip: *Serve this with all that nice barbecue-accompanying foods such as corn on the cob, slaw or salad, baked beans, and a green vegetable. Also, you can easily add extra barbecue sauces. Try mixing in a teaspoon or two of prepared mustard, molasses, brown sugar, orange juice, and other flavors you or your family will like.*

Turkey Burgers

Everyone is looking for the perfect turkey burger. This is it. Make it into meatballs or hamburgers and serve it like I do, on buns with tomatoes, onions, lettuce, mayo, and spicy ketchup, or if dieting, plain on the plate (with steamed vegetables or a salad). Because the ground turkey cooks up slightly dry, I added back some low saturated fat oil.

Preparation/Cooking time: *20 minutes*

Yield: *4 servings*

12 ounces lowfat ground turkey

⅛ cup finely chopped celery

⅛ cup finely chopped onions

½ teaspoon lite soy sauce

1 teaspoon Worcestershire sauce

¼ teaspoon garlic salt

Pinch each dried oregano and basil

1 In a large bowl, mix the turkey, celery, onions, soy sauce, Worcestershire sauce, garlic salt, oregano, basil, and any salt and pepper you want. Make 4 patties.

2 Lightly spray a large skillet with cooking oil spray. Add the patties and over medium heat, cook until slightly browned on each side, making sure that the burgers are cooked through.

Nutrition at a glance (per serving): *Calories 133.23 g; Protein 15.11 g; Carbohydrates 1.49 g; Dietary fiber 0.27 g; Total fat 7.05 g; Saturated fat 1.92 g; Cholesterol 67.19 mg; Sodium 240.17 mg.*

Lynn's tip: *These turkey burgers makes great meatballs for spaghetti and meatballs. Add 2 pinches (¼ teaspoon) each oregano and basil to give them more of an Italian flair.*

Chapter 8

Beyond the Ordinary Pasta and Rice: Grains that Are Out of This World

In This Chapter

▶ Incorporating the base of the Food Guide Pyramid into your diet

▶ Cooking pasta, grains, and rice

▶ Flavoring your grains

▶ Saving time with quick and healthy recipes

*T*his chapter shows you why grains are terrific stuff. You find out where grains fit in for your healthiest self. You discover lots of new grains, some you've never heard of but are readily available. Plus, you find out how inexpensive some grains are and how simple they are to cook. I also give you a long list of the most popular varieties of rice with a short explanation of how they taste.

In the recipe section, you find out about a really good wild rice that cooks in just five minutes and how to get arborio rice in a great risotto recipe on the table in ten minutes. In addition, I give you a list of really good lowfat commercial sauces and why to use them. From the earthy pearl barleys to the most silky fresh pasta, you see in this chapter that grains are just the most satisfying and simple food to eat and make.

When most people think of eating healthy, they think of eating rice, pasta, and grains. And although you're not limited to these foods, they are usually the staple of a healthy, balanced diet. In fact, grains form the bottom of the Food Guide Pyramid, with the USDA suggesting 6 to 11 servings daily from this category. But grains aren't limited to plain bread and rice. In this chapter, I show you how to jazz up your grains, like barley and couscous, rice, and pasta, with tongue-tantalizing recipes such as Wild Rice with Mushrooms and Cherries, Lemon Chicken with Risotto, and Couscous with Fresh Corn and Cumin, all made in a flash.

Eating Healthy: Start with the Bottom of the Food Guide Pyramid

If you're familiar with at the Food Guide Pyramid (see Chapter 1), you know you should be eating 6 to 11 servings of grains a day. That amount may sound like a lot. But 6 to 11 servings isn't that much — remember, a grain serving can include all foods made with grains. And those grains can be as plain-Jane as wheat, buckwheat, rye, rice, wild rice, corn, barley, and oats or as exotic as new quinoa, old kamut, and lots of other really interesting and delicious grains you may not have yet tried.

In addition, a serving isn't all that much. A serving is often 3 ounces (about the size of a deck of cards) or sometimes less such as a slice of bread, which is 1 ounce. So your breakfast waffles, two pieces of toast, or big bowl of cereal are all probably two servings. At lunch, your big sandwich with the two large slices of whole-grain bread made of wheat flour, wheatberries, and wheat bran might be three or four servings of grains. For dinner, you might have a few more servings of grains in the form of pasta, or brown rice, polenta or barley soup, and salad croutons. For dessert, your serving might be the pie crust, cake, or lowfat cookies — although grains, if they contain much fat or sugar, go into the Fats and Sweets area at the top. (Grains should ideally be whole grain and not sweetened or have added fats.)

Choosing Grains and Carbs for Better Health

Grains are carbohydrates. *Carbohydrates* are a broad category of starchy vegetables, fruits, grains, and sugars that the body turns to glucose for energy. Energy is good. Grains are good. Complex carbs are starchy food and are also sources of vitamins, minerals, protein, and fiber. Those with the fibers take somewhat longer to digest than *simple carbs,* sugars found naturally in fruit and milk or candy and soda pop. Carbs have half the calories as fat. Plus, carbohydrates like bread, rice, pasta, barley, and corn taste good and feel good in your tummy.

It's all in the diet

Rice is the grain most of the world grows and eats — including the people who stay alive the longest, the Japanese who live in Japan.

Americans consistently rank about sixth in longevity, as do Japanese-Americans. So health isn't necessarily genetic. Diet plays a huge role.

Complex carbohydrates are starchy foods and are also sources of vitamins, minerals, proteins, and fiber. Simple carbs are sugars. Some sugars are found naturally (like those in fruit and milk). Other foods (like soda, jellies, candy, and syrup) have sugar added. *Complex carbs* include lima beans, potatoes, bread, and pasta. Complex carbohydrates are not always better than simple carbs because fruits are simple carbs. However, fruits are better than soda pop. Carbohydrates are the body's preferred choice of energy. Your diet should include a variety of grains, fruits, and dairy or alternative sources of dairy if you don't want dairy.

Getting grains into your diet isn't difficult. Just check out the foods in Figure 8-1. Pasta is an American favorite. So is rice. Both are carbs.

Figure 8-1:
Eat 6 to 11 servings of grains daily.

If you're still not convinced about adding more grains to your menu, remember:

> ✔ **Chances are that you don't need more protein in your diet as most Americans eat 100 percent more than is recommended.** (For more information, see the section "But what about protein?" later in this chapter.) You need 8 to 10 grams per kilogram of body weight. Men 25 and over require 63 grams. Women 25 and older require 50 grams.

✔ **You can get protein in grains, beans, and even gelatin, although you won't find much in the latter.** But gelatin is an example that protein is in many places besides meat, so don't be afraid to substitute grains for meat, especially fatty meat, which probably should be very limited anyway.

✔ **Grains are nutritious and easy to cook.** Many grains come precooked, taking less than 15 minutes to prepare. (For some quick, fabulous recipes, see the section "The Cookin' Is Easy," later in this chapter.)

✔ **Grains can be very inexpensive.** If you have a big family and eat lots of rice, try buying it at an Asian store where 20 pounds can cost under $10. However, 8 ounces of Kamut available in fancy food stores can cost $5, but I think it's worth it.

✔ **Grains come in thousands of varieties and taste great.** In addition, grains fill the stomach and are a terrific source of energy for not only athletes but regular folks as well.

✔ **Grains contain little fat.** If you're watching your weight, grains are a great place to start (unless you add fat).

Which grains are best?

Grains are healthful and nutritious, as you can probably figure out from the Food Guide Pyramid (see Chapter 1). Some grains like whole grains are better to eat than others, so you need to eat a wide variety. Grains contain fiber, almost no fat, and no cholesterol. (Plants never contain cholesterol.) Fiber helps food move through the intestines quickly, so you want to eat plenty of it. Two to three servings of whole grains are recommended daily because they contain more than 18 vitamins and minerals, plus phytochemicals. In the case of refined grains, they are enriched with five nutrients after processing (B1, B2, B3, folate and iron), but that still leaves a deficit of nutrients.

If you want to eat the most healthful and nutritious grains that you can, keep the following in mind:

✔ **If you're concerned about fiber intake, eat oat bran, shredded wheat or bran, or wheat berries.** Bran contains close to the most fiber, while white rice contains the least. Recommended intake is 20 to 35 grams a day.

✔ **Pasta made from white flour is nearly as good as pasta made from whole wheat or unbleached flour.** Most pasta is made from white flour, and all white flour is enriched with vitamins and minerals. Whole-wheat flour has a small amount of additional fiber, but the difference is miniscule.

✔ **Brown rice is better for you than white rice, but the differences aren't great.** It's better to get white rice in your diet to take the place of high-fat junk food than to eat no rice at all. Most people who like rice eat both types.

If you want to know more about which grains are more healthful and nutritious, check out Table 8-1.

Table 8-1	Grains Are Everywhere But Pick and Choose 'Em For Your Health	
Best Choices for Health Benefits	**Okay Choices for Health Benefits**	**Poor Choices for Health Benefits**
Usually whole grains	Refined grains	High-fat rolls
Grits	Rolls	Biscuits
Rice noodles	White bread	Donuts
Polenta	Buns	Fried tacos
Rice cakes	Pretzels	Fried tortillas
Whole-grain cereals	White rice	Cookies
Wild rice	Lowfat waffles and pancakes	Danishes
Brown rice	Tortillas, rolled	High-fat corn chips
Buckwheat pancakes	Corn flakes	Sugar puffs
Whole grain crackers	Rice flakes	Fritters
Kamut	Rice flakes	Pastries
Barley	Saltines	Corn bread (if high fat and sweet)
Air popped popcorn	Light popcorn	

But what about protein?

Many grains contain almost all the proteins humans need, so don't keep asking, "If I don't eat meat, where will I get my protein?" (See Table 8-2.) Meat isn't the only food you can get protein from; in fact, you can get protein in lots of foods, such as grains and beans (see Figure 8-2). If you aren't sure whether you're getting enough protein, add a vitamin B12 tablet just to be sure. B12 is a vitamin found only in animal products.

Table 8-2	Choose Foods with Protein	
High-protein foods	*Medium-protein foods*	*Minimum or no protein foods*
Meat	Grains	Fruits
Dairy (including fatfree)	Vegetables	Fats, oils, margarines, butter
Beans	Fruits	Sugar

Remember, we don't need high protein. Just protein. And not all that much. An ounce of meat has 7 grams of protein, half a cup of kidney beans has 7 grams, and 1 cup of cooked wild rice has nearly 7 grams.

Grains and vegetables aren't complete proteins, but what is lacking in one you get in another. So combine beans and grains for complete protein, especially if you want to reduce saturated fat and lessen your cholesterol intake, which is in meat. And remember, meat contains no fiber. Grains and beans do.

Figure 8-2:
You can easily fit grains into your diet.

Pasta and Rice: The Two Most Common Grains

Hear the word "grains," and you probably instantly think of pasta and rice. But even though these two grains are so common, you don't want to go to the grocery store and pick up any old box. The following sections cover points you should keep in mind before you heat up your stove.

Grains, grains, and more grains

To widen your variety or renew your interest in grains, try some exotic ones (see the figure):

- **Quinoa** (keen'wa) is a tiny, round, white grain (actually part of the spinach family). It's the only complete "grain" protein as it contains all eight essential amino acids.

- **Millet** is a tiny, light tan seed with moderate protein. Sadly, it is used in America mainly for birdseed, but is a staple for one-third of the world.

- **Buckwheat** is not wheat but another grain. It's often made into great, earthy pancakes. *Groats,* which are also buckwheat, are made into *kasha,* a popular middle European dish. Kasha, unlike buckwheat pancakes, is for more cultivated taste because it has an unusual smell, at least to me. I'll only eat kasha when I'm very hungry, and then I like it!

- **Seitan,** called wheat meat, is a wheat gluten made into cakes, which can be formed to look and taste like many meat dishes. It contains protein and is easily formed into meat-lookalike foods. Vegetarians often use *seitan.* Bulgar or *bulghur* are wheat kernels that have been processed and crushed, used most often in Middle Eastern dishes. Most *bulgar* are precooked; farina as far as I know is not. Farina is a meal made from grains that when cooked in boiling water or other liquids makes a breakfast cereal with some protein. You can buy both these wheat-grain products in health-food stores.

- **Tempeh,** although made from soybeans, is usually mixed into cakes and used in place of meat.

You might also try spelt, sorghum, tritical, and fabulous *kamut* (a rice-shaped wheat form), all available in most fancy food markets. Or try teff, amaranth, emmer, and einkorn, which are all lesser known but ancient grains that kept people alive thousands of years ago.

All these grains are easy to fix, and most are really very good.

Pasta basics

One of the first things to consider is whether you want to make your own pasta or buy it. Fresh pasta is not better than dry; they just have different uses. (See the sidebar "Fresh pasta versus store-bought pasta.") I recommend that you make fresh pasta yourself. It is much better than store-bought fresh pasta, which has already dried somewhat and contains stabilizers to both keep it from drying and prolong the freshness, impacting the delicious texture and taste.

If you don't want to make your own pasta, but decide that you'd still like it to be fresh, you can always purchase fresh or soft pasta at the store. Store-bought fresh or soft pasta usually contains eggs and oil. If that bothers you, you might want to consider making pasta at home with less eggs and oil and fewer chemicals.

Keep in mind that boxed pasta can vary slightly in fat and cholesterol depending on whether it's made with eggs. But the amount you eat and the type of sauce — not the pasta — is usually what causes excess calories, saturated fat, total fat, and cholesterol. You can cut the fat by making more healthful cream sauces and keeping the basically healthy tomato sauces low in fatty meats. (See Chapter 11 for some terrific sauce ideas.)

Fresh pasta versus store-bought pasta

Fresh pasta (see figure) is better for delicate sauces and formed or stuffed foods like ravioli and tortellini. (Incidently, ready-made wonton squares stuff pretty well.)

Dried pasta holds its shape and is firmer when cooked, so it is better for chunky or robust sauces, long-cooking soups, and baked casseroles like macaroni where you don't want the pasta to turn to mush.

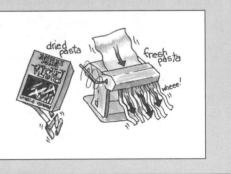

Making homemade pasta

Pasta is fun to make, whether you're using a hand-cranked machine to roll out the sheets or an electric appliance where you add everything in the top and it comes out as pasta (see figure). Just be wary of directions that say to add oil and eggs, which you can omit or cut in half. The best dried Italian or American pasta, just like the best Italian and French bread, doesn't contain oil or eggs.

Fresh Pasta

This is the way Italians made pasta for hundreds of years. Whether by hand or by hand-crank machine, this pasta is silky and so much better than the store-bought fresh or those made fresh with an electric appliance. Because it's made by hand, there is resting time. If you're making it with an electric appliance (the second best pasta) follow their ingredient directions. Sauce with your own sauce or a commercial sauce with your own extra additions to freshen it.

Preparation/Cooking time: *40 minutes*

Yield: *1 pound*

1⅛ cups flour plus 2 tablespoons	*2 large eggs*
¼ teaspoon salt	*1 to 2 teaspoons olive or canola oil*

1 Pour the flour into a mound on the counter or large cutting board. Mix in the salt with your fingers or a spoon and make a well in the center.

2 Add the eggs (you can omit 1 yolk) and oil, if using. Break the yolks or yolk with a fork and lightly beat in the flour well.

(continued)

3 With the fork, gradually draw the flour into the eggs until it is all absorbed, which takes 4 or 5 minutes. Let it rest for 5 minutes, covered lightly with gently tucked plastic wrap.

4 Uncover, move to 1 side, sprinkle 1 tablespoon more flour on the board, and knead the mixture for 6 to 8 minutes, until the dough is nice and silky. (You knead by continually flattening the dough with the heel of your palm, pushing and rolling it very hard, over and over.) Let it rest, this time covered lightly with plastic wrap, for 10 minutes, but it can be up to 30 minutes.

5 With a flour-covered rolling pin and board, roll the dough thinner than you would like your noodles to be, about the thinness of a dime. Let it rest for 8 to 10 minutes, uncovered, but don't let the edges become brittle. If they do, cover briefly with a damp towel.

6 You can now lightly flour the pasta and gently roll it up like a loose tube and cut the noodles with a sharp knife ¼-inch wide into thin strips. You can also make bows, use a cookie cutter for interesting shapes, make squares, or leave it flat and cut long strips with a ruler, whatever you like.

7 Either dry the pasta over a broom handle suspended between 2 chairs or better, boil it covered in several quarts of lightly salted water for 2 to 3 minutes.

If you opt to purchase pasta, you need to think about the type of flour that you want. Most American pasta is made from soft white flour. Imported or Italian-made pasta is available everywhere in the U.S. and is produced from *duram wheat,* a tougher flour. A few other pastas are made from whole wheat, oats or quinoa, but they aren't as popular and don't have the same mouth feel.

I use both Italian-made pasta, which, when cooked correctly, can have a real al dente texture, and American pasta, which, when cooked, is either soft and edible (but if not cooked enough, it is hard). There isn't much room for al dente with American pasta. It's either done and perfect, it isn't done, or it's too done and squishy. I make, eat, and love both Italian and American pasta.

Pasta comes in flavors ranging from basil, spinach, and artichokes to sun-dried tomatoes, asparagus, and black pepper and many others. And they are fun to try. I don't work with flavored pasta much. The pepper or spicy is too peppery, the tomato cooks up a strange wishy-washy pink color, the spinach is too yucky-looking, and only the inky, or squid, pasta is black and evil, which makes it delicious. And it has a taste. None of the others, at least to me, really do have much taste. I'd rather add my artichokes, tomatoes, or pepper to regular pasta. I don't even like whole-wheat pasta, which is always a squishy-outside, firm-inside thing.

Pasta comes in hundreds of shapes and sizes (see Figures 8-3 and 8-4). I love that the Italians use such graphic names for their pasta, such as linguine, which means tongues, orecchietta or little ear, and my favorite, vermicelli, or little worms.

Figure 8-3:
Various
shapes of
pasta.

Figure 8-4:
Still more
shapes of
pasta!

Rice know-how

Rice consumption goes back 5,000 years in India, China, and Thailand. Rice is interesting because some 7,000 varieties are available worldwide. It also has foolproof cooking methods and more inspiring approaches. Rice is not a fad food. Rice is a staple today to half the world's population and for decades was the base of the famous Duke rice diet, a medical plan for losing weight.

Nearly every large grocery market has the following kinds of rice:

- **Basmati (often aged):** This fragrant, long-grained rice can be stored and is tan in color. It can be aged between 5 and 40 years. It's valuable and given as wedding gifts in some countries.

- **Short-grained white or brown rice:** Should be eaten almost immediately or within a few weeks. If white, it has the husk, bran, and germ removed. Brown has slightly more nutrients and has only the husk removed.

- **Long-grained white or brown rice:** Considered to taste slightly better and slightly fancier than short grain and can be eaten within a few months of purchase. Again, if white, it has the husk, bran, and germ removed. If brown, which has slightly more nutrients, it has only the husk removed. If coated with starches (read the label), it needs to be rinsed many times.

Is instant quick rice worth the time you save?

Most quick rice is awful — no taste, no shape, no texture, no nothin'. A few companies have figured out how to make short-cooking rice that doesn't taste like it was cooked in coagulated dishwater. I think one of the best is Success 10-Minute Brown Rice and Success 10-Minute Brown and Wild Rice Mixture all in an easy boil-in-a-bag.

An excellent 5-minute wild rice comes from Gourmet Grains. Nag your market manager to get them for you. The Gourmet Grains 5-minute wild rice is great because it keeps the flavor and texture. Just add a few sautéed shredded onions, carrots, celery, and mushrooms, and you have a dish for a king.

✔ **Medium-grained white or brown rice:** A favorite in America, this rice is sticky. Use in risotto dishes.

✔ **Jasmine:** A delicate naturally aromatic rice often used in Asian cooking.

✔ **Pecan:** An aromatic hybrid rice, it's tan in color and smells like popcorn.

✔ **Arborio rice:** One of many starchy rices that are tiny and stubby. It needs to absorb liquid slowly and is used in risottos and other dishes where you want a more mushy or creamy texture.

✔ **Instant white rice:** Don't waste your time with this type. It tastes like it was cooked in dishwater or has no flavor, and it looks awful. (See the sidebar earlier in this chapter for more on instant rice.)

✔ **Instant brown rice:** Don't waste your time here, either. Better than the instant white, but it's often too mushy and lacking in flavor. (See the sidebar for more on instant rice.)

✔ **Ten-minute white, brown, or wild rice:** This rice is terrific! Success brand is terrific with its packets, and Uncle Ben's makes a very good medium-cooking time rice.

✔ **Five-minute wild rice:** This rice is terrific, too. This is almost as good as any long-cooking wild rice. The only reason to cook wild rice a long time is because you have the time and perhaps you want your own selection of wild rice types.

✔ **Wild rice:** This rice comes in short, medium, or 1-inch long and in many different colors. Although it takes 40 minutes, you have a choice of wild rices, which come in colors from light tan to nearly black, from ¼ inch to 1 inch long, and in flavors from mild and sweet to dark and nuttily earthy.

✔ **Sticky rice:** Usually used sweetened in desserts in Asian cooking, it is just that — sticky.

Incorporating Grains into Your Diet

You can use grain in many different foods.

✔ Appetizers

✔ Breads

✔ Breakfast foods

✔ Desserts

✔ Main dishes

✔ Salads

- ✔ Sides
- ✔ Snacks (see Figure 8-5)
- ✔ Soups
- ✔ Stuffing
- ✔ Toppings or garnishes
- ✔ With other grains

Figure 8-5: Add grains as snacks.

Try the following ways to incorporate grains into your menu:

- ✔ **Use grains to extend hamburgers, meatballs, or meat loaf.** To 1 cup ground lean beef, lean turkey, or lean pork, add ½ cup cooked brown or white rice, breadcrumbs, cooked barley, bulgar, or textured vegetable protein (also called TVP or TSP, which is mostly soy). Or reverse this mixture to lower the fat even further: ½ cup meat to 1 cup grains, such as breadcrumbs, rice, and TVP or TSP.

- ✔ **Toast some grains in a 325° oven for 10 minutes before cooking them in liquid.** Or lightly sauté grains misted with cooking spray in a skillet on the stovetop for 3 or 4 minutes for more flavor and texture and then cook them in liquid.

- ✔ **Rinse whole grains, including rice, in water.** Don't rinse grits, couscous, the uncommon teff, amaranth, or millet as they can clump, disappear down the drain, or have the vitamins washed off. My Japanese friends rinse and scrub their white rice with their hands, changing the pot water ten times or until the water is clear.

- ✔ **Be flexible.** Some rice (and other grains) — depending upon the size, how dry the rice is, or how long it has been stored — takes more or less water and slightly different cooking times than recommended. And some long-cooking grains, like dried corn or pisoli, can be soaked before cooking in liquid.

The Cookin' Is Easy

Cooking grains is soooooo easy. Grains need just two things: liquid and heat. The flavoring is up to you. (For more on flavoring, see the section "Flavoring Grains," later in this chapter.) The type of liquid (broth, water, or flavored liquids) usually doesn't matter, and usually the amount doesn't have to be precise.

The heat intensity for dried pasta does matter, and it has to boil in enough water to rehydrate. Once on a sailboat, I couldn't get the propane-fed burner up to a boil, but confident cook that I am, I put the pasta in the almost-but-not-quite simmering water anyway. Two hours later, the pasta was still a kind of melty mush exterior with a hard core. Rice might have worked.

But despite my pasta blunder, there is still no "absolutely correct" way to cook grains. Forget the "have-to-be-perfect" grain-cooking instructions in those snooty cookbooks that are intimidating. There is no "correct" way to cook grains.

Some cultures boil grains like rice, wheat, pisoli, or barley for hours in enormous open vats with great amounts of broth or water (see Figure 8-6). Then they drain it and eat it. Some cultures (and recipes) steam grains with very little liquid over extremely low heat in heavy covered pots. They throw in some meat, vegetables, and seasonings and have a "feel" as to when it is done. Some fry the grains in fat first and then steam it, as in rice pilaf.

Figure 8-6:
You can make rice in many ways.

Food for thought

I'd like to add an interesting comment about the use of grains. It was made to me from one of America's major grain growers, Dwayne Andreas, the then chairman of Archer Daniels Midlands when his Harvest Burgers brand was the major sponsor of my Low Cholesterol Gourmet television show for one of our four years on The Discovery Channel. Andreas said, "I don't know why we feed all these grains to animals just to eat the animals. We should bypass this middleman and just eat the grains for both health and resource management." Go, Dwayne!

You can do all of these, and it's fine. Little liquid. Lots of liquid. You can bake grains for hours or microwave them for minutes. Rice is easily cooked in electric rice steamers. Nearly all grains can be pressure cooked, even though it isn't always recommended. However, in my testing, I found that you can pressure cook everything. And some grains aren't cooked at all. *Couscous* just has hot water poured on top and sits for five minutes. And some grains are just popped. Couscous, a North Africa staple, is a flour-based granular semolina that is made into itty-bitty pebbles or curdy-looking things sometimes as small as the grains in grits, sometimes as large and even as round as bbs.

Best of all, nearly all grains like rice and pasta are forgiving. Not enough liquid? Add more. Too much? Pour some out. You might not want to peek at steaming rice, but if you do, no great harm. Just enjoy cooking grains. Take it easy, relax, the process is so simple. Grains are good.

The only things to keep in mind — pasta does need to boil, and rice needs to cook long enough so that it doesn't crackle.

If you like timelines when you're cooking, check out the following sections.

Quickest cookers

Short on time? These grains cook up in less than 5 minutes: rice noodles, cellophane noodles, wheat cereal, quick-cooking pasta, oats, quick-cooking wild rice, fresh gnocchi, Ramen noodles, instant white rice, dried pastitas (tiny little pasta shapes), most fresh pasta, rice cereal, and couscous.

Cooking instructions: Boil all these grains except the rice cereal and couscous in several inches of salted water, covered, for 3 to 5 minutes. The rice cereal takes 30 seconds.

For couscous, place 1 cup dry couscous in a bowl and cover with 2 cups boiling water, stir, and place a plate over the bowl.

Quick cookers

If you have 5 to 10 minutes, you can try these quick cookers: Angel hair pasta, orzo or riso, canned grits or cornmeal mush (lightly fried), polenta or grits in clear plastic tubes (faster if microwaved with a paper towel covering them loosely), thick plain or stuffed fresh pasta, mini pasta shells, thick pre-cooked pasta, quick-cooking grits, quick-cooking brown rice, quick-cooking oats, and quick-cooking wild rice.

Cooking instructions: Simmer the preceding dishes (except oats, grits, orzo, quick-cooking wild rice, and polenta) in several quarts water or liquid for 5 to 10 minutes, uncovered.

Oats and grits are cooked in simmering water, covered. Prepare orzo and quick-cooking wild rice according to package directions covered in boiling water, uncovered.

Slice polenta in plastic tubes, remove the plastic and then microwave (with a damp paper towel placed loosely on top as it pops), sauté, and brown, too, if you choose. (Boiling or steaming can disintegrate the slices.)

Medium cookers

The following dishes are ideal when you have only 10 to 25 minutes: white rice, sticky rice, cracked wheat cereal, most pasta, bulgar wheat, large or thick pastas, quinoa, pearl barley, and dry polenta.

Cooking instructions: Follow package directions for rice and wheat, but generally, add several quarts water or other liquid and boil or simmer uncovered. Most 1 pound amounts of pasta are cooked in 5 to 6 quarts boiling water for about 12 minutes. Large or thick pasta takes 15 minutes. Bulgar or cracked wheat takes 2 to 3 cups liquid and simmers for 15 minutes, covered. Quinoa and barley are boiled without a lid, covered with several inches of liquid.

Follow polenta package directions because it differs depending on the grit size and whether it's been precooked.

Long cookers

If you can spare 25 to 45 minutes, you have the following options: grits, wild rice, Irish oatmeal, brown rice, spelt, millet, large-sized barley, and buckwheat.

How to speedily flavor grains

My advice when it comes to quickly flavoring grains? Easy. Use commercial bottled or canned sauces. Here's why:

- Bottled or canned sauces are convenient and easy to use. Just heat and pour them on.

- You can use these sauces on any grain such as rice, kamut, polenta, and especially pasta.

- They taste as great as most restaurant sauces.

- They have already been cooked a long time right in the jar or can, and long cooking brings out flavor.

- Many contain very little fat (look on the label).

- Bottled or canned sauces are so varied, with hundreds of commercial sauces besides tomato sauce.

- You can easily freshen these sauces with your own sautéed garlic, onions, peppers, mushrooms, dried tomatoes, fresh tomatoes, carrots, parsley, chives, dried fruits, oregano, tarragon, sweet basil, lean meat or poultry, seafood, and whatever else you love.

- Bottled sauces, although not inexpensive, can be extended with your own additions, making them less costly, tastier, and more nutritious.

- If you're using a bottled or frozen sauce as a base, pasta and grain sauces are almost effortless.

- Bottled sauces are so good and so easy that many restaurants use them instead of making their own. (When visiting restaurant kitchens, I have spotted more than a few bottles).

Spelt is an ancient grain with a nutty flavor but with more protein than wheat and can be tolerated by those allergic to wheat. You find it in health-food stores.

Cooking instructions: To each cup of grains, add 3 to 5 cups water or liquid (or according to package instructions), cover, and cook.

Only begin grains such as oats in cold water and then bring them to a boil; if you want, it makes them a bit softer, smoother, or mushier.

Very long cookers

If time isn't of the essence and you have anywhere from 1 to 3 hours, then try the following grains: dry whole and cracked corn, including pisoli, kamut, and wheat berries.

Cooking instructions: To each cup of the preceding grains, add 4 to 6 cups liquid and simmer, covered. (You can also presoak these grains.) Pisoli takes the longest to cook, while kamut, at about an hour, is the quickest to make.

What about nontomato or cream-based sauces?

Keep in mind that commercially canned or bottled cream, cheese, or oil sauces, such as Alfredo, clam, and pesto, aren't as healthy as tomato-based sauces. For one thing, these types of sauces are too high in calories and fat (especially saturated fat). These sauces are also relatively expensive.

You can, however, use these sauces as a base and extend them with skim milk, evaporated skim milk, dry skim milk powder diluted in water or fatfree nondairy creamers, fatfree half-and-half, a variety of lowfat and fatfree cheeses, and a variety of sautéed vegetables and mushrooms.

If you want to extend commercial pesto, which is nearly all fat, use other liquids like chicken broth. If you extend pesto at home, you get the added bonus of a sauce with half the fat.

Flavoring Grains

You can flavor grains during cooking with vegetables such as onions, garlic, tomatoes, celery, and seasoning of herbs and spices. You can also boil grains plain in salted water with a flavorful pasta sauce poured on after cooking or, as in cooked cereal, you can add the strawberries and nonfat liquid nondairy creamer or skim milk after cooking.

Keep in mind the following tips when you flavor your grains:

- **Rice doesn't always need additional flavors.** Jasmine rice is terrific with nothing. This Asian-style, mildly fragrant white rice is purposely mild so that it can be used as an adjunct to other more highly spiced dishes that go with it or on it.

- **Don't overspice your meal.** You can use Hispanic-style, white, short-grain rice unflavored as a side for a hot and spicy bean or chili dish. East Indian or Indonesian-style basmati rice might have 20 more savory ingredients, or like couscous, the grain might be flavored more lightly with spices, a little meat, and some dried fruit.

  You can flavor basmati or Indian-style rice simply or with many ingredients.

- **Simple flavors enhance grains.** You can cook barley with my favorite triage of onions, celery, and carrots. You can even throw in exotic mushrooms. Corn on the cob is often simply flavored, with just butter or tub margarine (I use only the no-fat spray stuff) and salt and pepper. Grits taste good with small amounts of butter or margarine, salt, syrup, and fruit. Polenta can take almost any vegetable or maple syrup. Pasta can have any one of hundreds of sauces or flavors.

Fabulous and Easy Grain Recipes

Try these simple grain recipes.

Linguine with Creamed Clam Sauce

My testers said this rich and creamy dish was "by far the best recipe of this type they had ever tasted," so I pass it on to you with joy. Linguine is the traditional clam sauce noodle, but the wider pappardelle is my personal favorite. Garnish with chopped finely scallions and parsley or for a hot and spicy flavor, red pepper flakes.

Preparation/Cooking time: *25 minutes*

Yield: *6 servings*

1½ pounds pasta, such as linguine, pappardelle, angel hair, or ziti

3 large cloves garlic, minced

1 medium onion

3 inches of leek, or 2 shallots, finely chopped

6 ounces sliced fresh mushrooms

20 ounces fresh clams, chopped, liquid reserved, or 4 5-ounce cans baby clams, liquid reserved

¼ cup white wine (optional)

1 teaspoon fresh lemon juice

2 tablespoons cornstarch

2 tablespoons fatfree half-and-half, fatfree nondairy creamer, or light cream

¼ cup fatfree or lowfat ricotta

½ cup fatfree or lowfat cottage cheese

¼ teaspoon sugar

¼ cup coarsely chopped flatleaf Italian parsley, plus a few sprigs

1 In a large saucepan of salted boiling water, cook the pasta until al dente, about 8 to 12 minutes, depending on type and brand. Drain and set aside to stay warm.

2 Meanwhile, lightly spray a large skillet. Place over medium heat, add the garlic, onions, and mushrooms, lightly mist the vegetables, and sauté, stirring continually, for 3 to 4 minutes to avoid burning.

3 Add the clam stock (not the clams), white wine (if using), and lemon juice. Cover and turn the heat to low, stirring occasionally, cooking about 5 minutes.

4 Meanwhile, in a food processor or blender, add the cornstarch, cream, ricotta, and cottage cheese and puree on high 30 seconds or until velvety smooth, checking to make sure and blending more if needed.

5 To the skillet, add the clams, sugar, salt and pepper (if using), nonstick vegetable oil spray if needed, and stir well. Heat until very hot.

6 Add the pureed cream sauce and heat, stirring until hot and thick but not boiling (or it will curdle).

7 Drain the pasta and divide between serving plates, cover with clam sauce, and top with the parsley.

Nutrition at a glance (per serving): Calories 560.6; Protein 30.3 g; Carbohydrates 99.4 g; Dietary fiber 6.2 g; Total fat 3.2 g; Saturated fat 0.4 g; Cholesterol 33.8 mg; Sodium 128.8 mg.

Lynn's food info: Clams contain little fat — less than 2 grams per 3 ounces steamed. Their cholesterol is less than chicken. Clams are also good for teeth and jawbones because they promote lots of chewing.

And the winner is . . .!

The following are a few of the best tomato sauces, as rated by The Center for Science in the Public Interest in its April 1999 issue. (And these sauces also have only 0 to 3 grams fat for each ½ cup, making them generally healthier than many higher fat sauces.)

- ✔ Healthy Choice (except Alfredo)
- ✔ Ragu Light
- ✔ Enrico's Finest and Enrico's with Mushroom
- ✔ Classico Fire Roasted Mushroom and Garlic and several more
- ✔ Hunts Ready Chunky Special and Light Traditional
- ✔ Uncle Dave's Fat Free with Mushrooms and Uncle Dave's Tex Mex
- ✔ Tree of Life Organic and Fat Free Pasta Sauce Plus
- ✔ Progresso Red Clam with Tomato & Basil

Pasta with Italian Sausage and Green Peppers

This recipe has great Italian taste without all the usual fat because I used Italian sausage. (Turkey sausage doesn't have the punch to hold up in this flavorful sauce.) Make sure you defat the Italian sausage really well. You won't miss the fat. My testers voted this recipe an A+.

Preparation/Cooking time: *20 minutes*

Yield: *4 to 6 servings*

1 pound pasta, such as linguine, angel hair, pappardelle, ziti (¼ or ½ pound more pasta if serving 6)

8 ounces mild and lean Italian sausage

3 large cloves garlic, minced

1 large onion, finely chopped

1 green pepper, seeded and cut into 1-inch chunks

1 26-ounce jar bottled tomato pasta sauce, any flavor

½ teaspoon fennel seed

½ teaspoon red pepper flakes

1 In a large saucepan filled with boiling water and a little salt, boil the pasta until al dente, about 8 to 12 minutes, depending on type and brand. Drain and set aside to stay warm.

2 Meanwhile, lightly spray a large skillet. Place over medium-high heat and add the sausage, thinly sliced or squeezed out of the casing, breaking it up well with a fork or your fingers. Heat until thoroughly cooked, about 4 minutes. During cooking, blot the sausage and skillet with wadded paper towels. Turn out on a triple layer of paper towels, fold over, and press out any excess fat. Set the cooked sausage aside in the paper towels.

3 Wipe the skillet clean with the blotting towels, lightly spray again, and add the garlic, onion, and green pepper and cook, stirring, over medium-high heat, for about 8 minutes.

4 To the skillet, add the cooked sausage, pasta sauce, fennel seed, and red pepper flakes and cook, stirring, until very hot, about 4 minutes. Serve over the pasta.

Nutrition at a glance (per serving): *Calories 681.7; Protein 24.5 g; Carbohydrates 113.6 g; Dietary fiber 10.4 g; Total fat 13.6 g; Saturated fat 3.5 g; Cholesterol 22.6 mg; Sodium 1386.8 mg.*

Lynn's hint: *Thumb off pepper seeds into your skillet (or on salads). These seeds can be eaten cooked or raw because they are sweet and contain fiber. Don't use the pepper seeds if they are dark and moldy, although the pepper flesh may still be fine.*

Mexican Rice and Beans

This mild dish is fast and simple. The slightly sweet canned navy beans, pintos, or red beans give this dish its mild taste. You can always spice up the recipe with diced jalapeño peppers or hot sauce.

Preparation/Cooking time: *20 minutes*

Yield: *4 entree servings, or 8 side servings*

2 packets 10-minute quick-cooking brown rice, or 3 cups cooked brown rice

1 large white (strong or boiling, not sweet) onion, or 2 flat Mexican cibolas, coarsely chopped

2 cloves garlic, minced

1 green or red pepper, finely diced

2 tablespoons mild chili powder

1 teaspoon cumin

1 15 to 16 ¾-ounce can navy, pinto, kidney, or red beans, rinsed and drained

1 cup canned diced tomatoes, drained

1 6-ounce can diced green chilies

½ cup chopped scallions

2 tablespoons chopped fresh cilantro or parsley

1 Bring a saucepan filled with water to a boil and add the rice, cooking for 10 minutes or according to package instructions. When cooked, drain the rice from the packets and set aside lightly covered to stay warm.

2 Meanwhile, lightly mist a large nonstick skillet with spray. Add the onion, garlic, and green pepper, lightly mist the vegetables, and sauté over medium heat, stirring for 4 to 5 minutes. Add a tablespoon or 2 of water if needed.

3 Add the chili powder and cumin, stir well, and cook, stirring, for 2 minutes.

4 Add the beans and rice and ¼ cup water or fatfree chicken stock if needed to moisten and stir to mix well. Cover and simmer on low for 5 minutes.

5 Add the tomatoes, chilies, scallions, and cilantro, stir to combine, cover, and cook to heat thoroughly, about 2 minutes. Add any salt and pepper you wish.

Nutrition at a glance (per serving): *Calories 205.7; Protein 10.0 g; Carbohydrates 43.6 g; Dietary fiber 8.2 g; Total fat 2.2 g; Saturated fat 0.2 g; Cholesterol 0 mg; Sodium 814.6 mg.*

Lynn's fun food facts and lore: *Cibolas are strong Mexican onions. Navy beans are mild and sweet and are called navy beans because they were fed to sailors on ships. Some people call them Yankee beans or Boston beans, however, Bostonians prefer pea beans for their traditional Boston baked beans.*

Pasta e Fagioli

This is a great Italian pasta and bean dish tested by someone who never before really liked any pasta e fagioli mixture (see photo in color section). What a convert she turned out to be! It was so good the child of another of my testers ate her mother's entire portion.

Preparation/Cooking time: *30 minutes*

Yield: *6 to 8 servings*

8 ounces pasta, small shell, tube, penne, or ditalini

1 large onion, chopped

2 cloves garlic, minced

2 celery ribs, sliced

2 carrots, sliced

2 ounces pancetta (Italian bacon) or bacon, all fat cut off with a scissors

1 15 to 16.5 ounce can pinto, red, or pink beans, rinsed and drained

3 plum tomatoes, diced, or 1 cup diced, canned, and drained tomatoes

½ teaspoon honey or sugar

1 cup frozen peas, separate by banging on counter

1 teaspoon dried basil, or 1 tablespoon fresh basil

2 tablespoons chopped fresh parsley

3 tablespoons grated Pecorino, Romano, or Parmesan cheese

1 In a saucepan of boiling water, cook the pasta until very al dente. (The pasta cooks in the skillet for 5 additional minutes.)

2 Meanwhile, lightly mist a large skillet with spray. Add the onions, garlic, celery, and carrots (and season with salt and pepper, if you choose). Lightly spray the vegetables and sauté over medium heat, stirring for 5 to 7 minutes.

3 Add the pancetta, stir, and sauté for 3 to 4 minutes. If necessary, add 1 or 2 tablespoons water to prevent sticking.

4 Add the beans, tomatoes, and honey and stir to combine. Add the pasta and stir to mix. Cover and simmer for 5 minutes.

5 Stir in the peas, basil, and parsley and cover to heat for 1 or 2 minutes. Serve sprinkled with the Parmesan. Add any salt and pepper you wish. (The soup is very thick and you can stir in water to make it the consistency you like.)

Nutrition at a glance (per serving): *Calories 219.1; Protein 9.9 g; Carbohydrates 40.7 g; Dietary fiber 5.1 g; Total fat 2.3 g; Saturated fat 0.8 g; Cholesterol 5.6 mg; Sodium 297.1 mg.*

Lynn's food fact: *You can add frozen peas, mixed vegetables, and many other frozen small vegetables, heating just until hot as they have already been lightly cooked before freezing.*

Couscous with Fresh Corn and Cumin

If your family likes Tex/Mex food, corn, and pasta, this spicy but simple dish is one they'll love. It took me 15 minutes to prepare this recipe, but my testers did it in 10 so it can be really fast. (One tester did it in 25 minutes, though, so we compromised the time.)

Preparation/Cooking time: *20 minutes*

Yield: *4 servings*

1½ cups fresh whole kernel corn or thawed frozen whole kernel corn

1 cup dry couscous

1 clove garlic, minced

¼ to ½ teaspoon dried chipolte or fresh jalapeño pepper, seeded and finely chopped (if using dried chipolte, place in a dish with 1 to 2 teaspoons water for 2 minutes)

1 cup chopped red or green peppers

⅛ teaspoon ground cumin

1 tomato, diced

¼ cup chopped dried apricots (optional)

2 tablespoons chopped fresh cilantro or parsley

1 Place the corn in a small saucepan; add enough cold water to cover. Cook over medium heat for 3 to 4 minutes, or until tender. Drain and set aside.

2 In a medium saucepan, bring 1½ cups water to a boil. Stir in the couscous. Remove from heat, cover, and set aside for 5 minutes.

3 Lightly mist a large nonstick skillet with spray. Heat for 1 minute over medium heat. Add the garlic, peppers, and red or green peppers and sauté for 3 minutes over medium heat, stirring. Add the cumin, tomato, and salt and pepper and cook, stirring, for 1 minute. Add the corn.

4 Transfer the couscous to a large bowl; fluff with a fork, stir in the corn mixture, apricots (if using), cilantro, and any salt you wish

Nutrition at a glance (per serving): *Calories 235.7; Protein 8.1 g; Carbohydrates 50.5 g; Dietary fiber 4.8 g; Total fat 1.0 g; Saturated fat 0.2 g; Cholesterol 0 mg; Sodium 11.0 mg.*

Lynn's food fact: *If you have never had couscous, it is just a tiny little pasta. You can sub-stitute any pastita or tiny pasta such as orzo or little stars, but try to keep the pasta tiny. I've even seen tiny round bb-sized pasta also called couscous, which would be fun to eat.*

Macaroni and Cheese

Macaroni and cheese is a classic favorite and for homemade, my testers agreed this recipe is especially good. Plus, it is easy. This recipe successfully lowers the saturated fats without losing taste.

Preparation/Cooking time: *25 minutes*

Yield: *4 servings*

1 pound macaroni	*½ teaspoon prepared mustard*
2 cups fatfree or lowfat cottage cheese	*2 ounces sharp Cheddar cheese, grated or shredded*
1 cup fatfree half-and-half or fatfree nondairy liquid creamer	*1 tablespoon Parmesan cheese*
2 tablespoons flour	

1 Bring a large saucepan of salted water to a boil. Add the macaroni and cook according to the package directions until al dente. Drain, return to the saucepan, and set aside.

2 Meanwhile, in a blender or food processor, combine the cottage cheese, half-and-half, flour, and mustard. Process for 2 or 3 minutes or until velvety smooth. Season to taste with salt and pepper. Pour into a medium nonstick saucepan.

3 Bring to a boil, lower the heat, and cook, stirring constantly, for about 4 minutes.

4 Remove from heat. Add the Cheddar cheese and Parmesan and stir until melted. Let stand for a few minutes to thicken and pour over the macaroni, tossing to combine.

Nutrition at a glance (per serving): *Calories 608.4; Protein 32.5 g; Carbohydrates 96.4 g; Dietary fiber 3.9 g; Total fat 7.2 g; Saturated fat 3.6 g; Cholesterol 26.1 mg; Sodium 628.3 mg.*

Lynn's hint: *This dish can be eaten as soon as it is made, but for a buffet or casserole, pour into a shallow 1½-quart casserole, sprinkle on 1 cup herbed breadcrumbs, lightly mist them, and bake, uncovered, for 15 minutes in a 400° oven; instead of baking, you can also broil 4 inches from the heat for 2 to 3 minutes, or until crusty and golden brown.*

Orzo with Asparagus and Onions

Elegant and full of fiber and color, asparagus lovers will consider this an appetizing entree or side (see photo in color section). Look for my tip at the end of the recipe to find out how to make the creamed version. Orzo takes just a few minutes to cook, but you can use any small or even slightly larger pasta like little shells. One of my testers cooked the orzo in a mixture of water and fatfree chicken stock and liked a sprinkle of fresh lemon juice when the dish was finished.

Preparation/Cooking time: *20 minutes*

Yield: *4 servings*

1 pound orzo or star pasta	*1 tomato, diced*
1 onion, finely chopped	*¼ cup chopped fresh parsley*
2 cloves garlic, minced	*½ tablespoon diced red pepper*
2 cups 1-inch slices asparagus	*8 fresh basil leaves, thinly sliced*
1 6 to 7-ounce can mushroom pieces or slices, drained	*2 tablespoons grated Parmesan*

1 Bring a large saucepan of salted water to a boil over high heat. Add the orzo and cook about 6 minutes.

2 Four or 5 minutes into the cooking of the orzo, add the asparagus to the boiling pasta water and boil the asparagus with the orzo for about 2 minutes. Drain both and return the orzo and asparagus to the saucepan and set aside.

3 Meanwhile, lightly mist a large skillet with spray. Add the onions and garlic, mist them, and sauté over medium heat, stirring occasionally, for about 4 minutes.

4 Add the mushrooms, tomatoes, parsley, red peppers, and basil and a few tablespoons water or fatfree chicken stock to moisten if needed. Cover and cook for 4 to 5 minutes.

5 Add the orzo and asparagus. Season to taste with salt and pepper and toss to combine. Top with grated Parmesan.

Nutrition at a glance (per serving): *Calories 476.8; Protein 18.7 g; Carbohydrates 93.4 g; Dietary fiber 5.2 g; Total fat 3.2 g; Saturated fat 0.9 g; Cholesterol 2.5 mg; Sodium 183.7 mg.*

Lynn's tip: *For a creamed version, whisk together 1 cup fatfree liquid nondairy creamer or fatfree half-and-half or skim milk and 1 tablespoon flour to any of the liquids. Cook over medium heat, stirring, until thickened about 4 minutes. Add a pinch of ground nutmeg, toss with the other foods, and when served sprinkle on paprika for color (or cayenne for color and a spicy snap).*

Moroccan Saffron Rice and Chicken

Moist and creamy Moroccan saffron rice with just a touch of sweetness and lemon is a treat fit for you and guests alike. You can always use a little more saffron if you like its distinctive mild flavor. A pinch or 2 of the almost tasteless turmeric makes the dish more yellow and, unlike saffron, which needs long cooking, it can be added at any time. Garnish with chopped fresh parsley, chopped green scallions, or chives to give it a spark of color.

Preparation/Cooking time: *40 minutes*

Yield: *4 servings*

2 cups fatfree chicken stock

2 small chicken-flavored bouillon cubes

½ teaspoon saffron threads, crushed

1 cup diced skinless cooked or raw chicken breast

1½ cups chopped leeks or onions

2 cloves garlic, minced

1 teaspoon cumin

¼ cup white wine (optional)

1 cup long-grain white rice

¼ cup golden raisins or chopped dried apricots

1 cup pitted ripe black or Kalamata olives, cut in half

1 tablespoon lemon zest

1 Combine the stock, bouillon cubes, and saffron in a microwaveable measuring cup or medium bowl. Microwave on high power for 2 minutes, or until hot but not boiling. Remove and set aside.

2 Meanwhile, lightly coat a saucepan with spray and, over medium heat, add the chicken, leeks, garlic, and cumin and sauté, stirring about 3 minutes, making sure that the garlic especially doesn't burn.

3 Add the wine, if using, and boil. Add the rice and saffron stock, any salt and pepper you wish, and bring to a boil again. Reduce the heat, cover, and simmer for 20 minutes or until the rice is tender and the liquid absorbed.

4 Add the raisins and olives and stir. Garnish with the lemon zest.

Nutrition at a glance (per serving): *Calories 347.9; Protein 16.9 g; Carbohydrates 57.3 g; Dietary fiber 2.9 g; Total fat 5.6 g; Saturated fat 1.0 g; Cholesterol 30.1 mg; Sodium 1225.5 mg.*

Lynn's fun food fact: *Saffron is a gently flavored spice that is used worldwide, although not as much in America as in other countries. It is the world's highest priced spice because it takes 14,000 hand-picked crocus stigmas to make just 1 ounce. Unlike some spices and the herb dried oregano, which should be cooked quickly or it can get bitter, saffron should always be heated a long time to release the flavor.*

Spicy Spanish Green Rice

When food both tastes and looks good and takes only 15 minutes to fix from start to finish, it is a special treat. If you are a spicy food lover, this is your dish — although without the hot sauce and with a reduction of chili amount, it can be just flavorful green rice instead of spicy green rice. A squirt of lime at the end finishes it off.

Preparation/Cooking time: *15 minutes*

Yield: *4 servings*

2 cups fatfree chicken broth

1 to 2 packets brown 10-minute Success brand rice, or 2 cups cooked brown rice (1 packet makes 1½ cups)

1 cup ½-inch pieces cut green beans

¾ cup chopped fresh cilantro or parsley

½ cup finely chopped scallions including green

2 tablespoons canned chopped green chilies

Lemon or lime wedges

Green hot sauce

1 Add the broth to a saucepan and bring to a boil. Add the packet of rice, push it under the liquid several times, and simmer 10 minutes. (If using already cooked brown rice, reduce the stock amount to about half.)

2 Cut the bag open and add the rice to any remaining liquid.

3 Add the green beans, cilantro, scallions, and chilies and stir in well. Cover and, over very low heat, steam the beans for 2 to 3 minutes. If you don't have enough liquid, add a few tablespoons more. Add any salt you wish. Serve with lemon or lime wedges and hot sauce.

Nutrition at a glance (per serving): *Calories 107.7; Protein 3.7 g; Carbohydrates 23.1 g; Dietary fiber 2.6 g; Total fat 0.7 g; Saturated fat 0.0 g; Cholesterol 0 mg; Sodium 380.2 mg.*

Lynn's fun food facts: *Virtually unknown by most Americans 20 years ago, cilantro is the fresh version of dried coriander leaves, which have a completely different taste and have been used in America for a much longer time. Coriander seeds, used whole and ground, have an even more different taste than the leaves, and they have been used for centuries in Europe. Fresh cilantro is indispensable in the cuisines of both Asian and Latin American cooking.*

Wild Rice with Mushrooms and Cherries

Wild rice on the table in 10 minutes is a real treat. My tester's 10-year-old daughter loved it so much that she took this dish to school for her lunch the next day. Instead of cherries, you can substitute dried apricot pieces, cranberries, cherries, or dates pieces. Serve this as an entree or with skinless duck or turkey.

For holidays, add 1 cup roasted or boiled chestnuts. I received absolute raves when I stuffed my Thanksgiving turkey with this mixture of 1 cup each dates and chestnuts mixed into the usual bread, celery, and onion stuffing.

Preparation/Cooking time: *20 minutes*

Yield: *4 servings*

1½ cups chicken broth

1 packet 5-minute wild rice, or 1½ cups cooked wild rice

1 bay leaf

1 pound fresh mushrooms, sliced

1 cup chopped leeks or onions

1 stalk celery, thin-sliced

1 large carrot, thin-sliced or shredded

¾ cup fresh sweet cherries, pitted and quartered, or other dried fruit

1 Add the broth to a large saucepan and boil over high heat. Add the wild rice and bay leaf and cook according to the package directions or for 5 minutes.

2 Meanwhile, lightly spray a large skillet, add the mushrooms, leeks, celery, and carrots, mist the vegetables, and sauté for 5 minutes over medium-high heat, stirring often.

3 Remove and discard the bay leaf, cut the packet, add the wild rice to the liquid in the saucepan, and stir. Raise the heat to reduce the liquid, stirring, about 2 minutes. Add the sautéed vegetables and cherries and toss. Season with salt.

Nutrition at a glance (per serving): *Calories 222.5; Protein 7.7 g; Carbohydrates 46.8 g; Dietary fiber 4.3 g; Total fat 1.5 g; Saturated fat 0.5g ; Cholesterol 0 mg; Sodium 843.9 mg.*

Lynn's tip: *Pit your fresh or canned unpitted cherries with an inexpensive hand-held pitter, which I also use for pitting those small Kalamata olives. Or simply use a sharp paring knife, score the cherry lengthwise and around the middle, right down to the pit. Twist and peel off the sweet fruit.*

Lemon Chicken with Risotto

Creamy risotto rice, lemon, and chicken are great mixtures. A pressure cooker shortens the time by 15 to 20 minutes, but if you don't have 1, use cooked deli chicken and the skillet method. Both methods are given. If you pressure cook this recipe, my tester liked the addition of ½ cup chopped broccoli stirred into the hot food at the end.

Preparation/Cooking time: *15 minutes pressure cooked; 30 minutes skillet method*

Yield: *6 servings*

2 3½-ounce skinless boneless chicken breast halves, all visible fat removed, diced

2 inches leek, or 1 small onion, chopped

1 cup arborio rice

2 cups fatfree chicken broth

¼ cup dry white wine

1 teaspoon grated lemon zest

2 tablespoons fresh lemon juice

2 tablespoons chopped parsley

2 tablespoons grated or shredded Parmesan

Pressure Cooking Method

1 Lightly spray the pressure cooker with vegetable oil spray. Add the diced chicken breasts and leeks and brown over medium heat, stirring, about 4 minutes.

2 Add the rice, chicken broth, wine, zest, lemon juice, and any salt and pepper you want.

3 Put the lid on the pressure cooker according to the manufacturer's instructions. When steam steadily comes out of the hole, put on the pressure regulator, turn down heat slightly to medium, and cook for 8 minutes.

4 Turn off heat and let it rest until the hissing stops or place the cooker under cool running tap water until the cooker is quiet, about 2 minutes.

5 Remove the lid and stir in the parsley and Parmesan.

Skillet Method

1 Lightly spray a large skillet. Add the leeks and sauté, stirring, over medium heat for 3 minutes.

2 Add the rice and ½ cup broth, stirring, over medium to medium-low heat for 3 to 4 minutes until liquid is mostly absorbed. Add ½ cup broth and repeat stirring until absorbed, 4 to 5 minutes.

3 Add the wine, chicken, zest, juice, and ½ cup broth and heat, stirring, over medium to medium-low heat for 4 to 5 minutes. Add the rest of the broth in ½-cup increments, stirring each liquid addition until absorbed.

(continued)

4 Stir in the parsley and Parmesan and heat for 2 to 3 minutes or until all the liquid is absorbed.

Nutrition at a glance (per serving): *Calories 201.3; Protein 10.7 g; Carbohydrates 32.1 g; Dietary fiber 0.9 g; Total fat 1.4 g; Saturated fat 0.6 g; Cholesterol 19.9 mg; Sodium 269.6 mg.*

Lynn's tip: *You can add many other vegetables, such as asparagus spears, peas, snow peas, and sugar snaps, with the last ½ cup of broth. You can also make this recipe with long-grain white rice and quick-cooking pearl barley.*

Barley with Beef and Mushrooms

Earthy barley acquires an even deeper, richer flavor when simmered with dried mushrooms and beef. This is a side dish similar to rice. You can get the cooked beef thick-sliced at the deli or use leftover. If you don't have uncooked beef, one of my testers cooked cubed lean beef and browned them for a couple of minutes first, tossing right along with the barley.

Preparation/Cooking time: *15 minutes with quick-cooking barley; 35 minutes with regular barley*

Yield: *6 servings*

6 ounces dried mushrooms, porcini or any type

1 large onion, chopped

2 cloves garlic, minced

2 celery stalks, chopped

2 carrots, diced

3 cups sliced fresh button or cremini mushrooms

1 cup pearl barley or quick-cooking pearl barley

½ teaspoon dried thyme

¼ teaspoon dried rosemary, crumbled

1½ cups 1-inch diced cooked beef, deli or leftover, all visible fat removed

2 tablespoons chopped parsley

1 Place the dried mushrooms in a small bowl and rehydrate by adding 1 cup hot tap water. Set aside to soak for 10 minutes. When soft, remove the mushrooms with a slotted spoon, reserve the liquid, discard any tough stems, and chop the mushrooms.

2 Meanwhile, lightly spray a large skillet. Add the onions, garlic, celery, carrots, and fresh mushrooms and sauté, stirring, over medium heat for about 6 minutes.

3 In a large saucepan, add the barley, mushroom water, sautéed vegetables, all the mushrooms, thyme, rosemary, any salt and pepper you want, and 3 cups water or fatfree chicken stock (or as per package directions as barley sizes and times differ). Simmer on low heat for 15 to 20 minutes, covered or as per package directions if using quick-cooking barley.

4 Uncover, add beef, and adjust liquid by simmering to reduce if too soupy or adding water or broth by the tablespoon if needed. Stir in the chopped parsley.

Nutrition at a glance (per serving): Calories 266.7; Protein 16.8 g; Carbohydrates 46.9 g; Dietary fiber 7.7 g; Total fat 3.5 g; Saturated fat 1.0 g; Cholesterol 29.0 mg; Sodium 55.2 mg.

Lynn's food fact: Carrots, a member of the parsley family and eaten for hundreds or perhaps thousands of years, can be exceptionally sweet but are inexpensive. In Ireland, carrots are lyrically referred to as underground honey. Dried mushrooms can be expensive, and you may want to use only 3 ounces instead of 6 ounces.

Grilled Polenta with Sundried Tomatoes and Mushrooms

Bravo! said my testers. This robust and versatile dish can be a dinner entree with a few steamed spiced shrimp on top, a side dish anytime, fancy enough for brunch, served as an appetizer perhaps with sour cream, and eaten for a formal dinner, perhaps with caviar and a parsley sprig on top. See photo in color section.

Preparation/Cooking time: 20 minutes

Yield: 4 servings

4 ½-inch thick slices prepared fatfree polenta in a tube

6 ounces shiitake mushrooms, sliced

1 shallot, or 2 inches leek, or small onion coarsely chopped

2 cloves garlic, minced

4 sundried tomato halves, finely sliced or julienned

⅓ cup dry white wine or water

2 tablespoons chopped fresh chives or parsley

1 teaspoon grated Parmesan

(continued)

1 Lightly spray a large skillet. Add the polenta and cook 4 to 5 minutes per side, lightly browning each side on medium-high heat.

2 Meanwhile, in another skillet, lightly spray, heat, and add the mushrooms, shallots, garlic, and tomatoes. Sauté for 2 to 3 minutes on medium-high heat, tossing.

3 Add the wine or water to the skillet with the mushrooms and bring to a boil. Reduce the heat to low. Cook for 2 to 3 minutes or until the mushrooms are tender. Stir in the chives or parsley and Parmesan and any salt you wish.

4 Transfer the polenta to plates and spoon the sauce over the polenta slices.

Nutrition at a glance (per serving): *Calories 81.2; Protein 2.6 g; Carbohydrates 13.0 g; Dietary fiber 1.8 g; Total fat 0.2 g; Saturated fat 0.1 g; Cholesterol 0.4 mg; Sodium 187.9 mg.*

Lynn's health watch: *Check the label on tubes of prepared polenta. Some have more fat than others, and fatfree brands are available. Many are already seasoned with such things as mushrooms, sundried tomatoes, and jalapeño peppers, and you can use any of those in this recipe.*

Chapter 9

Fabulous Fruits and Desserts

In This Chapter

▶ Mixing lowfat and high-fat desserts

▶ Using sugar, substitute sugars, and sugarfree products with taste

▶ Making 25 easy and healthy desserts, all under five minutes

▶ Finding out what's available in your market for fast and healthy desserts

Something sweet after dinner is a given in most families, even if it is some terrible concoction. In this chapter, I give you 25 really good and simple assemblies or "throw togethers" that came from friends, testers, acquaintances, and other cookbook writers when I sent out the call for some fast, no-recipe desserts.

The dessert recipes in this chapter cost very little, are easy to make, a few are quite decadent, and as a bonus, they are all pretty darned healthy with reasonable calories (some more than others).

Creating Good-Tasting Lowfat Desserts

The secret to making a good-tasting, lowfat, low-calorie dessert is to use a few real ingredients. Desserts with fresh, real (not canned fruit or canned fruit pie fillings) always help lowfat recipes (see Figure 9-1). They may take a little longer to make than the canned ones, but the taste result is almost always worth it. If speed is a necessity, you can mix canned fruit with fresh or frozen. The fresh fruits that work best are blueberries, very thinly sliced apples or peaches, fresh lemon juice (for canned lemon meringue filling), and even thinly sliced plums.

A sweet but rather unusual pudding

Take 1 pint milk, 3 beaten eggs, ½ pound suet (beef fat), 1 teaspoon powdered sugar, ½ teaspoon salt. Add enough flour to make a thick batter. Boil for 2 to 3 hours. Serve with hot (fruit) sauce.

— 1879, *Housekeeping in Old Virginia,* dessert section

Figure 9-1: Use fresh fruits in your desserts.

Today we feed suet (beef fat) to the birds, and only a very few mincemeat pies still contain the obligatory meat and suet. For most, meals don't feel complete unless they end with something sweet. However, some chefs have elevated desserts to monstrous, tasteless, foot-high concoctions of chocolate leaves and squirts of this or that on the plate. I don't like them. I am full and simply don't want the extra calories and saturated fats. Instead, I wish talented chefs would use their considerable artistry to create more healthy desserts. Yes, I have occasionally had a fabulous blackberry or boysenberry tart or a chocolate something or other I couldn't resist, but usually, I like it simple and easy to make.

You can find lots of ways to sneak good, real flavors into any lowfat, low sugar, sugarfree, diet, or low-calorie dessert.

✔ If it can't be real whipped cream (and it can't because of the saturated fats, calories, and especially the contagious addiction), stir in a teaspoon of vanilla extract to an instant fatfree vanilla or chocolate pudding as you make it. Or shave some good chocolate on top of a fatfree or lowfat whipped topping or pudding. Or sprinkle on some cocoa or cinnamon or add fresh fruit to sugarfree gelatin desserts.

✔ To a lowfat or fatfree store-bought cake, make a rich raspberry sauce in 15 minutes (see recipe later in this chapter).

✔ Where juice is called for, use fresh squeezed orange, lemon, or real key lime juice instead of juice from concentrate.

✔ Add fresh fruits such as fresh blueberries, apples, or peaches to your canned instant blueberry, apple, or peach pie filling. The fresh fruits work even if they aren't precooked.

✔ If you have fabulous pears, no one will notice the fatfree chocolate sauce (into which you've stirred in a teaspoon of real vanilla extract).

✔ Top a sugarfree *glacé* (fruit ice) with real berries. A small sprinkle of fancy sugar crystals adds an authentic sugar taste, and the berries make a mound of plain yellow or orange ice more appealing.

Quick Lowfat Dessert Winners You Can Make in Five Minutes or Less

If you're looking for quickie lowfat winners, take a glance at these blue ribbon champs. They are all easy and very good. They are what I call assemblies. No recipes here. You just assemble them.

The following assemblies are 25 different and unique desserts that take only minutes. As an example, the kids will love the peanut butter and jelly "sauce" over ice cream. I also include lots of banana quickies. A few have liqueur, and one or two require a cornstarch and juice or berry sauce that you need to heat (which only takes a few minutes), but most are simple assemblies with only a couple of ingredients.

Keep the following in mind: All the ice creams, frozen yogurts, whipped toppings, cookies, wafers, graham crackers, puddings, custards, pie crusts, candies, and sauces like chocolate or butterscotch I mention are fatfree, lowfat, or reduced in fat. Nuts are regular nuts, and maple syrup is regular maple syrup.

Sugar substitutes

Most medical health letters say that artificial sugar or sugar substitutes used in small amounts — that means a packet or two once or twice a day — will not adversely affect you. If you feel one bothers you, discontinue using it.

Artificial sugars don't brown, and some don't hold up in baking although new ones are coming out continually that bake quite well. Some artificial sugars also taste slightly differently than real sugar. I don't use sugar substitutes in recipes in this book, but some of the products I use might contain them.

The original lower calorie (just as delicious) strawberry shortcake dessert

When the strawberries are in season, a quick strawberry shortcake recipe is a slice of angel food cake (which is fatfree), or other lowfat muffin, a large dollop of fatfree or lowfat whipped topping, a whole lot of sliced strawberries, another dollop of topping, and a final strawberry or two to grace the top of the fluffy topping. Eating lowfat strawberry shortcake can save about 200 calories and about 20 grams of fat, depending on the serving size.

✔ Ice cream cookie (two vanilla wafers filled with a ¼-inch slather of vanilla ice cream — try it between reduced-fat Oreos and graham crackers, too)

✔ Island fruits and ice cream (sliced mangoes, papayas, and kiwi over coconut ice cream — see photo in color section)

✔ Raspberries or raspberry sauce over vanilla ice cream

✔ Sliced cantaloupe with fresh lime juice and thin slivers of candied ginger and almonds

✔ Peach slices over ladyfingers with vanilla ice cream and whipped topping

✔ Fresh-pitted bing cherries over chocolate ice cream with whipped topping

✔ Melon, mango, and honeydew balls (with a splash of rum and orange juice for the grown-ups), and a big lemon sorbet ball for the kids

✔ Store-bought lemon sorbet tossed with fresh blackberries

✔ Oranges slices over ice cream and orange juice thickened with corn-starch and heated as a sauce

✔ Dates stuffed with walnuts or hazelnuts cut and served over vanilla ice cream (with a splash of Frangelica for the grown-ups)

✔ Tart apple slices with lemon glaze and Cheddar cheese

✔ Layered frappé in a tall glass with alternating layers of whipped topping and fruit (see photo in color section)

✔ Side by side small servings of several kinds of sorbet, such as mango, raspberry, and lime, with a mint sprig tucked in and a lemon twist on top

✔ Chocolate ice cream topped with whipped topping and lots of finely chopped walnuts (they look like so much more when finely chopped) and banana slices

✔ Bananas, lemon juice, and brown sugar cooked for 5 minutes, tossed with raspberries or blueberries (with a splash of rum for the grown-ups)

✔ Slice of pound cake, coffee ice cream, tiny marshmallows, chopped wal-nuts, and whipped topping

- Pear slices drizzled with hot caramel or butterscotch sauce topped with a dollop of vanilla ice cream or whipped topping

- Mango slices (bottled or fresh) on pineapple sorbet with a sprinkle of coconut (and a dash of rum for the grown-ups)

- Fresh peaches on reduced-fat Oreos with whipped topping and a big strawberry

- Partially thawed (frozen) bing cherries seasoned with lemon juice and a few tablespoons sugar (or Karo syrup, which isn't granulated) over vanilla ice cream with whipped topping and a sprinkle of cinnamon

- Fresh figs sliced over strawberry ice cream with maple syrup and slivered almonds to top it off

- Plain yogurt with sliced bananas or mandarin oranges and 2 tablespoons brown sugar mixed in the yogurt

- Ripe pears sliced over vanilla or chocolate ice cream, a drizzle of thick milk chocolate sauce (with a splash of pear brandy for the grown-ups), a teaspoon of whipped topping over the chocolate, and a sprinkle of nuts

- Peanut butter and jelly heated together, thinned with a teaspoon of canola oil and poured over vanilla ice cream with a sprinkle (about 2 tablespoons) of peanuts

- White chocolate candy bar pieces (about ¼ cup when broken into 1-inch pieces) heated just to melting, along with a few tablespoons thick nondairy creamer or half-and-half, poured over chocolate ice cream

- Graham cracker pie crust filled with ready-made chocolate or vanilla pudding, sliced bananas, and whipped topping

Fruit and Dessert Recipes

Many of the following recipes are dramatically sped up and reduced-fat versions of traditional recipes. Instead of trifle with enough high-fat whipped cream to keep you from rising out of the chair (and enough rum or brandy to stagger you when you do rise), you can make a fast, lush-looking lemon fluff.

Lowfat can still mean high calories

Remember, lowfat doesn't necessarily mean low calories. In fact, when it comes to desserts, my experience is that the calories are rather high in lowfat desserts (because of larger servings and extra sugar). And, beware of "reduced-fat" desserts. Although technically lower in fat, more often they can still be high in calories.

Lowfat dessert help around the corner right in your own market

High-fat, rich desserts are easy to find in any bakery department. Mine has candy bar cakes, thank you for nothing. Many have so many fillers and sugars, they don't even taste all that great. But worse than that, as skyrocket high-fat items, every bite is high in calories.

But when you begin to really look, you will see dozens and dozens of other, very convenient lowfat, nonfat, low sugar, or no-sugar desserts or dessert helpers ready for you, too. For example, you can find all types of ready-made whipped cream or whipped dessert toppings in all varieties of fat (none, to some, to low), and lowfat boxed toppings for you to whip, plus reduced-fat and fatfree cream cheese, frozen yogurts, ice cream bars, fruit bars, fatfree half-and-half, sugarfree maple syrup, reduced sugar fruit jellies and pie fillings, and many kinds of fresh and frozen fatfree and lowfat, and sugarfree cakes and cookies and other desserts.

So mix and match by serving sugarfree vanilla wafer cookies with lowfat coffee ice cream or a fatfree topping on a fruit crisp. The taste is there, but with fewer calories than expected.

Chocolate Eclair Cake

This rich, creamy, layered cake is better the next day (if you like a soft crust and soft layers). Eat it immediately if you prefer a crackly crust and layers. You will want to save the frosting recipe as it is outstanding.

Preparation/Cooking time: *20 minutes (plus 30 minutes to overnight to chill)*

Yield: *12 servings*

2 3-ounce boxes lowfat vanilla instant pudding

½ teaspoon vanilla

3 cups skim milk

8 ounces fatfree or lowfat whipped topping

1 cup fresh-squeezed orange juice, divided

1 box lowfat cinnamon graham crackers

1 cup sugar

⅓ cup unsweetened cocoa

¼ cup skim milk

Pinch salt

1 teaspoon vanilla

6 tablespoons reduced-fat cream cheese

1 In a medium bowl, add the pudding mix, vanilla, and milk and whisk for about 3 minutes or beat with an electric beater on the lowest setting for 2 minutes. Using a large rubber spatula, fold in the whipped topping.

2 Lightly spray the bottom of a 9-x-13-inch dish. Pour ½ cup orange juice on a flat plate. Dip each side of the graham crackers in the juice very quickly (for a more moist cake, dip both sides; for less moist, dip 1 side only). If dipping both sides of the graham crackers for a more moist crust, add more juice to the plate as needed.

3 Use ⅓ (you are making 3 layers) of the crackers, breaking them up to fit, making a nice bottom layer. Pour half the pudding mixture onto the graham cracker bottom and spread it evenly. Add a layer of graham crackers, pour on the remaining half of the filling, spreading it to make it even, and add the last layer of graham crackers.

4 In a small saucepan, add the sugar, cocoa, milk, and salt and stir well. Bring to a boil over high heat, stirring continually. Boil without stirring for 1 minute only. Remove from heat and let rest for 5 minutes. Stir in the vanilla and cream cheese. Spread over the top graham cracker top.

5 Cover with plastic wrap suspended with toothpicks or a high lid and refrigerate for 30 minutes until the pudding has time to set, or overnight.

Nutrition at a glance (per serving): *Calories 325.5 g; Protein 5.1 g; Carbohydrates 63.6 g; Dietary fiber 1.5 g; Total fat 3.0 g; Saturated fat 1.5 g; Cholesterol 4.9 mg; Sodium 475.9 mg.*

Lynn's tip: *For the big folks, add a tablespoon of orange liqueur to chocolate frosting.*

Apple Brie Pockets

This dessert is sophisticated enough for your fanciest diner or dinner, or you can make it with cream cheese or Cheddar and delight the kids with their very own little silver package (see photo in color section). For your fancy dinner, use parchment paper instead of foil. You can find parchment in most large markets near the waxed paper.

Preparation/Cooking time: *20 minutes*

Yield: *4 servings*

2 tart apples, cored and sliced	*1 tablespoon brown sugar*
4 ounces Brie cheese, cut into ¼-inch slices	*2 tablespoons toasted sliced almonds*

(continued)

1 Preheat oven to 400°. Fold the foil or parchment. Cut out a half heart that is 12 inches wide at the widest part of the heart (when opened) and 9 inches long. The hearts are fat, and you should closely follow the outside edge of the parchment paper (making it as large as possible).

2 Open the hearts and place on the counter, separated. Into the center of each heart half, add 4 to 6 slices of apple and top with cheese and a sprinkle of brown sugar.

3 Fold the empty heart half over the filled half and fold all the edges twice, making a double-folded hem all around the cut part of the heart edge. Make sure that it is tightly sealed.

4 Bake for 3 to 5 minutes, or until the cheese just starts to melt. To serve, cut a cross through the top of each packet and fold the 4 corners back. Sprinkle with almonds and serve hot.

Nutrition at a glance (per serving): *Calories 165.81 g; Protein 6.62 g; Carbohydrates 14.63 g; Dietary fiber 2.19 g; Total fat 9.65 g; Saturated fat 5.12 g; Cholesterol 28.35 mg; Sodium 179.99 mg.*

Lynn's tip: *To save some calories and fat (about 2 grams), substitute Camembert for Brie. Or use any lower fat cheese you want. Don't go for most fatfree brands because many don't melt, and if they do, most don't taste good enough yet.*

Berries on Gelatin

A great way to get kids to eat fruit, this fabulous fruit is easy because the gelatin is already pre-made, right from your market. Although the flavored gelatin cups can be found on the shelf, I prefer the refrigerated version because it is less watery and holds up when sliced. You can fancy this up by using your own dish and tucking in a mint sprig. Save a few berries for garnishing the whipped topping (and place a few of the prettiest berries on top).

Preparation time: *10 minutes*

Yield: *4 servings*

4 individual pre-made red gelatin cups

2 tablespoons lemon juice

2 bananas, sliced

1 cup fresh hulled and sliced strawberries

½ cup blueberries

½ cup raspberries

1 cup fatfree or lowfat nondairy whipped topping

4 mint sprigs for garnish (optional)

1 Run a thin sharp knife around the edge of the plastic gelatin cups and pour out into individual dishes or bowls. With the same knife, cut the gelatin into wedges down from the top. They will fall back, or you can help to separate them with the knife.

2 Sprinkle the lemon juice on the cut bananas and add to the top of the gelatin. Add the strawberries, blueberries, and raspberries (save a trio of the prettiest berries, though). Top with the whipped topping and a trio of berries. Tuck in a sprig of mint.

Nutrition at a glance (per serving): Calories 174.73 g; Protein 2.34 g; Carbohydrates 41.58 g; Dietary fiber 3.94 g; Total fat 0.59 g; Saturated fat 0.13 g; Cholesterol 0 mg; Sodium 63.75 mg.

Lynn's tip: If you like another flavor, buy the orange gelatin and add canned, drained mandarin oranges with a dollop of lowfat or fatfree whipped topping or try yellow gelatin and add green and red seedless grapes.

Raspberry Sauce

Raspberry sauce — shiny, thick, and sweet — is quite versatile. Perfect over angel food cake or under poached pears, this colorful and rich sauce dresses up lowfat or fatfree ice creams or frozen yogurts and even makes those store-bought fatfree brownies terrific.

Preparation/Cooking time: 15 minutes

Yield: 1½ cups sauce for 6 ¼-cup servings

1 pint cleaned raspberries

½ cup sugar

½ teaspoon fresh lemon juice

Pinch cinnamon

1 tablespoon cornstarch

1 To a processor or heavy duty blender, add all ingredients and process until smooth.

2 In a small saucepan, add the berry mixture and heat, stirring, until thick, about 4 minutes. Strain if you want a seedless sauce.

Nutrition at a glance (per serving): Calories 89.78 g; Protein 0.38 g; Carbohydrates 22.66 g; Dietary fiber 2.80 g; Total fat 0.23 g; Saturated fat 0.01 g; Cholesterol 0 mg; Sodium 0.29 mg.

Lynn's tip: To make the old-fashioned and charming late-1800s peach melba, add a scoop of lowfat vanilla ice cream. Place a fresh, ripe peach half (pitted) upside down on the ice cream, drizzle on this fresh raspberry sauce, and add a small dollop of lowfat whipped topping, and a couple more berries. Sprinkle with a few walnuts or pecans and tuck in a mint sprig.

Butterscotch Bananas in Maple Sauce with Ice Cream

This easy creation is always a hit with a party because it looks so spectacular. You can top with a big strawberry, raspberries, or blueberries. My liqueur tip at the end, for the grown-ups, is a winner and the way I personally make this.

Preparation/Cooking time: *15 minutes*

Yield: *4 servings*

4 ripe bananas

2 tablespoons maple syrup

½ cup fatfree or lowfat butterscotch sauce

1 teaspoon lemon juice

¼ teaspoon cinnamon

2 cups fatfree or lowfat vanilla ice cream or frozen yogurt

4 fresh mint sprigs (optional)

1 Cut bananas in half crosswise and lengthwise.

2 Lightly spray a large skillet with cooking spray. Add the maple syrup. Place the banana halves in the skillet, round side down, and cook over medium-high heat for 1 or 2 minutes. Turn over into the syrup and spoon on top.

3 In a small bowl, mix the butterscotch sauce, lemon juice, and cinnamon. Pour over the bananas, covering each. Lower the heat, cover, and cook for 5 minutes more.

4 Arrange 4 banana pieces on each of 4 dessert plates, spoon the sauce over bananas, and top each with a ½-cup scoop of ice cream. Garnish with the fresh mint.

Nutrition at a glance (per serving): *Calories 338.91 g; Protein 4.84 g; Carbohydrates 79.60 g; Dietary fiber 4.28 g; Total fat 2.63 g; Saturated fat 0.76 g; Cholesterol 5.42 mg; Sodium 195.20 mg.*

Lynn's tip: *To make this fancier, add some spirits to the sauce while it cooks. Try ¼ cup of any of the following: rum, Frangelico, coffee liqueur like Tia Maria, or an orange liqueur such as Triple Sec. For the kids, a plop of fatfree chocolate sauce is nifty.*

Lemon Cloud

Fluffy and soft on a graham cracker crust, this feels and tastes like a nice rich Midwestern dessert full of familiar flavors. An e-mail acquaintance, Tom Panciarello, sent a version of this easy and virtually fatfree dessert. He said, "Enjoy, it's like a cloud and delicious! Please give it a try, Lynn." I did, Tom, and I liked it.

Preparation/Cooking time: 10 minutes (plus 2 hours to chill)

Yield: 12 servings

2 boxes (small) lemon gelatin, sugar or sugarfree

1 12-ounce container fatfree whipped topping

36 to 38 cinnamon graham cracker squares

4 large bananas, sliced

⅓ cup lowfat cinnamon graham cracker crumbs

1 In a large metal bowl, dissolve the gelatin in 1 cup hot water. Add 1 cup ice water and pop into the freezer until cold or syrupy, about 5 minutes.

2 Fold the whipped topping into the cold gelatin in a steady stream until fully and incorporated.

3 Spray a 13-x-9-inch baking pan with cooking spray, wiping out any excess. Cover the bottom with a layer of graham cracker squares.

4 Cover the crackers with a layer of banana slices and pour in the whipped filling. Spread to make an even layer. Sprinkle the top with the graham cracker crumbs. Chill for 2 hours.

Nutrition at a glance (per serving): Calories 202.1 g; Protein 2.8 g; Carbohydrates 45.1 g; Dietary fiber 1.6 g; Total fat 1.0 g; Saturated fat 0.3 g; Cholesterol 0 mg; Sodium 165.2 mg.

Lynn's tip: You can change the flavor to any you like or add fresh fruit in between or on the side. Tom's original recipe was to make this with two 6-ounce cans very cold evaporated skim milk and ⅔ cup sugar, beating it into soft peaks and adding the gelatin in a stream. Chill as directed. His way works well, too, but I shortened the time and felt the taste was still great.

Banana Split Pie

This ice cream dessert will probably remind you of those special summer treats from your childhood. You can make this recipe over and over and never use the same combination of fruit, toppings, and nuts. Substitute butterscotch topping instead of chocolate, try strawberries with caramel topping and almonds or layer chocolate, vanilla, and strawberry ice cream. This came from my e-mail friend June Hughes.

Preparation/Cooking time: 5 minutes (plus 3 hours to freeze)

Yield: 6 servings

(continued)

1 banana, thinly sliced

1 8-inch reduced-fat graham cracker pie crust (save the plastic cover)

3 cup lowfat vanilla, vanilla ice cream, or frozen yogurt

⅓ cup fatfree fudge ice cream topping

1 cup container fatfree cold whipped topping

⅓ cup chopped peanuts

1 Arrange the sliced bananas all across the bottom of the pie crust.

2 Allow the ice cream to soften slightly and spoon it over the bananas, pressing very gently so that it fills the pie crust.

3 Drizzle the fudge topping over the ice cream. Top with the whipped topping and sprinkle with the nuts. Cover with the saved plastic cover and use it as a dome top (upside down) and freeze until hard, about 3 hours.

Nutrition at a glance (per serving): *Calories 394.72 g; protein 7.51 g; Carbohydrates 67.09 g; Dietary fiber 3.08 g; Total fat 10.37 g; Saturated fat 1.75 g; Cholesterol 5.01 mg; Sodium 286.94 mg.*

Lynn's tip: *If your crust didn't have a dome top, you may wonder how you can cover something with whipped topping without smushing the topping. Use toothpicks to elevate the plastic wrap.*

Key Lime Pie

This no-bake key lime pie was given to me by Ross Snyder of Delray Beach in Florida. It was so good, I ate a high, 5-inch wide 6-inch long slice and couldn't get enough. Purchase the crust already made or, for fewer calories, make your own with less fat. I have made it with both Persian limes and key limes, and key limes are better. A few shakes of green food coloring in the batter and decorated with a twisted lime slice on top with a little lime zest sprinkled around is especially attractive. Chill all the ingredients, pie shell, milk, and lime juice for a quicker setup time.

Preparation/Cooking time: *5 minutes (plus 3 hours to overnight to chill)*

Yield: *6 servings*

1 14-ounce can fatfree sweetened
condensed milk

2 8-ounce containers cold nondairy fatfree
whipped topping

⅔ cup fresh key lime juice

1 8 to 9-inch reduced-fat graham cracker
pie shell

1 In a large electric bowl with mixer, blend on slow the condensed milk and half of the whipped topping (one 8-ounce container) until well mixed but not thoroughly beaten. Add the lime juice and fold in carefully. The mixture will stiffen as you fold.

2 Pour into the graham cracker crust. Spread on top the amount of whipped topping you want.

3 Refrigerate for 3 hours to chill. Serve cold and refrigerate to keep.

Nutrition at a glance (per serving): Calories 453.28 g; Protein 7.30 g; Carbohydrates 89.36 g; Dietary fiber 0.11 g; Total fat 4.84 g; Saturated fat 0.67 g; Cholesterol 4.34 mg; Sodium 277.56 mg.

Lynn's tip: Make the same delicious pie with tangerine juice, lemon juice, or even pink grapefruit juice for a fabulous change. Use a drop or 2 of food coloring for each batter and a twist of the fruit or a candied version on top to identify the flavor.

Lowest fat graham cracker crusts

Make your own graham cracker crusts by processing broken graham crackers. Twenty crackers makes 1¼ cups, the perfect amount for a crust (use more if you like a thicker crust). If you don't have a processor, place the crackers between waxed paper or in strong plastic bags and crush them with a rolling pin. If you have a wand or hand blender, place the broken crackers in a strong large open plastic baggie, set in a bowl, and grind away inside the baggie. You need no margarine or butter when using the crumbs for a cheesecake crust, but for a key lime pie, you need to add 2 melted tablespoons of some kind of fat to keep the crumbs together.

Fried Fruit

This one is a little different, but my testers said it was a "smash hit." Jasmine tea bags are available in every large market in the Asian or regular tea section.

Preparation/Cooking time: *20 minutes*

Yield: *4 servings*

1 pint strawberries	*1 tablespoon minced or finely grated fresh ginger*
2 ripe peaches or nectarines, peeled and pitted	*2 tablespoons orange zest*
¼ pound fresh cherries, pitted	*1 tablespoon balsamic vinegar*
3 tablespoons cornstarch	*3 tablespoons sugar*
1 jasmine tea bag	*1½ cups fatfree whipped topping*

1 Wash all the fruit well and hull the strawberries, cutting them in half. Peel the peaches and cut into 6 to 8 wedges each. To a large bowl, add the hulled and sliced strawberries, peach slices, and whole pitted cherries.

2 In a small bowl, add the cornstarch and ⅓ cup cool water, mix, and set aside. In a glass measuring cup, place the tea bag and ½ tablespoon or 1½ teaspoons (or half) of the ginger. Add 1 cup boiling water and set aside to steep.

3 Heavily spray a large skillet with cooking oil spray. When hot, add the cherries, peach slices, strawberries, and orange zest and cook, stirring gently, for 2 minutes until the fruit is heated (you aren't cooking the fruit).

4 Add the ginger tea mixture, balsamic vinegar, and sugar to the skillet. Mix well and bring to a boil. Stir in the cornstarch-water mixture and cook, stirring over medium-high heat until the sauce thickens, about 1 minute.

5 Divide the fruit and sauce into 4 bowls and sprinkle the remaining orange zest over the top.

6 Fold the remaining ½ tablespoon ginger into the whipped topping and spoon over the fruit, serving immediately (or the topping melts).

Nutrition at a glance (per serving): *Calories 173.61 g; Protein 1.22 g; Carbohydrates 40.60 g; Dietary fiber 3.69 g; Total fat 0.61 g; Saturated fat 0.08 g; Cholesterol 0 mg; Sodium 32.60 mg.*

Quick and Easy Chocolate Mousse

This simple recipe is so delicious and versatile (see photo in color section). It's a recipe I get a request for continually. You can use many other flavors, depending upon the pudding you use. From butterscotch to my favorite, mocha, or the yummy lemon or one with nuts, you almost can't go wrong. Although you can eat it immediately, give the sugars and starches in the pudding time to melt and meld, which happens in the chilling time.

Preparation/Cooking time: *5 minutes (plus 2 hours to chill)*

Yield: *6 servings*

1 14-ounce can sweetened condensed fat-free milk	*1 4-ounce package fatfree instant chocolate pudding*
2 tablespoons orange liqueur (optional)	*3 cups fatfree or lowfat whipped topping*

1 In a medium bowl, add the milk, ¼ cup water, the orange liqueur if using, and the pudding mix.

2 Beat with an electric mixer for 2 minutes on low.

3 Carefully fold in the whipped topping until perfectly blended.

Nutrition at a glance (per serving): *Calories 311.32 g; Protein 6.28 g; Carbohydrates 68.48 g; Dietary fiber 0.55 g; Total fat 0.50 g; Saturated fat 0.12 g; Cholesterol 4.34 mg; Sodium 379.54 mg.*

Lynn's tip: *You can use any flavor of instant pudding mixture. With vanilla or chocolate, add ½ teaspoon vanilla extract. Add almond extract only with vanilla pudding. For mocha (my favorite), use a coffee liqueur and ¼ cup strong coffee instead of the ¼ cup water (all with the condensed milk). If you go for raspberry, use a raspberry liqueur, butterscotch, or hazelnut liqueur.*

Part III
New Fast and Easy (And Healthy) Ideas

The 5th Wave   By Rich Tennant

"I'm not sure we're getting enough iron in our diet, so I'm stirring the soup with a crowbar."

In this part . . .

Part III shows you how to make old favorites in brand new ways. You find out more than you ever knew about spices and condiments and where and how to use them. You also get terrific recipes for one-dish meals (hooray) and breakfasts. You can even find a chapter and recipes on slow cooking, which requires little prep time.

Chapter 10

Retro Foods: New Ways with Old Favorites

This chapter is filled with great retro recipes, recipes your mother and grandmother made (or maybe your father and grandfather). You can discover or rediscover them here, and they are worthy of any gourmet. These aren't the ersatz or fake foods or ham-type foods like Spam, but are instead, updated versions of mouthwatering dishes found from the 1800's on through the 1970s. You've heard of Salisbury steak, Swiss steak, and beef stroganoff. Well, they're here.

Finally, I give you tips on how to make almost any older-style, usually high-fat dish healthier . . . and faster.

Changing from Old to New

It was only 20 years ago that you expected to see your steaming bowl of chili with a half-inch of red grease floating on top. If you stirred it in, it kept floating back up, until the chili got cooler. When you stirred the lukewarm glob in again, it finally disappeared into the chili — then into your body to sit on your hips or in your arteries. People know today that food doesn't need all that fat to taste good. Now you can make a great chili with a terrific old-fashioned taste that contains almost no fat at all (see my recipe later in this chapter).

The "Ladies" food guide

"(1877) This little volume is sent forth in the confident belief that it is the Ne Plus Ultra of Cookboks or Guides to Housekeepers. Unlike the trashy cook and recipe books vended about the country for $1.50 or $2.00 a copy, "hashed"

up from irresponsible sources, more with a view to size and ashow than to practical utility . . ."

— The Home Guide, A Book by 500 Ladies, The Courier and Freeman, 1877

Today, for health-wise and time-smart people, everything has changed. You can cook the old recipes a new way — without the fat and with half the time. You can eat smaller portions when dining out, taking half the restaurant dinner home, and diluting the fat by adding your own fresh foods, maybe some canned or frozen foods, and even a handful of leftover diced lean ham or chicken for a very good meal. At half price.

Updating old recipes is easy. Here are a few guidelines.

Improving your health and saving calories

Keep the following guidelines in mind, and you'll improve your health and save calories.

- **Whenever it says to brown something in 2 tablespoons cooking oil, use a cooking spray.** Two tablespoons doesn't sound like much, but this small change can save you 240 calories. Don't spray for an hour, though. A spritz will do it. Lightly spritz the veggies as well as the pan.

- **If a dessert recipe says to cream the sugar and butter, forget switching to margarine.** Instead, switch to another dessert. Creaming means time, energy, fat, calories, and something that will taste good and tempt me, which I will then eat.

- **You can almost always use less meat than every general cookbook calls for.** When a recipe says 1 pound or 1½ pounds, you can almost always cut that in half or use only two-thirds. I use only a fourth. To make up for the bulk, be sure to add something else, like cooked mushrooms or brown rice, TVP (textured vegetable protein, found in all large supermarkets), or breadcrumbs, with suitable liquid to make it the same consistency. One of my tester's general rule is to use one-third lean meat to two-thirds vegetables, especially for a casserole.

- **Use smaller portions of meat.** If the recipe calls for two 6-ounce chicken breasts, use two chicken breasts that weight 3 ounces each after you skin them and remove the fat.

✔ **Substitute another meat.** If the recipe calls for 6 ounces of cube steak, use 4 ounces of flattened turkey breast for a saturated fat savings of more than 5 grams, which is a lot. If you still want to go with beef, then stay with the cube steak, which is a leaner cut. If it calls for chicken wings, skin them (and discard or use for soup the two end joints defatted after cooking).

✔ **Remove all fat from the meat.** From bacon fat, leg of lamb fat (butterfly it and cut it off), chicken fat (use scissors and paper towels to cut and pull off all the skin), pork fat, hamburger (mix with lean turkey breast or use as lowfat as possible), to the fat in canned meats like bottled wrapped tamales, just take it all off.

✔ **Don't change sugar amounts unless you're sure that you will like it less sweet.** If I'm not sure, I use one-sixth to one-fourth less sugar and add a few shakes of a sugar substitute, and it usually works. Sometimes I have reduced the sweetness so much, I have had to sprinkle more sugar on the dessert or lift a pie crust after baking it, adding it to the fruit, and then giving it time to melt in.

✔ **Use fatfree half and half or fatfree nondairy creamers.** Canned soups taste very good with these products. Or use skim milk for a thinner variety or evaporated skimmed milk, good with creamed mushroom, celery, and other creamed soups and desserts where its slightly sweeter taste contributes to the overall flavor. I like soy milk, too.

✔ **Use half skim and half nondairy creamer for a less blue milk in cereal.** Skim milk can look awfully grey or blue in your cereal bowl or can give coffee a "grayish" pall. Some of new "thick" skim milks are already avail able in large markets and are far creamier looking.

✔ **For whipped cream, try skim or regular milk, which both whip.** (One or 2 percent milk doesn't whip because the starches that keep it from separating also keep it from whipping.) Or use fatfree or lowfat whipped toppings in packages or tubs. Remember, it's fatfree only if you use the recommended amounts — usually 2 tablespoons. Go for 4 tablespoons, and you get some fat.

✔ **Use less fat and try the new nontrans fatty acid margarines.** Calories are nearly the same, and they contain no trans fatty acids and only .5 grams of sat fat in each 1 tablespoon serving so you have almost no hydrogenation.

✔ **Use the same kind of cheese but much less or mix fatfree and lowfat (or lowfat and regular).** Mixing a reduced fat (which usually isn't that low in fat) and a fatfree with half and half portions gives the best tastes with the least total fat and sat fat. Search for lowfat cheese that tastes good. Grated Parmesan is always good to use because of its concentrated flavor.

Butter versus margarine

Stick margarine contains less than half the saturated fat as does butter. Both have added salt and added color. Butter has cholesterol, margarine doesn't. Butter may contain antibiotics and hormones. Both may contain pesticides. Butter also has considerable transfatty acids, but not nearly as much as margarine. So which is better? Probably tub or diet margarine, according to the *Harvard Health Letter.* I use a fatfree spray, various oils, and nontrans fatty acid margarines.

Saving time and energy

The following tips can save you both time and energy.

- ✔ **Often, when recipes call for browning the meat first, you can reduce the steps in the recipe to just one step, simply by cooking everything at once, browning it all or not browning anything.** You may have a minor flavor loss.

- ✔ **You can save time washing dishes if you use less pans.** Simply move the foods to be browned to one side of the skillet and cook with only that side on the heat, adding the other foods later, or brown your foods in an extra-large skillet or Dutch oven so that you can add the rest of the foods to the same skillet when the meat or vegetables are browned (wiping out any extra grease with paper towels).

- ✔ **Try one of the new pressure or fusion cookers for faster cooking.** These cookers cut cooking time into a third or half in most recipes. The T-Fal fusion cooker doesn't even have any little pressure gauge to lose as it's in the lid.

- ✔ **Use a microwave to half-bake the potatoes (turn often), squash, and other foods and to half-cook many casseroles.** Then finish the dish in the oven for half the earmarked time with all the flavor and crisping oven-cooking gives.

- ✔ **Use a microwave to precook foods.** This method is great for boiling water quickly, melting margarine or butter, or softening fruits like lemons to juice them more easily.

- ✔ **Buy precut vegetables.** You can find them packaged in the vegetable or produce department or at your salad bar.

- ✔ **Ask your meat department to cut up any meat any way you wish, skin the chicken, butterfly the lamb, grind the pork, or defat the roast.**

- ✔ **To boil foods, cover the pot with a lid which makes for a higher temperature and no cool air on top, so that you have slightly faster boiling.** Or boil half the water in the microwave or use hot water to begin with.

> ✔ **When you're boiling eggs, sit your eggs in a bowl of hot tap water for a few minutes so that they don't crack upon immersion.** Then cook them in boiling water. Or begin them in cold water. Eggs take 20 minutes to cook through.

Making Then-and-Now Recipes

Using older recipes, especially those written before 1950, is fun and very interesting. These recipes are timely favorites, what your parents and grandparents loved, and I've already tweaked the ingredients while reducing the fat to make sure that the taste never gets lost.

Beef Stroganoff over Noodles

This is a quick stroganoff that is as yummy as it is easy (see photo in color section). Purchase lean beef that is already cut in strips and precut mushrooms and onions. Serve over noodles with a side of sliced tomatoes and a green vegetable like peas, green beans, broccoli, or asparagus.

Preparation/Cooking time: *20 minutes*

Yield: *4 servings*

10 ounces lean beef tenderloin, cut into strips

2 medium onions, thinly sliced

1 pound sliced mushrooms

1 tablespoon flour

½ cup beef broth or water

1½ teaspoons prepared Dijon mustard

2 sprigs fresh tarragon chopped, or ½ teaspoon dried

1 cup fatfree or lowfat sour cream

2 tablespoons chopped parsley

1 Lightly spritz a large skillet with cooking spray. Add the beef and any salt and pepper you wish and cook over medium-high heat for 3 to 4 minutes, turning to brown each side. Remove and set aside. (If the beef is overcooked, it will be tough.)

2 Respritz the skillet, add the onions and mushrooms, and lightly spray them with cooking spray. Cook over medium heat, stirring, until soft, about 7 minutes. Add the meat back to the pan.

3 Using a sieve, sprinkle the flour into the broth and whisk in well to remove lumps. Add the floured broth to the skillet and cook, stirring, over low heat for about 4 minutes, or until the sauce is thick.

(continued)

4 Stir the mustard and tarragon into the sour cream. Add to the skillet and heat for 1 or 2 minutes, mixing the foods together well. (Don't let the sauce boil or get too hot because it will curdle and the mustard will be bitter.) Serve over cooked noodles. Top with parsley.

Nutrition at a glance (per serving): Calories 246.5 g; Protein 23.2 g; Carbohydrates 24.0 g; Dietary fiber 2.2 g; Total fat 6.2 g; Saturated fat 2.1 g; Cholesterol 50.2 mg; Sodium 293.4 mg.

Lynn's tip: If you're using fresh tarragon instead of dried, to decoratively and easily cut it instead of chopping it, strip the tarragon leaves from their stems, pulling them off one by one. Stack the leaves and roll them up tightly. Slice the rolled leaves crossways. This technique is called a chiffonade of herbs.

Eggplant Parmesan

This is an Italian delight (see photo in color section). Use smaller eggplants for an attractive and interesting side. Each person gets half an eggplant, so buy them accordingly. The center of the eggplant is soft and custardlike. This recipe is easy to make, so don't let the ingredient list stop you — it's all for flavor. The even faster version is in my tip at the end of the recipe. It's the one I use myself, but my testers liked this version better, even though it is one of the longest cooking recipes in the book.

Preparation/Cooking time: 40 minutes

Yield: 4 servings

2 eggplants, about ½ pound each	1 teaspoon dried oregano
2 tablespoons olive oil, divided	1 cup bottled tomato pasta sauce
2 cloves garlic, minced	1 cup fatfree or lowfat ricotta cheese
2 tablespoons minced or finely chopped basil	½ cup grated fatfree or lowfat mozzarella cheese
2 tablespoons chopped parsley	¼ cup grated Parmesan cheese

1 Preheat oven to 350°. Remove the green tops of the eggplants and cut eggplants in half lengthwise. Make 8 or 9 deep cuts lengthwise, about ⅛ of an inch apart, across each half, not breaking through the skin but getting within ¼-inch of the edge. Then cut deeply again across the width, which makes a cross-hatch look or tiny squares where the cuts intersect, again taking care when you cut to not pierce the eggplant skin (or your hand).

2 Brush each cut side with the olive oil, using 1 tablespoon total for the 4 halves. Lightly salt and pepper if you wish and set aside on a lightly sprayed foil-lined cookie sheet.

3 In a small dish, add the remaining olive oil, garlic, basil, parsley, and oregano and mix. Poke the mixture into the slits. Cover each cut side of the eggplants with ¼ cup tomato pasta sauce.

Old-fashioned marzipan

Not that you're going to make almond paste everyday, but if you want to make a good olden-days dessert or party food, here's the recipe. Take 1½ cups finely ground almonds (processor), ¾ cup sugar, ¼ cup water, and a few drops almond extract, mix together, and cook on low heat for 20 minutes. Cool and make into figurines with food coloring, as they did from about the 11th century on, all over Europe.

What do you do with marzipan? Stuff it in dates or prunes. Lowfat? No! Healthy? Yes! Quick? Very! It's a recipe found in most 1800 cookbooks.

4 In a small dish, add the ricotta, mozzarella, and Parmesan cheese and spread on top of the tomato sauce. Bake for 30 to 35 minutes or until the eggplant is tender. (If you are a parsley lover, you can sprinkle more on before baking.)

Nutrition at a glance (per serving): Calories 219.6 g; Protein 16.1 g; Carbohydrates 17.3 g; Dietary fiber 4.0 g; Total fat 8.9 g; Saturated fat 2.2 g; Cholesterol 12.7 mg; Sodium 607.7 mg.

Lynn's tip: You can make a smaller, faster version by slicing large eggplants into 1 ½-inch rounds. Lightly brush with olive oil, shake on garlic salt, and microwave for 4 minutes to soften the rounds. Preheat oven to 350°, place the rounds on a sprayed foil-lined cookie sheet, fill with the same spices, sauce, and cheese mixture, and bake the rounds for 10 minutes or until fully cooked.

Creamed Corn with Diced Ham

This will be the best, sweetest creamed corn of your life, bar none, I promise. You make it the way it used to be made except without the cream. You can use frozen corn or corn that has been in the refrigerator for several days. Silver Queen corn makes the sweetest creamed corn. The diced ham makes it work as an entree.

Preparation/Cooking time: 20 minutes

Yield: 4 servings

4 ears corn shucked, kernels cut off

1 cup lean ¼-inch diced ham

¼ cup finely chopped red peppers or firm tomatoes for garnish

1 Divide the corn kernels in half. Place half in a food processor and process until smooth.

2 In a large saucepan, add the processed corn and kernels and heat over medium-low heat, covered, for 10 minutes. Add any salt and pepper you wish.

(continued)

3 Stir in the diced ham. Heat until the ham is hot. Sprinkle the red peppers on top of each serving as a garnish.

Nutrition at a glance (per serving): *Calories 124.1 g; Protein 9.5 g; Carbohydrates 18.0 g; Dietary fiber 2.6 g; Total fat 2.8 g; Saturated fat 0.7 g; Cholesterol 15.9 mg; Sodium 496.0 mg.*

Lynn's tip: *You can use leftover precooked, grilled, boiled, or steamed corn; the sugary starches from the precooking make an excellent creamed corn.*

Salisbury Steaks

My testers said these steaks are sooo good, moist, and full of flavor topped by a smooth and sassy sauce. They liked them best served with wide egg (yolkless) noodles. For a traditional meal, serve with noodles, peas, and fruit.

Preparation/Cooking time: *25 minutes*

Yield: *8 servings*

1 egg, slightly beaten

¼ cup fine herbed breadcrumbs

¼ cup finely chopped onion

2 tablespoons finely chopped red or green pepper

1 ½ pounds 93 percent fatfree lean ground beef

1 teaspoon butter or margarine

¼ cup ketchup

1 tablespoon lemon juice

1 teaspoon Worcestershire sauce

¼ teaspoon Tabasco sauce

1 teaspoon Dijon mustard

2 tablespoons sherry, or 1 teaspoon sherry extract

1 Preheat broiler. In a medium bowl, add the egg, breadcrumbs, onion, red or green pepper, and any salt and pepper you wish and mix well. Add the ground beef in pieces and mix well.

2 Shape the meat into 8 oblong patties, about ½-inch thick. Place on the broiler rack and broil 3 inches from the heat for 6 to 8 minutes on each side or until thoroughly cooked.

3 While the meat broils, in a small saucepan, add the butter or margarine, ketchup, lemon juice, Worcestershire sauce, Tabasco sauce, mustard, and sherry. Heat just to the boiling point. Pour over the cooked Salisbury steaks.

Nutrition at a glance (per serving): *Calories 169.9 g; Protein 19.1 g; Carbohydrates 5.7 g; Dietary fiber 0.4 g; Total fat 7.3 g; Saturated fat 3.1 g; Cholesterol 78.5 mg; Sodium 280.2 mg.*

Lynn's tip: *You can also use the sauce from the Swiss steak recipe, which follows.*

Corn facts

Although thousands of varieties of corn could be available, Americans only grow a few. This dangerous practice resulted in a surprisingly severe corn shortage in the United States only a dozen years ago when a blight affected the major variety grown. This same shortfall is reminiscent of 100 years ago in Ireland where a blight affected the one potato type harvested, resulting in the starvation of millions of Irish, or more than 10 percent of their population. Now, growers of many kinds of produce such as corn, potatoes, tomatoes, and apples are growing and offering for sale far more vegetable and fruit varieties. The result is that it keeps the genus strong and the supply steady and offers more interesting and varied types for the buyer. Heritage or olden days reserved seeds, older type fruits and vegetables grown by a few special people interested in preserving many varieties, have helped in this endeavor.

Swiss Steak with Country Gravy

Now called a cube steak, this is extra lean meat your market has cross-hatch scored to tenderize, and it makes a hearty dish my testers raved about. Don't add salt as the bouillon cube and Worcestershire have plenty. (Bouillon cubes are total retro and really do add flavor.) For a traditional meal, serve with cooked mashed potatoes (available in meat departments) or over bread or biscuits and a green vegetable. I pan-fry the steaks, but you can broil them or stove-top grill them just as well. The sauce is what makes the dish.

Preparation/Cooking time: 20 minutes

Yield: 4 servings

4 4-ounce cube steaks	*2 large onions, thinly sliced*
¼ to ½ teaspoon garlic salt	*2 tablespoons flour*
¼ teaspoon seasoned salt	*1 teaspoon Worcestershire*
1 beef bouillon cube	*2 cups fatfree half-and-half or skim milk*
1 pound mushrooms, sliced	

1 Lightly spray a large nonstick skillet. Place over medium-high heat. Add the steaks, sprinkle generously with garlic, and seasoned salt. Then, season with salt and pepper if you wish. Brown on 1 side, about 2 minutes, turn, season again, and cook until just done. Set aside on a hot plate and lightly cover with foil.

2 Meanwhile, lightly spray the skillet again and add a *scant* (retro word meaning slightly less) ¼ inch water. Over medium heat, melt the bouillon cube, stirring and mashing.

(continued)

3 Add the mushrooms and onions and cook over medium heat, stirring occasionally, covering them with the flavored water, for about 5 minutes. The water will evaporate, so lightly spray the mushrooms and onions with cooking spray to keep them from burning or sticking. Continue stirring and cooking for another 2 minutes.

4 While the mushrooms cook, in a medium bowl, add the flour, Worcestershire, and a little of the half-and-half or milk. Whisk until smooth before adding all the milk. Add the milk mixture to the nearly fully cooked mushrooms and onions and cook over low heat for about 4 to 6 minutes, stirring, until the flour is thoroughly cooked. Serve the meat and pour the mushroom sauce over the steaks and mashed potatoes or noodles.

Nutrition at a glance (per serving): Calories 356.3 g; Protein 32.4 g; Carbohydrates 29.4 g; Dietary fiber 2.7 g; Total fat 8.8 g; Saturated fat 3.0 g; Cholesterol 81.7 mg; Sodium 783.1 mg.

Lynn's lore: Called smothered steak in the British Isles around the 1930s through the 1950s, it is indeed smothered in mushroom sauce. This steak was originally thicker, double or triple the serving size (still pounded and scored however), but baked or braised for about 2 hours with a sauce that also contained tomatoes.

Chili con Carne

Comments ranging from, "Oh, my gosh, this chili is so good" to "My husband had no idea there was almost no meat (which he's not supposed to eat anyway) because it tastes so meaty" were the reports from my testers. To feed more people, pour the chili over cooked pasta, a baked potato, or a mound of corn or serve on a toasted bun for a retro Sloppy Joe sandwich.

Preparation/Cooking time: 25 minutes

Yield: 4 to 6 servings

4 ounces crumbled lean hamburger

1 large onion, chopped

2 cloves minced garlic

1 green or red pepper, diced

1 tomato, diced

1 heaping tablespoon chili powder

1 teaspoon cumin

1 ½ cups tomato juice or V8 juice

1 16 to 18.5-ounce can lowfat beef with beans or vegetarian chili

1 16-ounce can dark kidney beans, drained

1 Lightly spray a large 4-inch high-sided skillet or wide pot with cooking spray. Add the hamburger, fry over medium-high heat until cooked, about 3 minutes, rinse the cooked meat in a colander, and set aside.

2 Wipe out the skillet, lightly spray again, and add the onions, garlic, and green or red pepper. Sauté over medium-high heat for 8 to 10 minutes, tossing.

3 Add the cooked hamburger, tomato, chili powder, cumin, tomato juice, chili, and kidney beans and heat until the soup is very hot. Add any salt and pepper you wish.

Nutrition at a glance (per serving): *Calories 273.8 g; Protein 21.8 g; Carbohydrates 43.6 g; Dietary fiber 12.6 g; Total fat 3.6 g; Saturated fat 1.2 g; Cholesterol 19.0 mg; Sodium 756.2 mg.*

Lynn's tip: *For heat, season this chili with a half teaspoon crumbled chipolte (dried jalapeño), diced jalapeño (fresh chipolte), Cajun spice, hot sauce, or red pepper flakes. Throw some shredded lowfat cheese on top. You will never notice the cheese is lowfat the chili is so good.*

Sloppy Joes

This is a fun and healthy twist on the traditional 1950s Sloppy Joe recipe. You can prepare it ahead of time and when you're ready to eat, simply heat it and pour it over toast or toasted buns. The turkey and hamburger contain the same cholesterol, but the saturated fat differences are over 100 percent with the hamburger having more.

Preparation/Cooking time: *20 minutes*

Yield: *4 servings*

1 medium onion, chopped

2 cloves garlic, minced

8 ounces 93 to 97 percent lean turkey sausage or 93 percent lean hamburger

1 16-ounce can sliced mushrooms, drained

¼ teaspoon dried oregano

½ teaspoon dried basil, or 1 teaspoon chopped fresh basil

2 cups pizza or pasta sauce

4 hamburger buns

4 ounces shredded lowfat cheddar cheese

1 Lightly spray a large skillet with cooking spray. Add the onions and garlic and sauté over medium heat, tossing for 2 to 3 minutes, adding a few teaspoons water if it gets too dry.

2 To the onions and garlic, add the ground turkey or beef and any salt and pepper you wish and toss, mash, and mix with a fork so that it doesn't clump. Heat until the meat is thoroughly cooked, about 4 minutes. Add any salt and pepper you wish.

3 Add the mushrooms and toss for a minute or 2. Add the oregano, basil, and pizza sauce and, on medium heat, cook until hot.

4 Toast or steam the buns, open, pour the Sloppy Joe over the buns, and top with the shredded cheese.

(continued)

Nutrition at a glance (per serving): Calories 341.2 g; Protein 25.8 g; Carbohydrates 36.2 g; Dietary fiber 5.3 g; Total fat 10.6 g; Saturated fat 3.8 g; Cholesterol 40.1 mg; Sodium 1,290.5 mg.

Lynn's tip: You can make this recipe all vegetarian or more vegetarian by substituting half or a third with TVP (textured vegetable protein) or cooked brown rice for the meat. If you haven't tried using TVP (a soy granule found in any major market), you will be pleased because the texture is better than using canned meat lookalikes (also available in most large markets). Adding chopped celery and carrots with the onions boosts the fiber.

Peanut Brittle or Pulled Vinegar Candy

A favorite in the 1800s, originally called Pulled Vinegar Candy and Nuts, this recipe needed no changing. You pull it like taffy. It takes little time and is fun to make.

Preparation/Cooking time: 25 minutes

Yield: 14 pieces

2 tablespoons butter

2 cups sugar

¼ cup vinegar

½ teaspoon vanilla, or 6 drops peppermint oil

1 cup chopped unsalted peanuts

1 In a medium saucepan, add the butter and heat on high for 1 minute or until melted. Add the sugar and vinegar.

2 Have a bowl of cold water ready. Using the handle end of a spoon, drop a pearl-sized ball into the water occasionally. When it makes a hardened ball in the water, it is ready.

3 Remove from heat and pour onto a shallow, oiled platter. Sprinkle with the vanilla or oil and then the nuts.

4 Pull into bite-sized pieces. Roll each pulled piece in a long thin strip. Cut the strips in 1-inch pieces. Store in a tightly covered container.

Nutrition at a glance (per serving): Calories 125.6 g; Protein 0.0 g; Carbohydrates 28.8 g; Dietary fiber 0 g; Total fat 1.6 g; Saturated fat 1.0 g; Cholesterol 4.4 mg; Sodium 17.1 mg.

Lynn's tip: To make a browner color, add 1 drop of yellow, orange, and either blue or green food coloring to make the candy a light brownish color, reflecting the vinegar hue.

Chapter 11

Using Herbs, Spices, Condiments, and a Few Fast and Easy Sauces

. . . .

In This Chapter

▶ Working with almost every herb and spice — the mortar in the building blocks of flavoring food

▶ Using condiments and relishes

▶ Converting lowfat thin soups and sauces into thick lush soups and sauces

▶ Cooking with spirits

. . . .

*T*hink herbs, spices, salt and pepper, relishes, condiments, and sauces aren't very important? You think they just sit in your cupboard or take up space in your refrigerator door? Spices have been a major part of civilization for thousands of years. As far back as five thousand B.C., herbs and spices such as cinnamon and cilantro flavored common foods like roots, grains, beans, and poultry.

Still, many people are suspicious of or don't know how to use spices and herbs. I fix that in this chapter. Knowing how, where, and when to use spices and herbs is especially important in quick and healthy cooking where dishes don't simmer for hours. In this chapter, I tell you all that and more.

Working Magic with Herbs and Spices

Mystical feelings surround herbs and spices today. Think aromatherapy. The spice and herb trade is a multibillion dollar business (see Figure 11-1). They are plentiful, inexpensive, and easy to use when you know how to do so.

Figure 11-1:
You have
many herbs
and spices
to choose
from.

Americans have access to hundreds of thousands of available flavorings, spices, herbs, sauces, relishes, and condiments. You can find fresh and dried herbs, spices, wines, extracts, granules, essences, oils, vinegars, and other flavorings readily available and all relatively inexpensive.

Is it an herb or a spice, and what's the dif ?

Herbs are the green leaves of a plant like bay leaves, basil leaves, oregano, parsley, sage, rosemary, and thyme. The name herb even means herbage.

Spices are whole seeds, like fennel, mustard, and nutmeg; seed shells like mace; ground seeds like cumin, coriander, ginger, and dry mustard; flower parts such as saffron bark (bark cinnamon is one example); stalks or stems like lemon grass; buds such as cloves and capers; seed pods like rose hips; roots like ginger; and everything else that isn't the leaf or the stem close to the leaf.

Enjoyment of herbs and spices is picking up. Americans have developed a taste for Italian parsley, cilantro, lemon grass, wasabe, ginger, lemons pickled in cardamom, curry, chilies, sesame seeds, soy sauce, oyster sauce, five-star spices, fennel, and anise, and much more. And that's what herbs and spices do to food. They take a plain dish and give it much, much more.

If you don't know where to start . . .

If you've never used herbs and spices before, you'll probably want to err on the side of caution. Go slow. Use less rather than more. Use too few rather than too many. Use too little rather than too much. As an occasional judge of food contests, I've noticed that the biggest mistake good cooks and would-be cooks make is to use too many spices and herbs and to not use them in the proper or most tasty amounts.

I'm a professional, but when I'm not exactly sure what spices and herbs to use in a recipe, I experiment. I experiment continually. Here are my rules in finding the right herbs and spices for a dish. Begin by being very hungry (which is more important than you think).

The Ancient Romans didn't eat all that badly (if they were rich, that is)

"... for a sauce for roast meat, a quarter of an ounce each of pepper, lovage, parsley, celery seed, dill, asafetida root, hazelwort (an ancient bitter herb), turmeric, caraway, cumin and ginger ..."

— Ancient Classical Roman Sauce Recipe

1. **Fill four or five little custard cups with a few tablespoons of the food you want to add punch (some herbs or spices) to.**

2. **Add a pinch of a different herb or spice you think might work to each cup and stir them in, a smidgen (teeny tiny bit) at a time.**

3. **Label each cup with the spice or herb that you used, but hide the label under the cup.**

4. **Stir the herb or spice (or both) and taste each as you go along.**

   The next step is the mysterious process in getting to the right herb and spice for this particular dish.

5. **Go away and do something entirely different for about 5 minutes.**

   Purposely try not to think about which of the spices and herbs would be best.

6. **Go back into the kitchen for another taste.**

   The one you go to first, totally unconsciously and because you are hungry and want more, is always the correct one. You may want to fiddle with it more, but you have selected the right one.

Don't outthink yourself. Add the spices and herbs, wine, or extracts you've thought about and try them in the little cups first. You may find a magical signature mixture all your own. Just don't add them directly to the big soup pot until you're sure. I've ruined many a good dish by unthinkingly adding more of this or that.

One caveat. Don't experiment with black pepper. Use small amounts. Black pepper is one of those spices that expands in taste when stored. Put most of the amount you want on at the table. I've often peppered the soup, gravy, or sauce perfectly for the dinner. Next day at lunch I get surprised by an overly peppery soup, gravy, or sauce.

Also keep the following herb and spice rules in mind:

- Don't use too many herbs and spices together unless you're a pro. It's the biggest mistake noncooks make.
- Use both tarragon and garlic sparingly.
- Don't overly brown or burn the garlic. Unlike onions, which caramelize, garlic turns ugly and bitter when browned.
- Cook saffron a long time (over 20 minutes) to bring out the flavor.
- Cook dried oregano a short time, or it can turn bitter.

✔ Fresh basil is better than dried, but dried basil is better than none. (As a rule, fresh herbs generally taste better than dried.)

✔ Dried oregano is better than fresh, and Greek oregano is the best.

✔ Use double the basil to oregano when using both.

✔ Forget cooking with purple basil because it loses flavor when heated.

✔ Dried cilantro, dried parsley, and dried chives are blah.

✔ Fresh ground tellicherry pepper is the best-tasting pepper.

✔ Rub dried herbs briskly between your palms before tossing in the foods to release more flavor.

Matching up tried-and-true combinations

This section gives you an idea of which spices and herbs go with what foods. This is general, and if you have a favorite, write your own discovery or favorite in the margin, (then send it to me, too). A few vegetables like fresh onions and garlic are included in the herbs and spices, as are a few bottled condiments.

✔ **Beef:** Salt, pepper, onions, onion powder or salt, garlic salt, sugar, fresh garlic cloves, horseradish, parsley, bay leaf, thyme, tarragon, cayenne, sundried tomatoes, herbs de Provence, bouquet garni, bay leaves, red wine, Worcestershire, soy sauce, steak sauce, ketchup, and dry, prepared, or Dijon mustard

✔ **Fish and shellfish:** Salt, pepper, onions, onion salt, garlic, garlic salt, celery salt, basil, tarragon, oregano, dill, sundried tomatoes, mint, mayonnaise, and white wine

✔ **Ham:** Honey, preserves, maple syrup, brown sugar, dry or prepared Dijon mustard, soy sauce, Worcestershire, coffee, and bourbon

✔ **Lamb:** Salt, pepper, onion salt, garlic salt or powder, fresh garlic cloves, mint and mint jelly, soy sauce, steak sauce, relish, Worcestershire sauce, red wine, tarragon, and rosemary

✔ **Pork:** Salt, pepper, hot pepper, onion salt, garlic salt or garlic powder, sage, parsley, rosemary, oregano, mustard, white wine, sweet vermouth, plum sauce, brown sugar, and apple juice concentrate

✔ **Poultry:** Salt, pepper, hot pepper, onion salt, celery salt, celery seed, garlic salt or garlic powder, sage, parsley, rosemary, thyme, oyster sauce, Worcestershire, mustard, white wine, sweet vermouth, and plum sauce

✔ **Vegetables:** Salt, pepper, onions, garlic, celery, celery salt, bay leaves, tarragon, basil, oregano, parsley, thyme, rosemary, cinnamon, lemon, orange, hollandaise sauce, and mayonnaise

In addition, the following combinations are common regional, ethnic, or popular herb (see Figure 11-2) and spice suggestions. I pick just a few to illustrate what is usually or often used. Sometimes you don't know how to spark up a Tex/Mex dish or Chinese food and what flavors are appropriate. Hopefully, this list will keep you from adding vanilla to Mexican chili and may introduce you to grinding up walnuts or almonds in meat sauces or sticking a sprig of lemon grass into your chicken soup. I also added a few condiments to this list where appropriate.

- ✔ **American:** Salt, pepper, basil, parsley, ketchup, mustard, mayonnaise, steak sauce, salsa, and Tabasco
- ✔ **Caribbean:** Garlic, onions, hot sauce, lime, cloves, coconut milk, and curry
- ✔ **Chinese:** Garlic, onions, scallions and chives, water chestnuts, bamboo shoots, oyster sauce, fish sauce, rice wine, rice wine vinegar, soy sauce, chili paste, Chinese hot oil, hot pepper flakes, ginger, and cilantro
- ✔ **French:** Garlic, shallots, leeks, tarragon, thyme, rosemary, Herbs de Provence, bay leaves, bouquet garni, and paprika
- ✔ **Greek or Mediterranean:** Onions, garlic, cumin, basil, oregano, lemon, cinnamon, allspice, sundried tomato, paprika, fennel, anise, and rosemary
- ✔ **Indian:** Tamarind, coconut, curry, peanuts, dates, ginger, cashew nuts, almonds, cinnamon, and raisins
- ✔ **Indonesian:** Onions, garlic, bay leaves, peanuts, sambaloulek (a spice), cloves, lemon grass, curry, tamarind, soy, peanuts, saffron, and coconut
- ✔ **Italian:** Garlic, onions, sundried tomatoes, fennel seed, anise, Italian parsley, green and red peppers, basil, oregano, coriander, and sage
- ✔ **Japanese:** Onions, scallions, tofu, seaweed, sprouts, saki wine, ginger, wasabe, soy sauce, and chili paste
- ✔ **Middle Eastern:** Onions, garlic, cumin, raisins, apricots, pickled lemons, Kalamata olives (or Greek olives), curry, cayenne, paprika, almonds, basil, pistachios, pine nuts, turmeric, saffron, cinnamon, and mint
- ✔ **Southern American:** Liquid smoke, bacon, ham bouillon cubes, garlic, chives, red pepper flakes, and Cajun spices
- ✔ **Tex/Mex:** Onions, garlic, chili powder, cumin, chili peppers, bell peppers, jalapeño and other hot peppers, tomatoes, lime, oregano, basil, and cilantro

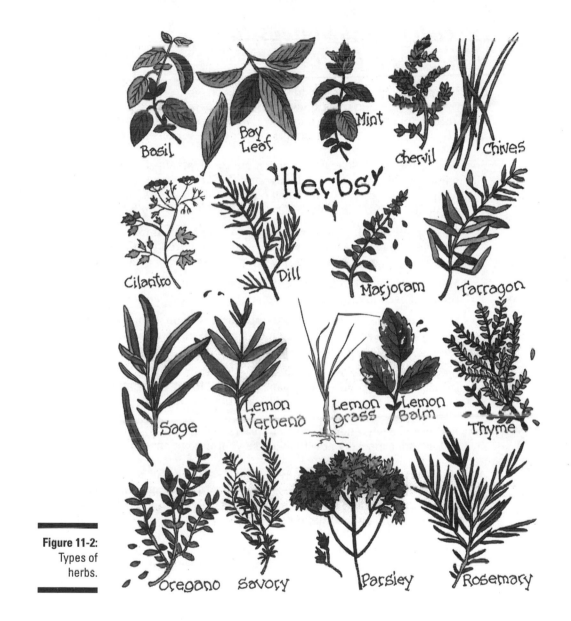

Figure 11-2:
Types of
herbs.

Discovering the intensity of herbs and spices

Here is a general idea of how mild or strong each spice, herb, and flavorings is. If you know you don't like spicy hot, you can avoid it. Likewise, if you love the subtle odors, those herbs and spices with the mild rating have a delicate flavor or smell that will please you. Here's how I describe each of the ratings:

- **Most mild:** Has a delicate flavor but not much smell, like turmeric, dried parsley (which is often used only for color or interest), saffron, or poppyseeds. When used in small or moderate amounts, imparts flavor or blends with other flavors but doesn't dominate.

- **Mild, medium mild, and aromatic:** If used in small amounts, it is mild and pleasingly aromatic, but like the gently flavored vanilla, sweet basil, or nutmeg, these can be overpowering if too much is used.

- **Medium spicy:** Like cinnamon, cloves, and oregano, can easily dominate the food even in moderate amounts.

- **Spicy but no heat:** Has a bite like raw garlic, cumin, lemon or lime, horseradish, wasabe, hot Asian mustard, and curry and can create a noticeable difference. Can easily dominate other flavors.

- **Spicy hot with heat:** Like jalapeño and all other hot peppers, chili paste, dried red pepper flakes, and black pepper, can burn or tingle the tongue and throat. Just a pinch too much can ruin a dish.

This list tells you what herb or spice to use (see Figure 11-3) and where, how strong it is, and especially how to increase your enjoyment of food.

Allspice: Mild and aromatic. Usually ground. Used in meat, roasts, chicken, duck, fish, stews, consommés, hams, vegetables such as potatoes and tomatoes, fruit, apple pie, and chutney, baked goods, and fruit juice. Resembles a blend of cinnamon, cloves, and nutmeg.

Almond: Mild and aromatic. Extract, oil, whole, chopped, peeled, unpeeled, and slivered. Used in French cooking. Extract in angel food cake. Whole used in Moroccan cooking, cookies, with curries, Middle Eastern dishes, desserts, marzipan, fish, and poultry.

Anise and anise seed: Mild. Whole-seed spice. Used in beef, pork, sausage, shellfish, soups, beets, turnips, cabbage, cauliflower, cabbage and cucumber salads, pasta, sauces, coffee cakes, cookies, and fruit juice.

Artificial butter-flavored sprays: Mild. Can also be extracts, oils, granules, and spreads. Used on vegetables, bread, toast, pastries, casseroles, and popcorn. Sometimes used in sautéing.

Figure 11-3:
Choose your
spice!

Basil or sweet basil: Mild and aromatic. Comes fresh, dried, or flaked herb. Used in meat, poultry, fish, seafood, omelets, soups, stews, sauces, especially pasta or Italian, Greek or other Mediterranean sauces, vinegar, stuffing, dips, salad dressing, and vegetable juice.

Bay leaf: Mild. Usually dried whole. Used in roasts, fish, beans, soups, stews, chowders, potatoes, vinegar, rice, tomato juice, gravies, bouillabaisse, sauces, and marinades. Usually removed before eating.

Black mustard seed: Spicy. Usually the whole seed, which is stronger than yellow mustard seed, is used. Used in mustards, chutneys, condiments, pickles, and corned beef.

Brown pepper: Spicy hot. Whole or ground. Often used in Szechwan food and other Asian foods, vegetables, meats, poultry, fish, stews, tofu, sauces, and dips.

Capers: Spicy. Not a spice or herb, but a salt-pickled shrub bud. Used in meat, poultry, fish, salads, salad dressings, vegetables, vinegars, soups, sauces, and dips and as a garnish.

Caraway seeds: Mild. Usually the whole seed. Used in German dishes, goose, onions, potatoes, noodles, sauces, dips, stews, stuffing, salads, sauerkraut, cabbage, vegetable juice, and rye and wheat bread. Can be added before, during, or after cooking.

Cardamom: Mild. Ground or whole. Used in meats, fish, curried fish, melon, fruit salads, pea soup, bean dishes, salad dressings, cookies, cakes, bread, pickled lemons, donuts, and Danish pastry.

Cashews: Mild. An oily nut used in Chinese foods, soups, stews, poultry, couscous, salads, candies, and desserts.

Cassia: Medium spicy and aromatic. Usually ground. A pale spice used as is cinnamon and is the primary ingredient in cinnamon. Used in stews, vegetables, sauces, fruit dishes, cookies, cakes, pies, and drinks.

Cayenne: Spicy hot. A ground spice used in chili, hot sauces, on or in meat, fish, pasta and macaroni dishes, soups, sauces, with cheese, vegetables, Asian and Tex/Mex foods, and on garlic bread and beans.

Celery seed: Mild. A dried spice used in meat recipes, poultry, soups, stews, salads, vegetables, vinegar, sauces, dips, slaw, herb breads, cottage cheese, relishes, bread, and vegetable juice.

Chervil: Mild. A fresh or dried herb similar to tarragon. Used with lamb, sausage, poultry, fish, shellfish, bouillon, meat, cottage cheese, soups, sauces, avocado recipes, omelets, vegetables, salads, salad dressings, and vegetable juice.

Chili powder: Medium spicy. A ground spice, which varies greatly, and is usually a combination of spices so that you get the blend you like. Used in Tex/Mex foods, chili, chili sauce, onions, guacamole, barbecue sauce, salsa, tomato soup, beans, potato salads, salad dressing, cottage cheese, stews, eggs, vegetable juice, and sauces.

Chilies: Usually spicy. A hot capsicum used fresh, dried whole, flaked, powdered, and paste form. Commonly available are ancho, habenaro, serrano, hari mirch, jalapeño, chipolte (which is dried jalapeño), and the hottest, scotch bonnet.

Chives: Medium spicy. Usually fresh or dried type of onion. Used as an herb with meat, poultry, fish and shellfish, and in soups, stews, chowders, omelets, sauces, dips, vegetables, vinegars, or anywhere onions might be used. Can be added before, during, or after cooking.

Cilantro or Chinese parsley: Medium aromatic or mildly spicy. A fresh herb (coriander is dried cilantro) used in salsas, sauces, salads, guacamole, soups, Asian dishes, Hispanic food, curries, stews, onions, spinach, tomatoes, cauliflower, and vinegar.

Cinnamon: Medium spicy and aromatic. Used in ground and stick form. Used in pork, ham, chicken, lamb, relishes, fruit pies and tarts, sauces, breads, cookies, spiced and mulled wine, punch, coffee, toast, coffee cake, applesauce, chutneys, pickles, gingerbread, pumpkin bread, vegetables such as onions, squash, pumpkin, tomatoes, sweet potatoes, yams, beets, noodles, rice, and many desserts with chocolate, gingerbread. Can be added before, during, or after cooking.

Cloves: Medium spicy. Usually aromatic ground or whole spice (cloves are the dried part of a flower). Used in beef, ham, pork, lamb, stew, stocks, vegetables, fruit pies, relishes, mincemeat pie, chutneys, cranberry juice, potpourri, corned beef, cakes, pumpkin pie, and cookies and in aromatic in *pomanders* (little spice bags you hang in closets, drop in soups, or clove studded apples to place in the kitchen to smell good).

Cumin: Medium spicy. Usually ground used in Tex/Mex, Middle Eastern, and East Indian dishes. Often used with chili and curry powder. Used in beef, lamb, pork, soups, stews, beans, chili, curries, sauces, vinegar, dips, bread, cakes, and salad dressings.

Curry powder or paste: Spicy. A ground blend that can differ in intensity. Used in beef, lamb, pork, sausage, chicken, seafood, couscous, rice, soups, dips, salad dressings, chutneys, relishes, cottage cheese, deviled eggs, curried eggs, fondue, vegetables such as cauliflower, onions, tomatoes, stuffing, noodles, and rice.

Dill: Mild and aromatic. Sometimes fresh, dried, or seed herb. Used in meats, poultry, fish, seafood, stews, sauces, dips, pickles, vegetables, salads, salad dressings, marinades, pickles, vinegar, cottage cheese, omelets, slaw, bean soup, chicken soup, and breads.

Fennel: Mild. Licorice-flavored spice. Seed used in Middle Eastern cooking and in meats, poultry, sausage, fish, seafood, stews, sauces, dips, vegetables such as cabbage, cucumbers, and onions, salads, salad dressings, pickles, bread, vinegar, pasta, cookies, and cakes.

Fenugreek: Most mild. Faint, curry-flavored, slightly bitter spice. Seeds, powder, whole-fresh, and paste. Used in Mediterranean and East Indian foods, in vegetables, sauces, and halvah (bread), and the seeds sprouted in salads.

Flowers: Mild. Sometimes slightly bitter, flowers are used fresh, dried, ground, the oil, essence, or extract. Used in salads, stews (squash flowers), molds, ices, and other foods. Roses, rose water, melon and squash flowers used in Middle Eastern and Asian cultures. Marigolds, nasturtiums, dandelions, lavender, violets, and many others used in wine, candied, sugared, in vinegar, sauces, soups, curries, jelly, rice, salads, wedding cakes, and cheeses. (Use only organic flowers).

Garlic: Spicy. An aromatic root used raw, cooked, in powder, with salt used in all cultures' cooking. Used in meats, game, poultry, fish, shellfish, vegetables, grains, bread, pasta, rice, beans, soups, sauces, salsas, salads, salad dressings, dips, eggs, and savory marinades and dishes.

Garlic powder: Spicy. Aromatic powder ground from garlic. Usually made with added salt and sugar. Used in meats, poultry, fish, seafood, ethnic foods, soups, stews, beans, pasta, rice, sauces, dips, vegetables, salads, salad dressings, breads, pizza, casseroles, and marinades.

Ginger: Spicy. Used fresh, ground, pickled, or candied. Used in Asian dishes and other ethnic cuisines and in meats, chicken, duck, soups, stews, stir-fries, fish and shellfish, vegetables, sweet and sour dishes, cakes, cookies, bread, gingerbread, pies, candy, drinks, chutney, and mulled or spiced wine. Pickled as a condiment for sushi and *churashi* (which means "thrown sushi").

Horseradish: Spicy, but no heat. Fresh, creamed, processed, dried in flakes, powdered root. Used with beef, ham, smoked fish, fish, shellfish, salads, egg salad, salads, and sauces. Can be added before, during, or after cooking. The Japanese green variety is called wasabe.

Hot sauce and chili paste: Spicy hot. In liquid, oil, or paste form. Used in Asian and Tex/Mex dishes, barbecue sauce, chili, Szechwan food beans soup, vegetables, guacamole, and the same foods as chili powder.

Juniper berries: Mild. Fresh or dried berry seed. Used in game, pork, poultry, stuffing, stews, apples, sauerkraut, sauces, potatoes, poultry, gin, vodka, and beer.

Lemon and/or lime: Spicy and aromatic. Citrus fruit fresh, bottled used for juice and pulp, the peel in extracts, oils, and zest. Used to flavor poultry, fish, shellfish, soups, sauces, beans, casseroles, fruit, guacamole, pastries, cakes, cookies, pies, juice, drinks, and desserts.

Lemon grass: Mild. Fresh and dried aromatic grass used in Asian and Middle Eastern foods, soups, meats, poultry, stews, rice, noodles, sauces, and vegetables.

Mace: Medium spicy. A ground spice, which is the lining of nutmeg. Used in fish, poultry, rabbit, sausages, soups, beans, pasta, fruit, vegetables such as Brussels sprouts, cabbage, and broccoli, chutney, sweet breads, cakes, cookies, and spiced wines.

Marjoram: Medium spicy. Fresh and dried herb used in meats, poultry, fish, seafood, stews, sauces, dips, many vegetables such as spinach, onions, carrots, squash, oyster stew, bread, stuffing, omelets, salads, and tomato juice. Wild marjoram, if from Europe, is what is known as oregano.

Marzipan: Mild. Almond paste used primarily in Europe in poultry, stuffings, desserts, and candies.

Mint: Mild and aromatic. Fresh or dried aromatic herb; many varieties (2,000 plus) such as the more common ones — peppermint, wintergreen, spearmint, curly mint, apple mint, garden mint, pennyroyal, water mint, lemon mint, chocolate mint, pineapple mint, and Corsican mint. Used in lamb, fish, poultry, ham, vegetables, salads, desserts, fruits, sauces, beverages such as mint julep, sorbet, jelly, tea, Middle Eastern foods, and with yogurt.

Mustard: Medium spicy. Ground or whole-seed spice. Used dry, mixed, or prepared (commercial mustard). American or Dijon-style, plus many other styles, such as honey-mustard, egg mustard, and so on. Used in meat, poultry, fish, shellfish, potatoes, pickling, condiments, relishes, deviled eggs, salads, salad dressings, vegetables, mayonnaises, marinades, sauces, dips, and cheese dishes.

Nutmeg: Mild. Whole or ground aromatic spice used in meat, meat loaf, meatballs, poultry, ham, pork, sausage, vegetables such as onions, squash, eggplant, mushrooms, and potatoes, pasta, dips, black beans, creamed soups, pea soup, sauces, eggnog, fruit, quiches, pasta dishes, cheese, cream soups, desserts such as cakes, cookies, doughnuts, and pies, and eggnog.

Onion powder: Medium spicy and aromatic. A ground root, often with added salt and sugar. Used in meat, fish, poultry, soups, stews, beans, casseroles, dips, sauces, vegetables, marinades, and salad dressings.

Oregano: Mild and aromatic. Fresh, ground, and dried herb (if European, is wild marjoram). Used in lamb, meat, pork, fish, poultry, vegetables, salads, mushrooms, desserts, fruits, sauces, beverages, vegetable juice, vinegar, omelets, and onions.

Paprika: Mild and spicy hot. A ground spice. Used in meat, poultry, fish, stews, chowders, Hungarian foods, deviled eggs, vegetables (especially potatoes, carrots, onions, and cauliflower), sauces, barbecue, salads, and salad dressings. Can be added before, during, or after cooking. Hot paprika is also occasionally available.

Parsley: Mild. A fresh or dried flaked herb. Used in meat, fish, shellfish, poultry, vegetables, salads, salad dressings, soups, stews, all vegetables, vegetable juices, cottage cheese, omelets, grains, stuffing, vinegar, and sauces.

Peanuts: Mild and aromatic. A legume used fresh, pickled, roasted, in brine, and ground in Chinese, Indonesian, Thai, and Mexican food, vegetables, couscous, pasta, soups, sandwiches, sauces, butters, cookies, and cakes.

Pecans: Mild. A fruit called a nut. Used in poultry, salads, entrees, soups, pies, fish, rice, sweet potatoes, vegetables like sweet potatoes, sauces, other desserts, and candy.

Pepper perfect

When you buy already ground black pepper, often it has been in the hold of a ship for many months and is a mixture of the cheapest black peppers. To get the flavor you really want in pepper, purchase several different kinds of whole peppercorns and try them in different pepper mills. Some come with their own little "mill" right in the top where you just invert the little spice bottle and grind away. Here are a few available in America. I buy them when I travel to savor different tastes.

Black: Under ripe whole berries.

Brazilian black: The most prevalently used pepper in the United States, but thought not to be the best. Usually sold by large spice companies. That's what you are usually buying in your store.

Green: Fresh, pickled, or freeze-dried

Lampong: Usually the whole black pepper

Malabar: Reportedly the best black pepper until tellicherry

Sarawak: Reported to be the best white pepper, but seldom available

Szechwan: Often a combination or blend of predominately red, reddish-brown berries, or peppercorns

Tellicherry: The best-tasting (and most expensive) black pepper

White pepper or Montoc: The core of the ripest, mature berries

Pepper: Spicy hot. Comes whole, pickled, cracked, ground, and in mixtures with other herbs and spices. Used in meat, fish, shellfish, poultry, vegetables, salads, desserts, on Proscuitto and melon, in sauces, salads, dips, grains, pasta, rice, vegetable juice, barbecue, savory and spicy dishes, marinades, and spice cake. (See the sidebar for more on the different types of pepper.)

Poppyseeds: Mild. A seed spice used in vegetables, salad dressing, bread, rolls, pasta, potato salad, sauces, grains, rice, egg dishes, vinegar, and coffee cakes.

Purple basil: Mild. A fresh herb to be used only as a garnish.

Red pepper flakes: Spicy hot. In flaked form. From the spice cayenne. Made from dried hot chili peppers. Used in Tex/Mex, Mexican, Middle Eastern, Oriental, and Cajun cuisines, as well as dips, fish, pasta, rice, beef, curry, pizza, sauces, soups, and French dressing.

Rose water: Mild and aromatic. A liquid made from roses and rose hips. Has a perfumey smell. Used in Eastern Indian recipes, Middle Eastern foods, Chinese soups, poultry, sauces, drinks, stews, vegetables, lemonade, gin fizzes, fruit salad, and desserts.

Rosemary: Mild and aromatic. Fresh, dried, and ground herb. Used in meat, poultry, lamb, fish, vegetables, salads, fruits, soups with potatoes, spinach, tomatoes, potatoes, sauces, breads, macaroni, marinades, stuffings, vinegar, vegetable juice, and bread.

Saffron: Very mild. Usually in threads or powder (the most expensive of all spices). Often used with turmeric in bouillabaisse, tomato soup, poultry, seafood, rice, paella, risotto, breads, cakes, cookies, curried foods, tea, stuffing, couscous, pilaf, and squash. Needs a long cooking time.

Sage: Mild. Fresh, dried ground, or crumbled aromatic herb. Used in most meats, rabbit, poultry, pâtés, soups, stews, lamb, pork, sausage, onions, peas, tomatoes, bulghur, vinegar, casseroles, pasta, stuffing, vegetables, cottage cheese, fondues, omelets, tomato juice, sauces, and bread.

Savory: Mild and aromatic. Fresh or dried herb. Used in meat, fish, shellfish, poultry, sauces, soups, stews, casseroles, beans, vegetables, vegetable juice, artichokes, asparagus, green beans, beans, rice, and pasta.

Sesame seeds: Mild. Also called benne, sesame paste, a ground spice (tahini), oil, or seed. Used in hummus, beef, poultry, salads, soups, breads, fish, rice, pasta, vegetables, Asian and Middle Eastern foods, noodles, cakes, and cookies.

Sesame oil: Mild. An aromatic oil that comes light and dark (dark used as a flavoring; light, as a cooking oil and flavoring). Used in Middle Eastern, Indonesian, Asian, Malaysian, and Thai cooking and in meats, poultry, fish, shellfish, noodles, rice, vegetables, sauces, soups, fondues, and cookies.

Shallot: Medium mild and aromatic. Usually a purplish or pale yellow bulb with a gentle garlic and onion flavor. Often used with French cooking and in meat, poultry, fish, sauces, soups, dips, relishes, vinegars, salads, and salad dressings.

Star anise: Medium spicy. Usually dried in the form of sliced pods, which contain licorice-flavored seeds. Used in soups, stews, sauces, dips, salad dressing, and Middle Eastern and Asian food.

Tamarind: Mildly sour. Used as a pod, ground, fresh, pulp, paste, or seed, often with some pulp. Used in meat, poultry, curry, chutney, pickles, and drinks.

Tarragon: Mild and aromatic. Fresh or dried herb. Used in meat, poultry, casseroles, fish, pasta, vinegar, stuffing, vegetables (such as asparagus, beets, carrots, green beans, onions, squash, mushrooms, onions, and squash), rice, grains, pasta, sauces, vegetable juice, salads, salad dressings, marinades, mayonnaise, mustard, and vinegar.

Thyme: Mild and aromatic. Fresh or dried herb of many varieties. Used in meat, venison, rabbit, poultry, fish, shellfish, casseroles, vegetables, pasta, cornbread, cottage cheese, omelets, gumbos, pea soup, tomato soup, vegetable soup, vinegar, stuffing, stews, salads, salad dressings, vegetables, sauces, and the liqueur Benedictine.

Turmeric: Very mild. Fresh, powdered, dried rhizomes (an underground stem). Often called Indian saffron. Used to enhance saffron or to give a yellow color to foods. Used in curried foods, deviled eggs, squash, couscous, rice, chutneys, mustards, dips, relishes, poultry, fish, salad dressings, sauces, and soups.

Vanilla: Mild and aromatic. A liquid, bean, pod, or extract. Used in desserts, puddings, cookies, cakes, sweet-style breads, ice cream, cakes, cookies, candies, pastries, milkshakes, eggnog, and sweet dishes.

Violet: Mild. Aromatic extract, fresh or dried, flaked or whole flowers, candied flowers used in sauces, liqueurs, and chocolates, and for decoration.

Walnuts: Mild. A fruit called a nut. Can be black or English, which has a different flavor. Used whole, in pieces, halves, crumbled, ground, or in oils. Used in meats, poultry, pesto, cookies, cakes, chicken, desserts, brownies, baked apples, apple pie, broccoli, green beans, and sweet potato. In Mexico, ground into meat sauces. Black walnuts have a slightly different flavor.

Wasabe: Spicy, but no heat. Horseradish root. Usually used for sushi, but can be added to vegetables, sauces, soups, relishes, salad dressings, and dips. Used mostly in Japanese food.

Just exactly what am I adding to my food?

You've probably already added a lot of these ready-mixed spices, herbs, and liquids to your food. But did you ever wonder exactly what you were adding?

Barbecue seasoning: A mixture of paprika, cayenne, sugar, garlic salt, black and white pepper, chili powder, and onion. The addition of celery salt is Southern; Tennessee uses Worcestershire and honey; North Carolina uses mustard, vinegar, cumin, lemon juice, and no chili powder; Georgia adds molasses; California-style is with orange peel; Mexico adds chocolate; and Florida adds lemon or orange juice. Used for meat, ribs, poultry, fish, potatoes, chips, celery, carrots, corn, popcorn, salad dressings, dips, beans, vegetables, sauces, and marinades.

Bouquet garni: A mild French blend of parsley, thyme, bay leaves, celery seeds, rosemary, and savory. Usually tied in a cheesecloth (or the outer leaf of a leek) and removed before serving. Used in soups, sauces, fish, beef, poultry, and vegetables.

Cajun spice: A spicy mixture of salt, cayenne, sugar, celery, garlic, and onions. Used for beans, soup, rice, legumes, meats, poultry, fish, sauces, casseroles, and oven-baked potato slices and in Cajun, New Orleans, or Creole-style foods.

Chinese five-spice powder: A sweet spicy combination of star anise, cassia (cinnamon), nutmeg, cloves, and allspice. Used in Asian, Middle Eastern, and Polynesian cooking and in stir-fried foods, stews, vegetables, meats, poultry, fish, and sauces.

Curry powder: A spicy blend that varies but always includes cloves, cinnamon, ginger, nutmeg, black pepper, chili, coriander, fenugreek, cumin, mustard seed, poppyseed, turmeric, cardamom, and curry leaf, but may include many more herbs and spices.

Garam masala: A spicy hot, East Indian blend of chili, coriander seed, black pepper, cloves, cardamom, and cinnamon. Used in stews, poultry, and soups.

Herbs of Provence: A mild combination of thyme or marjoram and sometimes basil, savory, tarragon, bay, fennel, and lavender flowers. Used in sauces, soups, and stews.

Hot sauce: A spicy hot liquid made up of several kinds of hot chilies in water, vinegar, extract, oil, or juice. Used in Asian, Cajun, and Tex-Mex cooking, guacamole, burritos, tortillas, meats, fish, poultry, soups, sauces, eggs, pasta, rice, salsas, dips, beans, vegetables, and vegetable juices.

Indian five-spice powder: A spicy Bengali mixture of cumin, fennel, fenugreek, nigell seed, and radhunio (a mustardlike spice). Used in Middle Eastern and East Indian dishes.

Italian seasoning: A mixture of oregano, basil, thyme, tarragon, sugar, and salt used in almost all Italian dishes (especially those with tomatoes), on salads as a good herb mixture, and in soups and stews.

Mexican seasoning: A spicy combination of cumin, oregano, flaked chilies, cilantro, garlic, onion, sugar, and salt. Used for Mexican or Tex/Mex guacamole, beans, rice, Mexican sauce, corn, corn bread, salads, salad dressing, salsa, chili con carne, tortillas, flautas, burritos, and barbecue sauce.

(continued)

(continued)

> **Pizza seasoning:** A mild or spicy seasoning of garlic salt, onion powder (or onion salt), celery salt, oregano, basil, sugar, and often thyme. Used for pizza, spaghetti sauce, and other Italian dishes, especially those with tomatoes (mixtures differ so if you see one with tarragon, you might want to skip it — while good, it doesn't always work on pizza or tomato sauce).
>
> **Soy sauce:** A flavorful essential in Oriental cooking. A mixture of fermented soybeans, wheat, and barley for dips, meats, marinades, poultry, fish, rice, and vegetables. (Lite soy which is low sodium, is also available.) Soy sauces differ, so over time, try several to see which one suits you best.
>
> **Worcestershire:** A flavorful originally English mixture of garlic, soy sauce, onions, molasses, tamarind, lime, vinegar, and anchovies. Used to season meats, gravies, sauces, soups, and vegetables. Worcestershire has less salt than sodium-reduced or lite soy sauce.

Adding Flavor with Gravy, Sauces, and Condiments

Without salsas, sauces, gravies, relishes, chutneys, and condiments, everyday meals, especially healthy foods, would be boring.

What's a lowfat hotdog or hamburger without mustard and relish or ketchup? Corn chips without salsa? Meat without a sauce or gravy? Pasta without sauce? Gravy makes an otherwise blah baked or mashed potato yummy. Sauces give vegetables like asparagus, cauliflower, broccoli, or beans — foods you may have had a thousand times — a totally different taste. If made nutritionally sound, sauces, gravies, and relishes are the frosting on the cake, the horse that pulls the cart.

Defatting

Because many sauces, gravies, and soups are made from the flavorful base of meat drippings, you want to first remove the fat. Fatfree or light sauces don't have to mean tasteless. The right herbs and spices will fix that notion (see preceding sections).

Thickness and luxuriousness isn't determined by the essence of fat. Good taste, when you know the right flavorings to use, has nothing to do with fatty foods or gravy filled with butter. Healthy usually does mean lowering the fat and fat is often found in gravies, sauces, and roux, a sauce base. Lowfat never means low taste or texture. Here's how:

✔ **Quickest way:** Use a defatting cup or pitcher. Pour the hot drippings or soup base where meat was cooking into the cup or pitcher, the kind with the spout at the bottom. When the fat rises to the top (2 seconds), pour off the safe, fatfree tasty drippings, which come from the bottom where the spout begins.

✔ **Simplest (but not as fast) way:** Put the cooking pot right in the freezer or refrigerator for 5 to 20 minutes. When the fat congeals at the top, remove it by hand or with a spoon.

✔ **Most labor intensive, time-consuming, and ineffective way:** Spooning the fat off the top.

✔ **Most fruitless way:** Paper towel dabbing. Unfortunately, paper towels can't tell the difference between the oily fat and the liquid the fat is floating on.

Thickening

Fatfree or lowfat also doesn't mean a thin runny sauce. You can thicken any cooked sauce, soup, or gravy with cornstarch, wheat, rice or tapioca flour, mashed potatoes, breadcrumbs, arrowroot, and all manner of thickeners. If you know how to keep your sauces, soups, and gravies thick and lush, no one knows the fat is gone — except your heart, arteries, and waist line.

✔ **To thicken gravy:** First defat the drippings. *For an opaque gravy:* Whisk 2 teaspoons flour to each ½ cup defatted drippings, add 1 cup water or skim milk, and heat, stirring, for 4 minutes. *For a clear and glossy gravy:* Whisk 2 teaspoons cornstarch in ½ cup defatted drippings liquid, add 1 cup water, and heat, stirring, for 2 minutes.

✔ **To thicken rouxs:** Rouxs are a cooked mixture of flour and various amounts of fat used to often thicken meat or cheese sauces, but flour and any skim milk works just as well. Whisk 1 tablespoon flour in each cup cool skim milk or 1 percent milk or fatfree nondairy liquid creamer, evaporated skim milk, or fatfree half-and-half. Cook over low heat for 4 minutes, stirring continually. You can also use a half cornstarch and half flour mixture.

Cook any roux, sauce, soup, or gravy thickener that contains flour at least 4 minutes so that the flour loses that doughy taste.

✔ **To thicken soup:** *For thick opaque soups like cream soups, potato or corn soups, and stews:* Whisk 2 tablespoons flour per quart of soup into 1 cup cool liquid. Add the lumpfree soup and flour mixture back to the soup and simmer, stirring, for 4 minutes *For thick clear soups like Asian chicken, consommé:* Whisk 3 tablespoons cornstarch or arrowroot into 1 cup cool soup broth, add the cornstarch and broth mixture back into the soup, and stir until it thickens, about 1 minute if the soup is already hot.

Your pan of the now thick gravy, sauce, or soup base will most likely taste better with a little salt and pepper. Other enhancing herbs or spices can include one, two, or sometimes more of the following: thyme, parsley, rosemary, garlic salt, celery seed or salt, liquid smoke, Worcestershire, soy sauce, steak sauce, ketchup, and dozens of other bottled sauces and flavorings.

Flavoring Food with Alcohol

Wines, liqueurs, champagne, sherry, and other alcoholic drinks such as beer and ale are commonly used for flavoring foods. Don't worry about getting drunk, though — alcohol is burned off or dissipated in cooking. Alcohol, wine without alcohol, or the extract of alcohol (available in many flavors such as sherry) can offer a greater taste variety to food. Following are common alcohol flavors that can spruce up soups and sauces, adding something new and delicious.

Use spirits sparingly — usually a tablespoon or two to each 8 ounces of liquid. And use only good quality spirit. Never use alcohol labeled "Cooking Sherry," or "Cooking Wine." They are of the poorest quality and may contain salt, and you are wasting all your good food with a poor addition. You would never put a rotten tomato in your soup, so don't use awful liquor.

With extracts, begin with a few drops to a half teaspoons. Table 11-1 tells you where to use some of the more common extracts.

Table 11-1	Using Common Extracts
Extract or Actual Product	*Where to Use It (Add During Cooking)*
Beer	Beans, soup, meat dishes, sauces, dips
Bourbon	Barbecue sauce, beef, stews
Brandy	Desserts, meat, sauces
Burgundy	Red meat, chicken, venison
Calvados	Pork, sauces, poultry, desserts
Cassis	Fruit, sauces, meat
Chambord	Desserts, poultry, fruit, sauces
Champagne	Meat, poultry, sauces, fruit, desserts
Cider, hard	Sauces, pork, fruit
Cider, regular	Sauces, fruit, pork, vegetables
Cognac	Red meat, sauces, fruit, desserts

Extract or Actual Product	Where to Use It (Add During Cooking)
Cointreau	Desserts, poultry, sauces
Drambuie	Desserts
Frangelico	Desserts, sauces
Grand Marnier	Desserts, poultry, pork, sauces
Grenadine	Sauces, desserts
Kirsch	Fruit, desserts, sauces
Medeira	Beans, vegetables, fruits, sauces, poultry
Marsala	Beans, vegetables, fruits, sauces, poultry
Pernod	Beans, sauces
Port	Red meat, desserts, sauces, stews
Red wine	Poultry, meat, sauces
Rum	White or dark desserts, chicken, sauces
Sherry	Poultry, desserts, sauces, soups
Vermouth	Sweet and dry meats, desserts, soups, sauces
Vodka	Meats, sauces, desserts, dips, poultry
Whiskey	Red meats, sauces, desserts

Making Fabulous and Easy Recipes

If you're ready to add flavor to your food, then the recipes in this section are for you.

Tartar Sauce

Tartar sauce really does enhances almost any fish or shellfish. It's also a great sandwich spread with the addition of fresh chopped onions. If you like it sweet instead of savory, substitute sweet pickle relish for the dill relish. If you're a green pepper lover, add ¼ cup diced.

Preparation time: *5 minutes (plus 1 hour to chill)*

Yield: *1¾ cups*

(continued)

1 cup fatfree or lowfat mayonnaise

¼ cup finely chopped onions or scallions, including the green

¼ cup finely chopped dill pickles

¼ cup finely chopped pimento or red pepper (optional for color)

¼ cup chopped parsley or watercress

1 teaspoon lemon juice

In a small bowl, add all the ingredients and stir. Chill, covered, for at least 1 hour.

Nutrition at a glance (per serving): *Calories 16.2 g; Protein 0.1 g; Carbohydrates 3.6 g; Dietary fiber 0.2 g; Total fat 0.0 g; Saturated fat 0.0 g; Cholesterol 0 mg; Sodium 146.7 mg.*

Lynn's tip: *Adding a few tablespoons chopped green Kalamata olives, drained capers, or chopped anchovies (or anchovy paste) gives the sauce a more savory, slightly different flavor.*

Fiery Hot Harissa

My testers said, "Unbelievable — the best sauce we ever had." They even made it one time with chipolte peppers, and it suddenly became their favorite Mexican sauce. Harissa is originally from Tunisia and is far more developed and delicious when freshly made than the usual canned variety. Serve with meat, over couscous and on bread with olive oil. If you make it Mexican style with chipolte peppers, it can go on anything Tex/Mex — in salsa and gazpacho and on beans, tacos, burritos, and fajitas.

Preparation/Cooking time: *10 minutes*

Yield: *1½ cups*

2 cloves garlic, minced

2 tablespoons finely chopped onion

½ teaspoon caraway seeds

1 cup fatfree chicken broth

3 tablespoons tomato paste

1 teaspoon ground cumin

½ teaspoon chopped fresh cilantro

½ teaspoon finely chopped jalapeño, small red hot peppers, or chipoltes

¼ cup finely chopped pimento

1 Lightly mist a medium nonstick skillet with nonstick olive oil spray. Add the garlic, onions, and caraway seeds and cook over medium-low heat, stirring for 3 minutes.

2 Add the chicken broth and tomato paste and whisk to mix well.

3 Add the cumin, cilantro, hot peppers, and pimento and cook over medium heat, stirring 2 to 3 minutes. Store refrigerated.

Nutrition at a glance (per serving): Calories 7.5 g; Protein 0.4 g; Carbohydrates 1.5 g; Dietary fiber 0.3 g; Total fat 0.1 g; Saturated fat 0.0 g; Cholesterol 0 mg; Sodium 86.7 mg.

Lynn's tip: For extra, extra hot harissa, use fat round habenero peppers, the hottest known to man. If you want to control the heat, add hot sauce by the drop. You can use harissa anywhere you like a spicy hot flavor.

Hollandaise Sauce

Hollandaise sauce is fabulous. Use it on asparagus and broccoli or over a whole steamed cauliflower, for substitute scrambled eggs benedict. You can make it in a skillet or saucepan instead of a double boiler; however, if your stove doesn't offer a very low temperature, the heat is harder to control with the skillet or saucepan. Continual testing with a finger in the pan does the trick. (It sounds awkward, but it works.) When the eggs become too hot for your finger, the hollandaise is at the magic moment to thicken, but remember, it gets thicker as it slightly cools, in about 3 minutes.

Preparation/Cooking time: 10 minutes

Yield: About 1½ cups

3 tablespoons stick margarine

3 tablespoons fresh lemon juice, room temperature

½ to ¾ teaspoon flour

1 cup substitute eggs, room temperature

Few sprinkles cayenne

1 In a small saucepan, heat the margarine until very hot. Add the lemon juice and flour to the margarine, whisking it in well.

2 Place the egg substitute in a bowl. Add to the bowl of eggs several tablespoons of the hot margarine mixture.

3 Using a whisk over very low heat (if you stop whisking, the eggs will solidify), slowly pour the bowl contents into the saucepan taking several minutes. As you're whisking, check the temperature with your finger (this isn't as awkward as it sounds). When your finger is too hot to hold in the saucepan egg mixture, it is getting to the right temperature and will thicken. Remove from heat and continue whisking about 3 minutes. It should be thick now. Stir in the cayenne and add any salt and white pepper you wish.

Nutrition at a glance (per serving): Calories 73.4 g; Protein 4.1 g; Carbohydrates 1.6 g; Dietary fiber 0.0 g; Total fat 5.7 g; Saturated fat 1.1 g; Cholesterol 0 mg; Sodium 149.9 mg.

(continued)

Lynn's tip: When reheating hollandaise, you can easily get curdled or rock hard eggs. Heat at a very low temperature, continually whisking and checking the temperature again with your finger. I have transferred barely warm sauce into a processor or whipped it with beaters or a hand blender and then put it back on a low burner, whisking and heating for just a minute or so, which also works fine.

White Sauce

White sauce is really good with its creamy and pale white color. It can be used as a base for many sauces including cheese, curry, dill, and rosemary, among others. Serve it over fish or chicken, cauliflower, broccoli, or wherever you want a basic white sauce.

Preparation/Cooking time: 12 minutes

Yield: 3 cups

1 tablespoon butter, margarine, or diet margarine

3 tablespoons flour

2 cups skim milk

1 cup fatfree nondairy liquid creamer

White pepper

1 In a saucepan, add the margarine, flour, and 1 cup milk and continually whisk over low heat for 2 minutes, being sure to smooth out any lumps.

2 Add the rest of the milk, creamer, and white pepper and simmer, whisking, until the mixture thickens, at least 4 minutes to cook the flour so that it doesn't taste doughy.

Nutrition at a glance (per serving): Calories 49.8 g; Protein 1.6 g; Carbohydrates 4.8 g; Dietary fiber 0.1 g; Total fat 1.1 g; Saturated fat 0.6 g; Cholesterol 3.3 mg; Sodium 37.5 mg.

Lynn's tip: Add ½ cup chopped fresh dill for dill sauce for fish or chicken. For macaroni and cheese or as a topping for a baked potato, pasta, toast, broccoli or cauliflower, omit the dill and add a mixture of ¼ cup fatfree shredded mozzarella and ¼ cup regular shredded mozzarella cheese while heating and whisking it. You can experiment with the cheese, using sharper Cheddars or milder varieties. Try and keep the full-fat versions to a minimum, mixing them with lowfat varieties.

Papaya and Mango Tropical Salsa

With both papayas and mangoes available in bottles all season, you don't have to wait for only the fresh. This is a great salsa with a spicy black bean dish or conversely, a plain bean recipe. It adds to both, chilling the tongue when with hot flavors, adding a sweet cool flavorful relish when the beans are bland. It is a treat with a plain white fish or skinless poultry.

Preparation time: *10 minutes*

Yield: *4 cups*

1 cup chopped fresh pineapple

2 small papayas or peaches, peeled and diced

1 cup chopped fresh mango

½ cup chopped scallions, including some of the green

½ finely diced red pepper

½ finely diced green pepper

2 tablespoons chopped fresh mint leaves

2 tablespoons chopped fresh basil

3 tablespoons fresh lime juice

Minced jalapeño pepper, or hot red pepper flakes to taste

In a medium bowl, combine all ingredients, add any salt and pepper you wish, and allow them to rest for about 30 minutes.

Nutrition at a glance (per serving): *Calories 45.8 g; Protein 0.7 g; Carbohydrates 11.7 g; Dietary fiber 1.8 g; Total fat 0.2 g; Saturated fat 0.0 g; Cholesterol 0 mg; Sodium 3.3 mg.*

Lynn's tip: *Mix in a clove or 2 of minced garlic to give this salsa an extra snap.*

Chicken, Turkey, Beef, or Ham Gravy

This gravy is so good. If you defat the drippings properly, it is nearly 100 percent fatfree and no one is the wiser. All the taste is still there, whether it is made from roasted or microwaved whole chicken (in a bag), Thanksgiving turkey, beef roast, lamb roast, or ham roast. To make the ham version a breakfast gravy, add ⅓ cup hot coffee (which makes it the traditional "red eye gravy").

Preparation/Cooking time: *12 minutes*

Yield: *About 2 cups*

(continued)

½ to 1 cup of liquid drippings (collect from the roasting pan or oven bag)

1 10-¾ can fatfree chicken or beef broth or stock (or homemade) or water or skim milk (for Southern gravy).

2 tablespoons cornstarch

2 tablespoons flour

½ teaspoon Maggi Seasoning, Bovril, Gravy Master, Kitchen Bouquet, or Spike (optional)

1 Defat the drippings using a defatting cup or placing them in the freezer for 5 minutes and removing the congealed fat.

2 To a nonstick saucepan, add the fatfree drippings, stock, cornstarch, flour, and seasoning, if using, including salt and pepper.

3 Begin whisking while cool. Turn the heat to medium, bring to a boil, and then reduce heat to a simmer. Whisk continually for 4 minutes (to thoroughly cook the flour or it will taste doughy) until thick.

Nutrition at a glance (per serving): *Calories 16.3 g; Protein 0.4 g; Carbohydrates 3.5 g; Dietary fiber 0.1 g; Total fat 0.0 g; Saturated fat 0.0 g; Cholesterol 0 mg; Sodium 101.8 mg.*

Lynn's tip: *If you've been so successful removing the fat from your beef or poultry that you don't have enough drippings to make ½ cup, add ½ hot water to the pan; deglaze by stirring the hot water and glaze; pouring it all into a defatting cup; defat; and use what you have. If you cook the skinned chicken or beef in an oven bag either in the microwave or oven you'll have plenty of drippings.*

Easy Chili and Steak Sauce

My most critical tester rated this sauce an A+. Spicy and cold, this unique mixture of what you already have in your refrigerator door is really incredible with steaks or roast beef, barbecued lamb, lowfat hotdogs, or veggie burgers. Stirring in several drops of hot sauce spikes it up. This sauce has lots of taste, looks, and texture.

Preparation time: *5 minutes*

Yield: *About 2 cups*

1 cup chili sauce or ketchup

¼ cup chopped green olives

¼ cup chopped pepperoncini peppers

¼ cup chopped ripe olives

¼ cup chopped onions or scallions

1 teaspoon fresh lemon juice

In a small bowl, add all the ingredients and mix well.

Nutrition at a glance (per serving): Calories 23.7 g; Protein 0.5 g; Carbohydrates 4.8 g; Dietary fiber 0.4 g; Total fat 0.5 g; Saturated fat 0.1 g; Cholesterol 0 mg; Sodium 349.8 mg.

Lynn's tip: The exact amounts aren't important, and you can add a tablespoon or 2 of many other condiments, such as chow chow relish, jalapeño peppers, and pickled or fresh chopped onions.

Barbecue Sauce

Thick, tangy and somewhat sweet, this basic sauce can be modified to a less sweet or spicier version by decreasing the sugar and increasing the chili powder, mustard, and hot sauce. Use in basting. For dipping, use the cooked version (both are given). Good for burgers, lamb, ribs (boil these first to lose some of the fat), poultry, fish, potatoes, chips, and for raw celery, carrots, corn, and as a topping for cooked beans.

Preparation time: 5 to 10 minutes

Yield: About 2½ cups

1 onion, chopped	1 tablespoon Worcestershire sauce
2 cloves garlic, minced	1 tablespoon low-sodium soy sauce
½ cup maple syrup or brown sugar	1 cup chili sauce or catsup
1 to 2 tablespoons cider vinegar	1 to 3 tablespoons chili powder
¼ cup sour cherry or apricot or other tart jelly	1 tablespoon prepared mustard
	Several drops Tabasco
½ teaspoon lemon juice	

For basting: In a medium bowl, add all the ingredients and mix well. *For dipping:* Lightly spray a saucepan, add the onions and garlic, and heat over medium heat, stirring for 3 minutes. Add all other ingredients, plus salt and pepper, and simmer over medium heat, uncovered, stirring occasionally, for 5 minutes.

Nutrition at a glance (per serving): Calories 102.4 g; Protein 1.1 g; Carbohydrates 25.4 g; Dietary fiber 1.0 g; Total fat 0.3 g; Saturated fat 0.0 g; Cholesterol 0 mg; Sodium 463.8 mg.

Lynn's tip: You can make lots of additions to barbecue sauce such as orange peel if you are a Californian, rum if you like a Jamaican sauce, or bourbon if you are from Tennessee. You can also add celery salt, honey, vinegar, cumin, lemon juice, molasses, and lots of hot sauce.

Basting or Dipping Spicy Plum Sauce

Cooked, this tangy sweet sauce is great for chicken and ham dipping; uncooked, it's just right for basting a whole chicken or ham, poultry tenders, fish, or barbecued vegetables such as onions, carrots, and peppers. Brush on fruits, such as grapefruit halves and pineapple slices, and bake or grill.

Preparation/Cooking time: *5 to 15 minutes*

Yield: *2½ cups*

½ cup brown sugar

1 tablespoon vinegar

1 16 to 18-ounce canned plums, pitted and chopped, with syrup

2 tablespoons fresh lemon juice

2 tablespoons Worcestershire sauce

1 ½ tablespoons low-sodium soy sauce

2 cloves garlic, minced

1 onion, finely chopped

1 tablespoon prepared mustard

Several drops hot sauce or chili paste

1 tablespoon cornstarch

Uncooked: To a large bowl, add the sugar, vinegar, plums, lemon juice, Worcestershire sauce, soy sauce, garlic, onion, mustard, and hot sauce (not the cornstarch) and mix well. Use uncooked for basting foods to be cooked. *Cooked:* To a small saucepan, add all ingredients except for the plum syrup and cornstarch. Mix the plum syrup with 1 tablespoon cornstarch and set aside. Over medium-low heat, simmer all ingredients, uncovered for 15 minutes, stirring occasionally. Add the syrup and cornstarch mixture and heat for 3 minutes, stirring. Puree when finished with a hand blender or in a processor or blender.

Nutrition at a glance (per serving): *Calories 47.8 g; Protein 0.3 g; Carbohydrates 12.2 g; Dietary fiber 0.4 g; Total fat 0.1 g; Saturated fat 0.0 g; Cholesterol 0 mg; Sodium 73.2 mg.*

Sweet and Sour Sauce

This recipe was voted the very best sweet and sour sauce my testers had ever had, and they don't mince words. A clever mix of cider vinegar and sugar, this sauce has both a light piquant and deep pungent taste.

Preparation/Cooking time: *10 minutes*

Yield: *2 cups*

½ cup cider vinegar

¼ cup brown sugar

½ cup thawed, frozen pineapple, lemon, or orange juice concentrate

¼ cup finely chopped onions

½ clove minced garlic

½ cup finely chopped green pepper, plus the seeds

2 tablespoons cornstarch

2 tablespoons low-sodium soy sauce

2 tablespoons finely chopped scallions

1 In a small saucepan, heat the cider vinegar, sugar, frozen juice concentrate, onions, garlic, green pepper, and pepper seeds over medium heat, simmer, stirring until the onions, pepper, and garlic are cooked, about 3 minutes.

2 Mix the cornstarch in the soy sauce and add to the mixture, stirring until it is thick, about 30 seconds.

3 Remove from heat and stir in the raw scallions.

Nutrition at a glance (per serving): *Calories 75.0 g; Protein 0.6 g; Carbohydrates 18.9 g; Dietary fiber 0.4 g; Total fat 0.0 g; Saturated fat 0.0 g; Cholesterol 0 mg; Sodium 137.4 mg.*

Lynn's tip: *You can add other flavors such as orange or lemon zest, canned crushed pineapple, diced Queen Anne cherries, ginger, or Chinese Hot Oil. You can also substitute brown sugar for the white sugar. Don't use fresh pineapple because the enzyme in it won't let it gel or thicken.*

Dill Dip

This dill dip is simple, good on sandwiches, fish, seafood mousse, and as a dip for many cold vegetables. It mixes together better if the ingredients are room temperature.

Preparation time: *5 minutes*

Yield: *1½ cups*

½ teaspoon dry mustard

½ cup lowfat sour cream,

¼ cup fatfree buttermilk

¼ cup reduced-fat cream cheese, room temperature

¼ cup finely chopped fresh dill, or ⅓ cup chopped dried dill

½ teaspoon onion salt

½ teaspoon cracked pepper

In a small bowl, beat together all the ingredients well and chill. Serve cold.

Chapter 12

Easy In, Easy Out: Basics for One-Skillet, One-Pot Meals

In This Chapter

▶ Making ready-to-cook meals

▶ Creating great one-skillet meals

▶ Using prepared foods healthfully and deliciously

▶ Getting out the extra salt while adding better flavor, more appeal, and even more fiber

*I*f you don't like to mess around in the kitchen, then this chapter is for you. Whether you're cooking for one, a couple, or a great big family, you get the magic formulas for making good food fast and simple.

In this chapter, I tell you the equipment you might want and the directions for cooking great meals — which are usually simply "put the food in the pan and turn on the heat." You also discover what kinds of foods to keep handy to make lots of easy fast meals and how to make those foods better and more nutritious.

What Are One-Skillet, One-Pot Meals?

When I say *one-skillet or one-pot meals,* I simply mean that you add all ingredients at the same time to one cooking vessel and cook them together. That's the ideal. Almost all the recipes in this chapter use only one pot, but sometimes you have two steps. However, none of these recipes takes any longer to prepare than 25 minutes.

One-skillet or one-pot meals from your store aren't the same old Rice-a-Roni and Hamburger Helper. Store-bought packaged meals have changed and expanded, and the changes are good. Numerous new shelf brands have popped into this fast-growing market. Old brands like Lipton's are offering several new packaged meals. There's a brand called Bean Cuisine, and there are others — mixtures of dried beans where can introduce your own additions, measure in some liquid, heat it, and voilà, you have a delicious meal in no time. Beans have never been so easy. Or so quick.

One-skillet or one-pot meals are a great starting point. Look carefully in your refrigerator and freezer cases. You'll see cold or frozen packaged meals, such as rice dishes with chicken strips, that cook in minutes. These prepackaged meals usually have only a meager amount of vegetables and serve only a few people. But you can round out the meal and increase the number of servings by adding vegetables, such as corn, green and red pepper, and diced tomatoes, plus a garnish of diced avocados and chopped onions. Making additions also dilutes the high salt content of these prepackaged meals and adds fiber and color.

With a few tips and hints, you won't need much convincing that one-skillet recipes and package meals available in markets are not only healthful and nutritious, but fast and quite tasty. So don't turn up your nose because the onions aren't first sautéed and caramelized or the chicken comes already cooked from the grocery deli department. Use these items to make your life easier, not to take the place of all your own freshly made foods.

Why you should try one-skillet or one-pot meals

Skillet and single pot meals require little effort, which is important for busy lives. And if you always, always vow to add a few (or lots) of your own fresh ingredients, which is often not suggested on the package, you reap the advantages of time saved, good-tasting food, extra fiber, and great nutrition. In addition, these simple, one pot, at-home food-preps have four great advantages:

- These meals are less expensive than eating out.

- You don't have to expend a lot of effort to make the meal.

- Your meal is on the table fast.

- You have little cleanup — only one pot or skillet (plus the dishes and silver).

Mastering One-Pot, One-Skillet Meals

Making one-pot or one-skillet meals is simple. You just need the right equipment. If you don't have one, consider purchasing a Crock-Pot, pressure cooker, or automatic rice maker. (If you need a new oven, you can even buy one with timed cooking. Or, simply get out the old electric frying pan for ease and speed.)

✔ **Crock-pots:** These great old-timey innovations have been rediscovered. They are slow cookers, which means that you cook foods a long time on low heat — a great flavor booster! Slow cooking brings out wonderful flavors in meats especially. The joy of these cookers is that they require very little of your time and do the cooking while you're away doing your living.

Sometimes, you can buy less expensive cuts of meat because the slow cooking makes them very tender. In the past, less expensive cuts were without fat, while expensive cuts were well marbled with fat. Today, it's the reverse. Less expensive cuts are now usually the fatty cuts, while more expensive cuts are zero trimmed and contain little fat.

Use your eyes. Select cuts with as little fat as possible.

Never heard of a crock-pot? Your grandmother did. Rival makes the original Crock-Pot, a crockery-style pot with a glass serving bowl insert (most are made of glass, plastic, and other materials), a lid, and a timer, but other manufacturers have begun to offer their own good versions of electric pot cookers. You plug them in, add your food, turn on the timer, and cook for 1 to 8 hours. It is good for foods that can stay at a certain temperature for many hours.

Not all crock-pot-style cookers have timers and letting meat sit for hours, unless the temperature is fairly high, is not good.

✔ **Pressure and fusion cookers:** These fabulous '40s innovations cook foods like stews, roasts, potatoes, artichokes, and other long-cooking foods in just a few minutes. Using a pressure or fusion cooker, you can cook many nutritious dishes easily. Today, pressure cookers are safe and secure. Many good companies make them. T-Fal makes an especially handy one called a *fusion cooker* with a securable lid (without that little extra thing on the top that always gets lost) and two different sizes of stainless steel pot bottoms.

Here is why you will love a pressure or fusion cooker. Spare ribs and vegetables cook perfectly in 15 minutes. (You have to spoon off the fat, however.) A whole chicken and vegetables cook perfectly in 15 minutes, the food tastes great, there is a fusion of flavors, and it's an easy cleanup. I regularly use my mother's 50-year-old 6-quart aluminum pressure cooker with a rubber gasket that is, remarkably, still good.

✔ **Automatic rice and vegetable steamers:** These are for rice alone or rice with onions, mushrooms, peas, and any meat so that the rice steams with all the other foods. Rice steamers don't cook rice any more quickly, but they save time as you don't have to guess or keep looking at it. Black and Decker makes a simple one for under $30, and other companies make them for near that price and every price up to $200. They are worth it if you love rice and want to make more rice, but don't want to watch the clock.

✔ **Electric frying pans:** These were popular 30 years ago, and they cook one-skillet meals pretty well, if you can find them (see Figure 12-1). They often are big and square with a heat grid on the bottom and controls in the handle. You put the food in the skillet, turn on the timer, cover, and cook about 25 minutes, or however long you want to. If the foods are low in fat, electric frying pans can be a healthy and easy way to prepare foods, although you need to add proper liquid or spritz with cooking oil spray before adding the vegetables.

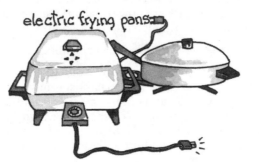

electric frying pans

Figure 12-1:
Electric
frying pan.

✔ **Countertop electric grillers:** A boon to singles and small families who like grilled foods quickly, most of these do simple grilling of meats, fish, fruits, and vegetables well. George Foreman's grill is tipped permanently so that the grease runs off (you can add little risers to make it level). The tipping of the Foreman grill is especially helpful for those who like hamburgers or chops occasionally, because nearly all are greasy. Some grills are slightly safer as the grease catch dish is attached. Once I forgot to even place the grease catching dish, and fat was everywhere. However, the less-tipped grills don't do as good a runoff job.

Improving Packaged Foods: What You Need

One way to make good meals on the table quickly is to purchase some of the many packages of dried or frozen foods to help you so that you don't have to slave over a sauce or try and figure out which spice to use. It's already done.

One way to make quick one-skillet meals is to keep the right kinds of foods available so that you can easily throw something together. One-pot or one-skillet meals don't take much planning, and it is often the way I cook most days. I am convinced stir-fries became popular because the whole meal (sans rice perhaps) was cooked in one wok — or skillet.

Keep the following foods on hand for easy one-skillet meals, which are really quick and healthy:

- ✔ Assortment of condiments, like ketchup, soy sauce, Worcestershire sauce, and mustard, to easily flavor foods

- ✔ Bottled pasta sauce for pasta and pizza

- ✔ Box of ready-made taco shells for quick tacos

- ✔ Boxes of semiprepared foods, where you add your own ingredients

- ✔ Canned baked beans (get the lowfat kind) to use as a base to make, extend, or improve homemade baked beans

- ✔ Canned pinto, kidney, and other beans to add to soups, salads, and cooked dishes

- ✔ Canned chicken to add to salads, stews, chicken soup, and other dishes

- ✔ Canned or frozen corn to add to soups, Mexican food, dishes with tomatoes, and beans

- ✔ Canned green beans to add to salads, soups, and casseroles

- ✔ Canned potatoes to add to soups, creamed dishes, and quick stews

- ✔ Canned soups (low sodium and lowfat) to use as a base to make homemade soup or to flavor casseroles

- ✔ Canned stew to use as a base to make soup or stew

- ✔ Canned tomatoes to add to chili, casseroles, beans, soups, and stews

- ✔ Canned tuna or salmon to add to any salad, casserole, and purees for dips (added to reduced-fat cream cheese) and to make patties

- ✔ Canned vegetarian chili to use as a base for chili and to make tacos

- ✔ Fresh and canned mushrooms to add to creamed dishes, pasta, stews, soups, and stir-fries

✔ Quick-cooking brown or white rice, barley, dried red lentils (they cook in 15 minutes), and canned lentil soups to add to nearly any dish

✔ Fresh and frozen chopped onions to add to any dish

✔ Fresh and frozen diced green peppers to add to any dish

✔ Fresh and frozen assortment of ready-to-cook vegetables to add to any dish

✔ Frozen vegetables with sauce (lowfat) to use as a base for other dishes

✔ Frozen mixed vegetables to add to any dish

✔ Frozen plain pizzas so that you can add large amounts of your own chopped mushrooms, onions, peppers, and pasta sauce

✔ Hard-cooked eggs whites to add to salads, creamed casseroles, semi-prepared dishes, deviled eggs, and egg salad (with the last two you still don't use the yolks)

✔ Quick-cooking pasta and lasagna noodles to make a fast pasta dish. It speeds up the time although it still has to be boiled or rehydrated with enough water for a microwave or oven-baked dish. The packages say "Quick Pasta" or "precooked pasta."

✔ Quick-cooking rice (white, brown, and wild) to add to any Asian, Mexican, Mediterranean, and Middle Eastern dish or any other dish or meal using rice

✔ Salsa for tacos, tortillas, chips, dips, Mexican food, and guacamole

Fixing Any Problems with Packaged Meals

The major markets carry on their shelves literally hundreds of packages of mixes ready to make into entrees or sides. From stuffing to rice mixtures, most can be made in less than 30 minutes. The refrigerated and frozen sections even carry entrees with meat, poultry, and shrimp already added. (I think they also need additions of fresh chopped vegetables.)

These packaged meals might be rice and lentils with flavor packets, pasta and rice with flavor packets, noodles alfredo, rice or pasta Parmesan, rice and beans with flavor packets, pasta and dehydrated chicken or beef, ramen noodles with flavor packets, and dozens and dozens more. With some, you just buy the flavor packets and add all your own chicken, pork, rice, noodles or whatever you want. With others, you add just a few items; with still others, everything is there — meat, vegetables, and rice — in the package.

But, as with anything, you may run into problems when you prepare these meals. Following are some common problems with dry packaged meals and ways to fix them:

- **Finished dish looks unappetizing or not like the picture on the package.** Don't worry about how the food will look. You can fix it. Your dish won't look like it does on the package. Stylists have arranged every morsel for that picture, and it is photographed so closely that a tiny cube of chicken looks like the whole breast. Upon closer inspection of the photo, you see the green is a parsley garnish and the red that made the photo so pretty is a slice of tomato on the plate.

  Answer: The photographer and stylist knew that the dish needed red and green, so take their tip and add your own red and green vegetables or garnish. For the green, add frozen peas, green beans, asparagus, or chopped parsley. If it needs red, too, add diced tomatoes, pimentos, red peppers, and so on. With a small dice, the vegetables won't even need cooking. Add them anyway for fiber and nutrients. Your food will be prettier than the picture.

- **The flavor isn't fresh or as good or as expected.** Dehydrated packaged foods, where liquid is removed, can sit for months on a shelf. They also contain many chemicals, most harmless, to retard spoilage, and that all affects taste. Plus, manufacturers don't always use appropriate herbs and spices like fresh parsley because they won't store unrefrigerated and dried herbs and spices can taste like grass.

  Answer: Add plenty of your own fresh ingredients, such as diced vegetables, raisins, grains, and maybe some of your own fresh or dried herbs and spices. If it's a lentil and rice dish, add your own carrots and onions during the cooking. If it's pasta Alfredo, add fatfree skim milk, fatfree half-and-half, or nondairy fatfree creamer (the last two have a creamier flavor), plus fresh peas, mushrooms, and diced tomatoes. The fatty cream sauce is diluted without becoming thin, you get more fiber, it goes further, you can have a larger portion, and it tastes better.

- **The flavor packets are stale or too salty.** Spice and herb packets can be old. Time usually doesn't affect the dried items, such as rice, beans, or pasta, but the ingredients in the flavor packets can taste stale. Many packages aren't dated.

  Answer: Smell the flavor packet as soon as you open it. Staleness can be detected because it smells like old grease (which is what goes stale). I use only one half the flavor pac anyway. You get less salt, and most flavor packets are too strong even when fresh. You can add the rest of the packet if it tastes okay.

Flavor packets are made to flavor instantly and don't need much cooking, so if the dish is cooked and you decide you want more, you can add it. If it really is stale — and many are — tell the market manager. They will refund your money. It's a good idea to buy foods with flavor packets in stores that have lots of business so that the turnover is quick and the packages don't sit on the shelves for months.

Too much salt? Companies also rely on adding excessive amounts of salt and sometimes, especially if it is an Asian flavor, sugar.

Answer: Read labels and compare the sodium content. The suggested daily upper limit is 2,400 mg; if the package contains 1,500 mg per serving for one meal, it's excessive. Sugar can't really be compared because the natural sugar from milk, fruit, and some vegetables are counted as sugar. Adding many fresh, frozen, or canned low-sodium vegetables and maybe even your own cooked rice, barley, pasta or canned drained beans dilutes the salt and other ingredients that aren't fresh. Fresh vegetables also add flavor and fiber.

✔ **Number of servings on the package is too small.** Often serving sizes don't match what the label says, Occasionally, the meal has too few servings. The serving sizes are set by the FDA with a goal of standardizing them and are based on what consumers eat from consumption studies. Check them anyway. I bought a package of small crackers, which said the serving size was 18 crackers, far too many for me at one sitting. But in most cases, entrees or side-dish packaged foods have serving sizes that go the other way. Many times a package will say it has four servings, and it barely serves two. One frozen entree package of a well-known brand of linguine alfredo said it served two and a half people. It barely served me. Manufacturers may want the calories to look low, so they may deliberately slightly decrease the serving size.

Creating One-Skillet or One-Pot Recipes

I know you can't always get every nuance of flavor cooking all the food together in one pot. A few dishes don't lend themselves to one-pot cooking, and they are in this book, too. But there are 500 more that do. So try it. Add your own favorite foods. Be bold. Your time and health is worth it.

One-Skillet Chicken Stew

There is nothing better than a great chicken stew. To speed up this recipe, use pre-chopped fresh onions, which are available in large markets and sold in packages marked stew or stir-fry onions, with mushrooms and peppers, or as frozen diced onions.

Preparation/Cooking time: 25 minutes

Yield: 4 servings

2 16-ounce cans fatfree chicken broth	*10 baby carrots, cut in half*
5 tablespoons flour	*2 stalks celery, thinly sliced*
8 ounces skinless, boneless chicken breasts, cut into bite-sized pieces	*1 clove garlic, minced, or 1 teaspoon bottled chopped garlic*
2 tablespoons diced red pepper or pimento	*2 tablespoons chopped parsley*
1 medium onion, chopped	*2 cups shell or gnocchi-style pasta, dry*

1 In a pressure cooker, large saucepan, or microwavable dish, add the broth and flour and whisk together.

2 Add the chicken, peppers, onions, carrots, celery, garlic, parsley, and pasta and any salt you wish. Pressure cook for 5 minutes; cook on the stove top for 12 minutes after boiling starts; or microwave for 8 minutes or until the pasta is cooked.

Nutrition at a glance (per serving): Calories 304.45 g; Protein 20.15 g; Carbohydrates 48.97 g; Dietary fiber 2.67 g; Total fat 2.38 g; Saturated fat 0.53 g; Cholesterol 31.33 mg; Sodium 663.65 mg.

Lynn's tip: To make this a soup instead of a stew, add another can of broth. For extra seasonings, add 1 tablespoon chopped fresh thyme (or ½ tablespoon dried) and one 2-inch sprig rosemary (or 1 teaspoon finely chopped) and stir in a chicken bouillon cube. For those who like it, a dash of sweet or dry sherry along with the seasonings makes this extra good.

Tex-Mex Chicken and Corn Sauté

Tex-Mex food with the mixtures of flavors is tempting for nearly everyone. (You can use this recipe for fajitas, too — just wrap in heated flour tortillas.) For a change from the salsa topping, garnish with a dollop of lowfat sour cream, diced onions and avocados, and a sprinkle of sliced black olives. You can substitute turkey or lean pork for the chicken. (See photo in color insert.)

(continued)

Preparation/Cooking time: 25 minutes

Yield: 4 servings

1½ tablespoons chili powder

½ teaspoon ground cumin

2 tablespoons lime juice or fatfree chicken stock

4 4-ounce skinless, boneless chicken breasts, cut in long, thin, but bite-sized pieces

1 medium onion, sliced (cut in half and then sliced with flat side on board)

2 medium green bell peppers, cut into thin strips

2 medium red bell peppers, cut into thin strips

1 10-ounce package frozen corn, unopened package hit on counter to separate kernels

1 cup bottled salsa or a few drops hot sauce (optional)

1 In a plastic bag or large shallow dish, add the chili powder, cumin, lime juice or chicken stock, and any salt and pepper you wish and coat the chicken and onions. (If you want, you can marinate or "keep" in the refrigerator for several hours.)

2 Lightly spray a large skillet with cooking oil spray. Over medium-high heat, add the chicken and onions and any spice mixture left in the bag or dish and sauté, stirring for 6 to 8 minutes.

3 Add the peppers and corn, lightly spray the vegetables, and stir, sautéing for 5 to 6 minutes.

4 Serve with the salsa or a few drops hot sauce over each serving.

Nutrition at a glance (per serving): Calories 235.1 g; Protein 26.7 g; Carbohydrates 26.8 g; Dietary fiber 5.7 g; Total fat 3.7 g; Saturated fat 0.9 g; Cholesterol 62.7 mg; Sodium 90.5 mg.

Lynn's tip: This is the perfect dish to look for packages of precut vegetables and strips of meat. Some brands have meat already grilled and cut into strips, cutting cooking time in half.

One-Pot Rice and Black Beans

Canned black beans usually don't have much added flavor, but they're easy to perk up. You can use other canned beans such as pinto, navy, field peas (which are a type of bean), or anything else interesting. Kidney beans might work, but I have never tried them.

Preparation/Cooking time: 10 minutes

Yield: 4 servings

2 packets 10-minute Success brand brown or white rice (makes 2 cups, cooked)

2 15.5-ounce cans black beans, drained and rinsed

1 large onion, chopped

¾ teaspoon dried oregano

Several dashes hot sauce

1 avocado sliced into 12 slices, coated with lemon juice (optional)

1 cup lowfat sour cream

1 tomato, diced

1 to 2 limes, cut into wedges

1 Cut the rice packets open and add to a large saucepan along with about 3 cups water (enough to cover the rice).

2 Add the beans, onions, oregano, and hot sauce, stirring to mix. Bring to a boil over medium-high heat, stirring occasionally.

3 Reduce the heat and simmer on low for 10 minutes, or until all liquid is absorbed. Fan 3 slices of avocado over the rice and beans, place a large dollop of sour cream in the center, sprinkle diced tomatoes, and serve with the lime wedge.

Nutrition at a glance (per serving): Calories 483.0 g; Protein 23.2 g; Carbohydrates 84.6 g; Dietary fiber 16.8 g; Total fat 7.2 g; Saturated fat 4.2 g; Cholesterol 20.0 mg; Sodium 416.0 mg.

Lynn's tip: You can add cooked fresh, frozen, or canned corn kernels under the beans and rice as a surprise or serve alongside this dish. If you have an onion or cilantro lover, add ¼ cup diced raw onions on 1 side of the serving dish next to the soup bowl and 2 tablespoons chopped cilantro (to be added in amounts desired while eating).

One-Pot Poor Man's Pasta

Easy and fast, this is a somewhat sweet dish (because of the carrots and barbecue sauce), yet it's very tasty and filling. It's also fresh-tasting with the crunch of the celery. You can vary the dish with some quick additions, such as a small can of drained mushrooms.

(continued)

Preparation/Cooking time: 20 minutes

Yield: 6 servings

½ pound ground 93 percent lean ground or diced top sirloin

1 medium onion, chopped

1 teaspoon minced garlic

½ pound angel hair pasta, broken in half

1 14.5-ounce can diced red tomatoes with Italian-style herbs (or 1 large tomato, diced, with 2 pinches each of oregano and basil).

1 cup shredded carrots

1 stalk celery, thinly sliced

1 10-ounce package frozen French-style green beans

¼ cup barbecue sauce

1 Lightly spray a pot or high-sided skillet (such as an iron frying pan or Dutch oven) with cooking spray. Brown the meat, onions, and garlic for 6 to 8 minutes over medium-high heat, stirring often.

2 Add 3 cups water and bring meat and water to a boil.

3 Add the angel hair, tomatoes, carrots, and celery and, over high heat, return to a boil. Reduce heat to medium-low. Cover and cook for 6 to 8 minutes or until the pasta is al dente.

4 Add the green beans and barbecue sauce and cook for 1 to 2 minutes or until green beans are heated.

Nutrition at a glance (per serving): Calories 252.4 g; Protein 14.6 g; Carbohydrates 39.8 g; Dietary fiber 4.0 g; Total fat 3.7 g; Saturated fat 1.2 g; Cholesterol 22.5 mg; Sodium 462.9 mg.

Lynn's tip: You can make this recipe with 10-minute brown rice or two 15-ounce cans of beans instead of the pasta.

Use any excuse to add fresh vegetables to packaged meals

Add fresh vegetables to every packaged, frozen, or canned meal as they dramatically improve the taste and look of packaged meals and dilute any excess salt or sugar. If you add fresh long-cooking vegetables like carrots, beets, celery, mushrooms, onions, or potatoes, be sure that they're cooked and hot first. Most frozen vegetables seldom need precooking because they're already lightly steamed at the company food prep site before freezing. All canned foods, including vegetables, are thoroughly cooked right in the can.

Chapter 13

Vigorously Healthy Vegetarian and Vegan Meals

● ●

In This Chapter

▶ Understanding the different types of vegetarians

▶ Discovering why you should eat veggies

▶ Creating fabulous vegetarian dishes

● ●

> **Recipes in This Chapter**
>
> ♂ Pasta Alfredo
> ♂ Beets in Pineapple Sauce
> ♂ Green Beans with Mushrooms
> ♂ Greek-Style Cauliflower
> ♂ Pasta with French Broccoli and Pine Nuts
> ♂ Peas and Cheese-Stuffed Baked Potatoes
> ♂ Spicy Island Carrots
> ♂ Tofu Mayonnaise
> ♂ Dinner Fruit Salad with Cantaloupe Dressing
>
> 🍴 🥚 ♂ 🥕 ≽

*1*n this chapter, you find only vegetarian and vegan recipes, in case you want to take healthy eating a step further. Conversely, you can add meat to all the recipes in this chapter.

In addition, if you're curious about the term vegan and some of the other terms used to describe certain diets such as macrobiotics, ovolacto, and such, you can find the descriptions here, too.

I also explain why eating vegetarian is not only less expensive than dishes with meat, but also how it can be easier, faster, and healthier.

There's Not Just One Kind of Vegetarian

You know vegetables are good for you. For health, religious, spiritual, scientific, or animal cruelty issues or reasons, you have to respect both vegetarians and vegans. They literally put their money where their mouth is. And their effort. Here are a few terms in case you're wondering what it all means.

What's a vegan anyway?

"Vegans (are) . . . the purest of the vegetarian world and who have the most limited diet, refuse to eat all animal derivative foods including butter, cheese, eggs and milk."

— *Food Lover's Companion,* Sharon Tyler Herst

- **Macrobiotic:** Originally thought to be a yin and yang balance, it is a diet consisting entirely of grains. (Not a balanced diet.)

- **Vegan:** Someone who eats no animal products whatsoever. (May not be a balanced diet.)

- **Strict vegetarian:** Someone who eats primarily grains, vegetables, fruits, and sometimes eggs, but may not eat cheese or other dairy. (Can be a balanced diet.)

- **Mostly or sometimes vegetarian:** Someone who eats primarily grains, vegetables, fungi, and fruits, but occasionally does eat cheese, eggs, fish, milk, and sometimes chicken. (Can be a balanced diet.)

- **Almost vegetarian or a plant-based dieter:** Someone who eats primarily grains, vegetables, and fruits, only occasionally takes a bite or two of red meat, and eats cheese, eggs, milk, poultry, and fish often. (Can be a balanced diet.)

Preparing Veggies

In addition to being healthy for you, vegetables are quick. They're plentiful and easy to prepare because most require simple cooking or little or no cooking. Even the hardest vegetables, like beets, potatoes, squash, and carrots, are easy to prepare. Vegetables should make up a large part of your diet.

Vegetarian Americans

Seven to eight percent of Americans are vegetarian, say the latest figures. Some folks call themselves vegetarians although they eat fish or chicken or both, so we don't have accurate figures on how many *strict vegetarians,* people who eat no animal products, there really are. We do know that a study of Seventh Day Adventists, a Protestant religious group that doesn't eat meat, pointed out that they live longer and with less incidence of heart disease than the general population who do eat meat. Seventh Day Adventists do eat cheese, milk, and other dairy.

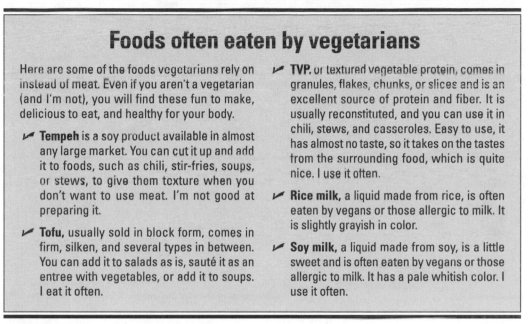

Foods often eaten by vegetarians

Here are some of the foods vegetarians rely on instead of meat. Even if you aren't a vegetarian (and I'm not), you will find these fun to make, delicious to eat, and healthy for your body.

✔ **Tempeh** is a soy product available in almost any large market. You can cut it up and add it to foods, such as chili, stir-fries, soups, or stews, to give them texture when you don't want to use meat. I'm not good at preparing it.

✔ **Tofu,** usually sold in block form, comes in firm, silken, and several types in between. You can add it to salads as is, sauté it as an entree with vegetables, or add it to soups. I eat it often.

✔ **TVP,** or textured vegetable protein, comes in granules, flakes, chunks, or slices and is an excellent source of protein and fiber. It is usually reconstituted, and you can use it in chili, stews, and casseroles. Easy to use, it has almost no taste, so it takes on the tastes from the surrounding food, which is quite nice. I use it often.

✔ **Rice milk,** a liquid made from rice, is often eaten by vegans or those allergic to milk. It is slightly grayish in color.

✔ **Soy milk,** a liquid made from soy, is a little sweet and is often eaten by vegans or those allergic to milk. It has a pale whitish color. I use it often.

Here are some veggie prep tips.

✔ Make sure that you wash your veggies well with soap and rinse them well.

✔ A few spoiled areas often doesn't mean that you need to toss the veggie. Cut them off.

✔ Don't overcook vegetables unless you want that particular flavor. Look for a brightened color for colored veggies and fork-tenderness for hard vegetables.

✔ Keep handy several ways to flavor vegetables so that you don't get tired of them.

Veggie Recipes You'll Want to Try

Because I have become more and more vegetarian throughout the years, I have selected vegetable and vegan recipes I like and make. These recipes contain no cholesterol and small amounts, if any, of saturated fat.

Why you should eat your veggies

Vegetables are what your body was primarily made to eat. You have long intestines, the same as other herbivores such as gorillas, apes, chimps, and other primates. You don't have advanced skills or tools like good night vision, claws, or proper canines to go through furry skin and bones. You live longer and do better with vegetables, fruits, and maybe occasional meats. These fruits and vegetables along with grains are your best foods. And the people that eat that way — for example, the Japanese that live in Japan — live the longest.

Vegetarian recipes are usually lower in fat (not always, though) than meat recipes, and if they have no dairy (cheese, egg yolks, whole milk, or cream), they are probably healthier. These recipes are all pretty easy and a lot of fun.

Pasta Alfredo

My testers were impressed with this creamy and tasty vegan alfredo, which doesn't contain cream or cheese (see photo in color section). If you aren't a vegan, substitute the soy for skim milk or fatfree half-and-half. One tester said she would love a sprinkle of Parmesan and a crumble of bacon or diced ham on this, but I like it as it is. Try it with the soybeans if you can find them. Peas or any other chopped green vegetable are great, too.

Preparation/Cooking time: *25 minutes*

Yield: *4 servings*

1½ cups small dry pasta, such as small shells or small macaroni noodles

1 10-ounce box frozen corn, defrosted

1 large onion, chopped

1½ cups plain soy milk

2 tablespoons flour

1 large tomato, diced

1 cup fresh or frozen shelled green soybeans or peas

2 tablespoons chopped parsley

Dash red pepper flakes

1 In a large saucepan of boiling water, add the pasta and boil until pasta is very al dente, about 10 minutes. (You may add salt to the water if you wish.) Drain and set aside.

2 Meanwhile, puree the corn in a processor or blender until very smooth.

3 Lightly spray a small skillet with cooking oil spray, add the onions, and sauté over medium-high heat, stirring, for about 5 minutes. Set aside.

4 Measure the soy milk in a 2-cup measuring cup. Whisk the flour into the milk. In the same saucepan with the drained pasta, add the milk and flour mixture and bring to a simmer, stirring continually. Cook for 4 minutes, or until thickened. Add any salt and pepper you wish.

5 Add the tomatoes, corn, soybeans, and parsley and stir gently to mix. Heat until hot, about 1 minute. Sprinkle on the red pepper flakes.

Nutrition at a glance (per serving): Calories 333.5 g; Protein 16.2 g; Carbohydrates 58.1 g; Dietary fiber 7.3 g; Total fat 5.9 g; Saturated fat 0.7 g; Cholesterol 0 mg; Sodium 28.2 mg.

Lynn's tip: Usually frozen, soybeans come hulled and unhulled. Out of the shell, these bright green beans are ready to add to any dish, taking about 2 minutes to steam. Slightly larger than a pea but smaller and greener and the same texture as a lima, they can be found in most Asian food markets. Called edamame in Japanese restaurants, they are offered as a refreshing appetizer. Served hot or cold and usually lightly salted, you put the pod gently in your teeth and slip the delicious bean out of the furry shell and down it quicker than you can say "saki."

Beets in Pineapple Sauce

This beet dish is so versatile you can serve it hot or cold, as a side dish to any rice or pasta entree, or as a salad on a bed of greens. If you want to use fresh beets (makes for a richer dish), scrub the beets well, but don't peel them. Microwave in the oven for 5 minutes and bake for 15 minutes in a 350° oven. Roasting them in the oven adds to their flavor.

Preparation/Cooking time: 15 minutes

Yield: 4 servings

1 8-ounce can crushed pineapple, reserving the juice

1 tablespoon red wine vinegar

1 tablespoon cornstarch

1 teaspoon grated fresh ginger

2 15-ounce cans whole beets, drained

1 To a cool medium saucepan, add the drained pineapple juice, red wine vinegar, cornstarch, and ginger and whisk well.

2 Cook over medium-high heat, whisking constantly, until the mixture thickens, about 4 minutes.

3 Add the beets and drained pineapple and cook until the mixture is heated, about 2 to 3 minutes.

(continued)

Nutrition at a glance (per serving): Calories 85.60; Protein 1.53 g; Carbohydrates 20.93 g; Dietary fiber 2.87 g; Total fat 0.25 g; Saturated fat 0.04 g; Cholesterol 0 mg; Sodium 273.43 mg.

Lynn's fun food fact: Don't try to use fresh pineapple or fresh pineapple juice if you want to thicken a sauce. Whether heating a dish or trying to get it to gel in the refrigerator, nothing will work if it contains fresh pineapple. An enzyme, which isn't in the canned pineapples (canned pineapple is cooked in the can destroying it), keeps the sauce or gelatin from thickening regardless of how much cornstarch or other thickeners you add.

Green Beans with Mushrooms

This is a simple and pretty dish, not highly seasoned, but with delicate and gentle flavors. It is just right in the winter. Serve it with baked or mashed potatoes, fish, turkey or chicken breast. If you are a vegan, go for brown rice and sliced tomatoes for a very colorful plate.

Preparation/Cooking time: 25 minutes

Yield: 4 large servings

1 4-inch block firm tofu, removed from water, cut into ½-inch cubes	2 cups defatted chicken stock
2 teaspoons soy sauce	1 pound green beans
1 large onion, finely chopped	½ cup sliced almonds
1 pound large button or brown mushrooms, sliced	2 teaspoons cornstarch
	2 tablespoons water

1 Lightly spray a large nonstick frying pan or saucepan with cooking oil spray. Add the tofu and lightly spritz all sides of that, too. Brown the tofu over medium heat, being careful not to break when turning. Add the soy sauce to the tofu, cooking 30 seconds to flavor the tofu. Remove the tofu to a plate and lightly cover with foil to keep warm.

2 Add the onions and 2 tablespoons water to the pan and cook over medium heat, stirring, for 2 minutes. Add the mushrooms and any salt and pepper you wish, stirring occasionally, and cook both for 6 minutes until the mushrooms are cooked through. If the mushrooms start to stick or get dry, add a tablespoon or so water.

3 Add the stock to the pan and bring to a boil. Simmer over medium heat for 10 minutes to reduce the stock by about half. Add the beans and almonds and any salt and pepper you wish. Cover and cook for 5 minutes, or until the beans are crisp-tender.

4 Place the cornstarch in a small dish. Add 2 tablespoons water and stir to dissolve the cornstarch. Add to the saucepan. Cook, stirring constantly, for 2 to 3 minutes, or until thickened. When serving, add the tofu to the top of the beans.

Nutrition at a glance (per serving): Calories 63.00; Protein 3.47 g; Carbohydrates 13.37 g; Dietary fiber 4.54 g; Total fat 0.46 g; Saturated fat 0.08 g; Cholesterol 0 mg; Sodium 331.05 mg.

Lynn's tip: Try all kinds of green beans in this recipe: haricot verte (the little ones), pole beans (the big ones), and Italian green beans, (wide and flat beans). Green beans are what I call a basic, because they go with almost any meal.

Greek-Style Cauliflower

Tender cauliflower takes to this zesty tomato sauce sparked with cinnamon, a signature spice in Greek cuisine. My testers raved about this. Garnish with some crumbled lowfat feta cheese if you are a vegetarian and not a vegan.

Preparation/Cooking time: 25 minutes

Yield: 4 servings

½ medium onion, chopped

2 cloves garlic, minced

1 teaspoon dried oregano

½ teaspoon crushed fennel seeds

¼ teaspoon ground cinnamon

1 small head cauliflower, green leaves removed, stem trimmed if needed

½ cup tomato sauce

1 tablespoon freshly squeezed lemon juice

1 6-ounce package Tofurella cheese, mozzarella, or Cheddar (or any other tofu-based cheese), shredded or sliced wafer-thin

¼ teaspoon crushed red pepper flakes (optional)

2 tablespoons chopped parsley

1 Coat a large saucepan (large enough for the cauliflower head to be steamed whole) with cooking spray. Add the onions, garlic, oregano, fennel seeds, and cinnamon. Cover and cook over medium-high heat for 3 to 4 minutes, or until the onions are soft. If necessary, add 1 or 2 teaspoons of water to prevent sticking.

2 Add the cauliflower, tomato sauce, lemon juice, and ½ cup water. Season with any salt and pepper you wish. Bring the mixture to a boil. Cover and reduce the heat to medium. Cook for about 8 minutes, or until the cauliflower is tender-crisp. Make sure that the water doesn't completely evaporate, adding more by the tablespoon if it gets too low.

3 Remove the cauliflower to a plate and immediately add the cheese to the top. Spray a square-foot square of aluminum foil with cooking oil spray. Using the foil, lightly cover the cauliflower and cheese making a tent, for 2 minutes to melt the cheese. (The spray keeps the cheese from sticking, and the foil keeps the heat in so that the cheese will melt.) Sprinkle with the red pepper flakes (if using) and parsley.

(continued)

Nutrition at a glance (per serving): Calories 56.68; Protein 3.70 g; Carbohydrates 12.06 g; Dietary fiber 3.92 g; Total fat 0.16 g; Saturated fat 0.02 g; Cholesterol 0 mg; Sodium 230.35 mg.

Lynn's lore: Creamy white cauliflower, a member of the cabbage family, is thought to have originated in Asia Minor and was grown domestically and eaten by the ancient Romans. It comes in green, white, and purple. It is high in vitamin A and other nutrients.

Pasta with French Broccoli and Pine Nuts

With just a whisper of garlic, the sweet fragrance of rosemary plays beautifully off the earthy crisp flavor of broccoli settled in among angel hair pasta. This is an attractive dish to serve, and it's simple to make. Steamed yellow (summer squash) makes a good side, and a salad completes the meal.

Preparation/Cooking time: 25 minutes

Yield: 4 servings

½ pound angel hair pasta

1 pound broccoli, cut into small florets, stems cut into rounds

3 tablespoons olive oil

2 teaspoons dried rosemary leaves

4 cloves garlic, peeled and crushed

2 tablespoons chopped toasted pine nuts

1 cup grape or cherry tomatoes cut in half

1 In a large pot, boil the pasta until al dente, about 6 minutes. During the last 3 minutes of cooking, add broccoli stems and cook for 2 minutes. Add the broccoli florets, cover, and cook for 1 minute.

2 Meanwhile, in an extra-large skillet, add the olive oil and heat on low. Add the rosemary to the olive oil.

3 Add the garlic to the heating oil with the rosemary. Raise the heat to medium and cook, stirring over medium heat, until the garlic is soft, about 3 minutes. Press down on the garlic to extract all the flavor swirling it around the pan. Remove the intact garlic cloves.

4 To the oil, garlic, and rosemary left in the skillet, add the pine nuts and tomatoes. Cook over medium heat, stirring frequently, for 1 to 2 minutes, or until the tomatoes soften. Remove the garlic.

5 Drain the pasta and broccoli and add the pasta to the skillet. Cook, gently stirring, for 1 to 2 minutes, or until hot. Use any salt and pepper you wish.

Nutrition at a glance (per serving): *Calories 372.1 g; Protein 12.0 g; Carbohydrates 51.9 g; Dietary fiber 6.2 g; Total fat 13.9 g; Saturated fat 1.8 g; Cholesterol 0 mg; Sodium 33.8 mg.*

Lynn's tip: *Cooking broccoli can be problematic because the tender florets often overcook before the stems are tender. But both parts can cook in almost the same time with this method: Cut off the florets where they join the stem; separate them into equal-sized florets. Slice the stem into ¼-inch-thick rounds. That way they are both about the same density. To cook broccoli with the most nutrients intact, stir-fry or steam. Broccoli stems contain fiber and flavor, but the most nutritious part of the broccoli plant is the leaves, so gather them up in the market and use them.*

Peas and Cheese-Stuffed Baked Potatoes

Preparing potatoes in both the microwave and oven offers the delicious taste of long-baking baked potatoes ready in a flash. Bursting with melting tofu cheese, scallions, and peas, these potatoes can be a whole meal or an attention-getting side. Nearly all large markets have tofu cheese, usually in 2 or 3 flavors. It doesn't have a strong taste but melts well. If you aren't a vegan, add ½ cup sour cream and diced lean ham to the mixture.

Preparation/Cooking time: *30 minutes*

Yield: *4 servings*

4 large baking potatoes	*1 teaspoon garlic pepper or garlic salt*
1⅓ cups peas, fresh or frozen	*½ cup chopped scallions, including the green*
1 cup shredded tofu cheese, such as Tofurella (in Cheddar or mozzarella flavors or use half Cheddar and half mozzarella)	*¼ cup chopped parsley*
	Paprika

1 Preheat oven to 400°. Pierce the potatoes and microwave, turning 2 or 3 times, for about 10 minutes.

2 Wet the potatoes thoroughly with cold water and place on a cookie sheet and bake for 10 to 12 minutes. Check the center with a thin knife for doneness.

3 In a microwavable bowl with a lid, add the peas and a few teaspoons water. Microwave for 1 minute on high, turning once, or until the peas are bright green. Remove, uncover, drain, and set aside.

4 Remove the potatoes from the oven. Cut off a top slice of the potato lengthwise, about ¼-inch thick, 3 inches long. Carefully scoop out the pulp, leaving ¼-inch potato in the shell.

(continued)

5 In a large bowl, add the potato pulp, cheese mixture, and garlic pepper and mash the potatoes into the cheese, mixing well. Add the scallions and any additional salt and pepper you wish. Add the peas and parsley carefully into the cheese and potatoes.

6 Stuff the potato shells with the cheese, peas, and potato mixture. Place the stuffed potatoes back into the microwave for 30 seconds to 1 minute, turning once or twice, to melt the cheese. Sprinkle with paprika.

Nutrition at a glance (per serving): *Calories 303.9 g; Protein 13.0 g; Carbohydrates 55.4 g; Dietary fiber 7.3 g; Total fat 3.3 g; Saturated fat 0.1 g; Cholesterol 0 mg; Sodium 786.5 mg.*

Lynn's tip: *Save the potato tops and refrigerate for another day when you want to make a potato skin appetizer. When ready, sprinkle on a mixture of lowfat tofu cheeses and scallions and bake for 10 or 15 minutes in a 350° oven. If you aren't a vegan, serve with sour cream and diced lean ham.*

Spicy Island Carrots

Spicy and slightly sweet, Jamaican jerk seasoning brings carrots alive. My testers raved about them. A pressure cooker speeds up the time by 10 minutes. If you are a vegetarian or vegan or want to try something new and healthy, add diced spicy tofu before serving and heat. A bright green vegetable and pasta or rice rounds out the meal. For nonvegetarians, chicken breast of a white fish like flounder goes well.

Preparation/Cooking time: *20 minutes*

Yield: *4 servings*

1 pound baby carrots, sliced or unsliced, or regular carrots, sliced

2 tablespoons brown sugar

1 teaspoon hot pepper sauce

1 teaspoon fresh lemon juice

1 teaspoon ground cumin

2 cloves garlic, minced

½ teaspoon chili powder

1 In a medium nonstick saucepan, add the carrots and cover with water. Bring to a boil over medium-high heat. Cook, stirring occasionally, for 10 minutes, or until the carrots are tender but still firm. Drain the carrots and transfer to a bowl.

2 Dry the saucepan and coat with nonstick spray. Add the brown sugar, hot pepper sauce, lemon juice, cumin, garlic, and chili powder.

3 Cook, stirring, for 2 to 3 minutes, or until the sugar bubbles and the spices are fragrant. Add the carrots. Toss or stir to coat the carrots with the sauce. Season to taste with salt and pepper.

Nutrition at a glance (per serving): Calories 74.58; Protein 1.20 g; Carbohydrates 16.96 g; Dietary fiber 2.25 g; Total fat 0.79 g; Saturated fat 0.12 g; Cholesterol 0 mg; Sodium 54.11 mg.

Lynn's tip: You can add lots of vegetables to this dish, but keep them small. Try diced celery, peas, chopped parsley, or chives. You can even add diced cooked poultry, ham, or beef if you want to use it as an entree with meat.

Tofu Mayonnaise

With any excuse (and if it tastes good and is easy), I'll use soy because of its health benefits. According to my testers, this is far tastier than any store-bought fatfree mayonnaise. Tofu, made from soybeans, one of the new yet ancient wonder foods, contains protein and is low in calories and fat. Use this anywhere you use mayonnaise.

Preparation/Cooking time: 5 minutes

Yield: 8 servings

8 ounces firm silken tofu	2 teaspoons prepared horseradish
¼ cup fatfree vegetable broth	2 teaspoons sugar
3 tablespoons lemon juice	1 teaspoon dried thyme
2 tablespoons olive or canola oil	1 to 1½ teaspoons Dijon mustard

1 Rinse the tofu in a colander and pat with a paper towel.

2 Over a processor or blender, squish the tofu through your fingers or mash with a fork and drop in the blender.

3 To the blender, add the broth, lemon juice, olive oil, horseradish, sugar, thyme, and Dijon mustard and season with salt.

4 Blend or process for 2 to 3 minutes to make very smooth. If made ahead, cover and refrigerate for up to an hour. Stir before using.

Nutrition at a glance (per serving): Calories 54.6 g; Protein 2.0 g; Carbohydrates 2.7 g; Dietary fiber 0.1 g; Total fat 4.2 g; Saturated fat 0.6 g; Cholesterol 0 mg; Sodium 49.4 mg.

Lynn's tip: If you haven't used tofu, you can find it in the vegetable department usually on the shelf above the veggies, eye level, in the open cooler bins. Look on the label and get the one with the lowest fat. Firm tofu is for soups, salads, and frying, so get the firm silken for mayo and dips. You can add a tablespoon or 2 of chopped onions, green and red peppers, and relish for a great sandwich spread.

Time-saving frozen vegetables

If you want to save time and several steps, use frozen vegetables such as green beans, cut asparagus, corn kernels, sliced okra, broccoli or cauliflower florets, butter beans, limas, and peas. These vegetables are often fresher than those at the market, having been frozen right next to the picking fields within hours of harvesting. They are already cut, washed, and lightly steamed. Bang the frozen box on the counter to separate, but don't bother defrosting. Being so small, they can be added to the pot on the stove, stirred in, and heated with just an additional minute or two, making the vegetables cooked perfectly.

Dinner Fruit Salad with Cantaloupe Dressing

If you've never had a creamy melon dressing, you're in for a treat. It is refreshing for any salad. If you use the dressing for anything other than a fruit salad, add a little salt and a good amount of cracked black pepper. Serve this salad plate with rice and bread.

Preparation time: *20 minutes*

Yield: *4 servings*

Dressing

½ cup fatfree lemon yogurt

2 teaspoons fresh lime or lemon juice

1 teaspoon Dijon mustard

1 tablespoon honey

1 3-inch wedge cantaloupe (rind removed), or about 1½ cups of cubed cantaloupe

Fruit Salad

4 bananas

1 tablespoon fresh lemon juice

2 ruby red grapefruit, peeled and cut into wedges

2 fresh pears, cut into chunks

1 cup blueberries

1 cup hulled and sliced strawberries

1 cup thinly sliced celery

2 kiwis, peeled and cut into wedges

2 plums, cut into wedges, or 2 small grape bunches

2 tablespoons finely chopped crystallized ginger

1 tablespoon finely chopped fresh mint

Mint sprigs for garnish

1 *Cantaloupe dressing:* In a processor bowl, combine the yogurt, lime juice or lemon juice, mustard, honey, and cantaloupe and process to the desired consistency or until most of the cantaloupe lumps are gone. Set aside.

2 *Fruit salad:* Cut the bananas into slices and place in a medium bowl; toss with the lemon juice. Arrange the bananas on a large platter. Add the grapefruit, pears, blueberries, strawberries, celery, kiwi fruit, and plums or grapes. Sprinkle on the ginger and mint. Drizzle with the dressing just before serving. Garnish with mint sprigs.

Nutrition at a glance (per serving): *Calories 291.76; Protein 5.27 g; Carbohydrates 72.17 g; Dietary fiber 9.76 g; Total fat 1.86 g; Saturated fat 0.25 g; Cholesterol 0.49 mg; Sodium 89.66 mg.*

Lynn's nutrition note: *If you're pressed for time, get the cantaloupe already cubed and packaged, available in most markets. Otherwise, use your nose to select the best cantaloupe or if they're too cold to smell, ask the green grocer to slice it for you and taste a sliver. Cantaloupe can be very bad and hard, too ripe, or absolutely luscious. Just 1 cup of cubed cantaloupe supplies more than 100 percent of the Daily Value for vitamins A and C.*

Chapter 14

Brighter Breakfasts

● ●

In This Chapter

▶ Deciding what's for breakfast

▶ Preparing fast and easy daily breakfasts

▶ Fixing lowfat but simple country inn feasts for brunch, weekends, or just once in a while

▶ Making omelets and scrambles healthy

▶ Substituting butter, eggs, bacon, and sausages

▶ Developing the breakfast that's right for you

● ●

*T*he investment you make in health today pays off in your largest and most important dividend tomorrow: better health. And it all starts with breakfast. That's why, in this chapter, I give you lots of quick and easy daily breakfast menus, as well as several lush, country inn-style Sunday morning feasts — feasts that are opulent but not laden in fats. You won't miss the calories with any of the lavish breakfasts here, and you won't be stumped as to what to eat quickly on weekdays.

You find out which breakfast meats are lowest in fat, how and why to use substitute eggs to lower your dietary cholesterol intake (and a simple recipe combining both regular and substitute eggs), why fruit is better than juice (but both are fine), and why breakfast is a good place to get your whole grains and fiber.

The suggested weekday menus show you how simple healthy breakfasts can be and how easy it is to make quick lush weekend breakfasts. I also give you lists of the healthiest breakfast choices and more healthy breakfast substitutions. You discover everything you need to know to help make this first meal of the day individual, yet quick and healthy.

Breakfast Every Day

"Lynn, what's a quick and easy healthy breakfast?" Surprisingly, that's the question I am asked most often when I do radio, give seminars, demos, and lectures, or do book signings. Dinners are certainly important on a lowfat or healthy eating plan, just as lunch is. But a good breakfast determines whether you're alert and feel your best all day or whether you get tired and lack energy. A daily habit of a simple lowfat breakfast of foods such as grains, lowfat dairy, and fruit is like money in the bank healthwise. Breakfast can help provide the nutrients your body needs to power your busy days. And breakfast needn't be tedious.

An easy healthy breakfast is simple — a no-brainer. And it can be varied.

I tell people, "Breakfast can be the easiest, quickest, and one of the most healthful of all meals."

A simple weekday breakfast can be low in calories, contain lots of fiber, lowfat dairy, and have the vitamins and nutrients you find in fresh fruit or juice — all in just three items: cereal or toast, skim milk, and fruit or juice.

Follow these tips when you're choosing these items for your breakfast, and you can't go wrong:

- **Cereal or toast:** Make it whole grain, from ½ to 1 cup (or 1 to 2 slices whole-grain toast or whole-wheat or high-fiber English muffins or whole-wheat bagels.

- **Skim milk:** You save 3 fat grams by using 1 cup skim milk instead of 1 cup 2 percent milk, and that's a lot. *Skim milk substitutions:* Soy milk, rice milk, fatfree nondairy creamer, fatfree half-and-half, or a mixture of any of these with skim milk.

- **Fruit:** A banana, apple, peach, mango, pear slices, berries, or even dried raisins are great fiber, carbohydrates, and tummy-filling food. *Fruit substitutions:* Orange or tomato juice (freshly squeezed preferably) or lemonade. You can switch occasionally to canned cranberry, peach, pear, pineapple, apple, mango, papaya, apricot nectar, or any one of a dozen others, but add the juice of half a fresh lemon for a fresh zing and extra vitamins.

Add coffee, tea, or water if you choose, and you have an easy, simple breakfast that you don't have to think about. All you need to do is make sure that you shop for these foods and have them on hand.

Midmorning Letdown

Some people get a mild letdown at around 11 a.m., especially when they eat a donut or two, a huge sugary muffin, or a "hearty" breakfast of a cheese omelet, sausage, and greasy, butter-filled biscuits. This midmorning letdown is probably because of the sugar high or high carbohydrate rush from the simple carbohydrates causing you to feel tired and even hungry. The sleepiness can be caused by the *tryptophan,* a natural amino acid that is contained in some of the more greasy foods. (Tryptophan is a natural sleep inducer found in milk, some meats, salmon, and other foods.)

The following list tells you why cereal, milk, and fruit make such an effective (and easy) breakfast:

- **Cereal and fiber:** Whole grains are better. Why? They have more fiber than other grains such as white flour or rice crispies or flakes. You need 20 to 35 grams of fiber a day. A small dish of whole-grain cereal, skim milk, and fruit or fruit juice is the best bet here and can supply 15 percent of your fiber needs. If you don't like a bowl of just all bran, try combining cereals or having all bran cereal one day and your favorite another. Look for a cereal with at least 5 grams of fiber per serving. Some cereals like Spelt, found in most major markets, can have even more.

- **Skim milk:** You get part of your daily need for calcium and the minerals and vitamins in milk (and, with skim milk, without the excess calories) and the other part from calcium supplements.

- **Fruit or juice:** Fruit is better than juice. Ideally, they are two different items, not interchangeable. For example, you would have some berries or half a banana on your cereal, *plus* a glass of fresh juice. One quart of juice is about 500 calories, and you'll probably drink 1 to 2 cups juice or between 150 and 250 calories (depending upon the thickness, sugar content, or dilution of the juice). An apple or banana is just 100 calories — more fiber, more satisfaction, and maybe more vitamins and minerals. If the juice is reconstituted, canned, bottled, watered, or some mixture, the real juice is only 10 percent and mostly sugar water. A glass of fresh juice is better than no fruit at all, but both for breakfast are ideal.

Because I'm often asked, I'll tell you what I eat in the mornings. My own breakfast is 1 or 2 slices of high-fiber toast (3 grams fiber per slice) in the summer, hot cereal in the winter, high-fiber flakes spring and fall, juice, and sometimes a banana, peach, or plum. I use a butterlike fatfree spray and, occasionally, cherry preserves. The bread type varies. One week it might be a nut-and-raisin high-fiber toast with the spray and no preserves (nut-and-fruit bread is higher in calories). Another week it might be whole-grain or wheatberry toast. I top the toast and fruit off with freshly squeezed orange juice and my assortment of vitamins, which I consume in my half-hour ride to an assignment or the gym.

Toast toppings

You can top whole-wheat toast, bagels, crumpets, or English muffins with jam, preserves, honey, apple butter, marmalade, cinnamon and sugar, or jelly, all of which are free of fat (but not calories).

Butter or margarine on toast? Diet or tub margarine over butter in regards to saturated fat and calories, but the best answer is neither.

If you're a coffee and tea lover, enjoy. That's what all the studies say about 2 to 3 cups a day. You could switch to Postum (a coffee substitute made popular during World War II and still selling briskly) or use half decaf half regular coffee, and new soy and coffee drinks are available and taste just like coffee with half the caffeine. Or drink Kava, a calmer downer. The latter two are available at health-food stores. Cream or half-and-half in your coffee or tea? It adds up more than you think. One month's worth of dairy cream in 3 cups of coffee a day is in excess of 50 grams of fat, most of it saturated, a very big amount. It's a place you can easily cut by using fatfree nondairy liquid or powder creamers or fatfree half-and-half.

Sunday Country Inn Breakfasts

We Americans are from a farm heritage and think an ideal breakfast is big and rich and definitely not complete unless it has such meats as bacon, ham, sausage, or steak even, corned beef hash, and especially eggs (and the egg bureau ads ditto this on radio and TV daily). Then you might also have hash brown potatoes (and lots of them), pancakes or waffles, and French toast with all the butter and syrup possible. Most people even want biscuits and maybe gravy, or donuts, Danishes, bear claws, or coffee cake. Today, these overly fatty and calorie-filled breakfast foods and our more sedentary lifestyle are a recipe for disaster. These foods mean extra weight, serious health problems, added costs, and going through life sleepy and lethargic.

But I like a rich breakfast on Sunday especially. And you can have it without the excess fat — and with the nutrients — and it will be delicious and healthy. Try my Pear French Toast (see recipe later in this chapter) with maple syrup and Canadian bacon, or my waffles with nuts and berries and not just six nuts. I don't skimp here.

Because few people do the strenuous manual labor of a century ago and you want the energy to do what you must, breakfast is a good place to begin to start your healthy day. The following sections contain some ideas. (Coffee and tea are not included, but you can add them.)

Breakfast on the go?

A bag of my orange granola (see recipe in Chapter 3) makes a handy breakfast companion that contains both grains and fruit. Or, for a quickie health drink, a banana smoothie is easy to whip up to sip on the way to the office, the gym or chores. (Cut a banana into chunks, puree in the blender or food processor with a scoop of fatfree vanilla frozen yogurt, a few strawberries, a tablespoon of honey or sugar, and a dash of cinnamon or nutmeg. Use skim milk to thin and ice cubes to cool).

What else can you eat for breakfast? The following menus are just some examples of breakfast. But you can eat anything — rice, pasta, potatoes, vegetarian pizza, a small amount of lean cold steak, carrots, stew, soup, salad, baked oysters, or just an apple. A regular defined breakfast is probably easier, but any nutritious food and some fruit are fine.

Weekday menus

Try a combination of these foods for your weekday breakfasts:

- Fresh fruit
- Whole-grain cereal with skim milk (5 grams fiber per bowl) and fresh fruit
- Toast (2 to 3 grams fiber per slice) and fresh juice
- Toast (2 to 3 grams fiber per slice) and fresh juice smoothie
- Whole-wheat bagel, whole-wheat English muffin, fatfree spray, and perhaps preserves

Weekend menus

Take a break from your weekday routine and time shortages by trying something different:

- Fresh fruit (a nice variety), or juice, or both
- Pancakes with fatfree butterlike spray or regular, lite, or regular maple or corn syrup
- Sausage or bacon made of turkey, vegetarian or lowfat plain or smoked

✔ Feather apple or strawberry waffles (see recipe later in this chapter) with regular or lite or regular maple or corn syrup

✔ Lean ham or Canadian bacon slices with fresh fruit or fruit or both

✔ Omelets with mushroom, onion, cheese, or any other addition (see recipe later in this chapter)

✔ Hash browns or potato pancakes served with applesauce and lowfat sour cream

✔ French toast with lite or regular maple or corn syrup

Easy Breakfast Substitutions

Making a very few changes can help you lower the fat and calories considerably and sometimes, even boost the nutrients. Table 14-1 tells you about some substitutions that you can make to improve your diet.

Table 14-1	Substitutions Worth Making
What You Should Have	*What You Could Have but May Not Be in Your Best Interest Healthwise or Caloriewise*
Bagels, whole wheat with lowfat cream cheese	Bagels with butter and full-fat cream cheese
Toast, whole grain with jam, no butter, but a butterlike spray	Toast with plenty of butter and jam
English muffins, whole wheat with small amount diet margarine and honey	English muffin with butter and preserves
Lowfat granola	High-fat granola
Whole-grain cereal with skim milk	Cereal with cream and, if hot, butter
Grits with syrup (or lite syrup)	Grits with butter and syrup
Waffles with syrup (or lite syrup)	Waffles made with excess oil, syrup, and plenty of butter
Pancakes with syrup (or lite syrup)	Pancakes made with excess oil, syrup, and plenty of butter between each pancake
Canadian bacon or trimmed bacon	Bacon
Turkey or lowfat sausage	Sausage
Lox or lean ham	Spam or fatty bacon

What You Should Have	What You Could Have but May Not Be in Your Best Interest Healthwise or Caloriewise
Egg white or substitute egg omelet with lowfat cheese	Whole egg and cheese omelet
Eggs Benedict with English muffin, Canadian bacon, lowfat hollandaise, scrambled substitute eggs	Eggs Benedict
Baked apple	Belgian waffle with whipped cream and strawberries
Baked oysters (without excess butter)	Baked oysters with butter, cream and cheese
Egg white and lowfat cheese souffle	Egg and cheese souffle
Bran muffins, 2 to 3 ounces, and not made with excess fat or sugar	Danish, cream donut or bearclaw, 3 to 4 ounces
Buckwheat pancakes with lite syrup	Buckwheat pancakes with chocolate chips, butter, and syrup
Cream of Wheat and skim milk	Cream of Wheat with cream
Crumpets with butterlike spray	Scones with margarine
Oven-baked potato wedges	Greasy fried hash browns
Muesli (lowfat) with skim milk	Sticky buns or rolls
Substitute eggs	Eggs

Additional quick and healthy breakfast choices

If you're not a fan of any of the breakfasts I describe in this chapter, the following breakfasts may satisfy you. I love and eat all of them at different times.

- Crumpets or lowfat muffins or scones, with small amount diet margarine or fatfree butterlike spray
- Cooked or dried fruit
- Grits or cornmeal mush
- Bacon (red part only), crisp, fat peeled off, 1 ounce
- Lox, 2 ounces
- Egg white omelet or egg white scrambled eggs

The recipes in this chapter look and taste as luscious as they are nutritious. In addition to the healthy breakfast substitutions in Table 14-1, you can substitute egg substitutes for regular eggs in all the egg dishes and use butterlike sprays for butter or margarine. These substitutions make the recipes nearly fatfree.

Egg substitutes

Egg substitutes, available refrigerated or frozen in cartons, are 99 percent egg whites with some betacarotene added for color. They're also pasteurized, which makes them safe to eat even when slightly undercooked, which is how some people prefer scrambled eggs. (Fresh eggs aren't safe undercooked because of salmonella, a nasty bacteria that has made hundreds of thousands in America very ill each year.) Some egg substitutes are nearly indistinguishable from eggs in the way they look, cook, smell, and taste. So don't give up on egg substitutes because you once tried some and they weren't quite right. Companies improve their formulas constantly. (My egg-filled tomatoes can change your mind, as can my Tex/Mex omelet.)

Why should you consider using egg substitutes?

- ✔ Egg substitutes contain no cholesterol, so they're great if you have a high blood cholesterol or want less dietary cholesterol.
- ✔ Egg substitutes contain no fat, so they can lower your dietary saturated fat or total fat intake if you eat eggs.
- ✔ Egg substitutes are primarily (99 percent) egg whites.
- ✔ Pasteurized, egg substitutes contain no salmonella, so they're safer to use.
- ✔ Egg substitutes contain few chemicals, pesticides, antibiotics, or hormones.
- ✔ Many brands of egg substitutes taste identical to regular eggs because they are.

If you aren't sure about egg substitutes on a regular basis, do as I do occasionally. Mix the substitutes with regular egg whites, which also contain no cholesterol, and omit all or most of the yolks. The next recipe shows you how.

Three-Egg Basic Scrambled Eggs

This recipe uses both substitute eggs and regular eggs. What do you save by using some substitute eggs? By omitting just 1 egg, you saved about 215 to 250 milligrams of cholesterol, almost as much as you should have in a whole day. In this recipe, you save more as you are eating more than one egg but less than an egg that contains cholesterol. You saved 5 grams of total fat per egg, and you haven't compromised the taste or the quality. One half cup of regular eggs (about 2 eggs) contains a conservative 430 milligrams of cholesterol. Plus, because the majority of your eggs have been pasteurized, chances are you will get less contamination if your omelet is slightly runny.

Preparation/Cooking time: *10 minutes*

Yield: *2 servings*

½ cup egg substitute   1 whole egg (including yolk)

2 egg whites

1 In a medium bowl, mix the ingredients well with a fork. Add whatever salt and pepper you would like or add the seasoning after the eggs are cooked. (Some people think salt added during cooking toughens eggs.)

2 Lightly spray a skillet with butter-flavored nonstick spray. Add the egg mixture to the skillet and over medium heat, stir, with a spoon or fork, especially the edges, cooking to desired consistency while heating over medium heat. Cook to desired dryness, pushing the eggs around the skillet. Serve plain or use any of the omelet fillings or toppings.

Nutrition at a glance (per serving): *Calories 167.90; Protein 25.26 g; Carbohydrates 3.30 g; Dietary fiber 0 g; Total fat 5.00 g; Saturated fat 1.55 g; Cholesterol 212.50 mg; Sodium 422.55 mg.*

Lynn's tip: *You can make this with all substitute eggs, half an egg yolk instead of a whole one (or none), or for a smaller omelet, the egg white from just 1 egg. Any variation works.*

Butter substitutes

New fatfree sprays such as "I Can't Believe It's Not Butter!" spray, plus Fleischmann's pour, Parkay's spray, and Country Crock's spray are terrific. Some don't say they are fatfree on the front label. Here's why they are so great.

- ✔ They work.

- ✔ They taste good.

- ✔ They are fatfree and have 0 calories using the recommended number of sprays.

- ✔ They are easy to use — just squirt or pour.

- ✔ You can use them on a variety of breakfast foods, such as toast, French toast, eggs while they are cooking, pancakes, waffles, grits, mushrooms, oatmeal, and vegetables (almost anywhere you would use butter or margarine).

If you add just 2 tablespoons butter for greasing a pan and for flavoring eggs in any recipe, each person could be eating an additional 4 grams of saturated fat. Butter is 51 percent saturated compared to soft tub margarine at 18 percent saturated fat. The extra fat is absolutely not worth it if the alternative light spritz of spray tastes just as good. Incidentally, both butter *and* margarine contain trans fatty acids (butter 3 percent, soft margarine 8 percent, and stick margarine 24 percent).

You're best off avoiding both butter and margarine most of the time. Diet or soft tub margarine is preferred if your choice is between butter and margarine. Diet or soft tub margarine contains almost two-thirds less saturated fats than butter. This information comes from the *Harvard Health Letter* (Vol 8 Oct 97). Plus, some new margarines contain no trans fatty acids and no hydrogenation. Hydrogenation in stick margarine hardens it and causes saturated fats, but butter still has by far the most sat fats (see Table 14-2). This information makes the new butter substitute sprays very attractive.

Table 14-2	Butter Substitutes: Calculate Your Savings	
Type of Spread	*Serving Size*	*Amount of Fat*
Butter	1 tablespoon	7 grams sat fat, 12 total fat
Margarine	1 tablespoon	2 grams sat fat, 11 total fat
Lite, diet, or soft tub margarine	1 tablespoon	1 gram sat fat, 5 total fat
Butterlike spray	5 sprays	0 grams sat fat, 0 total fat

Breakfast Recipes

These recipes are for weekends, Sundays, and brunches and for preparing ahead for quickie breakfasts. They are lots of fun to make and eat, especially because you know they are healthy and good for you. You can use the lowered fat ideas here as a base for making your own favorites.

Hot Oatmeal with Berries and Scalloped Apples

Plain hot oatmeal topped with berries (either raspberries, blackberries, or blueberries) and scalloped apples cooked in skim milk make this a higher calcium, fiber-filled breakfast. Serve with rich fatfree liquid creamer or the new fatfree half-and-half, both found in cartons near the milk. You can change the fruits if you want. My tester loved the blueberries, I loved the raspberries, and we both liked old-fashioned oats better than quick oats, which were mushier.

Preparation/Cooking time: *15 minutes*

Yield: *2 cups oatmeal and 2 cups fruit; 8½ cup servings*

Raspberries and Scalloped Apples

2 Granny Smith apples, thinly sliced, unpeeled or peeled

2 tablespoons freshly squeezed lemon juice

¼ cup sugar

½ teaspoon ground cinnamon

¼ teaspoon allspice

1 cup raspberries

Oatmeal

2 cups skim milk

1 cup old-fashioned or quick oatmeal

¼ cup water

1 tablespoon oat bran

1 To make the raspberries and scalloped apples: In a medium microwaveable bowl, combine the apples, lemon juice, sugar, cinnamon, and allspice. Leave out the raspberries. Cover loosely with microwavable plastic wrap and slit the wrap.

2 Microwave on high, stirring occasionally, for 5 minutes, or until the apples are almost tender. Add the raspberries and microwave for 1 or 2 additional minutes. Don't stir or the berries will bleed.

3 Meanwhile, to make the oatmeal: In a medium saucepan, add the milk, oatmeal, water, oat bran, and maybe a dash of salt and stir to mix. Bring to a full boil, stirring occasionally. Remove from heat, cover with a lid, and let sit for 3 to 5 minutes until it thickens.

4 Serve topped with the raspberries and apples and any creamy topping such as fatfree half-and-half or plain or hazelnut liquid nondairy fatfree creamer.

Nutrition at a glance (per serving): Calories 462.51; Protein 16.26 g; Carbohydrates 96.13 g; Dietary fiber 13.08 g; Total fat 4.07 g; Saturated fat 0.88 g; Cholesterol 4.41 mg; Sodium 129.55 mg.

(continued)

Lynn's health watch: *Oat bran, made from the outer layers of oat kernels, is rich in soluble fiber, which helps lower cholesterol and boost your fiber intake. Add it by the tablespoon (substituting it for a little of the flour) to oatmeal, cookies, cereals, pancakes, breads, muffins, yogurt snacks, or meat loaf.*

Pear French Toast

Pear slices under French toast is so easy and lush it's sure to become a weekend favorite (see photo in color section). You can add a dollop of fatfree or lowfat sour cream, toss on a few raspberries for color, and tuck in a sprig of mint for class. Serve with maple syrup, honey, nutmeg, hazelnut-flavored syrups, or any reduced-calorie or lite syrup. For an extra treat, add a dash of pear brandy to the syrup. Use at least a 12-inch skillet to cook the French toast so that you can do them all in just 2 batches. The oven keeps them warm, while the others are cooking but it isn't absolutely necessary.

Preparation/Cooking time: *25 minutes (variations can take 5 to 20 minutes)*

Yield: *2 servings (if using thick, wide French bread), 3 servings (if using French-sliced baguettes), or 4 servings (if using sliced bread)*

1 teaspoon butter	*¼ teaspoon vanilla*
1 ripe pear, cored and peeled or unpeeled	*Pinch of ground cinnamon*
½ cup fatfree egg substitute	*4 thick slices French bread, or 6 slices white bread*
1 egg white	
½ cup skim milk	*2 teaspoons confectioners' sugar*

1 Preheat oven to 200°. Lightly spray a large skillet with butter-flavored spray and add the teaspoon of butter, swirling it around over medium heat.

2 Cut the pears in half lengthwise and then in fourths lengthwise. Cut each fourth lengthwise into 3 slices. Add the 12 slices to the skillet, taking care not to break them. Cook over medium-high heat until a pale golden color, about 3 to 4 minutes per side. Remove and place carefully on a lightly sprayed ovenproof flat cookie sheet or plate, slices covered loosely in foil to keep warm. Set in the oven.

3 In a large shallow bowl such as a glass pie pan or dish, add the egg substitute, egg white, milk, vanilla, and cinnamon and whisk to combine.

4 Lightly recoat the skillet with a few spritzes of nonstick cooking spray. Heat to medium.

5 Dip the bread slices into the egg mixture, turning to coat both sides and to soak up as much of the mixture as possible.

6 Add to the skillet and cook for 4 minutes, or until golden. Flip and cook for 4 minutes, or until golden. If all the slices won't fit, do them in 2 batches. Keep the first batch warm in the oven, while the others are cooking.

7 When served, make a fan of 3 slices of the pears on each individual plate. Place the French toast on each pear fan but slightly off to the side so that you can see the top half of the 3 pear slices. Sprinkle with confectioners' sugar. If you like it sweeter, also use syrup around the edges, but add without disturbing the sugar.

Nutrition at a glance (per serving): Calories 188.79; Protein 8.79 g; Carbohydrates 31.95 g; Dietary fiber 2.07 g; Total fat 2.80 g; Saturated fat 1.01 g; Cholesterol 3.59 mg; Sodium 344.23 mg.

Lynn's lore: You have too much egg mixture for 4 pieces of sliced bread, so use 6 as suggested. Six slices serve 3 people, 2 slices per person. If using French bread, cut slightly thicker, depending on the diameter of the loaf. You can soak French bread for hours if family or guests are running late, or even overnight. You can't soak sliced bread, or it will disintegrate.

Eggs in Tomato Shells

This great recipe tests perfectly every time and is very easy (see photo in color section). Use it for Sunday breakfast, brunch, or even dinner, especially if you're a tomato lover. It's almost like a quiche, but the egg mixture is baked in the microwave in a tomato shell, making it a warm and inviting dish.

Preparation/Cooking time: 20 minutes

Yield: 4 servings

1 medium onion

4 large tomatoes, ½ inch of the top removed

1½ cups fatfree egg substitute

¼ cup chopped fresh parsley

4 ounces fatfree feta cheese, crumbled

½ teaspoon oregano

2 green onions, chopped

1 Lightly spray a skillet with nonstick cooking oil spray. Add the onions and cook on medium-high heat for 2 to 3 minutes, stirring occasionally. When finished, remove the skillet from the heat and place the skillet, if possible, on a cool surface like a stone counter or cool trivet.

(continued)

2 Scoop out the tomatoes, leaving ¼-inch around the edge. Don't pierce or cut the skin. Reserve the tomato pulp for another use — don't use it here as it makes the filling too watery. Place the tomato upside-down on paper towels to drain.

3 Make sure that the skillet is very warm to the touch, but not hot, or it will set the eggs. (You are bringing the mixture to slightly above room temperature.) Add the egg substitutes, parsley, feta cheese, oregano, and any salt and pepper you wish to the onions in the skillet. Stir to mix.

4 Lightly spray 4 custard cups.

5 Place a tomato shell, cut side up, in each cup. Pour the egg mixture into the tomato shells and leave about a ½-inch space at the top.

6 Place the filled tomato shells in the custard cups in the microwave and heat at 50% power for 2 minutes. Rotate and check every 2 minutes or less, even if you have a turntable, as they start bubbling very quickly (turn off heat immediately and rotate again). Heat, stopping again every 2 minutes, until a knife inserted in the filling comes out clean. Microwaving time takes between 5 and 10 minutes total, depending on the power of your microwave.

7 With a large slotted spoon or large rounded rubber spatula so you can get down under them, carefully remove the tomato shells from the custard cups and place on individual plates. Garnish with chopped green onions.

Nutrition at a glance (per serving): *Calories 127.40; Protein 17.16 g; Carbohydrates 15.08 g; Dietary fiber 2.66 g; Total fat 0.70 g; Saturated fat 0.10 g; Cholesterol 0 mg; Sodium 625.59 mg.*

Lynn's tip: You can add finely chopped green peppers and mushrooms to this dish, heating them first along with the onions. Also, try baking the filling for 35 minutes in a 350° oven in partially precooked hollowed zucchini halves, baby eggplant halves, or acorn squash halves. Make sure that the shells are partially cooked, or they will be hard and raw while the filling is done.

Grits (or Polenta), Blackberries, and Maple Syrup

My favorite breakfast is polenta with maple syrup and blackberries, lowfat sausage or bacon chards (meat only), fresh orange juice, and coffee. And polenta is my favorite easy dessert, too. Polenta with berries isn't as fancy as crepes, but it is delicious. Fancy polenta up by heating with the maple syrup 2 tablespoons orange juice, 1 tablespoon each triple sec, cornstarch, and ½ teaspoon orange zest all whisked into the syrup and heated for 2 minutes for what else? Grits Suzette.

You can serve this recipe with 2 ounces lowfat sausage, bacon with all the fat removed, lean ham, or Canadian bacon, coffee or tea, fresh juice, and green grapes.

Preparation/Cooking time: *10 minutes*

Yield: *4 servings*

1 8-ounce tube grits or polenta

1 cup maple syrup, heated

½ pint blackberries

1 Slice the grits or polenta into 8 slices, 1-inch thick slices each, and place them on a large microwave platter.

2 Place in the microwave and cover with a damp paper towel (or they may pop). Microwave on high for 4 to 6 minutes, or until very hot.

3 Serve 2 to a plate, pour on the syrup, divide the blackberries, and place on and around each slice.

Nutrition at a glance (per serving): *Calories 268.46; Protein 1.26 g; Carbohydrates 66.90 g; Dietary fiber 2.91 g; Total fat 0.30 g; Saturated fat 0.03 g; Cholesterol 0 mg; Sodium 132.64 mg.*

Lynn's tip: *I've tried both polenta and grits in the clear sausage tubes, side by side, eating one and then the other, and I can't tell the difference between the two except that the grits were less expensive.*

Hash Browns

The secret to good hash browns is high heat but not so high that the outside burns. Problem is, if the hash browns are more than ¼ inch thick and not greasy (which tempers the cooking) when you brown them, the inside is still raw. Using frozen packaged shredded potatoes and packages of chopped onions, available in all major markets, cuts the shredding and chopping time. Precooking the hash browns in the microwave cuts the cooking time and heats the center, too.

Preparation/Cooking time: *20 minutes*

Yield: *4 servings*

1 8-ounce package frozen shredded potatoes, or 2 medium potatoes, peeled and shredded

2 tablespoons flour or matzo crumbs

1 small onion, chopped, or 2 tablespoons frozen chopped onions

2 tablespoons chopped parsley

(continued)

1 In a large bowl, add 3 cups shredded potatoes, flour, onions, parsley, and any salt and pepper you wish and mix well. Make 4 flat rectangle or round pancakes.

2 Place them on a plate, cover with a damp paper towel, and heat in the microwave on high for about 4 minutes until cooked, turning often if they aren't too fragile.

3 Meanwhile, lightly spray a large skillet with cooking oil spray and heat to medium. When the potatoes are cooked, lightly spray them and add to the skillet. Heat until golden brown. Spray the top side, turn over with a spatula, and heat until golden, about 4 minutes each side.

Nutrition at a glance (per serving): *Calories 66.57; Protein 1.80 g; Carbohydrates 14.61 g; Dietary fiber 1.20 g; Total fat 3.56 g; Saturated fat 1.37 g; Cholesterol 0 mg; Sodium 19.44mg.*

Lynn's tip: *Top with lowfat shredded cheese, diced tomatoes, and chopped scallions. You can melt the cheese by topping the uncooked side and flipping on the cheese. (The cheese browns instead of the potatoes, however.) Add the tomatoes and scallions just before serving.*

Waffle variations for your sweet or savory tooth

Try these waffle variations whenever you make the Feather Apple Waffles, later in this chapter:

✔ Cover hot toasted waffles with thin-sliced mangoes and a lemon syrup made by heating 1 cup corn syrup with 2 tablespoons lemon juice, pinch of ginger, a shake of cinnamon, and a small amount lemon zest.

✔ Spread on hot toasted waffles a topping of fatfree chocolate syrup, chopped walnuts, sliced bananas, and a dollop of fatfree whipped topping.

✔ Spread on hot toasted waffles a room-temperature mixture of reduced-fat and fatfree cream cheese and apple butter and raisins.

✔ Pour on hot toasted waffles heated canned pie fillings such as cherry pie filling, blueberry pie filling, or apple pie filling. You can perk up the fruit in all three cans by adding a dash of cinnamon and 1 tablespoon or less fresh lemon juice. You can also add a squirt of whipped topping or a spoonful of fatfree or lowfat ice cream or frozen yogurt.

✔ Spread on toasted waffles a room-temperature mixture of reduced-fat and fatfree cream cheese, several overlapping thin-sliced tomatoes, several thin slices lox or smoked salmon, capers, and chopped scallions including the green part.

Blueberry Pancakes

Sunday breakfast lush and rich but with fewer calories than you'd expect is quick and easy with this pancake recipe. These pancakes are in all my books because they're the best. They aren't nice and tidy pancakes but thick and juicy, full of opulent sumptuous blueberries. You need to know strawberries and raspberries don't really work but blackberries cut in half with a sharp knife do work if you can stand the seeds. (I love them.)

You can serve these pancakes with 2 ounces cooked bacon chards (meat only, all fat removed), coffee or tea, fresh juice, and scrambled eggs.

Preparation/Cooking time: *25 minutes*

Yield: *4 servings (2 pancakes each)*

1 8-ounce carton liquid buttermilk pancake mix

1 pint blueberries

1 Place the blueberries on a large platter at the side of the burner you're going to use.

2 Lightly spray a large skillet with nonstick vegetable oil. When hot, pour in 4 medium pancakes. You will need to prepare the pancakes in 2 batches.

3 Immediately fill each of the still runny pancakes with 20 or 30 blueberries (depending on their size) so that each pancake is completely filled with berries.

4 When the bubbling of the batter stops, gently lift the edge of 1 and check the bottom. When the bottom is golden brown, turn the pancakes with a spatula, heating through the other side. Continue until each person has 2 to 4 berry-filled pancakes. Serve with maple syrup and extra blueberries. (Keep them warm on hot plates placed in a 275° oven, lightly covered with foil). Serve with maple syrup or sugarfree syrup heated with extra blueberries.

Nutrition at a glance (per serving): *Calories 130.92; Protein 3.25 g; Carbohydrates 28.29 g; Dietary fiber 2.86 g; Total fat 1.43 g; Saturated fat 0.36 g; Cholesterol 13.60 mg; Sodium 435.87 mg.*

Lynn's tip: *Take the batter out of the refrigerator for several minutes (or even an hour) before making. When you soap-wash the blueberries, rinse, drain, and pat them nearly dry with paper towels. Washing and rinsing with warm water slightly heats the berries anyway, allowing the pancakes to cook more evenly.*

Feather Apple Waffles

You can make these waffles with feather-thin sliced apples (or even with strawberries, which you don't cook). If you're an apple lover, you will love this dish. Make sure that you see the sidebar earlier in this chapter for some great waffle variations.

Preparation/Cooking time: *20 minutes*

Yield: *4 servings*

3 tart apples, cored and wafer-thin sliced (⅟₁₆-inch)

2 teaspoons fresh lemon juice

½ teaspoon cinnamon

4 teaspoons brown sugar

1 package frozen lowfat waffles (8 waffles)

½ cup maple syrup

Confectioners' sugar

1 Lightly spray a large skillet with butter-flavored nonstick spray.

2 Place the apple slices in the skillet and evenly sprinkle on the lemon juice, cinnamon, and brown sugar plus a few grains of salt if you wish.

3 Cook over medium heat, covered, for 5 minutes, checking to be sure that the apples don't burn and that they're cooked and soft. You can also microwave the apple mixture for 2 to 3 minutes. Meanwhile, toast the waffles.

4 Place 2 waffles on each individual plate. Carefully, so that they don't break, divide the apples and spoon on top of the waffles. Pour on the maple syrup and a shake of confectioners' sugar.

Nutrition at a glance (per serving): *Calories 366.90; Protein 6.22 g; Carbohydrates 82.24 g; Dietary fiber 3.96 g; Total fat 3.46 g; Saturated fat 0.08 g; Cholesterol 4.00 mg; Sodium 315.49 mg.*

Lynn's tip: *If you really want a rich birthday, Mother's or Father's Day, or "I love you" feast, add ½ cup chopped walnuts or pecans to the syrup and heat the syrup. As soon as it's hot, add ¼ cup raspberries to the skillet and remove the skillet from the burner. Don't stir or the berries will break. Pour on the nut-and-berry syrup, add a dollop of fatfree whipped topping, and tuck in a mint sprig at the edge of the waffles.*

Basic Omelet (or Scramble)

Omelets are one of the easiest and most versatile dishes for breakfast, brunch, lunch, or dinner and all of these variations are especially delicious. (See the sidebar "Omelet toppings or fillings," later in this chapter, for some great ideas.) You can place the toppings, made separately, in the center of the omelet, omelet folded over with a bit on top for decoration, or pour the whole filling on top or on the scrambled eggs. Only with the cheese omelet is it necessary to fold it over the cheese. I save you 250 milligrams of cholesterol and 4 grams of saturated fat by using primarily egg substitutes. Make sure that you have the toppings cooked and ready before you begin the eggs.

Preparation/Cooking time: 10 minutes

Yield: 4 servings (using 1-inch thick, 4-inches wide French bread)

1 cup egg substitute	*2 egg whites*

1 In a medium bowl, add the egg substitute, egg whites, and salt and pepper and whisk until slightly frothy.

2 Lightly spray an 8 to 10-inch skillet with nonstick vegetable oil spray and warm over medium heat. When the skillet is hot, immediately add the egg mixture.

3 Cook the eggs over medium-high heat for 3 to 4 minutes, lifting the edges of the egg mixture and tilting the pan several times to let the uncooked eggs run underneath. When the eggs are almost set, use a rubber spatula to once more loosen the edges. If you're using a filling (see the next sidebar), add it now to half the eggs, reserving a tablespoon or 2 for a dollop on top.

4 With the spatula, lift half the eggs and fold the eggs over the other half over the filling creating a half-moon, filling inside.

5 Reduce the heat to low and cook the folded omelet for 1 minute, or until the eggs are cooked through. (You can cover the pan for a minute.) Cut the omelet in half to make 2 wedges. Serve plain or add omelet fillings (see the next sidebar).

6 If scrambling the eggs (which means continual mixing with the fork while they cook), if you want any toppings or fillings, just add them attractively across the top after you serve the eggs.

Nutrition at a glance (per serving): Calories 38.32; Protein 7.76 g; Carbohydrates 1 17 g; Dietary fiber 0 g; Total fat 0 g; Saturated fat 0 g; Cholesterol 0 mg; Sodium 153.07 mg.

Lynn's tip: A little sprig of parsley or even a clean garden leaf tucked into the edge makes simple scrambled eggs look like a gourmet feast.

(continued)

Lynn's variation tip: To make an egg fritatta, prepare the filling and then the eggs. Set the cooked filling aside and begin cooking the eggs on the stovetop, but in an ovenproof skillet. Heat the oven to 350°. When the eggs are beginning to set, add the cooked filling directly on top of the eggs just before the eggs set (warm but still a little runny so that the filling settles on top gently, without disappearing into the eggs). Place the skillet with the eggs and filling in the oven and bake until the eggs are cooked and the filling reheated, about 12 minutes.

Omelet toppings or fillings

These toppings can really spice up a basic omelet or scrambled eggs. The cherry and Tex/Mex omelets (or scrambles when I forget to stir the eggs while cooking) are my favorites.

✔ **Cheese Omelet (or Scramble):** Add a pinch of nutmeg to the egg mixture instead of the pepper. Just before folding the omelet, sprinkle with 2 ounces shredded fatfree or lowfat Cheddar cheese or fatfree or lowfat mozzarella cheese. Fold and cook for 2 minutes, or until the cheese melts. Sprinkle with finely chopped scallions. If a scramble, sprinkle on top and cook covered until cheese melts.

✔ **Ham Omelet (or Scramble):** Just before folding the omelet, sprinkle with 2 ounces diced fatfree ham or Canadian bacon. Fold and cook for 2 minutes, or until the filling is hot. You can also add 2 tablespoons shredded lowfat cheese. Sprinkle with finely chopped fresh parsley. For a scramble, add to the eggs while cooking.

✔ **Bacon Omelet (or Scramble):** Cook 2 strips bacon per serving (or purchase already-cooked bacon) and remove absolutely *all* the fat before of after frying or microwaving. Chop and add only the lean bacon portion to the still liquid omelet (or scramble) as it cooks. Add salt and pepper. (This simple fat removal saves you about 8 grams of saturated fat, depending on how much bacon you use.)

✔ **Western Omelet (or Scramble):** In a separate skillet, spray and brown 1 chopped onion, green pepper, red pepper, and 1 large tomato (with the juices). Heat until the onion is soft. If the mixture sticks or gets too dry, add a teaspoonful or 2 of water or tomato juice. Stir in 1 tablespoon chili powder, a shake of cumin, a few tablespoons chopped cilantro, and salt and pepper, stir, and heat for an additional minute or two. Add to the center of the omelet, saving a few tablespoons to decorate the top. (For a scramble, mix the cooked ingredients into the liquid eggs and cook.)

✔ **Cherry Omelet (or Scramble):** Take a peek at this creation in the color section. Pit 1 cup fresh dark red bing cherries and chop coarsely, leaving a few whole cherries for garnish. If fresh cherries aren't available, use 1 cup canned tart cherries and reserve the juice. To a small cool saucepan, add 2 teaspoons cornstarch, 1 teaspoon fresh lemon juice, ¼ cup sugar, and 1 cup cherry or cranberry juice and whisk to mix. If using fresh cherries, add only 2 tablespoons sugar. Cook over medium heat for 2 to 3 minutes or until thick. Add the canned or fresh cherries and cook until hot, about 1 minute.

Leave the omelet or scramble flat. Add a dollop of sour cream to each omelet. Pour the cherry mixture over the sour cream topped omelet (or scramble).

✔ **Jelly Omelet (or Scramble):** Add ½ teaspoon sugar to the egg mixture. Omit the pepper but add a dash of salt. Just before folding the omelet, spoon 3 tablespoons jelly over the eggs. Fold and cook for 2 minutes, or until the filling is hot. Place a dollop of jelly on top to warn guest that, "This omelet is sweet. (For a scramble, add the jelly to the top.)

✔ **Mushroom Omelet (or Scramble):** Lightly spray a large skillet with no-stick spray. Add ½ pound fresh sliced mushrooms or one 16 to 18-ounce canned, sliced, drained mushrooms. If fresh, cover and cook over medium heat for 5 minutes (canned only take 2 to 3 minutes), or until the fresh mushrooms start to soften. Add salt and pepper. Sprinkle the omelet or scramble with fatfree Parmesan topping or Parmesan cheese. Perk up the mushrooms with a watercress sprig, clean leaf, or parsley sprig tucked under and edge or on top, because mushrooms always look so dank alone. For a scramble, add the cooked mushrooms into the liquid eggs, saving a few to decorate the top, and cook the eggs.

✔ **Parmesan Cheese Omelet (or Scramble):** To the basic omelet or scramble mixture, add ¼ cup grated Parmesan cheese. Sprinkle chopped parsley on top.

✔ **Onion Omelet (or Scramble):** Lightly spray a large skillet with nonstick spray. Add 1 cup chopped onions (several kinds if you choose). Spray the onions and add salt and pepper. Cover and cook over medium heat for 3 to 4 minutes, or until the onions start to soften. Add ¼ cup chopped parsley or a smaller amount of another herb such as snipped chives, basil, thyme or any other herb you like (or mix the herbs). Uncover and cook, adding 1 to 2 teaspoons water if needed to prevent sticking, for 2 to 3 minutes, or until the onions are golden. For a scramble, mix the cooked onions into the liquid eggs and heat.

✔ **Spanish Omelet (or Scramble) with Potatoes:** Finely dice 1 small potato and 1 small onion. Mince 1 small clove of garlic. Place in a microwavable dish and microwave the potatoes and onions on high for 2 minutes. Lightly spray a 10-inch skillet with no-stick spray. Add the potato and onion mixture, plus the small clove minced garlic. Lightly mist the vegetables with the spray and cook over medium-high heat, stirring occasionally, for 5 to 6 minutes, or until the potatoes are tender. Add a few teaspoons of water if the mixture gets too dry. Sprinkle the filled omelet or scramble top with several tablespoons finely diced tomatoes and chopped scallions including the green part. For a scramble, mix the cooked vegetables into the liquid eggs and heat.

✔ **Tex-Mex Omelet (or Scramble):** Lightly spray a large skillet with nonstick spray. Add ½ cup finely diced onions, ¼ cup finely diced green peppers, ¼ cup diced red peppers, ½ cup corn kernels, 1 teaspoon finely diced jalapeños, ½ cup finely diced tomatoes, and 1 clove minced garlic and a sprinkle of chopped cilantro. Mist with the spray and cook over medium heat, stirring occasionally, for 4 to 6 minutes, or until the peppers and onions are softened. Add a few teaspoons of water if the mixture gets too dry. Season with 1 teaspoon chili powder, ¼ teaspoon ground cumin, and ¼ teaspoon dried oregano. Serve the eggs on a bed of corn chips, spoon the mixture over the eggs, and add a dollop of fatfree or lowfat sour cream and a sprinkle of chopped black olives and more chopped fresh cilantro to the top (or poke a cilantro sprig under the sour cream). For a scramble, add the

(continued)

(continued)

cooked vegetables to the liquid eggs and heat. Garnish with a sprig of cilantro and a few diced tomatoes.

✔ **Huevos Rancheros Omelet (or Scramble):** Take 8-inch uncooked flour tortillas (heated) and add 1 or 2 large thin slices lean ham or very thinly sliced skinless chicken or turkey breast to the tortilla. Add the unfolded omelet or scramble on the ham, chicken or turkey and some heated chunky salsa to the eggs, fold, and sprinkle on shredded cheese, sour cream dollop, and chopped black olives. Place an avocado slice in the sour cream, ends sticking out. For a scramble, add the scrambled eggs to the meat slice on the tortilla and add the heated salsa and other ingredients to the top.

✔ **Greek Omelet (or Scramble):** Lightly spray a large skillet with nonstick spray. Add 1 cup torn spinach leaves, 1 chopped scallion and ¼ teaspoon dried oregano. Cook over medium heat, stirring for 2 to 3 minutes, or until the spinach wilts. Add a few tablespoons of water if the mixture gets too dry. Add 1 small chopped tomato. Cook for 2 minutes. After the omelet is filled and served, or the scramble is placed on a plate, sprinkle with 1 tablespoon crumbled lowfat feta cheese. Sprinkle with chopped fresh dill. For a scramble, add the cooked vegetables to the liquid eggs and heat.

Chapter 15

Slow Cooking in the Fast Lane

·····························

In This Chapter

▶ Getting better flavors with quick preps and unattended slow cooking

▶ Defatting long cooking and sometimes fatty meats and poultry

▶ Spicing secrets for slow cooking

·····························

Recipes in This Chapter

▶ Sausage and White Bean Soup

▶ Chicken Soup with Noodles or Rice

▶ Meat Loaf

▶ Long Baked Beans

Meats and poultry, even those that are tough and stringy, cooked a long time have a special, almost deeper flavor, are more tender, and can result in a fusion or blending of tastes. In this chapter, I concentrate on that premise with a few very good long-cooking recipes. I also tell you the kinds of foods and dishes that benefit from long cooking and give you the top secrets to good long cooking.

Why You Should Try Slow Cooking

Here's why slow cooking is a time-saver.

✔ You can cook all the food in one pot, over many hours unattended, while you do something else, coming home to a ready-made meal with little clean up and lots of saved time and energy.

✔ It's hard to make a mistake with long-cooked foods if you remember certain basics:

   • Beef works well with carrots, onions, garlic, celery, and tomatoes.

   • Chicken slow-cooks well with carrots, onions, garlic, celery, and perhaps sherry.

   • Pork slow-cooks well with onions and perhaps apple cider.

✔ Add any short-cooking vegetables during the last half hour. You can also add additional carrots, celery, plus potatoes, and other foods at any time as the same vegetables in the same dish can be cooked for different amounts of time.

Long, slow baking or cooking in liquid not only tenderizes and breaks up the texture of foods such as meat, it turns hard vegetables like potatoes soft. Cooking in liquid also imparts flavors into the meat, fish, or poultry. These flavors are herbs and spices or vegetables. Most quick cooking cannot do this as well, with the herbs staying mostly on the outside. This taste of long-cooked foods is highly pleasing and affords a type of caramelizing that only long cooking can bring. Tough, stringy meat falls off the bone and becomes imbued with a deliciously tasty ambrosia of flavors not available any other way. That's one reason why *demi glacés* (reductions of meat sauces), bouillon cubes, and meat and vegetable granules are great flavor boosters — you're adding flavor essences from foods that have been cooked a long time and reduced so that only the concentrated flavor is left.

Slow cooking several foods together in a slow cooker (see Figure 15-1) has many others benefits as well:

- ✔ Your meal cooks no matter what you're doing.
- ✔ Your whole meal is cooked at one time.
- ✔ You don't need to watch your meal because it doesn't burn.
- ✔ Your kitchen doesn't get hot.
- ✔ The flavor is infused and fabulous.
- ✔ Cheaper or less fatty meats become very tender.
- ✔ Your meals are nutritious and lowfat when you use lots of veggies and less meat.
- ✔ Spices and herbs infuse into the foods better.

In addition, you can slow-cook the following foods and dishes in slow ovens (225°), on the lowest heat on the stove (carefully check temperatures to be sure that your burner gets up to 225°, but not higher), or in slow cookers.

Figure 15-1:
A slow cooker saves you time.

applesauce and other apple dishes

breads and plum puddings

casseroles of all kind

chilies with dried beans from scratch

chowders

cobblers

cornmeal mush or polenta

curries

dried beans from scratch

fish

fricassee

lamb or mutton dishes

marinated dishes

meatballs

meat loaf

pork

potatoes

pot roast

puddings

rice

roast chickens and turkeys

root vegetables

sauerbraten (German-style beef)

soufflés

soups

spoon breads

stews

stuffings

tea

wild game

Mastering the Secrets of Slow Cooking

Slow cooking isn't hard to do, especially if you follow these basic tips:

- ✓ **To make the best soup from chicken, duck, or turkey, use poultry that has already been cooked or baked from a previous meal.** The cooked bones give it a mellow flavor found no other way.

- ✓ **If you're using turkey or chicken bones that haven't been baked or cooked, place them on a baking tray, separated and uncovered, and put them in a 425° oven for 1½ hours, or a slow oven (250°) for 4 to 6 hours.**

- ✓ **If you're using turkey or chicken bones for a soup or stew base that hasn't been baked or cooked, make sure that the bird simmers in liquid for 1½ to 2 hours, defatting the broth and adding any vegetables.**

- ✓ **If you're making a beef soup from fresh meat, cut one-fourth to one-third of the total amount of meat (if using a pound, dice 3 ounces) into ¼-inch dices and bake overnight in a slow (250°) oven, along with any bones.** Although the meat will dry out and harden, it will rehydrate when added to the soup or stew. The meat is small enough to give the stew a different consistency without the texture being intrusive.

- ✔ **If you're making a soup with fresh red meat bones that you didn't bake overnight, dust both the marrow bones and meat cubes in flour and salt and pepper and brown the bones along with the meat.** The browning releases additional flavors in the bones, too.

- ✔ **If a recipe calls for saffron, begin cooking the saffron early.** The flavors are only released after the first 30 minutes of cooking.

- ✔ **If a recipe calls for dried oregano, cook it a short time.** It can turn bitter after lengthy cooking.

- ✔ **Don't be afraid to add foods, such as onions or parsley, several times during the cooking.** Onions cooked 3 hours taste differently than onions cooked 1 hour or for just 10 minutes (or even diced raw on top).

- ✔ **Put longer cooking foods like meats in early.** Spoon off the fat religiously. Add shorter cooking foods later.

- ✔ **Don't let meats cook at very low temperatures (150°) for more than 3 hours because they can spoil.** Closely follow the manufacturer's directions for your slow cooker. Each manufacturer has tested the safety of the temperatures on its particular machines because temperatures vary.

You need to cut off, dig out, remove, peel away, and slice out every single bit of fat whether the meat is beef, poultry, pork, or something else. You don't need fat for tenderness — the long cooking takes care of that. You don't need it for flavor for the same reason. And why infuse everything with fat?

Trying Your Hand at Slow Cooking

The following recipes benefit from fast prep and long cooking to allow the flavors of the foods to meld together. Cooking in a slow cooker or on a stove also means that you don't have to heat the whole kitchen in the summer.

Sausage and White Bean Soup

A really long-cooking meat soup has a flavor that no other form of cooking can achieve. My testers loved this recipe (see photo in color section). It takes only a few minutes to prepare and is ready for dinner the next day. Presoaked beans speed up the cooking time by 12 to 16 hours. Most dried beans unsoaked cook easily in just 3 hours at a slightly higher heat — on the stove, for example. One of my testers says she cooks small white dried beans in about 1½ hours on the stove top. I did this recipe in a slow cooker.

Preparation/Cooking time: *15 minutes prep; 3 to 10 hours slow cooking, depending on the method*

Yield: *6 servings*

12 ounces ground sausage	*½ cup chopped celery*
1 pound dry white navy beans	*2 large carrots, sliced*
4 10½-ounce cans fatfree or lowfat chicken broth	*½ green bell pepper*
	1 tablespoon minced garlic cloves
1 bay leaf	*¼ cup red wine*
1 teaspoon dried thyme	

1 Lightly spray a large skillet with cooking oil spray. Cook the sausage on medium-high, about 12 minutes or until cooked. Blot up the fat with paper towels as it cooks. (To do so, remove the pan from heat and use wadded paper towels to blot excess grease once or twice during cooking). Place the cooked sausage on paper towels and blot again, pressing hard.

2 Fill a slow cooker or large oven dish (with a cover) with the cooked sausage, beans, chicken broth, bay leaf, thyme, celery, carrots, bell pepper, garlic, wine, and salt and pepper to taste. If you want it more like a soup, add 2 cups hot water.

3 Cook, covered, 8 to 10 hours in a Crock Pot; 3½ to 4 hours in a 275° oven; or 1½ to 2½ hours simmering on a very low burner on the stove top. If you use a larger dried bean, add more time and add more water, ¼ to ½ cup at a time, here and there as necessary to keep the moisture you want. Before serving, add any salt and pepper you wish and remove the bay leaf.

Nutrition at a glance (per serving): *Calories 388.3 g; Protein 22.3 g; Carbohydrates 51.5 g; Dietary fiber 12.3 g; Total fat 10.1 g; Saturated fat 3.4 g; Cholesterol 24.0 g; Sodium 954.2 mg.*

Lynn's tip: *Use any kind of sausage you want because you're precooking it and removing much of the fat, which causes the sausage to partially collapse and drain as it cooks. My favorite is Italian mild, but a spicy sausage is also good. Try to get the kind that has the least fat, which you can see by examining the sausage or reading the amount of total fat on the Nutrition Fact panels on commercially wrapped sausage packages. Serve with a large salad and good crusty bread.*

Tip: *If you're crazy about the flavor of salt pork or ham hocks in beans or chowders, boil ½ to 1 pound salt pork or ham hock in 2 or 3 quarts water for 20 to 30 minutes. Discard the pork and defat the flavored broth in a defatting cup and use that instead of clear water in this recipe for all flavor and no fat.*

Chicken Soup with Noodles or Rice

My testers didn't make a single change to this recipe, saying that this soup was "fabulous and takes surprisingly little work because you buy the vegetables already sliced from either the salad bar or vegetable department." You add the peas, parsley, and cooked noodles or rice at the last minute so that they don't overcook or get soft. You can add the peas still frozen if you first crack the box hard on the counter to separate them. Add 2 tablespoons sherry at the end of cooking if you like it (I do).

Note: The celery, onions, garlic, sage, parsley, bouillon, and bay leaves are divided. because half of each goes into flavoring the chicken as it boils. You discard those vegetables, along with the chicken skin and bones, because they're usually filled with fat. The remaining fresh vegetables go into making the soup. Making the recipe in 2 stages and defatting the cooking broth helps keep the fat content extremely low and the flavor incredibly high.

Preparation/Cooking time: 15 minutes prep; 3 hours slow cooking

Yield: 8 to 10 servings

1 pound noodles

1 3-pound whole chicken, tail and liver removed

2 cups sliced celery, divided

2 cups sliced carrots, divided

2 large onions, chopped and divided

10 cloves garlic, 5 whole and 5 minced

2 bay leaves divided

2 teaspoons crumbled sage, or 2 leaves fresh sage, cut into strips, divided

½ cup chopped parsley, divided

1 teaspoon dried or fresh rosemary

1 teaspoon dried or fresh thyme

2 chicken bouillon cubes, or 2 teaspoons chicken essence or demi glacé

1 cup frozen peas or corn (or a combination)

2 tablespoons cornstarch or flour

1 Cook the noodles according to package directions, drain, and refrigerate in a plastic bag until ready to use. You can do this a day or 2 ahead or when you're making the broth. (I cook extra pasta continually so that I have a bag of cooked noodles in the refrigerator, ready to use.)

2 Remove and discard all visible fat from the chicken (leave the skin). In an 8-quart soup pot or slow cooker, add the whole chicken and cover with water plus an additional 2 inches (about 4 quarts).

3 Add 1 cup celery, 1 cup carrots, 1 cup chopped onion, 5 whole cloves garlic, 1 bay leaf, 1 teaspoon sage, ¼ cup parsley, and any salt and pepper you wish. Cover and simmer on very low heat for 2 hours.

4 Remove the chicken to a plate. Scoop out the vegetables with a wide slotted spoon and discard if fat-filled (they are usually fat filled) or greasy. Defat the broth by using a defatting cup or by chilling and picking off the hardened fat.

5 Remove and discard the skin and bones from the chicken. Dice the meat and set aside. Add the reserved defatted liquid back to the pot.

6 Add the remaining 1 cup celery, 1 cup carrots, 1 chopped onion, 5 cloves minced garlic, 1 bay leaf, 1 teaspoon sage, ¼ cup parsley, rosemary, thyme, and bouillon cubes. (If you don't have about 2 quarts of liquid, add water or fatfree chicken broth to make 2 quarts.) Simmer on low, covered, for 40 minutes.

7 During the last 5 minutes of simmering, add the reserved meat and peas. In a small bowl, add ½ cup of the soup liquid, chill with an ice cube (or use cool water), and whisk in the cornstarch. Add the cornstarch mixture to the simmering pot and cook until thickened, about 1 minute. If using flour, add to ½ cup cool liquid, stir the flour mixture into the soup, and heat for 4 more minutes to cook the flour. Add the chicken back to the pot and sherry, if you want it.

8 When serving, remove the bay leaf, place the cooked noodles (or rice) in the bottom of each serving dish, and pour the hot broth and any vegetables over them.

Nutrition at a glance (per serving): *Calories 367.2 g; Protein 32.8 g; Carbohydrates 45.0 g; Dietary fiber 4.1 g; Total fat 5.5 g; Saturated fat 1.3 g; Cholesterol 123.3 mg; Sodium 431.6 mg.*

Lynn's tip: *If you add noodles to the soup during cooking, they will become mushy when stored overnight or for a few days in the refrigerator. Store the noodles or rice separately in a zippered plastic bag to keep them firm until you're ready to use them.*

Meat Loaf

This recipe makes a really fine meat loaf and got raves from my testers and their guests, who happily finished it off. If you aren't a ketchup lover, use any lowfat commercial tomato pasta sauce you like. You can also double the recipe or make mini-loaves, cooking for a slightly shorter time.

Preparation: *15 minutes prep; 1 hour, 20 minutes slow cooking*

Yield: *8 servings*

(continued)

1 pound 93 percent lean ground beef

1 cup finely chopped onion

2 cloves garlic, chopped

1 cup finely chopped celery

1 cup breadcrumbs

½ cup substitute eggs

1 teaspoon Worcestershire sauce

½ teaspoon sugar

1 cup ketchup, divided

1 Preheat the oven to 350°.

2 In a large bowl, add the meat, onion, garlic, celery, breadcrumbs, eggs, Worcestershire sauce, sugar, and salt and pepper to taste and mix well.

3 Lightly spray a 4-inch x 8-inch loaf pan. Add the meat mixture to the loaf pan.

4 Spread ½ cup ketchup on top of the meat loaf and bake for 45 minutes to 1 hour. After 1 hour, add the remaining ½ cup ketchup to the top, spreading it around, and bake for an additional 20 minutes.

Nutrition at a glance (per serving): Calories 187.4 g; Protein 15.7 g; Carbohydrates 20.5 g; Dietary fiber 1.1 g; Total fat 4.9 g; Saturated fat 1.9 g; Cholesterol 33.7 mg; Sodium 565.6 mg.

Lynn's tip: Make a vegetable or mushroom-layered meat loaf of sliced mushrooms, shredded carrots, slivered hard-cooked egg whites, black olives, red or green peppers, or almost any other vegetable that isn't too watery. First, divide in half the meat after the onions and other ingredients are well mixed. Put half of the mixture in the loaf pan, making a layer of about 1½ inches. Flatten it with your palm or fingers so that it is fairly even. Place a 1-inch layer of shredded carrots, cabbage, olives, peppers, thinly sliced mushrooms, or whatever julienned or thinly sliced food you're using and then top with the rest of the uncooked meat mixture, pressing it down slightly. Add half the ketchup or pasta sauce and bake as directed.

Long Baked Beans

Easy to make, delicious to eat, beans are a nearly perfect food and the long baking brings out all the rich flavor. High in fiber and protein, these beans are even better the day after they're cooked. Serve with all those barbecue foods like cole slaw or green salad, corn on the cob, carrots, and broccoli florets for a colorful and healthful meal. The beans will turn a dark, rich brown whether cooked simmering on very low on the stove top for 3 to 4 hours, in a slow cooker for 8 to 10 hours, or in a slow 275° oven for 8 or 9 hours. You may like your beans cooked slightly less with any of the preceding ways. A slow cooker on low may take longer than a slow cooker on high, too. It actually doesn't matter much. I have cooked mine for as long as 22 hours.

Preparation/Cooking time: *10 minutes prep; 3 to 22 hours slow cooking, depending on the method*

Yield: *8 servings*

2 teaspoons prepared mustard

¼ cup tomato ketchup

1 14.5-ounce can diced Italian-style tomatoes and juice

½ teaspoon liquid smoke

½ cup molasses

¼ cup brown sugar

1 teaspoon finely chopped garlic cloves

1 large onion, finely chopped

3 ounces lean smoked ham, cut into strips

1 large green pepper, diced (optional)

1 1-pound package pinto or white beans, carefully picked through to check for stones

1 Preheat the oven to 275° or plug in the slow cooker.

2 In a large baking dish or slow cooker, add the mustard, ketchup, tomatoes, liquid smoke, molasses, brown sugar, garlic, and 1 quart water and mix well.

3 Add the onions, ham, green pepper if using, beans, and salt and pepper to taste and stir around.

4 Cover with foil if baking (or the lid if cooking in the Crock Pot) and cook at 275° for 3½ to 8 hours in the oven. If using a Crock Pot, cook 8 to 10 hours, until the beans are tender. You must check the liquid and add more every few hours or so if needed, cooking until the beans are tender. Beans can vary in dryness, depending upon their age (meaning that they may take longer or shorter amounts of time to cook.) You can adjust flavor at any time during cooking.

Nutrition at a glance (per serving): *Calories 317.2 g; Protein 14.5 g; Carbohydrates 63.8 g; Dietary fiber 9.2 g; Total fat 1.4 g; Saturated fat 0.4 g; Cholesterol 5.6 mg; Sodium 591.0 mg.*

Lynn's tip: *If you want a real bacon flavor instead of ham, purchase precooked bacon. Using scissors, remove and discard all the fat from about 6 or 8 strips. Add the cooked bacon before heating. To shorten the cooking time, cook in a 300° oven, covered, for 8 hours, adding more water when needed, or on the stove top, covered, for 5 hours, over the lowest possible heat.*

Part IV
The Part of Tens
(And More)

The 5th Wave   By Rich Tennant

"It's a microwave slow cooker. It'll cook a stew all day in just 7 minutes."

In this part . . .

The best newsletters and Web sites are here. This chapter gives you their addresses, phone numbers, and a little critique on each newsletter so that you know what you are getting and which are the best.

Chapter 16

Ten Best Health Newsletters

● ●

In This Chapter

▶ Ten or so of the best health newsletters

● ●

*T*his is the chapter with the most long-lasting effects. I say long-lasting because when you get a subscription to one of the ten or so health letters listed here, you are arming yourself with the very best, up-to-date medical information . . . and it's continual. For as long as you have a subscription, you will get the newsletters you want each month. In this chapter, I give you the addresses and phone numbers so that you can get good nutrition and health information from the best health letters around.

Because I have a subscription to most of them and because I read each carefully every month, I also include my opinion about each health letter.

From the hottest food and health letter around — the Center for Science in the Public Interest's (CSPI) *Nutrition Action* — to the *Harvard Health Letter*, these are good investments in living and eating healthfully.

General Health Letters

Health letters are usually monthly and are between four and 12 pages with most running eight pages. However, *Health News* (from *The New England Journal of Medicine*) can have a whopping 30 pages and comes out every 3½ weeks. Health letters come in two styles. One style covers only a few subjects, but the writing is usually in depth (some newsletters do it so vaguely and with such a simplistic style that you don't really learn much). The other style is to write about many different subjects with just a few paragraphs about each. For me, this type is the more enjoyable newsletter, and I've noted those that do that. One, *Nutrition Action,* uses both styles, which makes it especially reader friendly.

For more in-depth scientific information that gives the name of who did the study, you can get the actual monthly medical journals the same as doctors and medical reporters do. The *Journal of the American Medical Association* (JAMA) and the *New England Journal of Medicine* are just two of the 3,000 or so other medical journals, all of which can be sent directly to you instead of their far less expensive excerpt-style health letters, which are written more for the layman. The cost difference is usually several hundred dollars for each journal.

The following are health letters I recommend.

You can call either the Boulder, Colorado, number or the Palm Coast number and order several newsletters as these large mailing houses handle hundreds of newsletters.

- ✔ **Consumer Reports on Health,** PO Box 56360, Boulder, CO 80323-6360, 1-800-234-2188. Well-written, full of information, a few more pages than most and has both long and short articles with a nice Q and A with four questions on the back page.

- ✔ **Environmental Nutrition,** Food Nutrition and Health, PO Box 420451, Palm Coast, FL 32142-0451, 1-800-829-5384. Monthly newsletter on nutrition, food, and health, written by registered dietitians.

- ✔ **Harvard Health Letter,** PO Box 420300, Palm Coast, FL 32142-0300, 1-800-829-9045. One of the most respected health letters. So successful it has spawned several offspring, from *Harvard's Mental Health Letter*, heart advisors, to *Harvard's Men's Health Watch*, and *Harvard Women's Health Watch*. It has only a few in-depth articles, but the subjects are topical.

- ✔ **Mayo Clinic Health Letter,** PO Box 53889, Boulder, CO 80323-3889, 1-800-333-9037. A lot of information in depth about just a few items. Nice color illustrations so that you can see what happens to your food or your rotator cuff. The last page has a Second Opinion, but contains only two questions.

- ✔ **Nutrition Action Health Letter,** 1875 Connecticut Ave NW, Suite 300, Washington, DC 20009-5728, 1-800-237-4874. This is one of my favorites because it gives you lots of information on many different subjects, focusing on one or two each month for in-depth reporting. And it yells at companies and organizations about their unhealthy products. CSPI played a primary role in getting Nutrition Facts panels on foods and healthier popcorn oils in movie theaters. CSPI also told the public that much Italian and Chinese restaurant fare wasn't very healthy.

- ✔ **University of California at Berkeley Wellness Letter,** PO Box 420148, Palm Coast, FL 32142, 1-904-445-6414. Many pages, short and long articles, covers everything from toilet seat covers to vitamin B, smoothies to fish and omega-3, alfalfa sprouts and free-range chickens. Well-written and full of good stuff with lots about food. One of my favorites.

More Specific Health Letters

Here are a few more health letters on more defined areas of health.

- ✔ **John's Hopkins Medical Letter Health After 50,** PO Box 420235, Palm Coast, FL 32142-0235, 1-904-446-4675. I like this one, but think many of the articles are more for people over 70 rather than 50. It has good little tidbits on new reasons to cut back on the amount of meat in your diet and in-depth articles, plus two Q and As on the back page.

- ✔ **Harvard Heart Letter,** PO Box 420234, Palm Coast, FL 32142-0234, 1-800-829-9171. Usually only four to five in-depth articles, well-written and on topical subjects such as "Extra Benefits from Diet," "Antidepressants and Quitting Smoking." Illustrations. For people who want to know more about their heart and how diet affects it, this is a good one.

- ✔ **The Cleveland Clinic Heart Adviser,** PO Box 420235, Palm Coast, FL 32142. 1-800-829-2506. Nice Q and A on the back. Good information, good illustrations.

- ✔ **Health News** (put out by the *New England Journal of Medicine*), PO Box 52924, Boulder, CO 80322-2924, 1-800-848-9155. Explains the latest medical research in newsletter form. You get 15 issues a year, about 30 pages each of a very complete and carefully written newsletter with one issue delivered every few weeks.

- ✔ **Tufts University Health and Nutrition Letter,** PO Box 57857, Boulder, CO 80322-7857, 1-800-274-7581. It provides reliable health and nutrition information.

- ✔ **Women's Health Advisor,** PO 420235, Palm Coast, FL 32142, 1-800-847-7131. This monthly publication covers menopause, anxiety, cancer, and myth- stopping truths concerning women's health issues.

Chapter 17

The Ten Best Health Web Sites

*I*f you buy this book for no other reason than having this Web site information, it is the best investment you can make. From government sites to the American Medical Association, this chapter shows you how to, literally, just reach out and touch the keys.

I give you almost three dozen fabulous Web sites. Because this is a Part of Tens chapter, you see ten Web sites first — but then I give you ten more, and then ten more still. I couldn't leave any out. And there are even more being developed daily on the Web.

And, of course, don't forget to check out my Web sites at LynnFisher.com or Lowfatlife.com.

A Personal Story Using a Web Site

Many of you have had personal experiences with health Web sites. My brother Bob was diagnosed with kidney stones, which apparently is one the worst pains known to man. His doctor told him to go straight to the hospital, so he did. But hospitals are busy and noisy all night long, and he got no rest, even with sedatives. He walked home five miles, hoping to pass the stones. They didn't pass.

He was frantic from the pain, tense with anxiety, and had no idea what he should do. Operate, wait, take medication — what else was available? He had no idea, and it was 5 a.m. He went to his computer, contacted several health Web sites, and found all the answers on everything he needed to know about kidney stones. He relaxed, went to sleep, and selected the doctor and treatment he thought would be best. It was all available on the computer. And he recovered quickly.

Kidney stones are relatively minor when compared to other very serious diseases. You can find information about every kind on illness or dietary situation from carrots to capsules, flatulence to fake foods, health questions, prescription medication, or pill interaction. You can find appropriate doctors or specialists in your area, discussion of rare problems, and especially, healthy eating information. Some sites are more helpful than others. Some are more thorough. Some are just interesting and fun. And be aware, there is also misinformation as anyone can post a health or medical site. Trust names and institutions you know.

Go into each site and put the ones you like in your "favorite places" file so that you can retrieve it at any time.

The following Web site by Tufts University, evaluates and rates healthy Web sites:

```
www.navigator.tufts.edu
```

Go to the General Nutrition area where you find updated information with many new sites. To get to them, just click on the one you want to see.

Sites You'll Want to Visit

The following sites are mostly by private organizations, like the American Heart Association's health news, and by government organizations, like the United States Department of Agriculture, which has a site where you can get information about the Food Guide Pyramid:

```
www.usda.gov/cnpp/pyrabklt.pdf
```

- ✔ **American Dietetic Association (ADA):** www.eatright.org
- ✔ **American Heart Association (AHA):** www.americanheart.org
- ✔ **American Medical Association (AMA):** www.ama-assn.org
- ✔ **Centers for Disease Control and Prevention (CDC):** www.cdc.gov
- ✔ **Food and Nutrition Information Center at National Agriculture Library United States Department of Agriculture (USDA):** www.nalusda.gov
- ✔ **National Heart, Lung, and Blood Institute (NHLBI):** www.nhlbi.nih.gov
- ✔ **National Institutes of Health (NIH):** www.nih.gov
- ✔ **World Health Organization/Health Topics (WHO):** www.who.int
- ✔ **Your American Cancer Society (ACS):** www.cancer.org

Ten More Sites for Good Measure

This second list has sites by mostly medical schools, like Harvard and Tufts, famous for their fine health newsletters (see Chapter 16).

- **Berkeley Education, Searchable Online Archive of Recipes:** `godzilla.eecs.berkeley.edu`
- **Columbia Medical School:** `www.goaskalice.colombia.edu`
- **Duke Medical School:** `www.mc.duke.edu`
- **Duke University:** `gilligan.mc.duke.edu`
- **Harvard Medical Center:** `dash.bwh.harvard.edu`
- **Mayo Clinic:** `www.mayohealth.org` (rated No. 1 by Tuft's Navigator site)
- **Medline:** `www.nlm.nih.gov`
- **MedTrial:** `www.medtrial.com`
- **Stanford Medical School:** `www.med.stanford.edu`
- **Tufts Medical Center:** `www.hnrc.tufts.edu`

And Still More

This third list is a hodgepodge, but it's not to be ignored. These sites contain mostly medical information. Some sites are by health and food nonprofits, like CSPI. Some sites, like CNN's, are from the media and for-profit companies. And some are simply Web sites, such as that from Dr. C. Everett Koop, that you just shouldn't miss.

- **About.com Health and Fitness:** `home.about.com`
- **CNN Health:** `www.cnn.com`
- **Cooking Light Online:** `cookinglight.com`
- **Cooks Corner:** `cookscorner.com`
- **CSPI Center for Science in the Public Interest:** `www.cspinet.org`
- **Diet Center Worldwide, Inc.:** `www.dietcenterworldwide.com`
- **Dr. C. Everett Koop:** `www.drkoop.com`
- **Glaxo Wellcome:** `www.healthylives.com`
- **HomeArts:** `homearts.com`
- **Home & Garden Television (HGTV):** `www.hgtv.com`

- ✔ **Light Living:** lightliving.com
- ✔ **Physician's Desk Reference, PDR's Getting Well Network:** www.pdr.net
- ✔ **Stanford University School of Medicine, Primary Care Teaching Module: Obesity & Weight Loss:** www.med.stanford.edu
- ✔ **Reuters Health Information:** www.reutershealth.com
- ✔ **Medical College of Wisconsin Physicians and Clinics, Using Diet to Lower Your Blood Pressure:** www.healthlink.mcw.edu

Glossary

Al dente: In Italian, means "to the teeth." Usually used to define pasta cooked firm but not mushy so that it has some texture to it.

Amino acid: Building blocks of protein. Eight essential amino acids, which your body cannot manufacture, must be included in your diet.

Blood cholesterol: Component in blood that comes from the dietary cholesterol you eat and the cholesterol that your body makes in the liver. High levels of blood cholesterol are a risk factor for heart disease.

Bouillon: A clear broth (see stock) usually made from the water in which meat, chicken, vegetables, or fish have been cooked. Also refers to commercially dehydrated products such as bouillon cubes, usually from condensed meat and salt, or granules of condensed meat.

Bread: A baked loaf of grains. To bread means to coat food with bread or cracker crumbs before cooking to give a crusty coating when cooked.

Brown: Cook food until the surface browns and crusts either by sautéing or placing under the broiler.

Butter: Cow fat made from cream into a spread. It is high in saturated fat.

Butter substitutes: Lower saturated fat products, such as margarine, sprays, butter/margarine blends, tub margarine, poured substitutes; any spread, solid, semi solid or liquid that substitutes for butter whether made from animal, vegetable fat, a mixture or another product.

Butterlike spray: Used in this book to mean a lowfat or fatfree butter substitute spray. (Actually, the spray isn't fatfree, but when used in recommended amounts the fat involved is negligible.)

Carbohydrates: Found in fruit and starchy foods like pasta, potatoes, lima beans, peas, rice, milk, yogurt, and bread.

Cholesterol: A waxy substance found only in animals and animal products. Can be implicated in forming cholesterol plaque, a substance that can line the inside of the arteries, narrowing them.

Cholesterolfree: Contains no animal products as all contain cholesterol (with the exception of egg whites, an animal product that contains no cholesterol).

Cornstarch: A floury powder made from corn used to quickly thicken soups, sauces, and pie fillings. It is more translucent than flour and has a shorter cooking time, thickening almost as soon as it is hot. 1 tablespoon cornstarch equals 2 tablespoons flour in thickening power.

Crock pot: A slow-cooking electric, timed vessel used to cook foods a very long period of time especially good for tough meats, meats with little fat. Also called a slow cooker. Crock Pot is also a brand name.

Cube: Cut into cubes ½-inch thick (larger than for dicing).

Dairy foods: Butter, margarine, sour cream, cheese, cottage cheese, yogurt and other products made from milk. Can include eggs.

Dash: A shake or two.

Demi-glacé: A highly concentrated flavorful reduced thick liquid. Usually made from beef or chicken, but sometimes vegetables, ham, or lamb. Used as a base for basting, gravies, sauces, and soups.

Dense: In meat, it means compact or thick meats without fat, such as Canadian bacon, tenderloin, and top round.

Dice: To cut food in square pieces, as in dicing tomatoes in the shape of dice or small square bits from ¼-inches, to large dice, at about ¾-inch square pieces.

Diet: A food plan for any number of food management issues such as weight loss, weight gain, weight maintenance, for food allergies eliminating nuts and fish, or other food-related health situations such as diabetes or rosacea (a skin problem associated with eating spicy foods and caffeine among others).

Dietary cholesterol: Found only in animal products.

Dieting: A food plan used to lower fats and serving sizes, usually associated with a program for weight loss.

Dollop: Usually used when discussing a garnish such as "add a dollop of whipped topping to the pudding." Most often, it is between 1 to 2 teaspoons on a single serving or as much as several tablespoons of sour cream or yogurt for soup in a tureen.

Extra lean: A meat and poultry term used to denote meat that is leaner than lean, which means less than 5 grams fat, 2 grams or less saturated fat, and less than 95 mg cholesterol.

Fat: Fat is the white or yellowish marbling in and on the edges of meat and poultry and in some fish (but seldom in shellfish). Fat is also bottled oil and the greasy substance left when cooking meat or cheese. All foods contain some fat, even radishes (which is miniscule), or avocados, which can be from 3 to about 15 percent. (Nearly all of it monounsaturated a fat with calories but not one that causes the formation of cholesterol plaque.) Fats contain double the calories as proteins and carbohydrates. The fats, which are usually in far greater amounts in meat and poultry products than in vegetables, are of three types: saturated, polyunsaturated, and monounsaturated. Saturated fat, for a healthy diet, should be limited for most.

Fatfree: A food with less than 0.5 grams fat per amount or per labeled serving size.

FDA: Food and Drug Administration, which is a regulatory agency for food, cosmetics, and medicines, among other things.

Fiber: Fiber is in the fruits and vegetables that grow on plants or trees. Meat, fish, shellfish, and poultry have none, rice little, and some grains more than others with some fruits or vegetables like pears containing quite a bit. It is the part that isn't completely digested. Studies show a diet high in fiber is healthier because it may help reduce blood cholesterol levels as well as being beneficial in certain types of cancer. The daily recommendation of fiber is 25 to 35 grams a day.

Finely chop: To chop or dice foods about ⅛ to ¼-inch in size.

Flour: Grain ground so fine that it becomes powdery. All-purpose flour is made from wheat, is white, and is used in this cookbook. It doesn't contain risers like salt or baking powder. Flour is the base ingredient of bread, pretzels, crackers, pasta, and couscous and is used to thicken gravy, soups, and sauces. Flour, unlike cornstarch, makes the thickened liquids opaque and needs to be cooked and stirred for at least four minutes so that it loses its raw, starchy taste. To flour a food means to coat lightly or dust with flour before cooking.

Fold: To gently stir one food into another, usually a whipped topping with anything else.

Food Guide Pyramid: The USDA (United States Department of Agriculture) food guide (see Chapter 1).

Fusion cook: Used to describe the new types of pressure cookers, which "fuse" the flavors together as well as quickly cook them.

Garnish: Foods used to adorn, embellish or enhance a finished dish such as sour cream on a thick soup, parsley sprinkled on a stew, a whipped topping on pies or cakes.

Gram (g): Metric unit of measure. 453.6 grams equals 1 pound.

Grate: Cut food such a cheese or cabbage into shreds, flakes, or tiny particles using a tool with sharp-edged holes, a knife, or a food processor.

Gratin: A casserole with a topping of bread crumbs and/or cheese.

Grill: To cook over or under flame, coals, or electric grilling rod.

HDL: High-density lipoprotein, a type of good cholesterol found in the blood, not in food. It is good because more helps remove the bad cholesterol (LDL) from the body. LDL causes the formation of cholesterol plaque, which lines the blood stream.

Herb: The leaves of usually aromatic plants used to season foods. They can be fresh, such as parsley, sage, basil, thyme, and rosemary, or sometimes dried whole or dried on the stem such as bay leaves and rosemary. Occasionally, you can buy dried stems of oregano and thyme. You can also find them freeze-dried, such as chives; dried and flaked or crumbled such as sage, basil, oregano, thyme, sage, and tarragon; or even ground such as ground oregano.

High-protein diet: A diet consisting of high protein foods such as meat, cheese and eggs. A diet too high in protein is harmful and can tax the kidneys and liver if they have even slight damage. Excess animal protein, which also means a high cholesterol and high saturated fat diet, may be implicated in heart and artery disease as well as osteoporosis, a bone thinning disease.

Hydrogenated: Hardened fats.

Lactose: Milk sugar.

Lactose intolerant: Difficulty digesting milk foods due to a deficiency of an enzyme needed to digest lactose. Symptoms often include flatulence and diarrhea.

LDL: LDL is low-density lipoprotein and a number that is part of the total cholesterol number that your doctor determines after taking a small amount of your blood to test. LDL should be less than 130. A healthy diet low in saturated fat and cholesterol combined with exercise helps to keep the number low.

Leavening: Anything that lightens and increases the volume of a batter or dough when heated — for example air (beaten into egg whites), yeast, or baking powder.

Low carbohydrate diet: A diet low in foods that are high in carbohydrates such as fruit, potatoes, rice, bread, beans, milk, yogurt, and some grains. All these foods are considered healthy. A diet low or extremely low in carbohydrates isn't considered healthy.

Low cholesterol or low in cholesterol: Low cholesterol means that there is less than 20 mg of cholesterol and less than 2 grams of saturated fat (both have to be low to be called low cholesterol) per reference amount customarily consumed (per serving).

Lowfat: Has a specific governmental meaning of less than 3 grams of fat usually per 3.5 ounces of food, but it can be per reference (amount of servings on the package) amount customarily consumed, which might be slightly more or less than 3.5 grams.

Macrobiotics: A way of eating loosely linked to Buddhism and more strongly linked to the ancient Chinese principles of yin and yang. The foods reflect Asian influences and include rice, sea vegetables, tamari, miso and umeboshi plum, daikon and lotus root.

Marbling: The small white lines, strias of white or yellowish fat in the meat of animals. To ensure the lowest fats, look for meat with the least marbling or white streaks (which is fat). Highly marbling meat used to be desirable and was more expensive. Today, highly marbled or fatty meat is considered inferior.

Margarine: A butter substitute that was created over 100 years ago and made popular during the World War II using the name oleo margarine. The healthiest margarines say on the package they contain no transfatty acids (butter contains transfatty acids) and little or no hydrogenation, which hardens the fats making them saturated.

Marinate: Tenderize and flavor food by soaking in a seasoned acidic and/or oily flavored liquid, which can be seasoned with herbs and spices, garlic, onions and other ingredients.

Meat: In this cookbook, includes beef, pork, and lamb, plus poultry, fish, and shellfish.

Microgram (mcg): Metric unit of measure. 1,000 micrograms equals 1 milligram.

Microwave: Cook using a microwave oven. You can cover foods cooked this way with a glass or special for microwave's cover, with damp paper towels, a microwavable plate, or vented plastic wrap, but not aluminum foil.

Milligram (mg): Metric unit of measure. 1,000 milligrams equals 1 gram.

Mince: Cut food in bits about ⅛-inch pieces, (smaller than if you chop them). Minced garlic means it comes from a garlic press.

Mix: Stirring and blending usually with a spoon or blenders.

Monounsaturated fat: One of the three fatty acids or fats in all foods. Although containing the same calories as the other two, saturated and polyunsaturated, not considered as harmful for heart and artery disease. Foods high in monounsaturated fats are avocados and canola oil.

Nondairy: Foods without milk, cheese, cream, eggs, and sometimes it means without any animal products. However, it usually just means without milk or cream-based products.

Nutritional Facts panel: Often called a food label, it's usually located on the back of the package. It gives serving size and food values, such as calories, total fat, saturated fat, cholesterol, sodium, and fiber.

Nutritionally sound: Containing all the necessary nutrients. A diet appropriate in calories, sodium, total fat, saturated fat, fiber, and cholesterol and usually means eating a wide variety of foods with very small amounts of oil and fats, sugar, fatty meats, and whole dairy, and larger amounts of basic foods such as vegetables, fruits, beans, grains, and cereals.

Obese: Describes an overweight person who weighs 30 percent or more than is recommended for their bone structure, sex, age, and body type. Technically, it is a body mass index (BMI) of 30 percent or greater. Some diseases such as heart, artery, arthritis, and diabetes can be exacerbated by obesity. Obesity comes from eating more food than one needs and is rarely caused by certain drugs and or disease.

Omega-3 fatty acids: Found in ocean fish, lower total cholesterol, and triglycerides. High intake prolongs bleeding times, so it is recommend that you consume fish on a regular basis instead of taking fish oil capsules.

Osteoporosis: A complex disorder characterized by a loss of bone mass often described as thinning of the bones or a loss of bone density, which becomes so great that ordinary activity can cause fractures. It is seen in women 15 to 20 years after menopause begins. It can affect both sexes. Calcium supplements taken throughout the day may help ensure that one can keep the body from losing calcium through natural causes or a high-protein diet. It is recommended that women and men over age 51 consume at least 1,200 milligrams of calcium a day through leafy green vegetables or lowfat dairy such as milk, yogurt, and cheese, calcium fortified foods such as juice or cereal, or calcium supplements to help keep bones strong.

Pan-broil, pan-fry, or dry-fry: In this book, means cooking lean meat, lean and skinless poultry, or fish briefly and rapidly in a pan with no added fat if the meat contains some, or lightly spraying with vegetable cooking oil spray if like fish, it contains almost no fat.

Pinch: Usually measures between $\frac{1}{16}$ and $\frac{1}{8}$ teaspoon. Technically, it is the amount you can hold between your thumb and forefinger.

Pith: The soft, white, often bitter skin between the peel and flesh of citrus fruit or the white membrane in green and red peppers. Be sure to remove it all when peeling oranges and the like.

Poach: Cook food in a liquid heated to just below the boiling point.

Polyunsaturated fat: One of the three fatty acids or fats in nearly all foods, and although with the same calories as all other fats, not considered as harmful as saturated fat. Oils high in polyunsaturated fats are corn oil, safflower oil, and sunflower oil.

Poultry: In this cookbook, it means bird flesh that it skinned with all visible fat removed including domestic poultry thigh fat, and can include or be used interchangeably with chicken, turkey, duck, pheasant, Cornish game hen, and quail.

Pressure cooker: A type of pot with a secure lid in which steam, under pressure, reaches a much higher temperature than the boiling point of water and therefore cooks faster.

Protein: The main function is to build and repair body tissue. Major sources of protein are meat (can be lean), dairy (can be skim), and dried beans and peas. There are small amounts of protein in vegetables, grains, and fruits and no protein in oils and butter. The body's need for protein is limited, and it is thought most Americans get double the protein they need, which may cause other medical problems.

Puree: Reduce food to a smooth, velvety pulp by pressing it through a sieve or food mill, or processing in an electric blender or food processor.

Quinoa: A very small, high-protein, calcium-rich seed related to the broccoli plant that contains all eight essential amino acids. It is often called a grain and cooks up like rice.

Recommended dietary allowance or RDA: Standards established by the Food and Nutrition Board of the National Research Council and are the recommended intake of essential nutrients that, based on scientific knowledge, will meet the known nutrient needs of most healthy people.

Red meat: Is the muscle meat of animals, such as cattle, sheep, lamb, pig, and deer, called red because the muscle usually is red, but used to denote all animals such as these even if the meat is more white or gray such as some pork and veal.

Reduced fat: Has a specific governmental meaning of 25 percent less fat than the usual food. Reduced fat can still be high fat.

Refresh: Quickly cool hot cooked food by rinsing or immersing it in ice water. It can also mean to add water and cover with plastic wrap and refrigerate wilted foods, such as lettuce, parsley, and even carrots and celery.

Registered dietitian (R.D.): The letters R.D. after a person's name signify that he or she has completed academic and experience requirements established by the Commission on Dietetic Registration, the credentialing agency for the American Dietetic Association (ADA), including a minimum of a bachelor's degree granted by a U.S. regionally accredited college/university, or equivalent, and an approved preprofessional experience program. R.D.s demonstrate their knowledge of food and nutrition by successfully passing a national credentialing exam and by completing ongoing continuing professional development.

Salt: Used as a flavoring and preservative. Salt is 40 percent sodium. Iodized salt has iodine added to it, which is beneficial in areas where iodine in the soil is limited.

Saturated fat: All foods contain basically three kinds of fats, saturated, monounsaturated and polyunsaturated. Saturated fats are solid at room temperature and are found mainly in animal products and the tropical oils (coconut oil, palm oil and palm kernel oil). This type of fat raises blood cholesterol levels more than anything else in the diet. It is found in butter, whole milk dairy, egg yolks, all meats and meat fat, most fish, and not in shellfish. It is also found in coconut, coconut oil, and palm oil and in smaller amounts in peanut, olive and corn oil.

Sauté: In French, sauté simply means to fry. With American cooking, sauté is usually associated with cooking with a very small amount or just a slick of oil, such as olive or vegetable oil, butter, or margarine, or a vegetable oil spray.

Score: Make shallow or deep cuts in a decorative pattern with a sharp knife. You score the thick part of whole fish with two or three slashes, slightly opening it and allowing heat to enter, so that part cooks as fast as the thinner areas. You score the top of bread for decorative reasons, and you score meat to allow herbs, spices, or marinades to enter.

Sear: Quickly brown the surface of food (usually meat) on, over or under very high heat to seal in juices and give a rich flavor.

Serving size: Are standardized for food labeling and based on RACC. The serving sizes on food labels may be different than what is on the Food Guide Pyramid and also what most people consider a serving size.

Shred: Grate or cut into very small pieces or long, even, thin strands.

Skim: Can mean to remove fat from the surface of a liquid or can mean the product contains no measurable fat.

Slow-cook: A method of cooking for a long time at low heat in the oven, a slow cooker, or on a very low burner on the stove top.

Sodium: A mineral, which your body needs. The estimated requirement for healthy individuals is 500 mg per day, and the mean daily sodium intake is 4,000 mg per day per person. The recommended intake is 2,400 mg or less.

Spice: The flower or stamen of a flower such as saffron; the seed such as mustard, coriander, or cumin; the bark such as cinnamon; or the root such as ginger (not actually a root but a rhizome) of a plant. Usually spices are sold ground.

Spray: Nonstick vegetable oil cooking spray, which can be olive oil, butter-flavored oil, corn oil, canola, or any other oil or mixture of oils. A light spritz contains unmeasurable calories. A spritz for five to ten seconds can mean as much as half a teaspoon, and the calories begin to rise.

Steam cook: Cook using a small amount of boiling water, which usually doesn't touch the food. Steam cooked foods often retain more vitamins and minerals than those covered in water and boiled.

Stew: Cook food slowly in a simmering, well-seasoned liquid in a covered pan. Also means a dish, such as beef stew, made by combining foods and cooking them together such as beef, potatoes, carrots, and celery.

Stir: Mix, usually with a spoon.

Stir-fry: Often used in association with Asian cooking. Means to use a very small amount of fat or other liquid to cook foods quickly, usually over high or medium-high heat, tossing them (stirring rapidly) as they cook.

Stock: Flavored broth made by simmering bones, skin, and scraps of meat, poultry, or fish with vegetables in water. This is what you get when you use a bouillon cube plus water.

Strain: Place food in a sieve to separate liquid from solids or force a soft food through a sieve to puree it and remove hard particles.

Substitute eggs: Egg products that contain no cholesterol, yolks, or fat, usually sold in a half pint or pint cardboard carton found in the egg or frozen food section. They are basically egg whites, 99 percent egg product, with beta carotene for color.

Sugar: A sweetener. Sugar comes in many forms, such as granulated, confectioners, powdered, light or dark brown, and raw. Other sweeteners are honey, jam, fruit and fruit juice concentrate, molasses, maple or corn syrup, and many other sugars. All sugars act the same in the body.

Supplements: Can be liquid beverages used to increase someone's calorie and nutrient intake, or they can also be vitamin and mineral pills.

Sweeteners: Besides sugar products, other sweeteners include fructose (the sweetest), glucose, sucrose, and artificial sweeteners, such as aspartame and saccharine.

Toss: To lightly or gently mix foods such as salad greens and other salad ingredients or to stir-fry vegetables while they are cooking so as to not break them up.

Total fat: On Nutritional Facts panels, signifies the aggregate amounts of saturated fat, polyunsaturated fat, transfatty acids, and monounsaturated fats. As an example, if the label says the food contains 1 g saturated fat, .5 g polyunsaturated fat, and .5 g monounsaturated fat, total fat would be more or less 2 g.

Trans fatty acids: Found in harder fats such as beef, butter, and milk fats and are formed in the process of hydrogenation. Stick margarine, shortening, commercial frying fats, and high-fat baked goods are the major food sources in the American diet.

Tofu: Also called bean curd. Soybean curd made from soybean milk by a process similar to that used for making cheese. Sold in blocks and comes in soft, firm, and extra-firm style. Use soft for whipping, blending, and crumbling; firm for slicing and cubing; and extra-firm for stir-fries and the like.

Triglycerides: Diet, estrogens, alcohol, obesity, untreated diabetes, untreated hypothyroidism, chronic renal disease, and liver disease can affect blood levels.

USDA: United States Department of Agriculture, which is a regulatory agency for some food products and monitors food labeling for meat and poultry products.

Vegan: A way of eating, which avoids all animal products including meat, fish, poultry, dairy, and eggs.

Vegetable oil: Oils such as canola, safflower, soy, olive, corn, peanut, any oil that is a vegetable oil. All oils have the same amount of fat and calories. Olive and canola oil are high in monounsaturated fats, which is good.

Vitamins: Needed by the body in small amounts and are components of metabolic processes. Must be included in the diet, because the body cannot make them.

VLDL: VLDL is very low-density lipoproteins, one of the lipoproteins measured when your total cholesterol number is given.

White meat: The meat of poultry such as chicken, turkey, Cornish game hens, and other poultry except duck. Does not refer to the meat of pork, which is red meat, called white meat in advertising to alert consumers that many cuts of pork are almost white when cooked.

Yogurt: A dairy product made by adding special bacterial cultures to milk. Yogurt comes whole, lowfat, or skim.

Zest: The outermost surface of the peel of a citrus fruit. Also a verb meaning to remove the outermost skin in tiny strips.

Index

Discover Dummies Online!

The Dummies Web Site is your fun and friendly online resource for the latest information about ...*For Dummies*® books and your favorite topics. The Web site is the place to communicate with us, exchange ideas with other ...*For Dummies* readers, chat with authors, and have fun!

Ten Fun and Useful Things You Can Do at www.dummies.com

1. Win free ...*For Dummies* books and more!
2. Register your book and be entered in a prize drawing.
3. Meet your favorite authors through the IDG Books Author Chat Series.
4. Exchange helpful information with other ...*For Dummies* readers.
5. Discover other great ...*For Dummies* books you must have!
6. Purchase Dummieswear™ exclusively from our Web site.
7. Buy ...*For Dummies* books online.
8. Talk to us. Make comments, ask questions, get answers!
9. Download free software.
10. Find additional useful resources from authors.

Link directly to these ten fun and useful things at http://www.dummies.com/10useful

For other technology titles from IDG Books Worldwide, go to
www.idgbooks.com

Not on the Web yet? It's easy to get started with *Dummies 101*®: *The Internet For Windows*®*98* or *The Internet For Dummies*®, 6th Edition, at local retailers everywhere.

Find other ...*For Dummies* books on these topics:
Business • Career • Databases • Food & Beverage • Games • Gardening • Graphics • Hardware
Health & Fitness • Internet and the World Wide Web • Networking • Office Suites
Operating Systems • Personal Finance • Pets • Programming • Recreation • Sports
Spreadsheets • Teacher Resources • Test Prep • Word Processing

IDG BOOKS WORLDWIDE BOOK REGISTRATION

We want to hear from you!

Register This Book and Win!

Visit **http://my2cents.dummies.com** to register this book and tell us how you liked it!

- Get entered in our monthly prize giveaway.

- Give us feedback about this book — tell us what you like best, what you like least, or maybe what you'd like to ask the author and us to change!

- Let us know any other *...For Dummies*® topics that interest you.

Your feedback helps us determine what books to publish, tells us what coverage to add as we revise our books, and lets us know whether we're meeting your needs as a *...For Dummies* reader. You're our most valuable resource, and what you have to say is important to us!

Not on the Web yet? It's easy to get started with *Dummies 101*®: *The Internet For Windows*® *98* or *The Internet For Dummies*®, 6th Edition, at local retailers everywhere.

Or let us know what you think by sending us a letter at the following address:

BESTSELLING BOOK SERIES

...For Dummies Book Registration
Dummies Press
10475 Crosspoint Blvd.
Indianapolis, IN 46256

(Top to bottom) Beets with Beet Greens and Oranges (Chapter 6),
Pasta Alfredo (Chapter 13)

Pan-Fried Barbecued Chicken (Chapter 7)

Apple Brie Pockets (Chapter 9)

(Top to bottom) Pasta e Fagioli, Grilled Polenta with Sundried Tomatoes and Mushrooms (both in Chapter 8)

(Left to right) Beef Stroganoff over Noodles (Chapter 10), Chunky Tomato Dressing (Chapter 4) and spinach

(Clockwise from top) Eggs in Tomato Shells, Cherry Omelet, Pear French Toast (all in Chapter 14)

(Left to right) Shrimp with White Wine Sauce (Chapter 7), Sugar Snap Peas with Mint (Chapter 6)

Tex-Mex Chicken and Corn Sauté (Chapter 12)

(Left to right) Quick and Easy Chocolate Mousse, Coconut Ice Cream with Mango and Kiwi, Fruit Layered Frappé (all Chapter 9)

Turkey Chili Tacos (Chapter 7)

Sausage and White Bean Soup (Chapter 15)

(Top to bottom) Orange Lentil and Wild Rice Salad (Chapter 4),
East Indian Luncheon Sandwich (Chapter 5)

Thai Peanut Dressing (Chapter 4) over halibut with sautéed vegetables

(Left to right) Eggplant Parmesan (Chapter 10),
Orzo with Asparagus and Onion (Chapter 8)